The Power of Cobol
for systems developers in the 21st century

By
Rui Bivar de Oliveira

A MigrationWare Product

First published in 2006

Edited by: Michelle Coetzee

Design and Typesetting: Jeanne Jollivet

André SC www.pixelplexus.co.za, incorporating an Apophysis spiral script by Niel Slater.

Publisher: BookSurge, LLC

ISBN 0-620-34652-3

Library of Congress Control Number: 2006905424
Publisher: BookSurge, LLC
North Charleston, South Carolina

NOTICE:

The author is preparing a CBT tutorial for students which should be available in 2007. This is a valuable audio-visual component offering added benefits to students. Watch out on our website for the announcement of its release.

FOREWORD

Coming across this book on the shelves of your local bookstore or online you may ask: "Why learn COBOL? Isn't it all replaced now by .NET or Java?". Well, firstly, if you have a bank account, an insurance policy, a pension or a loan, the chances are that the administration and control of your personal finances will be performed in COBOL. It has been estimated that 200 billion lines of COBOL code are in production today processing 75% of data on a global basis. In truth, of course, it is almost impossible to get a truly accurate picture of COBOL usage on a global scale but we can be sure that it is substantial and integral to our daily lives.

Secondly the COBOL today is not your father's COBOL. As a language, COBOL has continually evolved through both an active standards body and companies such as Micro Focus developing and extending the language. This means that while traditional COBOL systems retain their solid proven core business logic, they can now be extended and integrated with new technology. For example, many COBOL systems today are accessed directly or indirectly via the Internet, an Intranet or mobile devices, bringing new sets of users to traditional systems and rendering their functionality to an extended user base. Previously internally focused COBOL applications are now accessible across the enterprise, with COBOL business processes exposed in a Service Orientated Architecture (SOA), for example, as Web services.

This book draws on the author's long and successful experience in COBOL training and is, as the title suggests, a powerful and comprehensive study of the COBOL language, both the fundamentals of the language and new concepts such as Object Orientated COBOL. These concepts welded with new technologies such as .NET and Web services deliver the future of COBOL, both for new application development and the reuse and extension of existing COBOL assets.

John Billman
Product Director, Micro Focus Net Express
www.microfocus.com

PREFACE

COBOL is a programming language that is not only widely used in the computer industry but has also shown itself to be an excellent vehicle for teaching the art and science of programming. The reason for this is that it is a language of moderate complexity, and when using it, understanding the mechanism of programming is not unduly difficult.

Some years ago, attempts were made to rewrite or rehost many COBOL applications but these efforts proved unsuccessful. Instead, the idea of extinction was replaced with one of extension and inclusion. Fourth generation languages had come onto the market but none could match the power of COBOL. The fourth generation languages died a natural death. Instead, the languages to capture the market's fancy would be cryptic languages like C, C++ and, more recently, Java and the languages in the .Net stable. Nevertheless COBOL has retained a commanding position in spite of the noise made by its competitors against it. You may ask the reason for COBOL's resilience; I would say that it stems from the fact that being non-cryptic, it is easy to understand and therefore maintain. In addition, it is unequalled when it comes to processing large volumes of data and is also highly dependable and reliable.

COBOL is, to this day, the language that best handles applications that involve large amounts of data. As COBOL met the increasing demands of business the new standards introduced were always compatible with previous versions. This was not only the smart thing to do; it saved the IT industry large sums of money. Today a company's COBOL systems constitute a valuable asset.

Currently there are an estimated 3 million COBOL programmers in the world. Some say this figure is more likely for the United States alone.

The material in this book is presented in a manner that is both concise and to the point. Questions and exercises at the end of each chapter ensure that the reader will be able to write programs within a short space of time. Similarly, the wealth of live code examples ensures that thorough understanding of the subject is made possible.

How the Book is Organized

The book progresses from the simple to the complex. We have tried in the examples to never introduce topics that have not yet been covered. Sometimes this is not possible, but in these cases the example does not hinge on the material that has not been covered.

Clarity

The paragraphs have been purposely kept small so that your mind will not be flooded by a number of ideas at the same time. Similarly, examples have been kept small so as to emphasise the language statements being discussed. Regularly, the small examples will be incorporated into a larger program, enabling you to see how the different parts relate to one another. This is because I myself am discouraged by long examples. Chapters have been kept small to avoid overwhelming the reader with the volume of the task ahead.

Presentation of the Material

Logically, the book is split into three parts:

- Part 1 covers the language,
- Part 2 is directed at object orientation and
- Part 3 covers some of the advanced features of Net Express.

Each chapter starts with a list of the topics to be covered. Furthermore, the chapter ends in a summary of the material covered. The summary is followed by questions in the form of statements that need to be completed, True/False questions then follow. The chapter ends in a set of exercises that enable the student to implement what he has learnt. The examples presented in each chapter have all been solved and the solutions can be found on www.migrationware….. .

Structured Programming

We have included examples of the solution of logic problems encountered during programming. You should use the approach depicted when implementing procedural programming solutions. Note however, that even when using the object oriented approach you will see the advantage of using the logic learned with the procedural approach.

Software Requirements

We have used the Micro Focus product Net Express with .NET on the Windows platform, but you may implement most of the exercises using any of the compilers on the market. We have left .NET for a subsequent book so you may use compilers that do not include .NET.

Note however, that there are solutions for all the examples in the book but these will only run on Net Express with .NET. In addition, we have used mostly the .NET compiler for the examples. Collections and the database examples have been coded using Net Express 4.

Possible Errors

This is a new book and although we have made great effort to eliminate errors, it is possible that some might have slipped through in spite of our efforts. We apologize for the inconvenience and would be grateful if you would contact us by e-mail indicating the error as well as the page number where the error was found.

For the Future

You should make an attempt to master the material so as to become a competent COBOL programmer. Object orientation has become an important component of programming languages and you should make an effort to master it. It might not be easy at first but it will be an effort well worthwhile.

I wish you success in your study of the COBOL language and trust you will find it a worthwhile and exciting experience.

Rui de Oliveira
rui@migrationware.com.

Contents at a Glance

Contents

Chapter 1

Chapter 2

Chapter 3

Chapter 4

Chapter 5

Chapter 6

Chapter 7

Chapter 8

Chapter 9

Chapter 10

Chapter 11

Chapter 14

Chapter 15

Chapter 16

Chapter 17

Chapter 18

Chapter 19

Chapter 20

Chapter 21

Chapter 22

Chapter 23

Chapter 24

Chapter 25

Chapter 26

Chapter 27

Chapter 28

Chapter 29

Chapter 30

Appendix A

Chapter 1
Introduction to Programming

Topics Covered

- ❑ A Brief History of COBOL
- ❑ Course Organization
- ❑ Computing Basics
- ❑ Numbering Systems
- ❑ Files
- ❑ Processing of Data
- ❑ Program Testing
- ❑ Summary
- ❑ Complete
- ❑ True/False

A Brief History of COBOL

The word COBOL stands for **CO**mmon **B**usiness **O**riented **L**anguage - the upper case letters form the acronym COBOL. The choice of name indicates that the language was intended to satisfy the requirements of a business environment and this is true. However, COBOL has evolved to become an all purpose language with a business slant.

In 1959, a number of computer manufacturers and government agencies came together with the intention of creating a business language that would increase programmer productivity. Three committees were defined for the purpose; a Short Range, a Medium Range and a Long Range Committee. The task of the Short Range Committee was to develop a temporary solution while the Medium Range Committee would develop a more durable language specification. It turned out that the solution presented by the Short Range Committee became the accepted COBOL language.

At the time, the computer language in general use was the Assembler Language. Assembler could be described as a machine-oriented language because it is closer to machine language than any other computer language. This closeness means that, by and large, each Assembler instruction would generate one instruction in the machine language. What this implies is that Assembler is a cryptic language that could only be understood by Assembler programmers.

What was needed was a language that would be closer to a natural language, thus facilitating the communication between programmer and user. Such a language would be characterized by instructions where one instruction would generate a number of machine language instructions. Furthermore, it should markedly reduce the time taken to produce a running program. This was achieved by the first versions of COBOL, which came out in 1960.

That the Short Range Committee was successful is without doubt, in spite of doomsayers always predicting the imminent death of COBOL. That these predictions were erroneous is obvious from the fact that COBOL is probably the most widely used computer language in the world.

It is also true that COBOL has stood the test of time. Between 1960 and now many computer languages have come and gone, some say no less than a 1000, whilst COBOL has maintained a position of leadership up to the present and everything seems to indicate that it has a bright future ahead.

When you have a good recipe, after a time you will try to improve on it. This is exactly what happened with COBOL. In 1968 a new standard was established, with another version being published in 1974. When a new standard is published, the changes that are brought in are mostly of an incremental nature. A new standard was introduced in 1985.

The present work includes all changes introduced up to 2002. The most significant of these was object orientation.

Course Organization

I am using Net Express 4 as well as Net Express with .NET. For this reason, the examples in the book, which may be downloaded from the MigrationWare website, are Net Express projects. Most examples were created using Net Express with .Net, those that were not, did not function with .Net so Net Express 4 was used. Most of the book applies to COBOL, irrespective of the supplier used, because it reflects the Standard. Where topics reside outside the Standard, (database access is a case in point) the supplier decides on the implementation. Consequently, the examples will most probably not function except with Net Express. You may choose to copy the examples to a directory of your own and see exactly how the example operates. You may then alter the example and try out new things that may give additional insight into the topic covered.

Computing Basics

Programs process data and convert data into information. The program receives data, say a batch of unrelated invoices (data), and produces statements (information). To process data, it is necessary to store the data. Data are stored in bytes and computer storage is a collection of bytes. A character, i.e. an 'A', occupies one byte. Data are stored so that they may be processed. The processing of data is carried out by the Central Processing Unit, shortened to CPU.

 A byte consists of eight bits. A bit is a unit of storage that may be magnetized positively or negatively. If it has positive magnetization we say that its value is 1. If it has negative magnetization, we say its value is 0. Thus, a bit has two possible states, 0 or 1. A byte is also the smallest addressable unit of storage. This means we are not able to address individual bits.

 Two bits have four possible states namely, 00, 01, 10, 11. Eight bits in turn, have 256 possible combinations(2^8). Computer designers use these combinations to represent characters both numeric and alphabetic. In addition to these two, we need to specify special characters, such as punctuation and other characters as well. Furthermore, agreement had to be reached regarding what bit combination corresponds to each of the characters. Remember that at any time a byte will have some particular combination of bits on and off and each combination will correspond to one and only one character.

Numbering Systems

To see what values each bit has we will start by examining the numbering system with which we are best acquainted, namely, the decimal system. Consider that in the number 9090, the leftmost 9 has a value of 9000 and the rightmost has a value of 90. We reflect this situation with the following expression:

$$9 * 10^3 + 0 * 10^2 + 9 * 10^1 + 0 * 10^0$$

It follows that 90000 would be represented by $9 * 10^4$. Note that 10 to the power of 0 has a value of 1 arising out of the fact that 10/10 reflects a value of 1. Similarly, the value of 10^1 is 10, demonstrated by the fact that 100/10 is 10. We see that in a decimal system, each position on the left has a value which is 10 times greater than the position immediately to its right.

We can now look at the **binary** system. Because the bit has only two possible states, any position on the left is twice as great as its immediate position on the right. Assuming four bits with the value 1001, we would have the following expression:

$$1 * 2^3 + 0 * 2^2 + 0*2^1 + 1*2^0$$

The value would be:

$$1 * 2^3 = 8$$
$$0 * 2^2 = 0$$
$$0 * 2^1 = 0$$
$$1 * 2^0 = 1$$

The total value is 9.

The maximum value in four bits is: $8 + 4 + 2 + 1 = 15$

The values corresponding to each position in the byte, when the bit is on, are shown in the following table. The high order bit has a value of 128 and the low order bit has a value of 1.

128	64	32	16	8	4	2	1

As you can imagine, we often need to know, when programming, what value a byte contains. A collection of 0's and 1's would be very difficult for our minds to handle so we use the **hexadecimal** numbering system which is base 16. The digits 0 to 9 in the hexadecimal system correspond to the digits 0 to 9 in the decimal system.

Decimal	Hexadecimal
1	1
2	2
3	3
4	4
5	5
6	6
7	7
8	8
9	9
10	A
11	B
12	C
13	D
14	E
15	F
Table 01.01 – Decimal and hexadecimal correspondence – 1 of 1	

Because the byte contains eight bits, we can divide the byte into two parts of four bits each. We can represent each group of four bits with one **hexadecimal** character because the values that may be specified using four bits fall in the range 0 to 15. 0 signifies all bits off and 15, hexadecimal F, signifies all four bits on.

As designers struggled to agree as to what bit combinations corresponded to what characters, we have ended up with two character sets: the **ASCII** character set and the **EBCDIC** character set. ASCII stands for **A**merican **S**tandard **C**ode for **I**nformation **I**nterchange and is used on Unix, DOS-based operating systems and Windows. EBCDIC in turn stands for **E**xtended **B**inary **C**oded **D**ecimal **I**nterchange **C**ode and is used on IBM mainframes. Unicode is the latest standard and was introduced to enable a wider range of characters to be printed.

Unicode is an entirely new idea in setting up binary codes for text or script characters. Officially called the Unicode Worldwide Character Standard, it is a system for "the interchange, processing, and display of the written texts of the diverse languages of the modern world". It also supports many classical and historical texts in a number of languages.

Currently, the Unicode standard contains 34,168 distinct coded characters derived from 24 supported language scripts. These characters cover the principal written languages of the world.

We will now look at ASCII and EBCDIC. The value hexadecimal 31 corresponds to the value 1 in ASCII. The digit 3 is arrived at from the bit combination in the leftmost four bits. The digit 1, in turn, reflects the bit combination in the rightmost four bits. The bit combination hexadecimal F1 corresponds to the value 1 in EBCDIC. Hexadecimal F entails all bits turned on in the four high order bits, giving us a value of 8 + 4 + 2 + 1. What is high order? In the number 1234, 1 is the high order digit and 4 is the low order digit. 1 and 2 are the high order digits and 3 and 4 are the low order digits. The following table depicts the value 1 in ASCII and EBCDIC respectively:

ASCII

0	0	1	1	0	0	0	1

EBCDIC

1	1	1	1	0	0	0	1

We see that we need one byte to hold either an alphabetic character or a numeric character. Modern PCs have memory capacities of 256 megabytes and more, which means they are able to hold vast amounts of data, undreamed of only a few years ago. Note that 256 megabytes is at the low end of computer storage.

How many bytes of storage would we need to hold a name? Experience has shown that 35 bytes would be a reasonable size. We group bytes into units able to hold the data we need. These units we call **fields**. Thus, we would have a **field** for Student Number, one for the Student Name and another for Student Average.

To this point, we have seen that we group bits to form bytes and bytes to form fields. In addition, we group fields to form records. A record is described as consisting of related fields. You would find that Student Number is a reasonable field in a Student record. However, we would not expect to find Minimum Stock in a Student Record. This is what we mean by related fields. Furthermore, we group related records to form files.

Files

We have indicated that modern computers possess vast amounts of storage. However, this vast amount of storage is nothing compared to the amounts of data we need to keep. There is one additional factor that needs to be taken into account: When the power goes down, all that is stored in the memory of the computer is lost.

It is pertinent to note that there are two types of storage and that one is volatile and the other persistent. Volatile storage loses its state when the power goes down. Persistent storage, on the other hand, is not dependent on the availability of power.

The storage in the computer is volatile, the storage on your hard disk is persistent. Say your program is producing a list of the 20 000 students at a University, together with their marks. The data on 20 000 students need to be persistent because they will be required, not once but many times. Data that need to be kept from one program execution to the next, will be persistent data because they will be kept in **files**. You will agree that all 20 000 student records are related. Volatile storage may also be referred to as main storage and persistent storage as peripheral storage. Peripheral storage will be on disk, of the many types available, and on a mainframe may be on disk or magnetic tape.

When you need to process student records, your program will obtain the data from the Student file. You might also have files that are in some way related. These files may then be combined into a Database, where a Database will consist of related data. A Customer file and an Order file may presumably form part of the same Database. The files are related, but the relationship is not as close as the relationship between the records in a file where they all have the same format. By same format we mean that all the records in the file have the same fields, in the same positions.

Processing of Data

The computer processes data. It does this by, on the one hand, having data input and on the other, producing data on output. The processing is carried out by one or more programs residing in main storage. Programs are held in libraries or directories in the computer's hard disk. When we need a program to execute we ask the operating system to **load** the program into **main storage**. As you can see, the operating system will copy the program from peripheral to main storage. In our case, the operating system is Windows XP.

We should not *hope* that processing of good data will be correct; we must be *sure* that this will be so. With the logic techniques that you will learn. you will have no problem ensuring that your program will operate satisfactorily. However, there is another side to accurate results being obtained. The data that are coming in must be good. As we say in IT, 'Garbage In Garbage Out' or GIGO for short.

We differentiate between **data** and information. Data are not related in such a way as to make sense. When the data are processed in such a way as to make sense to a person, we say that information has been produced from data.

Program Testing

A program is only complete once it has been tested and seen to produce the expected results. To test the program, you must create test data and the test data must be structured in such a way as to ensure, as far as possible, that all critical parts of the program are functioning satisfactorily.

The program is written from a program specification detailing the inputs received, the processing requirements and the outputs expected. You only start tackling the problem when you are satisfied that you fully understand what is required. The next step is to solve the logic problems involved and only then should you undertake the coding task.

The question we now ask is, when do we prepare the test data? Let me say that few programmers enjoy preparing test data. But, to ensure that the program operates satisfactorily, we need good test data. The better we understand the specification, the more likely it is that the test data will be good. It is also true that preparing test data will, of necessity, assist us in understanding the requirements of the program. The conclusion is that test data should be prepared once you have understood the requirements of the program. This will be before you design the program solution.

The organization of the program must be such that when the program compiles and then executes it should automatically invoke the test data. The process will then be: compile and execute.

Summary

- Most COBOL statements may be understood by non-programmers.

- The number of possible states in a byte is 256. The range of values in a byte is 0 to 255.

- Operations inside the computer are carried out in binary. In communicating its contents the computer uses hexadecimal characters.

- The byte is split into two parts of four bits.

- The computer operates on two types of storage, volatile and persistent.

- The part of the computer that executes the program instructions is the Central Processing Unit, abridged to CPU.

- If garbage enters the program garbage will be produced on output.

- The hierarchy of data:

  - Bits are grouped to form bytes.
  - Bytes are grouped to form fields.
  - Related fields are grouped to form a record, i.e. leave-taken and salary.
  - Related records are grouped to form a file.
  - Related files are grouped to form a database.

Complete

1.   The number of possible combinations in a byte is 2 to the power of ____ .

2.   The maximum value that may be stored in four bits is ____ .

3.   ____ is the value corresponding to bit 3 where bit 0 is the rightmost bit.

4.   ____ is the part of the computer that processes the data.

5.   The bit representation 1100 0101 corresponds to the hexadecimal value _____ _____ .

6.   The bit configuration 0100 0000 corresponds to the decimal value _____ .

7.   Peripheral storage will reside on _____ or _____ .

True/False

1.   Operations in the CPU are carried out in hexadecimal.

2.   Hexadecimal 31 is equivalent to decimal 49.

3.   Decimal 38 is equivalent to hexadecimal 24.

4.   Generating test data should precede program design.

5.   Hexadecimal E is equivalent to decimal 13.

Chapter 2
COBOL Hierarchy

Topics Covered

- First Steps in COBOL
- The Coding Line
- COBOL is Hierarchic
- Some Coding Rules
- Rules for Name Formation
- The Environment Division
- Summary
- Complete
- True/False
- Exercises

First Steps in COBOL

Any COBOL statement will be placed within a division. There are four divisions, each serving a particular function. The nature of a statement will associate it with a particular division. The divisions follow.

- **Identification Division** - The division serves a single purpose, namely, to identify the program. The division header is mandatory according to the ISO standard but optional under Net Express.

- **Environment Division** - The division serves to identify the environment in which the program will operate. The files the program will use form part of the operating environment and will therefore be specified in this division.

- **Data Division** - All the data that the program will use will be defined in this division.

- **Procedure Division** - All the instructions that will manipulate the data reside in this division.

In a program, the divisions will appear in the preceding sequence. Note that if a division is not used, the division header need not be specified. The divisions grow in complexity as we go down the list. As you will see, the **identification division** has only one statement. The **environment division** has a few more and the **data division** and the **procedure division** considerably more. We can say that the last two divisions will comprise 95% of the program.

The Coding Line

The format of the COBOL coding line is a remnant from the old card systems that initiated the computer age. The card had 12 rows and 80 columns. For this reason, the cards were described as 80 column cards. Each column would be punched and the combination of the perforations on the column would determine the character that was punched.

We have progressed from this level but, since COBOL was around at the time and all data capture was done on these cards, we find these throwbacks. Although it won't carry on for much longer, it is the situation at present. The format of the coding line is as follows:

Columns	Purpose
1 – 6	Sequence number. Used with cards to allow sorting should the cards get out of sequence
7	Continuation column for the comment character
8 – 11	Area A, some statements start in column 8
12 – 72	Area B, most of the coding falls within this area
73 – 80	Program identification in case the cards get mixed up

Table 02.01 – COBOL Coding Line Format

The COBOL standard endorses free format, which allows you to start in column 1 and also gives a possible line length of 250 characters. Because of compatibility, Net Express 4 defaults to the preceding format, which is described as fixed. You may set format to be 'free' or 'fixed'. To secure free format, the following statement is required:

```
$set sourceformat"free"
```

The statement should precede the Identification Division.

COBOL Is Hierarchic

The division is at the top of the COBOL hierarchy. Within each division there will be sections and within each section there will be paragraphs. Note that sometimes paragraphs may appear inside a division without being inside a section. One such case is the identification paragraph that is in the **identification division**. Just for you to start getting a feel for things, we will look at a very simple COBOL program. You will not understand everything but don't let that worry you; it will still make sense to you.

COBOL Program

```
1        *Identification Division.
2        *Program-id. Chapter101.
3        *Procedure Division.
4            Display "Greetings to the world!"
5            stop run.
```

Listing 02.01

In column seven we have a comment character, the '*'. The asterisk will cause whatever appears on the line to be treated as a comment. Any comment will be bypassed by the compiler. Lines one and three are required by the standard but not by Net Express. Line two is not required either by the standard or by Net Express 4. One of the accusations leveled against COBOL is that it is verbose, requiring many lines of code for one particular requirement. As a matter of fact these apparently useless lines are doing some work - but the work will be done even if the lines are not coded. The compiler is able to do this because of the nature of the statements in any given part of the program. We call these lines that we omit **red tape coding**. The program could consist of lines four and five only. For the time being we will leave the red tape code in so that it is plain to you where each line of code belongs.

You see that the **identification division** contains the **program-id** paragraph, but the paragraph is not nested within a Section. Although unusual, as long as the **procedure division** contains only one paragraph, that paragraph need not be named.

Code in the procedure division exists in blocks called routines. Each block of code or routine will contain the code to satisfy some particular function. Note that we are not yet looking at object orientation and consequently ours is at present a procedural approach. When examining program logic using the procedural approach, we perform functional decomposition to arrive at the routines that need to be created to execute the required processing. For instance, in the preceding program, the purpose of the unnamed routine is to display a greeting.

Because our programs will be executing alone we use the instruction **stop run** to terminate execution. There are situations where we cannot execute stop run, but for the time being it will suffice. Before terminating we display the greeting. **Display** is a COBOL verb and not surprisingly it is used to display data.

Some Coding Rules

- The word division, in the division name, must be preceded by a space and followed by a period.
- The word section, in a section name, must be preceded by a space and followed by a period.
- A paragraph name must be only one word and it must end on a period. In COBOL the space is a word separator. It is for this reason that a program name must be one word.
- Any name, also referred to as an identifier (because that is what names do, they identify) must not exceed 31 characters.

In the program depicted in Listing 02.01, you see that the word division is always preceded by a space and followed by a period.

The paragraph name 'program-id' is only one word and ends on a period. The program name, in turn, is also preceded by a space and followed by a period. Remember, the space is a word separator. Had we coded "program id", the paragraph name would have been two words and this is unacceptable.

The paragraph name in the procedure division has a prefix 'A10'. The next paragraph, had there been one, might have been 'A20'. A program may have, say, 50 routines, and if the routine is prefixed 'Z30' you will know that you will find the routine at the end of the program.

We have included the name of the author of the program as a **comment**. In COBOL 74, 'Author' was an optional paragraph. At present, it may be included as a comment. If we need a comment on an existing line of code we use the floating comment indicator '*>'. The floating comment indicator may also replace the '*' in column seven.

Using Comments

```
 program-id. Chapter101.
*author. Tom Jones.
 procedure division.          *>Floating comment indicator
 A100-greeting.
     display "Greetings to the world!"
     stop run.
```

Listing 02.02

Columns 8 - 11 are referred to as area A. Columns 12 - 72 are in turn, referred to as area B. It is traditional to start division names, section names and paragraph names in column eight and all other statements in columns 12 and beyond. Furthermore, whenever we indent, it is normal for the indentation to be four columns to the right.

Rules for Name Formation

In forming the program name the following rules must be observed:

- The valid characters are :   A - Z
                                       a - z
                                       0 - 9

- The first character must be alphabetic.

- All other names abide by the same rules with the exception that the first character need not be alphabetic and the '-' may be used.

15

- A logical rule is that all names should be meaningful. Although 456 is a possible paragraph name in the **procedure division**, it is a bad name because it gives us no idea of what the routine does. Remember that in a routine, the routine name, which is also the paragraph name, should give us an idea of the work that the routine is doing. Which of the following would you select:

    - B20calcInterest.
    - 4567.

Note: A field name must contain at least one non-numeric character.

12345	Not valid
123-45	Valid but not recommended
123-AB	Valid but not recommended

In COBOL we have traditionally used the hyphen as a connector. Possible routine names would have been A100-calc-salary or A100-calc-overtime. You have several options and I suggest you adopt the one with which you feel most comfortable - unless, of course, you have to follow an imposed standard. The suggested options are:

- We leave out the hyphen, except in COBOL words over which we have no control. Instead, we start every word except the first with a capital. We would then have A100-CalcSalary and A200-CalcOvertime. This is called Pascal notation and predominates in PC languages. The reason for the capital A, at the beginning is to make it the same size as the digits which follow. We may also follow the traditional approach in COBOL and code the whole name in one case and separate the words using '-'. In that case, the '-' may be neither the first nor the last character in the name.

- You may choose to remain within the COBOL tradition and use the hyphen. When you use the hyphen there is no need to press the shift key for the capital. For this reason it is favored by many COBOL programmers.

For many years COBOL programs were coded in upper case. This no longer applies and it is much easier to just code everything in lower case. You will notice that when you go into OO COBOL there will be a tendency to drift away from the prefixing of the type A100 in a procedural program. However, you should stick to it because it assists in locating fields and routines.

The Environment Division

As earlier indicated, it is in the environment division that we specify the environment in which the program is to operate. There are two sections in the division, namely, the **configuration section** and the **input-output section**.

Both division and section statements may be omitted bearing in mind that they are red tape statements. If the division or section is not used, the statements may be left out. In Net Express, section names may be left out if the compiler is able to determine, from the nature of the statement, the section to which it belongs.

Additional Paragraphs

```
1        *Environment Division.
2        *Configuration Section.
3        *Source-Computer. IBM-370.
4        *Object-Computer. IBM-370.
5         Special-Names.
6              Decimal-Point is comma.
7         Input-Output Section.
8         File-Control.
9              Select payMaster assign to 'pay001'.
```

Listing 02.03

Source-computer is the computer in which the program was compiled and Object-Computer is the computer on which the program is intended to execute.

The **special-names** paragraph is used for a number of purposes. In the example, we show the code that would on output produce a ',' and not a '.' for the decimal point. Later on we will expand on other purposes for which the paragraph is used.

In the **input-output** section we specify the file environment in which the program is to function. A file is specified using the **select** statement. PayMaster, in the **select** statement, is the internal or logical name of the file. We say internal name because it is by this name that we will refer to the file wherever the file is referred to in the program. Pay001, on the other hand, is the external or physical file name, the name by which the file is known outside the program. Inside the program we never refer to the external name. The only reference to the external name is in the **select**.

There will be a **select** statement for each file used in the program.

Summary

- COBOL has four divisions.

- Sections are nested within divisions.

- Generally, paragraphs are nested within sections.

- The word division must be preceded and followed by a space.

- The word section must be preceded by a space and followed by a period.

- A paragraph name must be one word and must be followed by a period. A paragraph name may not contain any spaces.

- If a division is not used, its header may be omitted.

- The input-output section is used to specify the files used in the program.

- The files used in the program are specified by means of the select statement. The select specifies the internal name of a file and its corresponding external name. The external name is the name by which the file is known outside the program. There will be one Select statement for each and every file used in the program.

- In an identifier, the '-' may not be the first or the last character in the name.

- A program name may consist of the characters A - Z, a – z and 0 – 9.

- Identifiers, other than the program name, may consist of the characters A-Z, a – z, 0 – 9 and the -.

Complete

1.   The paragraph in the identification division is the _____ paragraph.

2.   The _____ precedes the word division.

3.   A _____ immediately follows the word section.

4.   The _____ character in a program name must be alphabetic.

5.   The _____ is a word separator.

6.   The _____ division is the third division in a program.

7.   The _____ immediately follows the word select.

8.   If the program uses three files, it will have _____ select statements.

9.   Area A comprises columns ____ to ____.

10.   The first section in the environment division is the _____ section.

11.   Another name for the external file is _____.

12.   Another name for the internal file is _____.

13.   If format is fixed, area B comprises columns ____ to ____.

14.   The hyphen may not be the _____ or the _____ character in a data name.

15.   Select statement is coded in the _____ section.

16.   Another name for the external file is _____ paragraph.

17.   The source-computer paragraph names the computer where the program will be
      _____.

18.   The object-computer paragraph names the computer where the program will be
      _____.

True/False

1.   The internal file name follows the keyword select.

2.   The select is part of the configuration section.

3.   The procedure division is the fourth division in a program.

4.   A routine may bear the name 67118.

5.   A field may have the name 3333-44.

6.   The program name 100Pay is valid.

7.   The environment division is compulsory.

8.   The program name may not contain numeric characters.

9.   Programid is a reserved word and may not be used as a field name.

10.   The field name 12345A is invalid

11.   The field name A12345 is valid.

12.   The field name 12345 is invalid.

13.   The field name 1234-5 is valid.

Exercises

1.   Name the divisions in a COBOL program.

2.   In which division is the data to be used by the program specified?

3.   Which section identifies the files to be used?

4.   Which is the division that has no sections?

5.   Name the valid characters for a program name.

6.   Name the rules for the formation of a field name.

7.   Write a program that will display your name.

8.   Name the sections in the environment division.

9.   Name the paragraphs in the configuration section.

10.   In which column must the following COBOL statements begin:

     a)   Section names
     b)   01 level data definitions
     c)   Continuation characters

11.   In which area may the following COBOL statements begin:

     a)   COBOL verbs
     b)   Subordinate data definitions

12.   Which of the following are not valid program names. Indicate what makes them invalid. If valid just write VALID:

     a)   prog-1.
     b)   2ndprogram
     c)   myfirst program.
     d)   tax % calc.

13.   Indicate, for each of the following data names, whether the name is valid or invalid. If invalid, give a reason why it is invalid.

      1.1.1   fielda
      1.1.2   1afield
      1.1.3   w01-this-field-us too-long
      1.1.4   section
      1.1.5   22-234
      1.1.6   data-
      1.1.7   cobol 1a
      1.1.8   w01_total
      1.1.9   01=w01-detail-line
      1.2.0   date

Chapter 3
Defining Data

Topics Covered

- Defining Data
- Types of Data
- Levels
- Numeric Data Type
- Nested Group Fields
- Filler
- Alphanumeric Data Type
- Alphabetic Data Type
- The Data Division
- The File Section
- The Working-Storage Section
- Defining Records
- A Complete FD
- Field Naming Conventions
- Summary
- Complete
- True/False
- Exercises

Defining Data

There can be no programming without data. It is now time to see how COBOL allows for the definition of data. All definitions of data take place in the **data division**. One drawback is that all data defined are visible to all the routines in the **procedure division**. If an instruction is responsible for corrupted data, that instruction can be anywhere in the **procedure division** and this makes it more difficult to locate the error. Object orientation, to which we will come later, overcomes this shortcoming.

Types of Data

There are types of data that have been with COBOL from its inception. Additional types have been introduced by the latest standard. We will start by looking at the former. Traditional data definitions fall into one of the following types:

- Alphabetic
- Alphanumeric
- Numeric

Levels

By allocating **levels** to data definitions, COBOL enables us to **group** items of data. **Levels** are numeric and go from 1 to 49. Traditionally, level 1 is specified in column 8, in area A. We may specify the level as 1 or 01. If we specify 01 then all level definitions use two digits. A definition will help to clarify:

Group Fields and Alphanumeric Fields

``
01   W10-date.
     05   W10-year
     05   W10-month
     05   W10-day
``

Figure 03.01

Numeric Data Type

The **level 01**, in the preceding definition, is a group item. **Group** items contain all lower items specified. Thus, W10-date contains the three items for W10-year, W10-month and W10-day. We would like the three level 05 items to be numeric. Let us see how we go about specifying this requirement:

The Picture Clause

```
01   W10-date.
     05   W10-year            pic 99.
     05   W10-month           pic 9(2).
     05   W10-day             pic 99.
```

Figure 03.02

Pic is an abbreviation for **picture** and, as the word indicates, it is used to specify to the compiler how it should picture the item. The 9 signifies a digit. Because we want two digits we specified 99. As W10-month shows, we can specify the two digits as 99 or 9(2). The 9 indicates a numeric field and in brackets is specified the number of digits to be catered for. Notice that every definition ends on a period.

Let us consider the situation where the numeric item we wish to define contains decimals. The 'V' specifies an **implied decimal point**. We say implied because the decimal point does not reside within the data, rather, the system will keep track of the number of decimal places for the item.

Integer and Decimal Data

```
01   W10-amounts.
     05   W10-capital         pic 999V99.
     05   W10-interest        pic V9(2).
     05   W10-total           pic 9(4)V9(2).
```

Figure 03.03

Assuming that W10-total contains the value 123.45 we can graphically represent the contents of the field as shown.

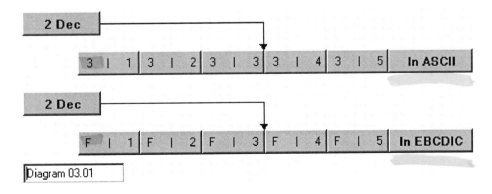

Diagram 03.01

Hexadecimal 3 indicates a digit in **ASCII** and hexadecimal F indicates a digit in **EBCDIC**. What about signing the data? If we are talking about a person's age it is always positive, but many values may need to be signed because the value may at times be positive and at others negative. Temperature is a case in point. An 's' is used in the picture to indicate the presence of a sign. Note that it makes for greater efficiency in execution if all numeric fields are signed.

Signing Numeric Fields

```
01   W10-amounts.
     05   W10-capital        pic S999V99.
     05   W10-interest       pic V9(2).
     05   W10-total          pic S9(4)V9(2).
```

Figure 03.04

The hexadecimal digit 3 stands for **ASCII** + and the hexadecimal digit 7 stands for **ASCII** -.

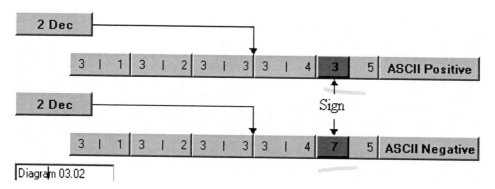

Diagram 03.02

The hexadecimal digit C stands for **EBCDIC** + and the hexadecimal digit D stands for **EBCDIC** -.

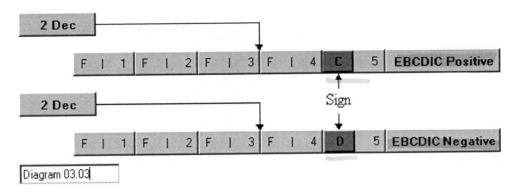

Diagram 03.03

In the preceding cases each digit occupies one byte. We describe this format as unpacked or display. This is the default format. If you do not specify a usage then 'display' is assumed. Note that the word **usage** may be dispensed with when specifying the usage.

The Usage Clause

```
    01   W10-amounts.
         05   W10-capital  pic S999V99 usage display.
         05   W10-int      pic V9(2).
         05   W10-total    pic S9(4)V9(2).
```

Figure 03.05

With respect to size of numeric fields we must distinguish between the COBOL 85 standard and the present standard. COBOL 85 and preceding standards established the maximum size of a numeric field to be 18 digits. The modern standard caters for a maximum of 31 digits.

Nested Group Fields

You will have noticed that a **group** field does not have a picture clause. This is because a group field is defined in terms of its subordinates. Subordinates of a group field may be group fields or **elementary** items. An elementary item does not contain subordinates and contains a **picture** clause.

27

Length of a Group Field

```
01   W10-amounts.
     05   W10-initial-amount          pic S9(7).
     05   W10-intermediate-amount     pic S9(7).
     05   W10-final-amount            pic S9(7).
```

Figure 03.06

The length of the group field in figure 03.06 is 21 bytes and it behaves as an alphanumeric field. The following code snippet depicts a nested group field.

We have referred to the maximum size of a numeric field. You may ask: What is the maximum size of an alphanumeric field? For all practical purposes, it is allowed a size that is given by the size of storage available in the machine.

Nested Group Fields

```
01   W30-amounts.
     05   W30-emp-id                    pic X(3).
     05   W30-emp-name                  pic X(35).
     05   W30-emp-leave.
          10   W30emp-leave-startdate   pic 9(6).
          10   W30emp-leave-enddate     pic 9(6).
     05   W30-emp-salary                pic S9(7).
```

Figure 03.07

The field W30-amounts has a length of 57 bytes and the field W30-emp-leave has a length of 12 bytes.

Filler

Assume that you have a record definition and that you are only interested in some of the fields. It would be unwise to burden the compiler with field definitions that are not required. Consider the following definition:

Filler

```
01   emp-rec.
     05   emp-key.
          10   emp-br-code     pic   X(3).
          10   emp-code        pic   9(4).
     05   filler               pic   X(72).
     05   emp-salary           pic   S9(5).
```

Figure 03.08

We used the word **filler** to indicate that between the field emp-code and the field emp-salary there are 72 bytes of storage. Had we not indicated this, it would appear that the two fields were positioned one next to the other. COBOL 74 requires the use of the word **filler**. COBOL 85 does not require the use of the word. Blanks may then replace the word filler. Furthermore, if the group field emp-rec is never used, we may replace it by the word filler or we may leave the name blank. This is illustrated in the following example:

Filler at Level 01

```
01.
     05   emp- key.
          10   emp-br-code     pic   X(3).
          10   emp-code        pic   9(4).
     05                        pic   X(72).
     05   emp-salary           pic   S9(5).
```

Figure 03.09

Alphanumeric Data Type

The characters in an **alphanumeric** field may have any bit configuration possible. This means that an alphanumeric field may contain any character. With regard to size, an **alphanumeric** field may be any size as long as it will fit into the available memory.

The following definitions illustrate the use of alphanumeric fields:

Alphanumeric Definitions

```
01   W20-messages.
     05   W20-msg1     pic X(12)          usage display.
     05   W20-msg2     pic XXXXXXXXXXXX        display.
     05   W20-msg3     pic X(12).
```

Figure 03.10

29

Note: A group field behaves like an alphanumeric field. Whatever we can do with an alphanumeric field, we can do with a group field. Almost.

Alphabetic Data Type

Alphabetic fields, up to and including COBOL 85, could only contain alphabetic characters and the space. This limitation is maintained but note that an **alphabetic** field may be specified wherever an **alphanumeric** field appears. If an **alphabetic** field appears in an unauthorized operation, it will be treated as an **alphanumeric** field. The following code snippet exemplifies definitions of the **alphabetic** data type:

Alphabetic Data Type

```
01  W20-messages.
    05  W20-msg1    pic A(12)            usage display.
    05  W20-msg2    pic AAAAAAAAAAA          display.
    05  W20-msg3    pic A(12).
```

Figure 03.11

We already know that field definitions appear in the data division. We will tackle the division as follows:

The Data Division

The **data division** contains seven sections. For the time being we will concentrate on the use of two of these sections. The two sections in question are:

- File section
- Working-storage section

The File Section

The **file section** caters entirely for items that are part of input or output operations. Any files that the program uses must be defined in the section. There will be one definition for each **select**. The file name used is the internal or logical file name. The internal or logical file name is the name by which the file is known inside the program. The file is defined using an **FD** or file definition statement.

FD Definition

```
Environment Division.
Input-Output Section.
File-Control.
    Select pay-master assign to pay001.
Data Division.
File Section.
fd  pay-master
    label records are standard.
01  pay-record                    pic X(75).
```

Figure 03.12

The logical file name is **pay-master** and it is specified following the **select** keyword as well as in the **FD** statement. Following the **FD** is a record definition. We specified 75 as the length of the record. This means that every time data are passed to the program, or from the program, 75 bytes of data will pass.

There are other clauses in the **FD** but they do not concern us at this point.

Working-Storage Section

The field definitions for numeric, alphanumeric and alphabetic fields, which we encountered earlier, all belonged in the **working-storage** section. All fields that are not part of input or output are defined in the **working-storage** section. When we come to look at other sections we will realize that this is not always true but, to this point, it is entirely true. An earlier definition inserted into the **working-storage** section follows:

Working-Storage Section

```
Data Division.
Working-Storage Section.
01  W10Amounts.
    05  W10Capital          pic S999V99 usage display.
    05  W10Interest         pic V9(2).
    05  W10Total            pic S9(4)V9(2).
```

Figure 03.13

Defining Records

In the **file section** we had a record definition of 75 bytes. We may define the record in detail in the File section or in the **working-storage** section. Below we will show the two definitions. Firstly we will show the record defined in the file section:

Record Definition

```
Data Division.
File Section.
fd  pay-master.
01  pay-record.
      05  pay-studentNo          pic X(5).
      05  pay-studentName         pic X(35).
      05  pay-studentAverage      pic 9(3).
```

Figure 03.14

The program retrieves records from disk by reading them. We must distinguish between **physical** and **logical reads** as well as between **physical** and **logical records**. A **physical read** will retrieve more than one **logical record** at a time. We say that a block of **logical records** is retrieved. The **blocking factor** determines how many **logical records** will be present in a **physical record**. The block of records is in an area called the **buffer** area. To speed up sequential processing, for every file there are two **buffers**. Double buffers are represented graphically below:

Buffer 1

StNo 1	StNo 2	StNo 3	StNo 4	StNo 5

Buffer 2

StNo 6	StNo 7	StNo 8	StNo 9	StNo 10

Note the following:

1. The first read will fill both buffers and pass record for StNo 1.
2. Subsequent reads will present subsequent records.
3. Once record for StNo 5 has been processed the next record, record StNo 6, will be presented to the program on the next read.
4. While the program is processing record StNo 6, the system is also busy loading buffer 1 with new records.
5. The records previously in buffer 1 have already been processed and may now be overwritten.
6. Below are the new contents of buffer 1:

Buffer 1

StNo 11	StNo 12	StNo 13	StNo 14	StNo 15

On an **IBM** mainframe the blocking factor is specified in a JCL statement. JCL stands for **Job Control Language** and is used to call programs into execution, providing all the information required for the programs to run.

To assist us in understanding record buffering we will compare buffering to a non-computerized activity. Imagine an accountant doing the accounts for a small chemist. The transactions reflecting purchases and payments are on the desk at which the accountant is sitting. The customer accounts are in a drawer. The accountant, being a reasonable person, would go to the drawer and bring a bunch of customer records to the desk and start updating them. It would be highly inefficient to get up and go to the drawer for every customer record to be updated. Record buffering is similar: Each time a physical record needs to be retrieved we get a block of records rather than a single record.

The buffer is **not directly addressable** by the program. A logical read is intercepted by the **Input Output Control System** and the next record in the buffer presented to the program. Because the buffer is not directly addressable by the program we cannot look at a previous record once a new record has been given to us.

As an alternative we may define the record in the **FD**, not in detail, and define it in detail in working-storage. The following example depicts this situation:

Record Definitions

```
File Section.
fd   student-master
     label records are standard.
01   student-record          pic X(43).

Working-Storage Section.
01   student-area.
     05   student-no          pic X(5).
     05   student-name        pic X(35).
     05   student-average     pic 9(3).
```

Figure 03.15

The group field student-area is addressable by the program and this has advantages. There is a form of the **read** that will retrieve a record and place it in the designated field in **working-storage**. The latter solution is preferable to the former.

A Complete FD

The **FD** may be more elaborate than the one depicted. Below we provide an **FD** containing additional clauses:

A Complete FD

```
File Section.
fd   student-master
     block contains 15 records
     record contains 43 characters
     data record is student-record
     label records are standard.
01   student-record            pic X(43).
```

Figure 03.16

- The **block contains** clause – On **IBM** mainframes it is customary to code "block contains 0 records", the desired blocking factory being coded in the JCL. The clause is also not required where the physical device provides for only one record size.

- **Record contains** 43 characters – Not very useful. You can see from the definition that the record contains 43 characters.

- **Data record is** student-record – Equally not very useful since we can see the name of the record from the 01 level under the fd.

- The **label records** clause is mandatory in COBOL 74 and optional in subsequent versions. The clause defaults to **label records are standard**. Label records are records that contain information about the file, including its location on disk.

Field Naming Conventions

You will have noticed that we used the prefix Wxx. The W indicates that the field has been defined in the **working-storage**. We code upper case W so that it will be the same size as the number that follows. The xx is a sequence number. Definitions specifying W50… will follow definitions containing W40. Remember that the data division may be extensive and unless we use a means of sequencing our definitions, time will be wasted locating an item. We may use an additional prefix: for employees we might have W15-emp-salary. When seeing W15-emp-hours-worked we would know that the field belongs to the same record definition as W15-emp-salary.

Summary

- We looked at **numeric**, **alphanumeric** and **alphabetic** data types.

- Levels enable us to group data items.

- **Levels** start on 1 and extend to 49.

- For **levels** between 1 and 9 we may specify 01 ... 09.

- A definition of a signed numeric field containing decimals:

-   - 05   amount   pic S9(5)V99.

- The maximum size of numeric fields is 18 digits according to the 85 standard. The new standard stipulates a maximum of 31 digits.

- A definition of an alphanumeric field:

-   - 05   lastName   pic X(20).

- The maximum size of an alphanumeric field is given by the size of the memory of the computer on which the program is running.

- A definition of an **alphabetic** field:

-   - 05   lastName   pic A(20).

- The maximum size of **alphabetic** fields is given, as for alphanumeric fields, by the size of the memory on which the program is running.

- Group fields behave as **alphanumeric** fields.

- In numeric fields, the decimal point is implied.

- By **buffering** records on input and output operations processing is accelerated.

- Records may be processed in the buffer or in **working-storage**.

- Processing in the buffer obviates the need to transfer the record to **working-storage**.

- Processing the record in **working-storage** has other advantages because the working-storage is under program control.

- The **label records** clause is not mandatory and defaults to Label records are standard. Label records are records which provide information concerning the file.

- The **block contains** clause is seldom used. Instead, the information is provided by JCL statements when the program is executed.

Complete

1. When processing sequentially, we _____ input/output operations.

2. According to the COBOL 85 standard the maximum size of a numeric field is ____ bytes

3. According to the COBOL 2002 standard the maximum size of a numeric field is ____ bytes

4. The picture of a numeric signed field with 5 integers and 3 decimal positions is _____.

5. In a numeric field, we have an _____ decimal point.

6. For every sequential file we will have ____ buffers.

7. The highest numeric level number possible for a group field is ____.

8. A byte in an alphanumeric field may have any of the ____ possible combinations.

9. Select statements are coded in the _____ section.

10. In a numeric field the ASCII code for a negative value is ____.

11. The highest level, numerically, for a numeric field is ____.

12. The data in an alphanumeric field may have ____ of the ____ possible bit configurations in a byte.

13. The possible characters in an alphabetic field are ____ to ____ and the _____.

14.   Under the FD we would define fields that are part of _____ and _____.

15.   Fields that are not part of input or output are coded in the _____ section.

True/False

1.   The maximum size for an alphanumeric field is 160 bytes.

2.   The maximum size of a numeric field is 32 bytes.

3.   If a program reads a file and writes to a file two Select statements will be required.

4.   The number of records in a buffer is given by the blocking factor.

5.   A group field may or may not have a picture clause.

6.   Elementary fields have a picture clause.

7.   A level 01 is always a group field.

8.   A level 49 may be a group field.

9.   Fields that are part of input or output are defined in the Working-Storage section.

10.   In the FD we specify the physical file name.

11.   An input/output file needs two selects.

12.   A group field having only numeric subordinates is implicitly numeric.

13.   It is possible to have a group field without subordinates.

14.   In a signed field, the sign takes up one additional byte.

15.   The data type of a group field is implicitly alphanumeric.

16.   The FD contains a period at the end of each line.

17.   A group level field should be defined starting in column 8.

18. An identifier bearing the following name '12345' may be described as having a stupid name but it will at times be a valid identifier.

Exercises

1. You need to define a field where you will keep a record of the number of records read. Define the division, the section and the field.

2. Define a working storage field at level 05 capable of containing the value 9375. The field should not be signed.

3. Define a working storage field at level 05 capable of containing the value between 9375.25 and –4500.00.

4. Define a working storage field that must be initialized to the value –5732.57.

5. Show the record definition in the FD for the following record.

   The file is called CREDIT-MAST and has the record CR-REC, on which the following fields are found:

customer number	8 characters
current balance	8 numeric, 2 decimals
amounts owing	made up of 4 different fields signed
30 days	5 numeric, 2 decimals
60 days	7 numeric, 2 decimals
90 days	9 numeric, 2 decimals
over 90 days	9 numeric, 2 decimals
postal address	made up of the following items.
3 address lines	20 characters each
postal code	4 characters
card date	made up of the following items:
application	8 numeric
granted	8 numeric
expiry date	4 numeric
customer key	in the following sequence. each field is 4

   characters in size - account, branch, store, region

   How many bytes will this record occupy?

6.   Name the four divisions that appear in a COBOL program in the order in which they must appear.

7.   Which division has no sections?

7.   What are the rules for determining a valid program name?

9.   What characters are valid as alphanumeric?

10.   What is the maximum size for a numeric field?

11.   What is the default type of a group field?

12.   How many bit configurations are possible in one byte?

Refer to the following schematic representation of an employee record

LEVEL	01	A							
	05	B1	B2	B3	B4		B5		
	10	C1	C2	C3	C4	C5		C6	C7	C8	C9

The essential information about each elementary item for the employee record is as follows:

C1 – department code	2 characters
C2 – employee number	5 digits, unsigned
C3 – employment date – day	2 digits, unsigned
C4 – employment date – month	2 digits, unsigned
C5 – employment date – year	2 digits, unsigned
B3 – leave due	5 digits, 2 decimal places
B4 – tax number	5 numeric bytes
C6 – address line 1	20 characters
C7 – address line 2	20 characters
C8 – city	15 characters
C9 – postal code	4 digits, unsigned

Given the following portion of a DATA DIVISION

```
01      field-one
        05      field-two                pic x(5).
        05      field-three
                10      field-four       pic 9(5).
                10      field-five       pic x(15).
        05      field-six                pic s9(5).
```

12.1   Name the group items.
        Name the elementary items.
        Give an example of a group item in the above structure that is part of a more in-
        clusive group.

12.2   How many bytes are there in the structure described by FIELD-ONE?

12.3   In each of the following cases, give the number of bytes occupied by the field
        WZZ-FIELD.

```
12.2.1    01    wzz-field        pic  s9(5)
12.2.2    01    wzz-field        pic    9(5)v99.
12.2.3    01    wzz-field        pic  s9(5).
12.2.4    01    wzz-field        pic    9(5)v99.
12.2.5    01    wzz-field        pic  s9(16)v99.
```

Chapter 4
File Processing

Topics Covered

- First Steps in File Processing
- The Open Verb
- The Close Verb
- The Read Verb
- Reading a Single Record
- Constants
- Literals
- Figurative Constants
- The Copy Statement
- The Copy with the Replacing Option
- Summary
- Complete
- True/False
- Exercises

First Steps in File Processing

Files have existed since the beginning of computerized data processing. Remember that computer memory is volatile, meaning that it needs a continuous power source. Since our experience tells us that sooner or later power will go down, it is essential that we be able to keep data in a persistent state between program executions. Before the advent of disk storage, data were kept on punched cards between executions. The files were then card files. We now use disk storage which, besides being compact and fast, has additional advantages.

The verbs that follow are all concerned with file processing.

The Open Verb

Opening the file makes it available to the program. If it is an input file, a pointer to the next record to be read is positioned at the beginning of the file. If it is an output file, the pointer will be positioned appropriately so that the first record may be written to the file. Note that opening a file already open will cause the program to terminate abnormally.

Three options are available to the programmer to indicate the type of operations that can be carried out:

- The file may be read - this is an input operation.
- The file may be written to - this is an output operation
- The file may be updated - this means that a record will be retrieved from the file, changed and then written back to the original position.

In the **open**, we must specify the mode of operation to be carried out by the **open** as well as the name of the file to be processed. The name of the file will have previously been made known to the program via the **select** statement. The name specified will be the logical or internal file name. The code below depicts opening of the three files, each with its particular mode of processing.

The Open Verb

```
open input   tran-file
open output  emp-hours-worked
open I-O     emp-master-file
```

Figure 04.01

The preceding code uses three opens. It is more efficient to use one **open** instruction for the three files rather than one for each of the files. You will have noticed that when coding we try to align instructions so as to give the code a pleasing appearance conducive to a better understanding.

One Open, Multiple Files

```
open input    tran-file
     output   emp-hours-worked
     I-O      emp-master-file
```

Figure 04.02

In the preceding example, we are processing one file in each mode. It sometimes happens that we have more than one file for each mode. The code below depicts the situation:

Another Open

```
open input    tran-file-east
              tran-file-west
     output   emp-hours-worked-east
              emp-hours-worked-west
     I-O      emp-master-file
```

Figure 04.03

COBOL 85 requires that we should first specify input, then output, then I-O files. Although you may choose to maintain this sequence this is not required by the 2002 standard. Note that the **open** secures **buffers** for the file, although no records are read. It is the first read that will fill both buffers.

The Close Verb

The **close** verb closes the file. Output buffers that have not been written out will be written out when the **close** executes. For this reason it is particularly significant that you close all output files. In addition, closing a file releases buffer storage. Consequently, you should close files as soon as they cease to be required.

COBOL 74 required explicit closing of files. This requirement was set aside but its usage still persists. Specifying a **stop run** will cause all open files to be closed.

COBOL 74

```
close tran-file
      master-file
stop run
```

COBOL 85 and 2002

```
...
stop run
```

The Read Verb

For a start, we will be looking at the **sequential read**. The read presents a logical record to the program. Assuming that the file has 20 records, the twentieth read will return the twentieth record. The **read** has been successful just as all the preceding reads. It is only on the twenty-first read that end of file (EOF) is detected. Let us have a look at the sequential read:

The Read

```read fileName```
```   at end```
```   imperative statements```
```   not at end```
```   imperative statements```
```end-read```

Figure 04.04

The fileName is the logical or internal file name. It is customary to indicate what should be done when the file ends but the '**not at end**' is not used as frequently. You will have noticed that '**at end**' and '**not at end**' are conditions. In the presence of a condition we have to specify the scope of the condition, in other words, where do the actions to be carried out when the condition is true end? Terminating the scope of the **read** is the function of the **end-read**.

As indicated earlier, we may choose to process the record read in working-storage. The format of the read which follows allows us to do this. The format of the read means that a record is to be retrieved and then placed in the named field in **working-storage**.

comment indicator

Read Into

```
read fileName into field-name *> field in w-s
    at end
        imperative statements
    not at end
        imperative statements
end-read
```

Figure 04.05

This format of the **read** uses up more CPU cycles. However, it has the advantage that if the program terminates abnormally and a dump is obtained we can more easily locate the area. On an IBM mainframe, if the program terminates abnormally, a dump is produced. A dump is a listing of all the main storage positions occupied by the program. By examining a dump we are able to locate different areas of storage and determine the cause of the abnormal termination. Different companies have different standards and whereas some will prefer processing in the buffer, others will go for processing in **working-storage**.

Reading a Single Record

Having become acquainted with a number of verbs dealing with file input and output, this is perhaps the right time to look at a complete program that reads a single record. You will see the **environment division** with the **input-output** section and the latter with the **file-control** paragraph. In the paragraph we find the **Select**. Notice that we specified the full path.

Then follows the **FD** and, in the Procedure Division, the Open, the Read and finally the **stop run**. This last instruction will cause all open files to be closed before terminating the program.

Elementary File Processing Program

```
program-id. Prog0406.
environment division.
    input-output section.
    file-control.
        select emp-list assign to "c:\cobnet\emp001".
data division.
fd  emp-list.
```

Figure 04.06 – 1 of 2

Elementary File Processing Program

```
01  emp-rec.
    05  emp-id          pic X(5).
    05  emp-name        pic X(10).
    05  emp-salary      pic S9(5).
procedure division.
start-paragraph.
    open input emp-list
    read emp-list
     display emp-id "   " emp-name "   " emp-salary
     stop run.
```

Figure 04.06 – 2 of 2

Constants

A constant refers to storage that has been set to some value at compile time. We used a constant in the first program you encountered. "Greetings to the world" is the constant and it forms part of the code. If we need to change the message we have to change it and then recompile the program.

```
Display "Greetings to the world!"
```

There are two types of constants:

- Literals
- Figurative constants

Literals

Literals, in turn, are of two types

1. Numeric literals - Valid characters are:

   0 to 9
   + or - if present, must be the leftmost character.
   . - decimal point, if present, may not be the rightmost character.

   Maximum length for numeric literals is 18 digits for COBOL 85 and 31 digits for COBOL 2002.

2. Alphanumeric literals
   - any kind of literal enclosed in single or double quotation marks.

Examples of literals:

```
05   W10Amt1          pic 9(6) value 123456.
05   W10Amt2          pic X(6) value "123456".
```

W10Amt1 is a numeric literal. W10Amt2 is an alphanumeric literal because it is enclosed in quotes. In the example we used double quotes because that is what was previously required. At present either single or double quotes will do. An alphanumeric literal is able to contain any of the possible characters. In the example, the literal contains digits.

The maximum length for an alphanumeric literal is 160 characters. Note that literals have a value at compile time but may be changed programatically.

Figurative Constants

A **figurative constant** is a constant to which COBOL has allocated a name. The figurative constants follow:

- High-Value/ High-Values   Hexadecimal FF
- Low-Value/Low-Values   Hexadecimal 00
- Space/Spaces   ASCII   Hexadecimal 20
                    EBCDIC   Hexadecimal 40
- Zero/Zeros/Zeroes ASCII   Hexadecimal 30
                    EBCDIC   Hexadecimal F0
- Quote/Quotes
- All "literal" where literal is any alphanumeric literal

Literals are described as hard-coded because to change a literal, the program has to be re-compiled.

High-values represent the highest value a byte may contain. This means all bits on, represented in hexadecimal as FF. Similarly, **low-values** represents the lowest value in the collating sequence. This implies all bits off in the byte, represented in hexadecimal as 00.

The Copy Statement

It sometimes happens that there are files that are used by many programs. Defining all the fields in the records can be an arduous, discouraging task. The **copy** verb comes to our assistance. We keep the record definition in a directory accessible to all. The files in this directory are referred to as **copy text** or **copy books**. Instead of coding the definition, in its place we code a copy statement. The copy book normally does not include a 01 level. This allows the programmer to name the record in the way found most appropriate.

Consider the following example:

Contents of emp-rec.

```
05  emp-id        pic X(5).
05  emp-name      pic X(10).
05  emp-salary    pic S9(5).
```

The code to incorporate the copybook.

```
fd  emp-file.
01  emp-rec.
    copy emp-rec.
```

After compilation the copybook would have been incorporated.

```
fd  emp-file.
01  emp-rec.
    05  emp-id        pic X(5).
    05  emp-name      pic X(10).
    05  emp-salary    pic S9(5).
```

The Copy With the Replacing Option

Sometimes we would like to have the record definition incorporated into the program but we would like to change something in the copybook. Generally, changes have to do with the names. One change that comes to mind is changing the names to incorporate a prefix.

```
working-storage section.
01  emp-rec.
    05  emp-id        pic X(5).
    05  emp-name      pic X(10).
    05  emp-salary    pic S9(5).
```

We wish to change the prefix emp to W20-emp. The following code would accomplish the task:

```
working-storage section.
01  W20-emp-area.
    copy emp-rec replacing 'emp' by 'W20-emp'.
```

The listing would reflect the following:

```
working-storage section.
01   W20-emp-area.
     05  W20-emp-id          pic X(5).
     05  W20-emp-name        pic X(10).
     05  W20-emp-salary      pic S9(5).
```

Naturally, for obvious reasons, we have selected a short record description with only three fields. Note that, in practice, record definitions can be extensive and a definition with 20 fields is not exceptional.

Summary

- Files are important because they enable us to store data between one execution and the next.

- Main storage is volatile and peripheral storage is not. This means that when power goes down all data present in volatile storage are lost.

- To make the file accessible to the program, it must be opened. The operation also acquires buffer space. The **open** requires us to name the manner in which the file is to be opened. A file may be opened as input, output or I-O.

- The **close** will cut the link between the program and the file and will release buffer space. Naming of the way the file has been opened is not necessary.

- To retrieve records from a file we use the **read** verb. We are able to specify what is to be done while there are still records to process and what is to be done when there are no more records in the file.

- Constants refer to storage that has been set to a value at compile time. To change that value the program needs to be recompiled. There are two types of constants: **literals** and **figurative constants**.

- **Literals** may be numeric or alphanumeric. Alphanumeric literals are enclosed in inverted commas whereas numeric literals are not.

- A **figurative constant** consists of a value to which COBOL has assigned a name. Thus, **high-values** is the name given by COBOL to the highest value in the collating sequence.

- The **copy** verb enables us to incorporate a file into the program. The file to be incorporated is referred to as a **copybook**. The copy may also be used with the **replacing** option. The option replaces named text followed by the replacing text.

Complete

1.   In the case of volatile storage, data are lost when the _____ goes _____.

2.   The **open** secures _____.

3.   The **open** positions the _____to the beginning of the file.

4.   The _____enables us to specify actions to take when there are no more records to read.

5.   The _____enables us to specify actions to be taken when there are no more records to be read.

6.   The _____enables us to specify while there are still records available.

7.   The **open** acquires _____ space to hold the records read.

8.   The **close** releases _____ space.

9.   The **read** enables us to process records in working-storage or in the _____.

10.   **Literals** may be _____ or _____.

11.   Alphanumeric **literals** are enclosed in _____.

12.   In a numeric **literal** the '.' may not be the _____ character.

13.   The '+' or the '-' sign, when present, must be the _____ character.

14.   **Low-values** is a _____ constant.

15.   The **copy** verb is used to incorporate a _____ _____ into the program.

16.   When using the **replacing** option with the **copy**, the replacing text _____ the text to be replaced.

True/False

1. The **open**, for different types of I/O, requires that we specify input files, followed by output files, followed by I-O files

2. The **open** establishes a link between the program and the file.

3. The maximum length for a numeric field in COBOL 2002 is 31.

4. The **open** positions the file pointer to point to any record in the file.

5. The maximum length for a numeric field in COBOL 85 is 16.

6. The open acquires **buffer** storage and fills both buffers with records.

7. In the **close** we specify the name of the internal file.

8. A numeric literal may only contain the characters 0 to 9 and the sign.

9. An alphanumeric literal may contain any value in the collating sequence.

10. The first read will fill both buffers.

11. COBOL 85 does not require a **close** statement if the stop run is being used.

12. The logical and the internal files are different types of files.

13. The **close** will cause any unwritten records to be written to the file.

14. In the **read** we specify the name of the external file.

15. The FD, Select and Open set must all name the same file.

16. If you no longer need a file you should immediately close it.

17. The **stop run** will close all open files to ensure that all files are closed before the program terminates.

18. Alphanumeric literals must be enclosed in double quotes.

19.   The copy verb incorporates a copybook into the program.

20.   In **all literal** the literal may be numeric.

Exercises

1.   Code a **read** for file emp-file. Use both 'at end' and 'not at end' clauses.

2.   Code an **open** for files emp-in, an input file, emp-out, an output file and emp-master which is I/O. Use the COBOL 85 standard.

3.   Code a **close** for the preceding files.

4.   Code an alphanumeric literal with the value 'End of File'.

5.   Code a numeric literal with the value 123456.78.

6.   You have copybook emp-rec. It contains definitions of fields starting at level 05. The file is emp-file. Code the FD, and the copy statement.

7.   Code a **select** in respect of the preceding statement.

8.   Indicate the paragraph in which the **select** is to be inserted.

9.   Indicate the **division** in which the **select** belongs.

10.   Name the figurative constants that you know.

11.   Name the categories into which literals fall and give examples of each.

12.   What are the valid characters in a numeric literal, and what are the constraints that apply.

13.   Define a group field with two numeric subordinates each capable of containing the value 99999. Code the procedure division statement that will place binary zeros into the two numeric fields.

14.   Define a group field with two numeric subordinates, each capable of containing the value 99999. Code the procedure division statement that will place hexadecimal 'FF' into the two numeric fields.

15.   List the figurative constants.

Chapter 5

Designing a Program

Topics Covered

- ❏ Introducing Program Design
- ❏ The Perform Verb
- ❏ With Test Before and With Test After
- ❏ The Read Routine
- ❏ The Display Verb
- ❏ The Accept Verb
- ❏ Summary
- ❏ Complete
- ❏ True/False
- ❏ Exercises

Introducing Program Design

In the preceding chapter we saw how to read and display a single record. The next task we are going to tackle is reading all the records in a file. Unless we get our logic right we might not process the first record, or perhaps the last. In addition, we might miss records in the middle, although this is more difficult.

Whatever the approach we adopt, be it OO, or procedural, we are attempting to reduce complexity. The procedural approach uses functional decomposition to reduce complexity. We ask, what does the program need to do? Read a record, display the record, print a cheque, etc. We construct routines to resolve each of the functions we have detected. Sometimes it is inevitable that a routine will tackle more than one problem. Cohesion refers to the degree to which a routine handles one function. A highly cohesive routine will process only one function. We should strive to build cohesive routines. We will modify the preceding program to illustrate this point.

The approach to file processing we are going to adopt was introduced by Michael Jackson, a British industrialist who devoted a great deal of attention to programming and to systems design. What he said was:

- We start by reading a record from each and every file that is to be processed sequentially.

- We read the next record when we have finished processing the preceding one.

Next, we show a graphical representation of the logic involved in processing a file sequentially. We will start with the first record, and proceed record by record, until the end of the file is reached. This type of representation is known as a hierarchic chart.

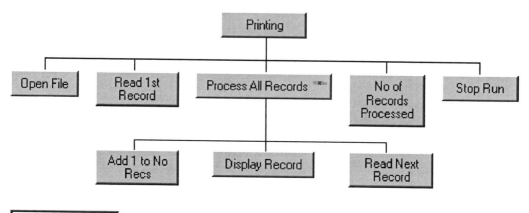

Diagram 05.01

Notice that on the left of the **iteration** we show what is done before the iteration. The iteration is shown by an '*' in the top right hand corner, although we have some times used a question mark. An iteration is a loop and what is done while the loop persists is what is specified in the level below. On the right of the iteration and at the same level, we have what is done once the iteration ends. It follows that printing the number of records processed will only take place once all the records have been processed. We will show the code that will implement the preceding design. For that we must look at the COBOL verb that is used for the purpose.

The Perform Verb

What the **perform verb** does is to execute a block of code. In the perform we name the routine to be executed. Return from the named routine is to the first instruction following the perform. If the **perform** implements a loop, it will repeat execution of the named routine until the condition is satisfied.

It follows that each time the routine is executed, execution returns to test the condition. If the condition is satisfied, execution falls through to the first instruction following the loop. Note that because return to the point of departure is automatic, the **perform** implements a controlled branch. A banned instruction is the maligned **go to,** which provides an uncontrolled branch. An uncontrolled branch is one without a return mechanism. This makes it a dangerous branch.

Formats of the perform:

- Perform RoutineName -
  Executes the named routine and then returns.

  ```
  perform read-tran
  ```

- Perform RoutineName ctr times -
  Executes the named routine the specified number of times.
  The number of times may be specified as a literal or as a field name.

  ```
  perform read-tran 5 times
  ```

- Perform RoutineName until ctr > limit
  If ctr starts with a value of 1 and limit contains 5, the loop will
  execute 5 times. Inside the loop we have to increment ctr by 1 each
  time. Before entering the loop, we have to set ctr to an appropriate
  value.

```
Perform Varying

    Move 0 to ctr
    perform read-tran until ctr > limit
    perform routine-name
        varying ctr from 1 by 1
            until ctr > 5
```

Figure 05.01

When using this version of the perform, we need to initialize and increment inside the loop.

- The in-line perform – The **in-line perform** does not cause a branch to a named routine. Instead, it will execute the code that immediately follows until an **end-perform** is reached. The snippet of code that follows depicts the **in-line perform**. Notice also that we have used the **varying** clause. The clause enables us to initialize the loop control variable as well as to implement the increment. We may initialize the loop control variable to any desired value, positive or negative. Similarly, the incremt may be positive or negative

```
In-line Perform

    perform varying from 1 by 1
        until ctr > 5
            display "The value in ctr is: " ctr
    end-perform
```

Figure 05.02

The program that follows implements an in-line perform. Notice that in-emp-mast is the logical file name. Consequently, it is this file name that is used wherever a file name is required. This will be used in the **FD**, in the **Open** and in the **Read**. Notice that in the read we use the file name. The format of the read instruction calls for us to read a file but in fact what we want, and what happens, is that we want a record and it is a record that is received and not the file. Examine the perform. You will see that the instructions to be executed reside between perform and end-perform. Four records are read – that is the number of records in the file. We did not execute till **end-of-file**, you will soon see why.

In-line Perform

```
identification division.
program-id. chapter101.
environment division.
input-output section.
file-control.
    select in-emp-mast assign to "c:\cobnet\emp001".
data division.
file section.
fd  in-emp-mast.
01  in-emp-record              pic X(20).

working-storage section.
01  ctr                        pic X(09).

procedure division.
first-paragraph.
    open input in-emp-mast
    read in-emp-mast
        perform varying ctr from 1 by 1 until ctr > 4
            display in-emp-record
            read in-emp-mast
        end-perform
    stop run.
```

Listing 05.01

Test Before and Test After

As you might have noticed, the forms of the instruction that we covered so far had the test executing before execution of the loop. If the test proved true, the loop was bypassed. Sometimes, however, we need to go into the loop at least once. In such instances, the test should not be carried out before we enter the loop but after each execution of the loop. Graphically represented, we will show what happens when we specify **with test before** or **with test after** when coding the **perform**. On the left we have with test after and on the right, with test before. With test before is the default.

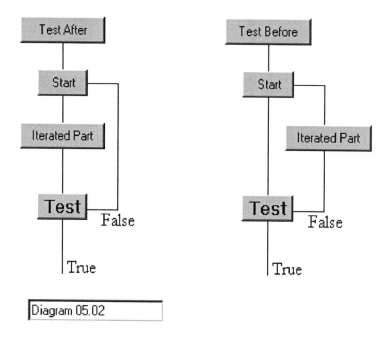

Diagram 05.02

The very small program that follows illustrates the difference between the two:

Test Before and Test After

```
program-id. Chapter0601 as "Chapter0601".
data division.
working-storage section.
01   W10-ctrs.
     05   W10-ctr0      pic 9(2) value 1.
     05   W10-ctr1      pic 9(2) value 0.
procedure division.
A100-start.
     perform with test after until W10-ctr0 = 1
         display "Test after, condition satisfied."
     end-perform
```

Listing 05.02 – 1 of 2

Test Before and Test After

```
    perform with test before until W10-ctr1 = 1
        display "Test before, condition not satisfied."
        compute W10-ctr1 = W10-ctr1 + 1
    end-perform
    accept W10-ctr1
    exit program.

 end program Chapter0601.
```

Listing 05.02 – 2 of 2

```
c:\ Command Prompt                                    _ □ ×
Test after, condition satisfied
Test before, condition not satisfied
```

Both messages printed once. As indicated, we may explicitly specify **with test before**, but because that is the default it is not essential. The cases where we have to test after are not all that common.

The Read Routine

The **read routine** is one that should normally be made highly cohesive. There is no valid reason for introducing additional functionality into the read routine.

You may on occasion encounter huge read routines where a great deal of work is carried out. Please do not follow this approach. It does not follow good programming principles and can only lead to serious problems.

A Read Routine

```
Z100-read-file.
    read in-emp-mast
        at end move high-values to in-emp-record
    end-read
```

Figure 05.03

Because **at end** is a condition, the **end-read** which terminates the scope of the **read** is mandatory. High-values represents the highest value in the collating sequence and being hexadecimal FF, cannot be entered from the keyboard, implying that no record can possibly have a key of that value. We will incorporate a test against high-values in our perform. In the example we depict only the procedure division because everything else remains the same:

Implementing the Read

```
procedure division.
A100-start.
    open input in-emp-mast
    perform Z100-read-file        1 read
    perform until in-emp-record = high-value
        display in-emp-record
        perform Z100-read-file    numerous reads
    end-perform
    stop run.

Z100-read-file
    read in-emp-mast
        at end move high-values to in-emp-record
    end-read.
```

Figure 05.04

Whenever we encounter a loop we have to think of what it is that we have to do before entering the loop. In our example, we had to open the file and read the first record. Had we not read the first record the condition in the perform would have been meaningless. Unless we have read a record, in-emp-record contains garbage.

Reading before embarking on the loop introduces the principle of **reading ahead**. Because we have read ahead, when we enter the loop we have a record to process. Were the file to be empty, in-emp-record would be equal to high-values, the condition would be satisfied and the loop would not be entered.

If we are inside the loop it is because we have a record to process. We process the record. There is no more work to do inside the loop. We read the next record. You see that the last thing we do inside the loop is read the next record. Inside the loop, processing may be more or less extensive. In the example, processing was limited to a display. We must also consider what it is that needs to be done when we exit the loop. In our example we did nothing. Generally this is not the case.

Typical of procedural languages is the presence of routines containing unrelated instructions with only one thing in common; they must all be done at one particular time. You might say that such a routine has little cohesion and this is true. OO does away with such routines. In procedural code we live with these routines and say that they have **temporal cohesion**, where temporal refers to time.

We will break our simple program into additional routines. We have the routine

A200-init bearing **temporal cohesion**. Let us look at the program:

Temporal Cohesion

```
procedure division.
A100-start.
    perform A400-accept-ctr
    perform A200-init
    perform A300-process
    stop run.
A200-init.
    move 1 to ctr
    open input in-emp-mast
    perform Z100-read-file.
A300-process.
    perform until ctr > st-ctr
        display ctr in-emp-record
        perform Z100-read-file
        add 1 to ctr
    end-perform.
A400-accept-ctr.
    display "Please enter No of records to be displayed:   "
    accept st-ctr.
Z100-read-file.
    read in-emp-mast
        at end move high-values to in-emp-record
    end-read.
```

Figure 05.05

You will notice that A100-start performs a number of unrelated tasks with one common characteristic: They must all be done at one particular time. The exception is the **stop run.** One point worth mentioning is that every division name, section name and every paragraph name must end on a period. The last instruction in every paragraph ends on a period.

The Display Verb

The **display** verb is used when low volumes of output are involved. It may be used to send output to the screen or to the printer. We may display literals or fields. The items will be displayed in the same sequence as they appear in the display. The 2002 standard has introduced exception clauses. If somebody does something to us that we don't like we might say: "I take exception to that!". It is in this sense that the clause is used. If the system is unable to execute a given instruction it will throw an exception. The exception clause, when coded, will cause the exception thrown to be caught and what is specified will be executed. We modified the display to integrate the **display** with the exception clause. Because a condition is involved, we needed to include **end-display**.

The Display

```
display in-emp-record
    on exception
        display "Wow!"
    not on exception
        add 1 to ctr
end-display
```

Figure 05.06

"On exception" means "if the instruction could not be executed". In the example we displayed "Wow!" - not very useful, you might say. When the **on exception** exit is taken we will do what is required to correct the error. The normal exit is the "**not on exception**" exit, which indicates that the instruction executed successfully.

The display incorporates a carriage return. This means that every display starts on a new line. If we eliminate the carriage return, a subsequent display will start on the same line as the preceding display. To eliminate the carriage return we code the **no advancing** clause.

We may place an accept following a display with no carriage return. In this case the data entered by the user will appear on the same line as the display. The following example shows the use of the clause. The message displayed and the user's response will appear on the same line. We will be looking at the accept shortly. As the statement indicates, the accept is used to accept data by the program.

No Advancing

```
program-id. disp001.
working-storage section.
01  W10-date.
    05  W10-msg1    pic X(24) value
                            "Please enter your name".
    05  W10-msg2    pic X(35).
```

Figure 05.07 – 1 of 2

No Advancing

```
procedure division.
A100-start.
    display W10-msg1 " " no advancing
    accept W10-msg2
    display W10-msg2
    stop run.
```

Figure 05.07 – 2 of 2

The Accept Verb

The **accept** verb is intended for low volume input and allows for one, and only one, field to receive the data. When the accept instruction is encountered execution stops and waits until data are entered and the enter key depressed. Normally, the **accept** is preceded by a display so that the user knows what is expected of her.

```
accept amount
```

In addition, the **accept** enables us to retrieve the **date**, the **time** and the day of the week from the system. The next example retrieves the **date**. If we do not specify a pattern for the **date**, a two digit number for the year of the century is returned. Specifying a pattern returns 2004, without a pattern 04 will be returned.

Accepting the Gregorian Date

```
program-id. Acc001.
working-storage section.
01   W10-date.
     05   W10-yy              pic 9(4).
     05   W10-mm              pic 9(2).
     05   W10-dd              pic 9(2).
01   W20-date                 pic X(6).

procedure division.
A100-start.
    accept W10-date from date  yyyymmdd
```

Figure 05.08 – 1 of 2

Accepting the Gregorian Date

```
    accept W20-date from date
    display "Date is: " W10-date
    display "Date is: " W20-date
    display W10-yy ':' W10-mm ':' W10-dd
    stop run.
```

Figure 05.08 – 2 of 2

Date returns the **Gregorian date**; **day,** which now follows, returns the **Julian date**. Again, if a pattern is not specified, a two-digit year is returned that excludes the century.

Accepting the Julian Date

```
01   W10-date.
    05  W10-yy                   pic 9(4).
    05  W10-dd                   pic 9(3).
procedure division.
A100-start.
    accept W10-date from day yyyyddd
    display W10-date
    display W10-yy ':' W10-dd
```

Figure 05.09

Time returns two digits each for hours, minutes, seconds and hundredths of a second. **Day-of-week** returns a number between 1 and 7, where 1 is Monday and 7 is Sunday.

```
    accept W20-time from time
    accept W20-dow  from day-of-week
```

The **accept** also caters for exception raising by including the on exception/not on exception clauses.

Summary

- The procedural approach uses **functional decomposition** to reduce complexity.

- A **cohesive routine** closely follows the principle of one routine, one function.

- The **read ahead** principle ensures that we have a record when we enter the loop to process the records.

- The **read ahead** principle goes together with the principle that we read the next record when we have finished with the preceding record. This means that the last thing we do inside the loop is read the next record. Furthermore, unless we read ahead the condition in the perform will not be valid because it involves the record key, present in the record.

- We read before the loop. If the file is empty, high-values will be returned and the loop will be bypassed.

- We covered the following forms of the **perform**.

```
perform A200-process-all
perform A200-process-all ctr times
perform A200-process-all until ctr > limit
perform A200-process-all
     varying ctr from 1 by 1 until ctr > limit
```

- The **perform with test after** always executes at least once. If the loop is to execute 5 times the condition would be until ctr = 5.

- The default **perform** or **perform with test before** will bypass the loop if the condition is satisfied. For the loop to execute 5 times, the condition should stipulate until ctr > 5.

- The **display** is for low-volume output. We may display literals and fields.

- The **accept** names a field that will receive data from the keyboard. When an accept is encountered, execution pauses. When the enter key is depressed the data in the keyboard buffer will be placed in the named field and execution will proceed. We may also accept system values for date, time and day of week.

Complete

1. The **procedural approach** uses _____ _____ to resolve complexity.

2. **Cohesion** means one routine for ____ function.

3. The type of cohesion we find when a set of diverse operations needs to be executed at the same time is called _____ cohesion.

4. An in-line perform must end on _____.

5. If the condition in the perform says 'until ctr > limit' then every time the routine executed control returns to _____ the condition.

6. The with **test after** clause forces execution even if the _condition_ is satisfied.

7. The with **test before** causes execution to be _bypasse_ if the condition is satisfied.

8. The **display** is for _low volume_ output.

9. The clause that will enable two displays to display on the same line is the _no advancing_ clause.

10. To **accept** the date with a 4 digit year we code a picture of _XXXX_.

11. To get a seven digit **Julian date** we code a picture of _XXXX DDD_

12. The **display** incorporates a _carriage return_

13. If an **accept** follows a display, for data to be entered on the same line as the data displayed, we would code the clause _no advancing_

14. If the **day-of-week** is returned, _1_ is for Monday and _7_ is for Sunday.

15. If two displays follow one another, the data will be displayed on _2_ line/s.

16. A read that incorporates a condition must end on _end read_

17. The field that receives **high-values** must be of type _alphanumeric_

True/False

1.   A perform until... executes while true.   *F*

2.   The clause with test after bypasses the loop if the condition is already satisfied.   *F*

3.   In a hierarchy chart 'Close File' would appear on the left of the iteration.   *F*

4.   In a hierarchy chart the read follows the open.   *T*

5.   A perform ... varying does not require prior setting of the condition field.   *T*

6.   The inline perform may end on an end-perform or a period   *F*

7.   The display verb has an explicit carriage return.   *T*   *F*

8.   The accept... from date returns a four digit year.   *F*

9.   We may use the accept to place data into one or more fields.   *F*

10.   A perform varying ctr from 1 by 1 until ctr > 5 will execute 4 times.   *F*   *5*

11.   A perform varying ctr from 1 by 1 until ctr > 5 will execute 5 times.   *T*

12.   A read must always end on end-read.   *F*   *?*

13.   The advantage of the in-line perform is that we can follow the logic without looking at another part of the program.   *T*

14.   The accept catering for time returns hours, minutes and seconds.   *F*   *?*

15.   With the perform varying you must always vary from 1.   *F*

16.   With the perform varying you may vary by whatever value you find appropriate.   *T*

17.   With the following code: perform until ctr > 5 you must increment ctr inside the loop.   *T*

18.   In the preceding question you do not need to set the ctr before the perform.   *F*

Exercises

1.   Write a program that implements a loop to accept msg from the user. Display the message, as well as the date and time of day. The loop should execute five times. The output should look as follows: msg Date is: 20040612 Time is: 11:55:22

2.   Write a program that will accept:

>   i.   emp-id, five characters alphanumeric.
>   ii. emp-name 35 characters alphanumeric
>   iii. emp-salary five digits numeric.

3.   Repeat three times. Before accepting each item, output a message describing what is expected. Once all three items have been accepted display all three, identifying each one.

Chapter 6
Arithmetic Operations

Topics Covered

- Arithmetic Statements
- The Compute Verb
- The Add Statement
- The Subtract Statement
- The Multiply Statement
- The Divide Statement
- Finding the Remainder
- Summary
- Complete
- True/False
- Exercises

Arithmetic Statements

Most arithmetic operations are of the format:

> operation operand1 connector operand2

In an **add** the connector will be **to**. Note that operand1 may consist of one or more fields. Similarly, operand2 may consist of one or more fields. It is operand2 that receives the result. Optionally, the result may be placed not in the second operand but in a named alternative.

The Compute Verb

In preceding examples we have used the **compute**. The **compute** is the most comprehensive of all COBOL arithmetic statements and is, for this reason, widely used. One of the reasons for its popularity is that, most of the time it is able to replace the remaining arithmetic instructions. When replacing other arithmetic operations, there is a marginal drop in efficiency that, it is felt, is amply compensated by its clarity and ease of use.

Format

```
compute field1 rounded = arithmetic expression
      on size error
            imperative statement
end-compute
```

- **Rounding** - Assume the operation yields a result with three decimals. For rounding to be effective, the receiving field should have two decimals. Consider the values:

    ```
    - Result:     123.456
    - Rounding:      .005
    - Rounded:    123.46
    ```

- Adding five to the rightmost digit, causes the carry to increase. In the result the value of the rightmost digit increases by one. If the result had been 123.453, the rounded result would have been 123.45. In rounding a negative number we should add -.005.

    On size error, in a compute, may occur for either of two reasons:

    - The expression contains a division by zero
    - The expression yields a value that exceeds the maximum value possible for the field

The clause operates very much like the on exception, since an exception is raised and caught by the clause. If the clause is not used, division by 0 will cause the program to terminate abnormally.

- The arithmetic expression may contain any of the following arithmetic operators:

+	Addition
-	Subtraction
*	Multiplication
/	Division
**	Exponentiation e.g. ** 3 signifies cubed.

Order of precedence in the **compute** uses the following rules:

- First do everything that is in brackets
- Exponentiation is done going from left to right
- Multiplication and division follow also from left to right
- At the lowest level of precedence we have addition and subtraction, also evaluated from left to right.

Consider the following compute:

```
compute amount = (A + B **3) + (C + D * X) + (E - F / Y)
```

Sequence of computation:

1.   B ** 3 = L   A + L = M

Going from left to right, we do everything that is in brackets, so we start with the rightmost expression. Within the expression, we first do exponentiation. B ** 3 = L, L is the result. We then carry on with the rest of the operation in brackets. A + L = M.

2.   D * X = N   C + N = O

In the next bracketed operation we start with multiplication, D * X = N. The result N is then added to C producing the result O.

3.   F / Y = P   E - P = Q

We start with division yielding P. From E we subtract P yielding Q.

73

4.   `amount = M + O + Q`

The last step consists in adding all the intermediate results to produce a final result.

When we use the **on size error** clause the **end-compute** is required as for any condition.

Note the following points:

- All arithmetic operators, as well as the equal sign, must be preceded and followed by a space.

- Left brackets cannot be followed by a space and right brackets cannot be preceded by a space.

The Add Statement

In the **add**, as well as in other binary operations, the second operand receives the result.

Format 1.

```
add jan-sales to first-quarter
```

The result will be placed in first-quarter.

Add	First Operand	Second Operand
Initial	100	500
Final	100	600

```
add jan-sales feb-sales mar-sales to first-quarter
```

The result will be placed in first-quarter.

Add	First Operand	Second Operand
Initial	100 200 300	1500
Final	100 200 300	2100

```
add jan-sales feb-sales mar-sales to first-quarter
                                   year-total
```

Add	First Operand	Second Operand
Initial	100 200 300	1500 5000
Final	100 200 300	2100 5600

The results will be placed in first-quarter and year-total. All formats may include the **rounded** clause as well as the on size error clause. The example shows this situation:

Rounded and On Size Error Clause

```
add jan-sales to first-quarter
              year-total rounded
    on size error
        display "Destination field too small"
end-add
```

Figure 06.01

The **rounded** will apply only to the destination field for which it was specified. In the example we specified **rounded** in respect of year-total, so year-total will be rounded. First-quarter will not be rounded. We may specify **rounded** for all the output fields if we so wish.

The Giving Clause

```
add jan-sales feb-sales mar-sales
    giving first-quarter rounded
        on size error
            display "Receiving field too small"
end-add
```

Figure 06.02 – Format2

Assume we have the following data definitions:

Fields With the Same Name

```
01  year-totals.
    05  first-quart     pic S9(4) value 7500.
    05  second-quart    pic S9(4) value 9000.
    05  third-quart     pic S9(4) value 0.
    05  fourth-quart    pic S9(4) value 0.
01  half-year-totals.
    05  first-quart     pic S9(4) value 3000.
    05  second-quart    pic S9(4) value 4500.
```

Figure 06.03

You will notice that there are two group fields and that some of the same names are present in both. The **corresponding** clause will add all fields with common names.

Corresponding may be shortened to **corr**. Consider the statement:

Format 3.

```
add corr half-year-totals to year-totals
```

In the group field year-totals, the fields first-quart and second-quart received 3000 and 4500 respectively. We may specify the **rounded** and **on size error clauses**.

The Subtract Statement

In the **subtract**, as in the add, the second operand receives the result.

Format 1.

```
subtract jan-sales from first-quarter
```

The result will be placed in first-quarter.

Subtract	First Operand	Second Operand
Initial	1000	5000
Final	1000	4000

```
subtract jan-sales feb-sales mar-sales from
                first-quarter
```

The fields jan-sales, feb-sales and mar-sales are added together and the result subtracted from first-quarter. The result is then placed in first-quarter.

Subtract	First Operand	Second Operand
Initial	500 600 700	5800
Final	500 600 700	4000

```
subtract jan-sales feb-sales mar-sales
              from first-quarter rounded
                    year-total
```

The fields jan-sales, feb-sales and mar-sales are added together and the result subtracted from first-quarter and year-total. The result will be placed in the second operand namely, first-quarter and year-total.

First-quarter was rounded but year-total was not. It is also possible to include the on size error clause. Including the clause will cause an exception to be generated if the value generated will not fit into the receiving field.

The **rounded** will apply only to the destination field for which it was specified. In the example we specified rounded in respect of first-quarter, so year- total will not be rounded. First-quarter will be rounded. We may specify rounded for all the output fields if we so wish.

The Giving Clause – Format 2

```
subtract jan-sales feb-sales mar-sales
    from year-total
        giving three-quarters
          on size error
              display "Receiving field too small"
end-subtract
```

Figure 06.04

The **giving** clause places the result in the field specified following the **giving**. Both operand1 and operand2 remain unchanged. Because the receiving field does not participate in the arithmetic, it need not be numeric.

As for the add, assume we have the following data definitions:

Fields with the Same Names

```
01   year-totals.
     05   first-quart      pic S9(4) value 8000.
     05   second-quart     pic S9(4) value 9000.
     05   third-quart      pic S9(4) value 0.
     05   fourth-quart     pic S9(4) value 0.
01   half-year-totals.
     05   first-quart      pic S9(4) value 3000.
     05   second-quart     pic S9(4) value 4000.
```

Figure 06.05

Again, the **corresponding** clause will subtract all fields with common names. Consider the statement:

Format 3.

```
subtract corr half-year-totals from year-totals
```

In the group field year-totals, the fields first-quart and second-quart will now have the value 5000 in both fields. We may specify **rounded** and on size error.

The Multiply Statement

In the **multiply**, the first operand may be one field only. The second operand may be more than one field. As before, the second operand receives the result.

Format 1.

```
multiply interest by capital
```
The result will be placed in capital.

Multiply	First Operand	Second Operand
Initial	1.15	10000
Final	1.15	11500

```
multiply interest by south-sales north-sales
```

The result will be placed in south-sales and north-sales.

Multiply	First Operand	Second Operand
Initial	1.15	10000 20000
Final	1.15	11500 23000

Format 2.

```
multiply interest by capital
     giving  south-cap north-cap
```

The result will be placed in south-cap and north-cap. The values in interest and capital will remain unchanged. The result fields initially contain garbage:

Multiply	First Operand	Second Operand	Result
Initial	1.15	10000	00## !8%
Final	1.15	10000	11500 11500

We may specify the rounded and on size error clauses as shown in the code snippet that follows. **On size error** forces the use of the **end-multiply**.

Arithmetic Clauses

```
multiply interest by capital
    giving south-cap
            north-cap rounded
            east-cap
            west-cap  rounded
    on size error
          display "Overflow on multiply"
end-multiply
```

Figure 06.06

The Divide Statement

In the **divide**, the first operand may be one field only. The second operand may be more than one field. As before, the second operand receives the result.

Format 1.

```
divide no-of-people into capital
```

The result will be placed in capital, no-of-people remains unchanged.

Divide	First Operand	Second Operand
Initial	5	1500
Final	5	300

```
divide no-of-people into capital
                        shares rounded
```

No-of-people remains unchanged, capital and shares receive the result.

Divide	First Operand	Second Operand
Initial	5	1500 3000
Final	5	300 600

Rounded was specified for field share-wage, so the result would have been rounded, if required.

Divide Format 2

```
divide no-of-people into capital
    giving  share-salary
            share-wage rounded
    on size error
        display "Division by zero or field too small"
end-divide
```

Figure 06.07

Divide	First Operand	Second Operand	Result
Initial	5	1500 3000	%@ 9X
Final	5	1500 3000	300 600

Share-salary and share-wage receive the result, no other fields will change.

Divide Format 3

```
divide capital by no-of-people
    giving  share-salary
            share-wage rounded
    on size error
            display "Division by zero or field too small"
end-divide
```

Figure 06.08

The result will be the same as that given by the preceding example. Note that **by** may be used only with the **giving** clause. The format of the **divide** below, which provides for a **remainder,** may be used only with the **giving** option

Divide Format 4 – Giving and Remainder

```
divide no-of-people into capital
    giving  shares
        remainder small-bit
        on size error
        display "Division by zero or field too small"
end-divide
```

Figure 06.09

The following format of the divide is like the preceding format but replaces the **into** by **by.** Of course, the sequence of first and second operand is reversed.

Divide Format 5

```
divide capital by no-of-people
    giving  shares
        remainder small-bit    on size error
        display "Division by zero or field too small"
end-divide
```

Figure 06.09

Finding the Remainder

To find the **remainder** the following operations are carried out:

-	The dividend is divided by the divisor.	30 / 7
-	The result is placed in the quotient field.	4
-	The quotient is multiplied by the divisor	28
-	The result obtained is subtracted from the dividend	30 - 28
-	This result is placed in the remainder field	2

Assume the following definitions with decimal positions:

```
05  A          pic S999      value 175.
05  B          pic S99       value 32.
05  C          pic S99V99    value 0.
05  D          pic S99V99    value 0.

divide A by B giving C remainder D

175/32 = 5.46875
5.46875 placed in C, C will contain 05.46
05.46 * 32 = 174.72
175 - 174.72 = 0.280
A = 175, B = 32, C = 05.46, D = 0.28
```

Assume we ask for rounding and remainder. Further assume fields defined as follows:

```
05  field1      pic S999V99    value +3.2.
05  field2      pic S999       value +518.
05  field3      pic S999V99    value 100.
05  field4      pic S999V99    value 200.
```

```
        divide field2 by field1
            giving field3 rounded
                remainder field4
```

After execution:

```
05   field1        pic S999V99    value +3.2.
05   field2        pic S999       value +518.
05   field3        pic S999V99    value 161.88.
05   field4        pic S999V99    value .01.
```

Summary

- The **compute** calculates the result of an expression and returns the value into one field. The result may be rounded. The keyword rounded follows the receiving field.

- Coding `add 1 to res` is slightly faster than coding `compute res = res + 1`.

- The **add** and the remaining arithmetic operations may place the result into one or more fields. The results may be rounded selectively; that is, following the field name we place the keyword rounded.

- When a number of fields is subtracted from a field, the fields to be subtracted are added and the result provides the value to be subtracted.

- The first operand of the **multiply** may only be one field.

- The second operand is not changed when using the **giving** option.

- The first operand of the **divide** may be only one field.

- The **remainder** clause in the divide calls for the use of the giving option.

- When using the **giving** option we may code `add X` **to** `Y giving Z` or alternatively we may leave out the **to** and code `add X Y giving Z`.

- When using **divide by**, the giving clause must be used.

- A **literal** may not be a receiving operand.

Complete

1.   The corresponding clause may be used only with the _____ and the _____.

2.   The corresponding clause references _____ fields.

3.   The corresponding clause operates only on fields with the _____ name.

4.   The second operand in an arithmetic statement may name _____ than _____field.

5.   The field or fields following the giving clause may be of type _____ or _____.

6.   Assume the following code:

```
01  A       pic S9(03)V99    value 214.
01  B       pic S9(03)V99    value 31.
01  res     pic S9(03)V99    value 0.
01  rem     pic S9(03)V99    value 0.

divide A by B giving res remainder rem
```

After execution res would contain _____ and rem would contain _____.

True/False

1.   The clause with test after bypassess the loop if the condition is already satisfied.

Assume the following fields with the specified values for the questions that follow.

```
Flda (S999) = 100+
Fldb (S999) = 200+
Fldc (S999) = 300+
Fldd (S999) = 200-
Flde (S999) = 000+
```

2.   Given the statement: add flda to fldb, after execution fldb would contain 300.

3.   Given the statement: `add fldb to flda`, after execution flda would contain 300.

4.   Given the statement: `add flda fldb to flde`, after execution flde would contain 300.

5.   Given the statement: `add flda fldb to fldd flde`, after execution fldc would contain 500 and fldd would contain 300.

6.   Given the statement: `add 500 to flda fldc fldd`, after execution flda = 600+ fldc = 00+ fldd = 500+.

7.   Given the statement: `add 100.5 to flda`, after execution flda would contain 200.

8.   Given the statement: `add flda to fldd`, after execution fldd would contain 100.

9.   Given the statement: `add flda to fldd giving flde`, after execution flde would contain 100.

10.   Given the statement: `add flda to fldc`, after execution fldc would contain 400.

Exercises

Provide the COBOL statements to execute the following. Do not use the compute statement and use only one statement for each question.

1. Deduct int-amount from total-amount and put the result in total-amount.
2. Deduct bonus from tot-received and put the result in tot-salary.
3. Add bonus to salary and subtract the sum obtained from tot-remuneration. Place the result in commission-received.
4. Find the sum of km-road, km-rail and km-water. Deduct the result obtained from total-km and place the result in total-km.
5. Add rental-rates and electricity to produce a figure for tot-expenditure.
6. Subtract deductions from gross-income with net-income as the result field.
7. Add capital to 15 and put the result in capital.
8. Subtract the value in amount from 89.2 and put the result in new-amount.
9. Add the values of first-quart and second-quart, subtract the sum obtained from quarter-3 and place the result in final-value.
10. Add 75 to the sum of the values of rate-a and rate-b. Subtract that sum from rate-c and place the result in rate-c.
11. Place the sum of normal-sales and special-sales in total-sales.
12. Add the fields over-60, over-30 and current and put the result in amount-owing.
13. Add the fields salary-to-date and bonus and put the result in salary-to-date.
14. Determine what is wrong, if anything, with the following statements. If you find nothing wrong, please indicate this by writing "NOTHING WRONG".

```
14.1   add 3.5 to g giving d rounded
14.2   divide a by b
14.3   divide x by 0.5 giving y z rounded
14.4   subtract p and q from r
14.5   compute b = d x a - c
14.6   compute d = c + d rounded
14.7   add a b d tp d
14.8   multiply c rounded by d
14.9   multiply -0.5 by b c d
14.10  divide -3.2 into c rounded
```

15. Using the following arithmetic statements, give the name of the result field(s) and the result value(s). Leading and trailing zeroes and assumed decimal points (indicated by A) must be shown clearly.

The following field definitions apply to each arithmetic statement.

FIELD	PIC	VALUE
P	S999V99	010ʌ00
Q	999V99	090ʌ00
R	999V99	030ʌ00
S	999	040

```
15.1      add 5 r giving p
15.2      add q 12.456 to r rounded
15.3      subtract p from q giving r
15.4      subtract p from q giving r
               on size error move 1 to s
          end-substract

15.5      subtract 1520.036 from r rounded
                          on size error move 1 to s
          end-subtract
15.6      multiply q by r
15.7      multiply q by r
                          on size error move 1 to s
15.8      divide r into q
15.9      divide 11 into s, r rounded
15.10     divide 11 into r giving s remainder q
```

Chapter 7

Move, Logical & Relational Operators

Topics Covered

- Introducing the Move
- Introducing the If
- Relational Operators
- The Continue
- Nested Ifs
- Class Tests
- Sign Test
- Logical Operators
- Implied Subject
- Implied Subject and Relational Operator

- The Not
- Not with Same Operator
- Not with Different Operator
- Not with the Class Test
- The Write Verb
- Writing to the Printer
- Summary
- Complete
- True/False
- Exercises

Introducing the Move

The **move** verb enables us to copy data from one field to one or more fields. We say copy and not transfer because the data remain in the source field.

Format

```
move source-data to dest-a, dest-b, dest-c...
move 'literal' to dest-d, dest-e...
move 125 to limit
```

Note that the destination must represent storage. For this reason, a literal may not follow a **to** in a **move** statement. The significance of moving a literal to a literal is that it is equivalent to saying make 7 equal to 10. 10 cannot possibly be changed to anything else.

Source	Destination
Numeric	Numeric
	Alphanumeric
Alphanumeric	Alphanumeric
	Alphabetic
	Numeric
Alphabetic	Alphabetic
	Alphanumeric
Table 07.01 – Permissible moves	

Although the preceding moves are permissible, it is up to the programmer to ensure that the data are acceptable to the destination field. You see that a numeric field may be moved to an alphanumeric destination. Note, however, that the numeric field may not contain decimals. Net Express signals an error but allows the operation.

Alphabetic data items, in the 1974 and 1985 standards, could only contain alphabetic characters and the space. The 2002 standard allows any alphanumeric character. Nevertheless, we cannot move a numeric field to an alphabetic destination.

Introducing the If

The **if** is classed as a COBOL verb and enables us to establish one or more conditions which will enable us to choose between different courses of action. The **if** is generally used in conjunction with one or more relational operators.

Without relational operators, the if is meaningless. A table of **relational operators** follows:

Relational Operators

As the name indicates, a **relational operator** establishes the relationship between two fields. Such relationships are either true or false, and as such must be used in conjunction with **if** statements.

Relational Operator	Abridged	Condensed
Greater Than	>	Greater
Not Greater Than	Not >	Not Greater
Less Than	<	Less
Not Less Than	Not <	Not Less
Equal To	=	Equal
Not Equal To	Not =	Not Equal
Less Than or Equal to	<=	Less or Equal
Greater Than or Equal	>=	Greater or Equal
Table 07.02 – Relational Operators		

An example illustrating the use of the **if**:

The IF Statement

```
if   rec-code  = 1
     move rec-amount to pr-debit
else
     move rec-amount to pr-credit
end-if
```

Figure 07.01

Notice how we indent the code to enhance clarity. It is usual to reduce the amount of typing by using the = sign rather than the verbal form shown below.

```
if   rec-code  is equal to 1
```

For every **else** there must be an **if**. The reverse is not true; if there is no alternate action, the else may be dispensed with. There is a **next sentence** clause that is used to fill an empty condition.

Next Sentence

```
if  rec-code  = 1
    next sentence
else
    move rec-amount to pr-amount
end-if
```

Figure 07.02

COBOL 74 does not use the **end-if**. Instead, it uses the period to terminate the scope of the **if**.

The Period to Terminate the If

```
if  rec-code  = 1
    next sentence
else
    move rec-amount to pr-amount.
```

Figure 07.03

The **end-if** brings advantages as we will see shortly. If statements may get more complicated, and in such cases, the **end-if** offers greater flexibility.

The Continue

The **continue** replaces the next sentence clause. It was introduced with the 85 standard. In the following example we could have used next sentence without paying a penalty but, as we will see later, this is not always the case.

Next sentence carries execution to the first period found, whereas **continue** carries execution to the first instruction following the **if** in which it is inserted.

Continue

```
if  month  = 'dec'
    continue
else
    move 0 to bonus
end-if
```

Figure 07.04

Nested Ifs

When we want to execute a routine where more than one condition is true and we need an else for each of the conditions, we would nest the ifs, one inside the other, as shown in the example:

Nested Ifs

```
if  doc-date not > todays-date
    if  new-bal not > limit
        perform A100-update
    else
        perform B100-reject-bal
    end-if
else
    perform B100-reject-date
end-if
```

Figure 07.05

Interpreting the above we would say: If the first **if** is true, execute the second **if,** otherwise execute the **else** and perform B100-reject-date. If the second **if** is true, execute A100-update, otherwise perform B100-reject-bal. When coding, we always attempt to align the **else** with its matching **if**. The same may be said of the **end-if** which is also aligned with its matching **if** and **else**.

Class Tests

The **class test** examines the specified field to see if it belongs to the class specified in the test. In the alphabetic test the field is tested for the presence of characters in the range A to Z, upper and lower case and the space. Any other characters will be regarded as not belonging to the class. We are able to narrow the alphabetic test to determine if the characters in the field are upper or lower case. We will leave this aspect till later.

Alphabetic Test

```
if  W10-msg not alphabetic
    display "Error in W10-msg"
end-if
```

Figure 07.06

An item of data may also be examined to determine if all its characters fall within the range zero to nine. This test is the test for numeric.

Numeric Test

```
if  W10-value numeric
    display "Value is satisfactory."
end-if
```

Figure 07.07

Sign Test

COBOL offers the possibility of ascertaining the sign of a numeric field. The tests available to us are as follows:

- Test for **positive** - **Positive** means a number greater than zero.

    ```
    if  W10-value positive
    ```
    or
    ```
    if  W10-value not positive
    ```

    Not positive means zero or negative

- Test for **zero**

    ```
    if  W10-value zero
    ```
    or
    ```
    if  W10-value not zero
    ```

    Not zero means positive or negative

- Test for **negative** - **Negative** means a number less than zero.

    ```
    if  W10-value negative
    ```
    or
    ```
    if  W10-value not negative
    ```

    Not negative means zero or positive

Logical Operators

Logical operators bring power to the **if** by enabling us to establish compound conditions. Of course, we only use compound conditions when simple conditions will not do the job. Compound conditions increase complexity exponentially because the number of fields involved tends to double in number.

The logical operators are:

- and
- or
- not

Let us see how these operators work by looking at examples depicting different aspects of the use of the operators.

1.   `if (a > b) and (c < d)`

In an **and**, as above, for truth to be returned, it is necessary that both expressions evaluate true. If the first expression evaluates false, then it is pointless to evaluate the second expression for it is no longer possible that both expressions evaluate true. It is often convenient to bracket for clarity. In the case above it would make no difference to the result.

2.   `if (a > b) or (c < d)`

In an **or**, as above, for the evaluation to return true it is enough that one of the expressions be true. Consequently, if the first expression is true it is pointless to evaluate the second expression. In an **or**, the second expression will be evaluated only if the first expression proves to be false. Assume the following values:

```
W = 100, X = 50, Y = 100,
Z = 200, WW = 10, XX = 20
if W > X or Y > Z and WW = XX
```

Because `W > X` yields true and the expression is followed by an **or**, no further evaluations are effected. Such problems may be overcome by appropriate bracketing. After bracketing, as shown below, everything becomes clear and the expected result of false would be received.

```
if (W > X or Y > Z) and WW = XX
```

Implied Subject

When we have more than one relational condition connected by a logical operator, the subject may be omitted from all except the first relational condition:

```
if x = y and = z   is equivalent to  if x = y and x = z
```

Implied Subject and Relational Operator

In the preceding example we dropped the subject. It is also possible to drop the relational operator.

```
if x = y and z   is equivalent to  if x = y and x = z
```

The Not

- "Not" with Same Operator

Ambiguity may result when using **not** coupled to abbreviation. If the relational operator remains the same in the second expression, the **not** is carried across

```
if x not = y and z is equivalent to  if x not = y and x not = z
```

- "Not" with Different Operator

Once the relational operator changes, the **not** fails to be carried across.

```
if x not = y and < z is equivalent to
```

```
if x not = y and x < z
```

- "Not" with the Class Test

The **implied test** is not allowed for the class test, as exemplified below:

```
if x = y or numeric
```

The code should be replaced by the following:

```
if x = y or x numeric
```

The Write Verb

The **write** verb caters for high-volume output both to the printer and to disk. COBOL is unparalleled in its ability to process large volumes of data, which is what is to be expected of a language directed at satisfying business needs. We first look at writing to disk.

In writing, a number of devices are involved so it is possible that the **write** will not be successful. The **invalid key** is the exception processing clause. If the write is unsuccessful this situation will be detected by the **invalid key** clause.

Since **invalid key** is a condition, we need to limit its scope. The scope is limited by **end-write**. If we do not include the **invalid key** clause, the exception raised will not be caught by the program. Instead, it will be caught by the operating system and the program will terminate abnormally:

Writing to the Printer

```
    write record-name
    or
    write record-name
        invalid key
            display "Unsuccessful write, file is NEWMAST".
    end-write
```

Figure 07.08

One point to remember is that you **read a file** and **write a record**. What we mean by this is that in the **read** we mention the file name, but have a record returned. In the **write** we refer to the record name and write a record.

Writing to the Printer

When writing to a file on disk, the first record will be written to the first position in the file. The second record will be placed adjacent to the first record and so on, until end of file is reached. When we are writing to the printer, every time we write we have to know where the line we are printing will come to rest on the page.

One of the things we must be able to detect is bottom of page. It follows that we must keep count of the lines printed. On a mainframe, the standard page is 66 lines in length. We want to leave some space at the top, say six lines. Following, we would have headings occupying, say six lines. Headings serve to identify the report and describe the columns in the report. Time and date would also be part of the heading information. Assume further that we leave four lines blank at the bottom, we would then have the situation depicted below:

Paper is   66 lines
Top of page   -   6
Bottom of page -   4
Headings   -   6   16
Lines on page   50

Before printing a **detail line**, namely the line containing the data to be printed on the report, we need to ascertain whether the page can hold the line. If the number of lines already printed on the page is greater than 49, we need to go to the top of the next page, print headings and only then will we be in a position to print the detail line we have prepared.

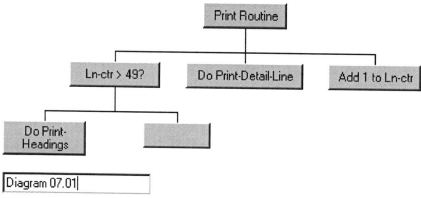

Diagram 07.01

Interpreting the chart, when branching to the print routine, we start by testing the line counter. If it exceeds 49, we have already printed 50 lines so we branch to print headings. There may be an 'o' in the top right hand corner indicating selection we have used a question mark. We are deciding between two courses of action where in one we do nothing and in the other we print the heading line. On return we print the detail line we had readied for printing. We add one to line counter. Notice that in the print-headings routine, the last thing we do is to move zero to the line counter. The chart for the heading routine follows:

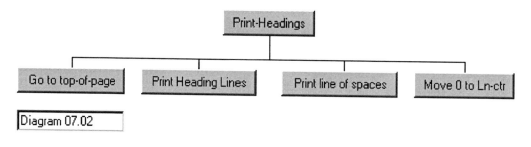

Diagram 07.02

In the example that follows, we read a file and print it. Notice that we define a detail line. We need to move the data from the record we have just read to the detail line we defined. At this point we are ready to print the detail line. Notice that we set the value of the line counter to a value greater than 50. This will force headings to be printed before the first detail line is printed. We will analyse parts of the program, after which the full program will be shown.

Note the following points:

- In defining the heading lines we only name the fields that we need to name because we will be moving data to them – the rest are fillers.

- In the detail line we do not initialize any fields to spaces because, when required, we move spaces to the whole area.

- A routine was created to handle all the things that need to be done at the beginning, before we embark on the loop to process all records in the file. Notice that all the actions reflected in this routine need to be done only once:

  - Open files
  - Get and assemble the date
  - Read the first record

- We create a routine that will perform the actions that need to be done once the loop has executed:

  - Close the files
  - Print total salaries

- We have routines to:

  - Perform a main loop, which controls what to do and when.
  - Ready the detail line for printing and add to total salaries.
  - Test to see if headings need to be printed and print the detail-line.
  - Read a record.
  - Go to top of page and print headings.

Print Program

```
        program-id. Chapter0701 as "Chapter0701".

        environment division.
        input-output section.
        file-control.
            select print-file assign to printer.
            select emp-file  assign to "c:\cobnet\emp100".

        data division.
        file section.
        fd  print-file.
        01  print-rec          pic X(80).
        fd  emp-file.
        01  emp-rec            pic X(20).

        working-storage section.
        01  W10-emp-area.
            05  W10-emp-id      pic X(5).
            05  W10-emp-name    pic X(10).
            05  W10-emp-sal     pic S9(5).

        01  W20-heading-line1.
            05                  pic X(20) value spaces.
            05                  pic X(25) value
            06                            "Our First Report".
            05  W20-yyyy        pic X(4).
            05                  pic X      value '/'.
            05  W20-mm          pic X(2).
            05                  pic X      value '/'.
            05  W20-dd          pic X(2).

        01  W30-heading-line2.
            05                  pic X(10) value spaces.
            05                  pic X(7)  value "Emp. ID".
            05                  pic X(10) value spaces.
            05                  pic X(8)  value "Emp Name".
            05                  pic X(10) value spaces.
            05                  pic X(10) value "Emp Salary".
        01  W40-heading-line3  pic X(80) value all '-'.
```

Listing 07.01 – 1 of 3

Print Program

```
    01  W50-detail-line.
        05                   pic X(10).
        05  W50-d-emp-id     pic X(5).
        05                   pic X(10).
        05  W50-d-emp-name   pic X(10).
        05                   pic X(10).
        05  W50-d-emp-sal    pic S9(5).
    01  W60-date.
        05  W60-yyyy         pic X(4).
        05  W60-mm           pic X(2).
        05  W60-dd           pic X(2).
    01  W70-line-ctr         pic 99.
    01  W80-total            pic S9(7).

    procedure division.
    A100-start.
        perform B100-init
        perform until W10-emp-id = high-values
            perform M100-prepare-print
            perform M200-write
            perform Y100-read
        end-perform
        perform Z100-final
        goback.

    B100-init.
        open input emp-file
        open output print-file
        accept W60-date from date YYYYMMDD
        move 60        to W70-line-ctr
        move W60-yyyy to W20-yyyy
        move W60-mm    to W20-mm
        move W60-dd    to W20-dd
        move 0         to W80-total
        perform Y100-read.

    M100-prepare-print.
        move W10-emp-id    to W50-d-emp-id
        move W10-emp-name to W50-d-emp-name
        move W10-emp-sal   to W50-d-emp-sal.
        add  W10-emp-sal   to W80-total.
```

Listing 07.01 – 2 of 3

Print Program

```
        M200-write.
            if  W70-line-ctr > 5
                perform Y200-print-heading
            end-if
            display W50-detail-line
            write print-rec from W50-detail-line
            add 1 to W70-line-ctr.

        Y100-read.
            read emp-file into w10-emp-area
                at end
                    move high-values to W10-emp-id
            end-read.
        Y200-print-heading.
            write print-rec from W20-heading-line1
                after page
            write print-rec from W30-heading-line2
                after advancing 2 lines
            write print-rec from W40-heading-line3
            move spaces to W50-detail-line
            write print-rec from W50-detail-line
            move 0 to W70-line-ctr.
        Z100-final.
            move spaces to W50-detail-line
            move W80-total to W50-d-emp-sal
            write print-rec from W50-detail-line
                after advancing 2 lines.

        end program Chapter0701.
```

Listing 07.01 – 3 of 3

Summary

- The **move** copies data from a source field to one or more destination fields.

- A literal may not be the receiving operand in a **move**.

- A numeric field may be moved to a numeric field and also to an alphanumeric field. It is up to the programmer to ensure that the alphanumeric field does not end up with invalid data such as spaces.

- An alphabetic field may be moved to an alphabetic or an alphanumeric field.

- Every **if** should end on an **end-if**. An **if** may have a corresponding **else** – however, an **else** must always have a corresponding **if**.

- To specify the condition in an **if** statement we use relational operators. To connect two or more conditions, we will use logical operators. The logical operators are **and** and **or**. The **not** is used for negation.

- The **continue** carries execution to the first instruction following the **if** in which it is inserted. The next sentence takes execution to the first instruction following the first period encountered.

- The **alphabetic test** tests for A-Z, upper and lower case and the space.

- The **numeric test** tests for the characters 0 – 9.

- The **sign test**, tests for positive, negative and zero. Bear in mind that 'not negative' is zero or positive and 'not positive' is zero or negative.

- When printing, we need to be able to determine when going to the next page is required. To go to the top of the next page we use the **after advancing page** in conjunction with the **write**.

Complete

1.   A numeric field may be moved to a _____ and to an _____ destination.

2.   An alphanumeric field may be moved to a _____, _____, _____ destination.

3.   An alphabetic field may be moved to a _____, _____ destination.

4.   The condition 'not greater than or equal to' may be expressed as _____.

5.   The condition 'not less than or equal to' may be expressed as _____.

6.   The alternate way of showing 'not less than' is _____.

7.   Assume that if month is 12 we don't do anyting otherwise we add 1 to ctr.
if month = 12 _____ else...

8.   You have: 'move '999' to alfanum', defined as pic X(3). The test 'if alfanum numeric' display 'OK' would display _____.

9.   If x = y and z could be replaced by _____.

10.   If x not = y and < z is equivalent to _____.

11.   Not negative means _____ or _____.

12.   Not positive means _____ or _____.

13.   A numeric field may not be moved to an alphanumeric field if it contains _____.

14.   A _____ may not serve as a destination in a move statement.

15.   The return from a perform is always to the _____ instruction _____ the perform.

True/False

1. An alphanumeric field may be moved to a numeric field.

2. A numeric field may not be moved to an alphanumeric field.

3. An alphabetic field may be moved to a numeric field.

4. Where we use a literal we may use a field name.

5. Where we use a field name we may use a literal.

6. 'Greater than or equal to' may be replaced by 'not less than'.

7. An **in-line perform** may have no more than one period between perform and **end-perform**.

8. When we code: perform rout-x 5 times, the word times may be dispensed with.

9. You have defined Source pic X(5) and Dest pic X(4). Source contains 'SMITH'. Furthermore, you code move Source to Dest. After execution, Dest will contain the value 'SMITH'.

10. A period is always required at the end of a paragraph.

11. We may initialize fields defined in working-storage at compile time.

12. We may initialize fields defined in the file section at compile time.

13. The value clause is only used in the working-storage section.

14. The word **filler** provides addressability to the area.

15. The **continue** statement operates like the **next sentence**.

16. An **if** must always have a matching **else**.

17. An ELSE must always have a matching IF.

Exercises

1.   Prompt the user to enter the name of the candidate. Prompt the user to enter the height. If the height is less than 1600mm display: "Sorry! Too short". If the height exceeds 1800mm display: "Sorry! Too tall". If the height falls within the two values display: "Congratulations! You have been accepted".

2.   In the preceding exercise, before checking the value for height ensure that the value is numeric.

3.   Prompt the user to enter a message and check that it is alphabetic.

4.   Repeatedly prompt the user to enter a temperature. To end, the user should enter 999. Check the temperature and display whether the temperature is positive, negative or zero.

5.   Repeatedly prompt the user to enter weight and height. To terminate enter 99 for both weight and height.

   a)   If the weight is less than 60 and the height is greater than 180 display: "Sorry! Too thin".

   b)   If the weight is 65 and the height is 178 display "Excellent! You are just right".

   c)   If the weight is equal to 65 and the height not equal to 178, display: "Sorry! Just missed."

Chapter 8
Data Types

Topics Covered

- ❑ Internal Format Data
- ❑ Moving Alphanumeric to Alphanumeric
- ❑ Moving Numeric to Numeric
- ❑ Moving Alphanumeric to Numeric
- ❑ Moving Numeric to Alphanumeric
- ❑ Moving a Group Field to a Numeric Field
- ❑ Moving a Literal to an Alphanumeric Field
- ❑ Moving "All" Literal
- ❑ The Justified Clause
- ❑ Constants Revisited
- ❑ The Figurative Constant Spaces
- ❑ Summary
- ❑ Complete
- ❑ True/False
- ❑ Exercises

Internal Format Data

We have defined numeric data before and we noticed that we used one byte to define one digit. When data are in this format we say that they are in the **external format**. The format is described as external because when data come from the outside, say from the keyboard, they come in this format. If we consider the byte as consisting of two four-bit components, each component is able to hold a digit. In this way a byte will be able to hold two digits. When data are in this format, two digits per byte, we say that they are in the **internal format**.

Data in the **external format** are also said to be in the **unpacked** or **display** format. On the other hand, data in the **internal format** are said to be **packed**. Each format has its own usage, as shown below.

Internal Format
Usage is comp-3
Usage is computational –3
Usage is packed-decimal
External Format
Usage is display
No usage specified – default applies
Table 08.01 – Basic Numeric Formats

Comp-3 is an abbreviation of **computational-3** and, not surprisingly, the extended form is seldom used. **Usage is display** is the default so it is normally left out. Also, the words **usage is** need not be coded, it being sufficient to specify the usage. The following examples depict the situation described:

```
        05   W10-amt        pic S9(5)V99 usage is comp-3.
    or
        05   W10-amt        pic S9(5)V99 comp-3.
    or
        05   W10-amt        pic S9(5)V99 packed-decimal.
    or
        05   W10-amt        pic S9(5)V99 computational-3.

    and

        05   W10-amt        pic S9(5)V99 usage is display.
    or
        05   W10-amt        pic S9(5)V99.
```

When we pack data we must be able to determine how many bytes the data will occupy. Let us consider the previous definitions:

```
05   W10-amt        pic S9(5)V99.
05   W10-amt        pic S9(5)V99 comp-3.
```

We can see that the data in the display format will have used seven bytes. To determine the storage required by the packed data definition we have to do some arithmetic. Before we do that, however, let us see what the two definitions look like in storage.

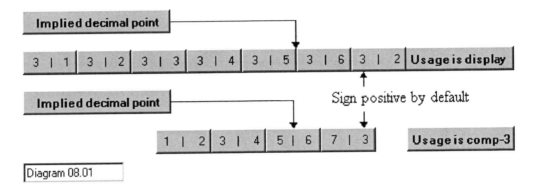

Diagram 08.01

You will recall that the high order four bits in a byte are referred to as the zone bits. The low order four bits are referred to as the digit bits. Notice that in the unpacked field the sign occupies the zone bits of the low order byte. In the packed field the sign occupies the digit bits of the low order byte. In fact, in a packed field it is as if the sign had been appended to the data. The sign follows the data.

We see that in the packed field definition we have catered for seven digits. In addition we must allow for the sign, so we have:

No. of digits   7
Sign   1
Total   8 / 2 = 4

The field would occupy four bytes. What if the picture for W10-amt said pic S9(6)V99? Our arithmetic would look as follows:

No. of digits   8
Sign   1
Total   9 / 2 = 4.5

107

Note, however, that we cannot have half a byte so the field would occupy five bytes. Half a byte, the zone of the high order byte would **not** be used. The number of digits in your definition should always be odd. Graphically the storage would look as follows:

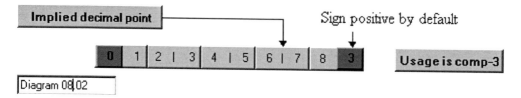

Diagram 08 02

The instruction "move 1123456.78 to W10-amt" would cause the field to contain the value: 123456.78. The program is precluded from using the zone of the high order byte. The program will consume extra cycles to ascertain what it is able to use. Consequently, make sure that you define the field in such a way that there is never half a byte unused. The preceding definition should be: pic S9(7)V99. The arithmetic would then be:

No. of digits	9
Sign	1
Total	10 / 2 = 5

The number of digits in the definition of a packed field should always be odd. (Above: 7 + 2 = 9)

More on the Move Statement

- Moving Alphanumeric to Alphanumeric

One important point to note is that in a **move**, the rules that apply with respect to alignment are the rules that apply to the receiving field. Data in an alphanumeric field align on the left. Thus the first byte to be moved from the source will be the leftmost byte and it will be moved to the leftmost byte in the destination. The move will proceed byte by byte, from source to destination, until all bytes have been transferred or until all bytes in the destination have received data. In this latter case data in the destination would have been truncated. Consider the following definitions:

```
05   W10-source      pic X(04) value 'SAME'.
05   W10-dest1       pic X(07) value 'Michael'.
05   W10-dest2       pic X(03) value 'Roy'.
```

The instruction:

```
move   W10-source   to      W10-dest1
                            W10-dest2
```

Graphically we have:

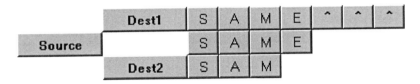

We have used the '^' to represent a space.

When the data were moved to dest1, they were aligned on the left and once all the data had been transferred, the remaining bytes were filled with spaces. In the case of Dest2, the destination is shorter than the source so the data were truncated.

Moving Numeric to Numeric

In moving a numeric source to a numeric destination, data are again moved byte by byte, but in this case alignment is on the decimal point. If a decimal point is not present, alignment will be on the right.

If the destination is shorter than the source, the data will be truncated. If the destination field is longer than the source field, unused bytes in the destination will be zero filled.

Assume the following definitions:

```
05   source           pic S9(04) value 1234.
05   dest1            pic S9(07).
05   dest2            pic S9(03).
```

The instruction: move source to   dest1
                                          dest2

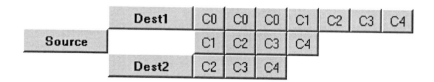

Dest1 is longer than source, the data was moved byte by byte, starting on the right, unused positions on the left were zero filled. On the other hand dest2 is shorter than source. This time truncation took place. The leftmost digit was truncated.

Let us now consider the situation where the definitions contain a decimal point. We know that alignment will be on the decimal point.

```
05   source          pic S9(03)V99 value 123.45.
05   dest1           pic S9(05)V9.
```

Graphically represented we have:

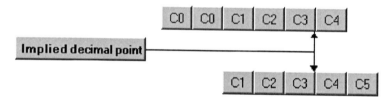

On the right there was truncation, the low order decimal position was lost. On the left the positions left blank were zero filled. The receiving field had extra integer positions and was short on the decimal positions. In the next example we will have extra positions on both sides of the decimal point.

```
05   source          pic S9(03)V9  value 123.4.
05   dest1           pic S9(05)V99.
```

Graphically represented we have:

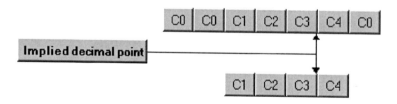

We had zero filling on the right and on the left - the bytes that did not receive data were zero filled.

Moving Alphanumeric to Numeric

Remember, in a move the rules that apply are the rules of the receiving field. The points to note are that data will be aligned on the right and that the sending field may not contain spaces. In the following definition the two rightmost positions will contain spaces. In this case there will be an attempt to move these two spaces to the receiving numeric field. This will be invalid data and the program will terminate abnormally.

```
05   alfa-num        pic X(06) pic '1234'.
```

Assume the following definitions:

```
05   alpha-num       pic X9(06) value '123456'.
05   num             pic S9(04).
```

The instruction:

```
Move alpha-num   to num
```

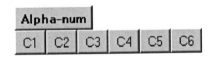 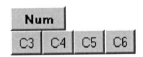

In moving from an alphanumeric source to a numeric destination it is the responsibility of the programmer to ensure that only valid data are moved to the destination. In the preceding example did the programmer expect 1234 to be transferred or did he expect the value 3456? We suggest that both source and destination be the same size.

Moving Numeric to Alphanumeric

The leftmost position in the numeric source will be moved to the leftmost position in the alphanumeric destination. Note also that the source may not contain a decimal point. If the source is longer than the destination there will be truncation. If the destination is longer, the unused positions on the right will be space filled.

```
05   W20-alpha-num pic X(06).
05   W20-num1       pic S9(04) value 1234.
```

The instruction:

```
move W20-num1 to W20-alpha-num
```

The graphical representation:

We may move a packed field to an alphanumeric field as long as it does not contain decimals. The field will be unpacked into the alphanumeric field.

Moving a Group Field to a Numeric Field

You will recall that a group field behaves as an alphanumeric field. We have already said that in a move the rules followed are the rules pertaining to the receiving field. Regrettably, when it comes to the move from a group field to a numeric field this does not apply; the rules that follow are the rules for an alphanumeric destination. Assume the following definitions:

```
01   an-group                              value '1234'.
       05   an1              pic X(02).
       05   an2              pic X(02).
01   nums.
       05   num1             pic S9(04).
       05   num2             pic S9(03).
       05   num3             pic S9(05).
```

The instruction: `move an-group to num1`

Since the two fields are the same size, the results are acceptable and execution proceeds without a hitch.

```
move an-group to num2
```

The destination is smaller than the source; truncation takes place but execution is successful.

```
move an-group to num3
```

Execution is not successful. Because the numeric field is being treated as an alphanumeric field, data are moved in starting on the left and vacant positions are space filled. When moving of a space to a numeric field is attempted, execution is interrupted and the program terminates abnormally.

Moving a Literal to an Alphanumeric Field

Moving a literal of type numeric is the same as moving a field of type numeric. The move to an alphanumeric field is permitted as long as the literal does not contain a decimal point. The definition and the instruction follow:

```
05  alpha-num            pic X(05).
move 1234 to alpha-num
```

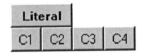

The data were moved in accordance with alphanumeric moves. Alignment was on the left and the vacant position on the right was space filled. Had we coded the move as follows, it would have been successful. ASCII hexadecimal 2E is the decimal point

```
move '123.4' to alpha-num
```

What was moved was not a numeric source but an alphanumeric source.

Moving All 'Literal'

The move transfers the named literal repeatedly to the destination field. The literal may be numeric or alphanumeric - but, if numeric, it may not be packed. The literal may consist of one or more characters. Irrespective of the type of the destination, the rules are the same as for the alphanumeric move. Assume the following definitions:

```
05  alpha-num1           pic X(06).
```

113

```
      05  alpha-num2              pic X(07).
```
The instruction.

```
   move all 'AB' to alpha-num1
```

Graphically represented:

The literal was moved repeatedly, starting on the left, until the destination was full. Let us now see what will happen if the size of the destination is not a multiple of the size of the literal.

The instruction:

```
   move all 'AB' to alpha-num2
```

Graphically represented:

Transfer stops when the last position in the destination receives a character.

Assume the following definitions:

```
      05   num1              pic 9(05)V99.
```

The instruction:

```
   move all '12' to num1
```

Graphically represented:

 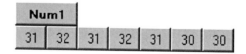

The literal was moved repeatedly, starting on the left, until the integer component was full. Transfer stopped and the decimal component was zero filled. Note that the literal must be an integer.

114

The Justified Clause

The **justified** clause is applied to elementary fields of type **alphanumeric** or **alphabetic**. The clause is used to force alignment on the right as against the natural alignment of these types on the left. The clause may be shortened to **just**. We may also specify **right**, as shown below:

```
05   alpha-num1          pic X(06) just.
05   alpha-num2          pic X(06) just right.
```

The instruction:

```
move 'Yes' to alpha-num1
move 'No' to alpha-num2
```

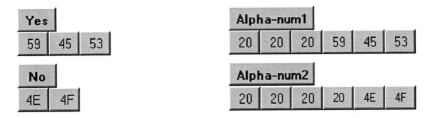

The values shown for the characters are the ASCII equivalents. The data were aligned on the right and the vacant positions were space filled. What will happen if the destination field is shorter than the literal?

```
move 'October' to alpha-num1
```

Truncation was now on the left.

If the **move all 'literal'** is applied to a field for which the justified clause has been specified, the justified clause will not be respected. Consider the following code:

```
05   alpha-num2          pic X(07) just right.
move all 'Yes' to alpha-num2
```

The graphical representation:

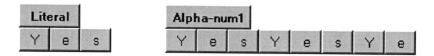

Because the last character on the right is an 'e' it follows that the first character moved was the 'Y' and it was moved to the leftmost position in the destination.

Constants Revisited

We have seen constants specified at elementary level as well as at group level. We have seen the **figurative constant zero** specified at elementary level. What we are going to investigate now is the effect of specifying the figurative constant at group level. We will also see if specifying the literal '0' will also have the same effect. Consider the definitions:

```
01   W20-group                            value zero.
        05   W20-num1          pic S9(03).
        05   W20-num2          pic   X(03).
        05   W20-num3          pic S9(03).
```

Graphically represented we would have:

We see that specifying the figurative constant zero caused a zero to be placed in each and every byte in the group, including W20-num2. Let us now see the effect of specifying the literal zero instead of the figurative constant **zero**. Consider the definitions:

```
01   W20-group                            value 0.
        05   W20-num1          pic S9(03).
        05   W20-num2          pic S9(03).
        05   W20-num3          pic S9(03).
```

The compiler expects an alphanumeric literal and rejects the code.

The Figurative Constant Spaces

Specifying the value clause with the figurative constant spaces at group level has the effect of moving spaces to the whole field. It is true that specifying the literal ' ' has the same effect. Consider the definitions below:

```
01  W20-group                               value spaces.
      05  W20-num1           pic S9(03).
      05  W20-num2           pic  X(03).
      05  W20-num3           pic S9(03).
```

All bytes in the group field would contain spaces. Of course, W20-num1 and W20-num3 are numeric and must contain appropriate values before they can be used.

Summary

- Numeric data may be in the **internal** or the **external format**. In the external format, a digit occupies one byte. In the **internal format**, a byte is capable of holding two digits. Data in the **internal format** are said to be **packed** and data in the **external format** are said to be **unpacked**.

- In a **packed** field, the digit component of the low order byte holds the sign. In an unpacked field, the zone component of the low order byte holds the sign.

- To find out how many bytes the number will occupy, divide the total number of digits, integer plus decimals plus one for the sign, by two and round upwards.

- The number of digits, integer plus decimals, should always be odd.

- In moving data, alignment in the receiving field follows the rules of the receiving field.

- For alphanumeric fields, alignment is on the left; vacant positions on the right are space filled. For numeric fields alignment is on the right or on the decimal point; vacant positions on the left are zero filled. If there are decimals and all decimal positions are not filled, vacant positions on the right will be zero filled.

- For alphanumeric fields, if the data do not fit, truncation is on the right. For a numeric field truncation is on the left. If there are decimals and they do not fit, truncation on the right will also occur.

- In moving alphanumeric to numeric, the alphanumeric field may not contain spaces. Data in the numeric field will align on the right.

- In moving numeric to alphanumeric the leftmost position will be moved to the leftmost position in the destination. If there is truncation, it will be on the right. If the destination is longer than the source, there will be space filling on the right. The numeric source may not have decimals.

- When a group field is moved to a numeric field, the rules followed are as for an alphanumeric destination. Alignment will be on the left. If the destination is shorter than the source there will be truncation on the right. If the destination is longer, vacant positions on the right will be space filled or the program will terminate abnormally.

- Moving a numeric literal to an alphanumeric field is the same as moving a numeric field to an alphanumeric field. The literal may not contain decimals.

- In moving **ALL 'Literal'**, the literal will be moved repeatedly until the receiving field is full. If the size of the receiving field is not a multiple of the size of the literal there will be truncation.

- In moving **ALL 'Literal'**, if the literal is numeric it may be moved to a numeric destination. If the destination contains decimals, the decimal positions will be zero filled.

- The **justified** clause is applied to an alphanumeric field to cause alignment to be on the right.

- If the ALL 'Literal' is applied to a field for which the **justified** clause has been specified, the **justified** will not be respected.

- Specifying '**value zero**' at group level will zero fill the group field. If 'value 0' is specified for a group field, the rightmost position of the group field will receive a '0' and the remaining bytes will be space filled. It may also happen that specifying the literal will cause unsuccessful compilation.
- Specifying 'value spaces' at group level will fill the whole field with spaces.

Complete

Show a space as a caret ('^').

1.   A numeric packed field may be moved to an alphanumeric field if it does not contain _____.

2.   Moving a packed numeric field to an alphanumeric field will _____ the data.

3.   In moving a numeric field to an alphanumeric field, if the destination is longer than the source _____ will occur on the right.

4.   If you define a numeric field with the picture 9(5)V99 and you move the value 7523.9 to it, the value in the receiving field will be _____. (Show all bytes)

5.   You have defined a field with the picture X(6) **justified**. You move the value September to it. After the move the field will contain the value _____.

6.   You have defined a field with the picture X(7). You move **all** 'Yes' to the field. After the move the field will contain the value _____.

7.   You have defined a field with the picture X(7) **justified**. You move ALL 'Yes' to the field. After the move the field will contain the value _____.

8.   You have a group field and its subordinates contain the value 98765. You move the group field to a numeric field with picture 9(4). After the move, the numeric field will contain _____.

9.   You have an alphanumeric field defined with the picture X(06). After moving the value 'Five' to it, it will contain _____.

10.   The sign in a packed field is in the _____ component of the ___ _____ byte.

11.   The sign in an unpacked field is in the _____ component of the ____ _____ byte.

True/False

1. We may not move a packed field to an alphanumeric field.
2. Data moved to an alphanumeric field align on the left.
3. Numeric data moved to a numeric field always align on the right.
4. Moving packed data to a numeric unpacked field will unpack the data.
5. If you move 5000 to an alphanumeric field defined as X(6) after the move, the field will contain 500000.
6. When packed data are moved to an alphanumeric field, the data are unpacked.
7. We may move an alphanumeric field containing packed data to a numeric unpacked field and the data will be unpacked.
8. If, for a group field, we code 'value zero', the group field will be set to all zeros.
9. If, for a group field, we code 'value 0', the group field will be set to a zero on the left. The remaining bytes will be set to spaces.
10. To determine the size of a packed field given its picture, we divide the number of digits by 2, subtract 1 and round upwards.
11. You have a numeric field defined as 9(3) containing the value 123. You move this field to a field defined as X(6). You move the alphanumeric field back to the numeric field. The numeric field will now contain the value 000.
12. We may not use the **justified** clause on a field defined as numeric.
13. Specifying the **justified** clause on an alphanumeric field will cause the data to align on the left.
14. **move all** 'Literal' does not respect the **justified** clause.

Exercises

Assume the definition:
```
05   work1           pic A(06).
05   work2           pic X(06).
05   work3           pic 9(06).
```

1. Describe the contents of each of the following. If you think the operation is not valid write 'Not valid'. Show all bytes. Show a space as '^'.

```
move 'One'       to work1
move 'One Two'   to work1
move 100         to work1
move 'spaces'    to work1
move 'R '        to work1
```

2. Describe the contents of each of the following. If you think the operation is not valid write 'Not valid'. Show all bytes. Show a space as '^'.

```
move 100         to work2
move 'One'       to work2
move 'One Two'   to work2
move spaces      to work2
move 'zero'      to work2
```

3. Describe the contents of each of the following. If you think the operation is not valid write 'Not valid'. Show all bytes. Show a space as '^'.

```
move 'One'       to work3
move 123         to work3
move 100.00      to work3
move 'B '        to work3
move zero        to work3
```

4. What will the following items contain when initialized as shown? Show all bytes. Show a space as '^'.

```
01   Group1                          value 0.
     05   amount1     pic 9(5).
     05   amount2     pic 9(5).

01   Group1                          value zero.
     05   amount1     pic 9(5).
     05   amount2     pic 9(5).
```

5.   What will the following item contain when initialized as shown? Show all bytes. Show a space as '^'.

```
05   space-field  pic X(5) value 'spaces'.
```

6.   What will the following item contain when initialized as shown? Show all bytes. Show a space as '^'.

```
05   amount2      pic 9(5)     value 0.
```

7.   What will the following item contain when initialized as shown? Show all bytes. Show a space as '^'.

```
05   space-field pic X(6)      value spaces.
```

8.   What will the following item contain when initialized as shown? Show all bytes. Show a space as '^'.

```
05   space-field pic X(8)      value '415'.
```

9.   What will the following item contain when initialized as shown? Show all bytes. Show a space as '^'.

```
05   msg         pic X(8)      value 'Yes'.
```

10. What will the following item contain when initialized as shown? Show all bytes. Show a space as '^'.

```
05   space-field pic X(8)      value all 'Yes'.
```

11. What will the following item contain when initialized as shown? Show all bytes. Show a space as '^'.

```
05   amount      pic 9(2)V9.
     move 138.55 to amount
```

For each of the following, give the number of bytes occupied by W1-number:

```
11.1  01   w1-number        pic S9(5)v99   comp-3.
11.2  01   w1-number        pic S9(9)v99   comp-3.
11.3  01   w1-number        pic 9(5).99-.
11.4  01   w1-number        pic S9(5)v99.
11.5  01   w1-number.
           05   w1-no1      pic 9999.
           05   w1-no2      pic 99.
```

```
    1.6    01    w1-number          pic 9999.
                 88    w1-no1              value 9999.
                 88    w1-no2              value 99.
```

12.   Given the following data fields:

Name	Picture	Contents
field-b	S9(3)	345
field-c	9(5)	30000
field-d	999	670

Complete receiving-field value for all legal moves below. Indicate which moves, if any, are illegal.

Move to receiving-field

		PICTURE	VALUE
12.1	all " xyz"	x(5)	?
12.2	"xyz"	x(5)	?
12.3	"zero"	x(5)	?
12.4	field-b	9(3)	?
12.5	all "xyz"	9(3)	?
12.6	field-c	9(3)	?
12.7	field-d	9(3)	?
12.8	field-b	S9(2)	?
12.9	field-d	xx	?
12.10	field-b	S9(5)	?

13.   Given the following data fields for _each_ MOVE.

```
        01    field1.
              05    field1-a    pic 99      value 7.
              05    field1-b    pic 9       value 8.
        01    field2            pic 9(4)    value 12.
```

Complete the receiving field value for all legal moves below. Indicate which moves, if any, are illegal. Show leading/trailing spaces and zeros clearly.What will **field1** contain after execution of each of the following?

13.1   move field2 to field1

13.2   move "ab" to field1

13.3   move field2 to field1-a

13.4   move "ab" to field1-a

13.5   move "1" to field1

13.6   move field2 to field1-b

13.7   move all "ab" to field1

13.8   move all "ab" to field1-a.

what will **field2** contain after execution of the following?

13.9   move field1 to field2

13.10   move 12345 to field2

Chapter 9
Binary Fields & Bitwise Operations

Topics Covered

- Binary Fields
- Alignment of Binary Fields
- New Numeric Types
- Float
- Comp-5
- Bitwise Operations
- Bitwise AND
- Bitwise OR
- Exclusive OR
- The Not
- The COBOL Standard
- The Right Shift and the Left Shift
- Summary
- Complete
- True/False
- Exercises

Binary Fields

We have learnt to define numeric data in the packed and unpacked formats. These formats are traditionally associated with languages running on mainframes and, so far, with COBOL running on PCs. The **binary data** traditionally offered by COBOL are specified using the structure provided by the **pic** or **picture** keyword.

When we use **pic**, we specify the maximum number of digits the field is expected to contain. If the maximum value the field is to contain will not exceed 9, we would specify **pic 9**. Note that the picture enables us to specify maximum and minimum values. We are not able to specify intermediate values. If we need a field to keep the days of the month it would have to have a **pic 99** picture, although values in the field would never exceed 31. The following table depicts the maximum and minimum values associated with the different pictures:

Picture	Value Range
Pic S9	-9 to +9
Pic S99	-99 to +99
Pic S999	-999 to +999
Pic S9999	-9999 to +9999
Pic S99999	-99999 to +99999
Table 09.01 – Field capacities	

The **binary** fields in COBOL are fixed length as opposed to the variable length fields with which we have become acquainted. The lengths are as follows:

Field Type	Length
Halfword	2 bytes
Fullword	4 bytes
Doubleword	8 bytes
Table 09.02 – Binary field types	

When using **packed** and **unpacked** formats, four bits are used to specify a digit in the range 0 to 9. In the binary format the situation changes. A **binary** field has a value that is established by the bits that are on. The leftmost bit determines the sign. If the bit is on, the value is negative; if the bit is off, the value is positive. Let us start by seeing the value associated with each bit position. We will look at a 16 bit field.

	16384	8192	4096	2048	1024	512	256	128	64	32	16	8	4	2	1
	15	14	13	12	11	10	9	8	7	6	5	4	3	2	1

We are accustomed to using the decimal system. In a decimal system every digit position has a value that is 10 times the value of the digit position of its right-hand neighbor. In the binary system, base 2, each bit position has a value that is twice as large as the value of its right hand neighbor. Whereas in the decimal system every position reflects a power of 10, in the binary system each value is a power of 2. The following table depicts these powers and associated values:

Powers	Values
2 to the power of 0	1
2 to the power of 1	2
2 to the power of 2	4
2 to the power of 3	8
2 to the power of 4	16
2 to the power of 5	32
2 to the power of 6	64
2 to the power of 7	128
2 to the power of 8	256
2 to the power of 9	512
2 to the power of 10	1024
2 to the power of 11	2048
2 to the power of 12	4096
2 to the power of 13	8192
2 to the power of 14	16384
Table 09.03 – Values as powers of 2	

If all the bits are on we should be able to store a maximum value of 32767 given by the sum of 15 bits when they are all on. But you know that in COBOL we are not able to specify intermediate values. The range of values will be given by pic S9999 or pic S99999. If we say pic S99999 the maximum value we can specify is 99 999, but we only have two bytes and 99 999 will not fit. Then, in two bytes, the maximum value we are able to store is given by a picture of S9999. The following table shows the values we are able to store for each of the binary field sizes.

Picture	Value
Pic S9 to Pic S9(4)	9 to 9 999
Pic S9(5) to Pic S9(9)	99 999 to 999 999 999
Pic S9(10) to Pic S9(18)	9 999 999 999 to 999 999 999 999 999 999
Table 09.04 – Pictures and associated ranges	

Let us investigate the usages that are associated with binary fields.

Usages
Usage is binary
Usage is comp
Usage is comp-4
Table 09.05 – Binary usages

The following program depicts the pictures and values associated with each definition. In each we have at all times shown the maximum value allowed for the definition. It is unusual to employ the keyword 'usage' in our data definitions. In the example below, we used the keyword in the first definitions only.

Binary Fields

```
program-id. Chapter0901.

working-storage section.

01  W10-types.
    05  W10-bin-half    pic S9(4)   usage binary value 9999.
    05  W10-bin-full    pic S9(9)   usage binary value
                                    999999999.
    05  W10-bin-double  pic S9(18)  usage binary value
                                    999999999999999999.

01  W20-types.
    05  W20-bin-half    pic S9(4)   comp value 9999.
    05  W20-bin-full    pic S9(9)   comp value 999999999.
    05  W20-bin-double  pic S9(18)  comp value
                                    999999999999999999.

01  W30-types.
    05  W30-bin-half    pic S9(4)   comp-4 value 9999.
    05  W30-bin-full    pic S9(9)   comp-4 value 999999999.
    05  W30-bin-double  pic S9(18)  comp-4 value
                                    999999999999999999.
```

Listing 09.01 – 1 of 2

Binary Fields

```
procedure division.
A100-start.
    display 'Binary half word     : ' W10-bin-half
    display 'Binary full word     : ' W10-bin-full
    display 'Binary double word   : ' W10-bin-double
    display 'Binary half word     : ' W20-bin-half

    display 'Binary full word     : ' W20-bin-full
    display 'Binary double word   : ' W20-bin-double
    display 'Binary half word     : ' W30-bin-half
    display 'Binary full word     : ' W30-bin-full
    display 'Binary double word   : ' W30-bin-double
    stop run.
```

Listing 09.01 - 2 of 2

```
Binary half word     :   +9999
Binary full word     :   +999999999
Binary double word   :   +9999999999999999999
Binary half word     :   +9999
Binary full word     :   +999999999
Binary double word   :   +9999999999999999999
Binary half word     :   +9999
Binary full word     :   +999999999
Binary double word   :   +9999999999999999999
```

Binary fields may contain decimals. The following code reflects the preceding definitions now containing decimal positions:

Binary Fields with Decimals

```
01   W10-types.
     05   W10-bin-half     pic S9(2)V99   usage binary value 9999.
     05   W10-bin-full     pic S9(7)V99   usage binary value
                                          999999999.
     05   W10-bin-double   pic S9(16)V99  usage binary value
                                          99999999999999999999.
```

Figure 09.01 – 1 of 2

129

Binary Fields with Decimals

```
01  W20-types.
    05  W20-bin-half    pic S9(2)V99  comp value 9999.
    05  W20-bin-full    pic S9(7)V99  comp value 999999999.
    05  W20-bin-double  pic S9(16)V99 comp value
                                      99999999999999999.
01  W30-types.
    05  W30-bin-half    pic S9(2)V99  comp-4 value 9999.
    05  W30-bin-full    pic S9(7)V99  comp-4 value 999999999.
    05  W30-bin-double  pic S9(16)V99 comp-4 value
                                      99999999999999999.
```

Figure 09.01 – 2 of 2

Alignment of Binary Fields

How alignment takes place depends on the type of hardware on which the program is running. Mainframes are word machines, whereas PCs are byte machines. In a byte machine a field aligns on the next available byte. Word machines align on an appropriate word boundary. Boundaries are **half word**, **full word** and **double word**. Binary fields, in a word machine, must align on a boundary that is divisible by the size of the binary field. Thus a binary half word field may be aligned on a half word, a full word or a double word. A full word binary field may be aligned on a full word or on a double word boundary. A double word binary field may only be aligned on a double word boundary. A 01 level field will be aligned on a double word. On a word machine we may force alignment by using the keyword **synchronized**.

The following definitions secure automatic alignment. All the fields below align on an appropriate boundary:

Alignment of Binary Fields

```
01  W10-binary-fields.
    05  W10-double   pic 9(18)  comp.
    05  W10-full     pic 9(9)   comp.
    05  W10-half     pic 9(4)   comp.
```

Figure 09.02

Of the definitions that follow, only the first is aligned. We force allignment by using the keyword **synchronized**. The keyword may be shortened to **sync**.

130

Synchronizing

```
01   W10-binary-fields.
     05   W10-half          pic 9(4)   comp.
     05   W10-full          pic 9(9)   comp sync.
     05   W10-double        pic 9(10)  comp synchronized.
```

Figure 09.03

New Numeric Types

The 2002 COBOL standard has taken into account the tremendous expansion in the commercial use of the PC and the new languages that are now in general use on the PC. Characteristic of these languages is that they use data types that differ from those used in COBOL. If programs in the different languages are to communicate it would be advantageous if both COBOL and these languages were able to use the same data types.

Following, we show the new **binary** types introduced by the COBOL standard to provide compatibility with corresponding types present in PC languages. Note that PC languages do not have total uniformity with regard to data types. One example of a difference is that Java does not have unsigned numeric variables, whereas C has unsigned numeric variables. To favour compatibility you should sign all your fields. Notice that the keyword **pic** is not used in the definitions.

New Data Types

```
program-id. chapter0902.
working-storage section.
01   W10-types.
     05   W10-bin-char     usage binary-char signed value 127.
     05   W10-bin-uchar    usage binary-char unsigned value 255.
     05   W10-bin-short    usage binary-short signed value
                                 32767.
     05   W10-bin-ushort   usage binary-short unsigned value
                                 65535.
     05   W10-bin-long     usage binary-long signed value
                                 2147483647.
     05   W10-bin-ulong    usage binary-long unsigned value
                                 4294967295.
     05   W10-bin-double   usage binary-double signed.
     05   W10-bin-udouble  usage binary-double unsigned.
```

Listing 09.02 – 1 of 2

New Data Types

```
procedure division.
A100-start.
    display 'Binary-char signed     : ' W10-bin-char
    display 'Binary-char unsigned   : ' W10-bin-uchar
    display 'Binary-short signed    : ' W10-bin-short
    display 'Binary-short unsigned : ' W10-bin-ushort
    display 'Binary-long signed     : ' W10-bin-long
    display 'Binary-long unsigned   : ' W10-bin-ulong
    compute W10-bin-double  = 2 ** 63
    compute W10-bin-udouble = 2 ** 64 - 1
    display 'Binary-double signed   : ' W10-bin-double
    display 'Binary-double unsigned: ' W10-bin-udouble
    stop run.
```

Listing 09.02 – 2 of 2

The execution of the preceding program yielded the following results:

Of the new types we have considered so far, none will allow a fractional component; they only store integers. Note that to this point we have looked at usages employing the **comp** or **computational** keywords. Their uses so far are:

- For **binary** fields we specify either **comp** or **comp-4**.
- For **packed** fields we specify **comp-3**.

We are still left with **comp-1**, **comp-2** and **comp-5**. We will be looking at these usages in a short while.

Float

Binary-double occupies 64 bits, does not allow decimals and is high precision. The float type is a **floating point** type and consequently allows for decimals. **Float** allows for both low and high precision. The following table depicts the options available for types catering for decimals:

Usage	Precision
Float-short	7 digits
Float-long	16 digits
Float-extended	16 digits
Comp-1	7 digits
Comp-2	16 digits
Table 09.06 – Precision in calculations	

The next program depicts the use of the types catering for decimals and the output reveals their level of precision. Precision to seven digits implies that the seventh digit will be rounded. Float-extended is simply another name for float-long because the results produced are exactly the same when using either of the types. Furthermore, as you can see, **comp-1** pairs with **float-short** and **comp-2** pairs with **float-long**. Precision to 16 digits means that the 16th digit will be rounded.

The Float Type

```
program-id. chapter0903.

working-storage section.
01  W20-types.
    05  W20-float-short      usage float-short value
                             123.45678901.
    05  W20-float-long       usage float-long value
                             123.456789012345678.
    05  W20-float-extended   usage float-extended value
                             123.456789012345678.
01  W30-types.
    05  W30-float-short      usage comp-1 value 123.45678901.
    05  W30-float-long       usage comp-2 value
                             123.456789012345678.
```

Listing 09.03 – 1 of 2

The Float Type

```
procedure division.
A100-start.
    display 'Float short    : ' W20-float-short
    display 'Float long     : ' W20-float-long
    display 'Float extended: ' W20-float-extended
    display 'comp-1         : ' W30-float-short
    display 'comp-2         : ' W30-float-long

    stop run.
```

Listing 09.03 – 2 of 2

```
C:\ Command Prompt                                        _ □ ✕
Float short    : 123.4568
Float long     : 123.456789012346
Float extended: 123.456789012346
comp-1         : 123.4568
comp-2         : 123.456789012346
```

We see the same degree of precision in **float-short** as we see in **comp-1** and in **float-long** we see the same degree of precision as in **comp-2**.

Comp-5

Using **comp-5** provides us with another way of defining the **binary** fields we have been learning about. By combining the usage with the picture we are able to define the different binary types with which we have become acquainted.

Note that the picture and the **usage** together determine the type. However, PIC S9(2) does not mean a maximum value of 99. The following table depicts the **usage**, the corresponding picture and the maximum values associated with each.

Equivalent	Picture + comp-5	Maximum Values
Binary-char	Pic S9(2) comp-5	127
Binary-short	Pic S9(4) comp-5	32767
Binary-long	Pic S9(9) comp-5	2147483647
Binary-double	Pic S9(18) comp-5	2^{62}
Binary-long unsigned	Pic X(4) comp-5	4294967295
Table 09.07 – Usage Comp-5		

134

The following program depicts the use of comp-5 and the output clearly shows that comp-5 produces the values associated with the corresponding binary fields.

The last item depicted in the table is a Net Express type equivalent to binary long unsigned. You will notice that it is coded as Pic X(4) although it is numeric. Because it is unsigned it is able to contain a value double the value in the signed field plus 1.

Comp-5

```
program-id. chapter0904.

working-storage section.
01   W40-types.
        05   W40-char      pic S9(2)   comp-5 value 127.
        05   W40-short     pic S9(4)   comp-5 value 32767.
        05   W40-long      pic S9(9)   comp-5 value 2147483647.
        05   W40-double    pic S9(18)  comp-5.
        05   W40-picx      pic X(4)    comp-5 value 2147483647.

procedure division.
A100-start.
     display 'Binary char    : ' W40-char
     display 'Binary short   : ' W40-short
     display 'Binary long    : ' W40-long
     compute W40-double = 2 ** 63 - 1
     display 'Binary double  : ' W40-double
     compute W40-picx = 2 * W40-picx + 2
     display 'Pic X(4)       : ' W40-picx
     stop run.
```

Listing 09.04

```
Binary char    : +127
Binary short   : +32767
Binary long    : +2147483647
Binary double  : +223372036854775807
Pic X          : 4294967295
```

Although binary-char corresponds to char in C, its behaviour is not entirely the same. Whereas in C a type char may receive any value, say '65' or 'A', both having the same bit configuration, in COBOL a binary-char may only receive data that are numeric.

Bitwise Operations

The introduction of bitwise operations into COBOL stresses the fact that, as indicated earlier, the language started off as a purely business language but today has become an all purpose language with a business slant. As you know, the byte is the smallest addressable unit of storage. Bitwise operations, however, enable us to manipulate bits. **Bit manipulation** is not a common requirement in a commercial application but writers of non-commercial software have welcomed the introduction of bitwise operations.

All integer data types allow bit manipulation. This means binary-char, binary-short and binary long. Although we may apply bitwise operations to type binary, the type only allows reference to the four rightmost bits in a byte because it is tied to the 'pic 9' structure. For this reason we will not look at bitwise operations affecting the binary type. Because it is easier to depict, we will work mostly with **binary-char**.

We will start by looking at how Micro Focus handles bitwise operations. The COBOL standard handles the operations in a slightly different manner. When we look at the standard we will provide you with a table that will make clear the difference between the two.

The following code illustrates the definition of a **binary-long** field appropriately initialized. Notice that a **B** prefixes the initializing value. The B must always precede the binary value.

```
01  W80-bool        binary-long unsigned value
                    B"10000000000000001000000000000001".
```

If the field had not been initialized we could have used a move to set it to the desired value. The following code will do this:

```
01  W90-amask           binary-long unsigned.
    move B"10000000000000001000000000000001" to W90-amask
```

The Bitwise And

In most bitwise operations we want to change values or ascertain values. To do this we need a mask. We will set the mask field to the particular bit configuration that will achieve the desired objective. The examination starts on the left and proceeds bit by bit until all the bits have been examined. The target receives the result of the examination and also provides the mask. If we need to repeatedly use the mask, we need to replenish it each time we use it.

The truth table for the **and** follows. For true to result, corresponding bits must be on.

Source	Target	Result
0	0	0
1	0	0
0	1	0
1	1	1
Table 09.08 – And truth table		

In the next example we have a field W10-num containing the bit value '00111001'. This is the hexadecimal value corresponding to 9. You will recall that digits in the unpacked format have 3 in the high order four bits and the digit value in the low order four bits. This is what we have: The high order four bits contain '0011' which is binary for decimal 3. The low order four bits contain '1001' binary for decimal 9.

The mask contains '00001111'. Since in an **and** both bits must be true, any value in the four low order bits will be retained. The high order four bits all contain zero which means that 0 will be returned each time. Let us look at the program and then at the output:

The Bitwise And

```
program-id. Chapter0904.
data division.
working-storage section.
01  W10-num        binary-char unsigned value B"00111001".
01  W10-amask      binary-char unsigned value B"00001111".
procedure division.
A100-start.
    display "Source: " W10-num
    display "Mask  : " W10-amask
    call "cbl_and" using W10-num W10-amask by value 1
    display "Source: "W10-num " Mask: " W10-amask
    stop run.
```

Listing 09.05

```
Command Prompt
Source: 057
Mask  : 015
Source: 057 Mask: 009
```

Notice the line of code that is responsible for most of the work done and certainly for all the anding work.

```
call "cbl_and" using W10-num W10-amask by value 1
```

We use the verb **call** when we want to ask another program to do work for us. The name of the program is "**cbl_and**' and the program we are invoking expects to receive two fields and a literal that depicts the length of the fields being passed. We will later go into the intricacies of calling programs; for the time being this short explanation should suffice. You will notice that for each of the bitwise operations we do we will be calling on the services of another program. You will also notice that the value in the mask has been changed; the value it now contains is the result of the anding operation. The 1 is the length of the arguments being passed.

The program that is called expects to receive the arguments in the sequence shown, namely value, mask and length of arguments.

The Bitwise Or

For the bitwise **or** to yield true it is enough that only one of the bits in the comparison be true. The truth table for the **or** is:

Source	Target	Result
0	0	0
1	0	1
0	1	1
1	1	1
Table 09.09 - Or truth table		

We are now reversing the operation conducted by the preceding **and**. The lines of code containing the data follow.

```
01  W10-num      binary-char unsigned value B"00001001".
01  W10-amask    binary-char unsigned value B"00110000".
```

W10-num is the source and it contains binary 9. We wish to convert it to unpacked 9. Unpacked 9 has the hexadecimal value 39, from which we see that the mask must have the value 3 in the high order four bits. The four low order bits contain zeros so that the original data in the source will not be changed. Remember, in an **or** only one of the items needs to be true, so the mask contains all zeros. The call that does all the hard work for us is:

```
call "cbl_or" using W10-num W10-amask by value 1
```

Because we are working with **binary-char**, the length is always one, hence the value one.

The Bitwise Or

```
program-id. Chapter0906.

data division.
working-storage section.
01  W10-num         binary-char unsigned value B"00001001".
01  W10-amask       binary-char unsigned value B"00110000".
01  W10-char        pic 9 redefines W10-amask.
procedure division.
A100-start.
    display "Source: " W10-num
    display "Mask  : " W10-amask
    call "cbl_or" using W10-num W10-amask by value 1
    display "Source: "W10-num " Mask: " W10-amask
    stop run.
```

Listing 09.06

Notice that 57 is the binary value of hexadecimal 39. In decimal the 3 has a value of 30. In hexadecimal, which is base 16, the 3 has a value given by 3 * 16, which is 48. Adding 9 to the figure results in 57.

Exclusive Or

In the **exclusive or**, if both bits are the same, 0 results. True results when only one of the bits is on. In assembler and in other languages that have the exclusive or, the most frequent use of the facility is for the toggling of a bit on and off. The truth table for the **exclusive or** looks like this:

Source	Target	Result
0	0	0
1	0	1
0	1	1
1	1	0
Table 09.10 – Exclusive Or		

In our example we start with both source and mask having a value of one. This means that zero is going to be returned. The mask now contains zero. Since the mask is now zero, the exclusive or will return one and so on. Let us look at the program:

The Bitwise Exclusive Or

```
program-id. Chapter0907.

working-storage section.
01   W10-num        binary-char unsigned value B"00000001".
01   W10-amask      binary-char unsigned value B"00000001".
procedure division.
A100-start.
    perform 5 times
        call "cbl_xor" using W10-num W10-amask by value 1
        display "Source: "W10-num " Mask: " W10-amask
    end-perform
    stop run.
```

Listing 09.07

```
Command Prompt                                    _ □ ✕
Source: 001 Mask: 000
Source: 001 Mask: 001
Source: 001 Mask: 000
Source: 001 Mask: 001
Source: 001 Mask: 000
```

The Not

The **not** will invert all bits giving us the one's complement. The program will perform this operation whenever it needs to convert a number from positive to negative or vice versa. If we have the value 1, invert all bits using **not** and add 1, we get the two's complement, which gives us −1. In the program we start off with a value of 1.

The Bitwise Not

```
program-id. Chapter0908.
data division.
working-storage section.
01  W10-num          binary-char signed value B"00000001".
01  W50-pause        pic x.

procedure division.
A100-start.
    display "Number: " W10-num
    call "cbl_not" using W10-num by value 1
    compute W10-num = W10-num + 1
    display "Number: " W10-num
    accept W50-pause
    stop run.
```

Listing 09.08

We will use a graphical representation to depict what happens.

0	0	0	0	0	0	0	1	Starting value of 1
1	1	1	1	1	1	1	0	All bits inverted now add 1
1	1	1	1	1	1	1	1	Final value −1

We will assume that we start off with a value of 2 and then proceed as in the preceding example.

0	0	0	0	0	0	1	0
1	1	1	1	1	1	0	1
1	1	1	1	1	1	1	0

Starting value of 2
All bits inverted now add 1
Final value –2

Let us consider a starting value of 3:

0	0	0	0	0	0	1	1
1	1	1	1	1	1	0	0
1	1	1	1	1	1	0	1

Starting value of 3
All bits inverted now add 1
Final value –3

You will see that the negative value is given by the value of the bit that is on and is to the immediate left of the leftmost zero, subtracting all the bits that are on to the right of the leftmost zero. We will consider a starting value of 4.

0	0	0	0	0	1	0	0
1	1	1	1	1	0	1	1
1	1	1	1	1	1	0	0

Starting value of 4
All bits inverted now add 1
Final value –4

The first bit that is on and is to the left of the leftmost zero has a value of 4. Since there are no bits on to the right of this one there is nothing to subtract. Finally, we will look at a starting value of 5.

0	0	0	0	0	1	0	1
1	1	1	1	1	0	1	0
1	1	1	1	1	0	1	1

Starting value of 5
All bits inverted now add 1
Final value 8 – 3 = -5

The COBOL Standard

The standard defines the types on which we have been performing bitwise operations as Boolean. The definition of a Boolean type follows:

```
01   W10-bool      pic 1111  usage bit value B"1001".
01   W10-true      pic 1     usage bit value B"1".
```

- The field W10-true, because it has a length of 1 bit may be used in an **if** as follows:

```
if  W10-true        *> without a relational operator
    move. . .
```

   or

```
if  W10-true = 1
    move. . .
```

- The field W10-bool occupies four bits and is followed by an implicit filler of four bits. An implicit filler of seven bits follows W10-true.

- The following table relates the Micro Focus calls to the Standard's equivalent operators:

Micro Focus Call	Standard Operators
CBL_AND	B-AND
CBL_OR	B-OR
CBL_XOR	B-XOR
CBL_NOT	B-NOT
Table 09.11 – Bitwise calls	

- Because the standard uses operators it is able to use the Boolean operators in a compute.

```
Compute W10-result = W10-num B-OR W10-amask
```

Right Shift and Left Shift

COBOL does not offer right and left shift operations. Because in binary data one shift to the right is equivalent to a division by two, we can create functions that will implement a right shift. A left shift, on the other hand, is equivalent to a multiplication by two.

   As we have indicated, the sign in a binary field is carried in the high order bit. Let us consider an initial value of -16 and a shift to the right of one position:

| 1 | 1 | 1 | 1 | 0 | 0 | 0 | 0 | Bit value of -16
|---|---|---|---|---|---|---|---|
| 0 | 1 | 1 | 1 | 1 | 0 | 0 | 0 | Shift one position to the right

   We see that shifting one position to the right would cause a zero bit to be gained on the left. The result is that the number changed from negative to positive. This is what used to happen with the right shift in C. Java overcame this problem and there was a lot of bragging about this huge step forward. C has since also overcome the problem.

As indicated, we can implement right and left shifts in COBOL using simple division and multiplication and the sign will always be respected.

Right and Left Shift

```
identification division.
program-id. chapter0909.
data division.
working-storage section.
01  W10-types.
    05  W10-bin        usage binary-short signed value 128.

procedure division.
A100-start.
    display 'Value before positive right shift: ' W10-bin
    perform right-shift
    display 'Value after positive right shift : ' W10-bin
    display 'Value before positive left shift : ' W10-bin
    perform left-shift
    display 'Value after positive left shift  : ' W10-bin
    move -128 to W10-bin
    display 'Value before negative right shift: ' W10-bin
    perform right-shift
    display 'Value after negative right shift : ' W10-bin
    display 'Value before negative left shift : ' W10-bin
    perform left-shift
    display 'Value after negative left shift  : ' W10-bin
    stop run.
right-shift.
    compute W10-bin = W10-bin / 4.
left-shift.
    compute W10-bin = W10-bin * 4.
```

Listing 09.09

Summary

- **Binary** fields are fixed length. They are two, four or eight bytes in length. To these lengths correspond the descriptions halfword, fullword and doubleword respectively.

- Although a **halfword** should be capable of holding a value of 32767, this is not so because we specify pic S9(4) or pic S9(5). There is no way of specifying an intermediate value.

- Binary fields employ the usage **binary**, comp or comp-4.

- A **binary** field may contain decimals.

- On a PC we have byte alignment so alignment is automatic. Mainframes are word machines and on these machines, binary fields need to be aligned on a proper boundary. A proper boundary is one that has an address that is divisible by the length of the field.

- The 2002 standard introduced types that are present in PC languages, the definitions of which do not use the picture clause.

- The types are:

  - Binary-char   - 1 byte
  - Binary-short   - 2 bytes
  - Binary-long   - 4 bytes
  - Binary-double - 8 bytes

- None of the preceding types allows for decimals.

- **Float**, as the name implies, is floating point and therefore allows for decimals. Float offers low precision, seven digits and high precision, 16 digits.

- We may use **comp-5** to define fields of type binary-xxx, where xxx may be replaced by char, short, long and double. The definition uses the picture clause in conjunction with **comp-5** usage.

- For bit manipulation, we use any of the binary-xxx types.

- For bitwise operations we use a mask. Note, however, that the **not** does not require a mask.

- The mask will have a value and therefore a structure, suited to the purpose.

- The **and** requires that both bits be true.

- The **or** requires that at least one bit be true.

- The **exclusive or** requires that only one of the bits be true.

- The **not** inverts the value of each bit.

- For **right** and **left shift** we may implement our own routines.

Complete

1.   You want to use a binary field to store temperatures in the range – 20 to +50. The field would be defined as PIC S_____ comp.

2.   For a binary field definition, we may employ the usage COMP or _____ or _____.

3.   On a PC binary, fields align on a _____.

4.   On a mainframe, the address of a binary halfword must be divisible by _____,

5.   On a mainframe, the address of a binary fullword must be divisible by _____,

6.   You need to place a value of 95000.74 into a binary field. The picture for the field would be PIC S_____ binary.

7.   The _____ clause causes binary fields to be aligned on a proper boundary.

8.   Using the new binary types introduced by the standard, to store a value of 25325 you would define the field as usage _____.

9.   Using the new binary types introduced by the standard, to store a value of + or - 25325 you would define the field as usage _____ _____.

10.   Float-short corresponds to _____ and float-long corresponds to _____.
11.   You wish to place the value 1,234,567 into a binary field. The picture should be PIC S_____ comp-5.

12.   Anding 1111 0000 with 0110 1001 produces _____.

13.   Oring 1111 0000 with 0110 1001 produces _____.

14.   Not 1111 0000 is _____.

15.   Exclusive oring 1100 0110 with 0011 0110 produces _____.

True/False

1. Binary fields may not contain decimals

2. The PIC clause enables us to specify maximum and minimum values as well as intermediate values.

3. A signed fullword binary field may hold a value of 4294967295.

4. Fullword fields align on a boundary that is divisible by 4.

5. Usage is comp and usage is binary yields the same results.

6. To a signed binary-char field, we may assign any character that has a bit configuration not greater than 127.

7. Binary-char occupies two bytes.

8. The value 1001 0110 anded with 0110 1001 yields 1111 1111.

9. The value 1001 1111 ored with 1111 0000 will yield 1111 1111.

10. The value 1001 1111 exclusive ored with 1111 0000 will yield 0110 1111.

11. Float-extended and binary-double have the same size.

12. You have a field defined as float short. You move the following value to it: 123456789987. If you display the field, the following would be displayed 123456790000000000.

13. The precision for float-extended is 16 digits.

14. The Net Express program that carries out anding is 'cbl-and'.

15. To interpret a negative binary number we find the value of the bit position to the immediate left of the leftmost zero. To that value we add all bits on to the right of that bit.

16. The not implements the two's complement.

Exercises

1. Explain why the maximum values in a binary field are always odd.

2. Create a routine to do a right shift and another to do a left shift. Ask the user for a number and a code to signify division or multiplication. Say 1 is division and 2 is multiplication. The user must also indicate the even value by which the number is to be divided or multiplied.

Chapter 10
Editing

Topics Covered

- Editing
- Alphabetic Editing
- Alphanumeric Editing
- Numeric Editing
- Zero Suppression
- Comma Insertion
- Inserting Blanks
- Signing an Edited Field
- Edited Field with Sign on the Right
- Edited Field with Sign on the Left
- Floating '+' Sign
- Floating '-' Sign

- The CR and DB Symbols
- The Fixed '$' Sign
- The Floating '$' Sign
- Cheque Protection
- Scaling
- Editing the Date
- Blank When Zero
- The Special-Names Paragraph
- Culturally Specific Editing
- Summary
- Complete
- True/False
- Exercises

Editing

Editing is concerned with the formatting of data so as to make it easy to understand the data. Seeing an amount depicted as '00958720' is not as informative as '$ 958.72'. COBOL is prominent among computer languages for the facilities it provides for the formatting of data. This is not surprising because of the importance that adequate reporting has in the commercial world.

There are two types of editing categorized by the action taken. The categories are:

- **Insertion editing** – In insertion editing a character that is not in the source is inserted into the edited result.

- **Suppression** with **replacement** – In this type of editing, a character in the source will be replaced by a different character in the edited result.

Furthermore, insertion editing will be of one of the following types:

- Simple insertion
- Special insertion
- Fixed insertion
- Floating insertion

As we examine different examples of editing we will identify the different types of editing involved.

Alphabetic Editing

Alphabetic is the simplest type of editing. Editing uses a number of characters, each indicating the intended result. The following table shows the edit characters allowed in **alphabetic editing**:

Edit Character	Purpose
A	Each character in the picture will be replaced by a character in the source.
B	**Simple insertion** – a space is inserted at the specified point. There is no corresponding character in the source.
Table 10.01 Alphabetic edit characters	

The following code illustrates alphabetic editing:

Alphabetic Editing

```
01  W10-msg              pic A(15) value "Thisandthat.".
01  W20-edit-msg         pic A(4)BA(3)BA(5).
    move W10-msg to W20-edit-msg
    display "The edited result is: " W20-edit-msg
```

Figure 10.01

```
Command Prompt                                    _ □ ×
The edited result is: This and that.
◄                                              ►
```

The first four characters in the source will come to occupy the first four positions in the edited field, represented by 'A(4)'. Then we have the insertion character 'B' which will cause a space to be inserted in the edited field at that point. The same applies to the remaining characters so as to produce the edited result shown.

Alphanumeric Editing

Alphanumeric editing is slightly more involved than alphabetic editing. The following table shows the edit characters allowed in **alphanumeric editing**.

Edit Character	Purpose
X	Each character in the picture will be replaced by a character in the source.
B	Simple insertion – a space is inserted at the specified point. There is no corresponding character in the source.
9	Each digit in the source will replace each 9 .
0	Simple insertion – a 0 will occupy the position. There is no corresponding character in the source.
/	Simple insertion – a slash will be inserted into the edited field at this point, before the next character is processed

Table 10.02   Alphanumeric edit characters

The following code illustrates alphanumeric editing and the use of the alphanumeric edit characters.

Alphanumeric Editing

```
01   W10-info              pic X(13) value "XK12020040614".
01   W20-edit-info         pic X(5)B00BX(4)/XX/XX.
     move W10-info to W20-edit-info
     display "The edited result is: " W20-edit-info
```

Figure 10.02

```
Command Prompt                                        _ □ ×
The edited result is: XK120 00 2004/06/14
```

The first five characters in the source will come to occupy the first five positions in the edited field, represented by 'X(5)'. Then we have the insertion character 'B', which will cause a space to be inserted at that point in the edited field. The same applies to the remaining characters so as to produce the edited result shown.

Note that the '/' may also be used in alphabetic editing although it is not strictly an edit character belonging to the alphabetic editing set. This is because the compiler will treat the alphabetic field as an alphanumeric field, if this becomes necessary.

Numeric Editing

Numeric editing is considerably more involved than the editing in the preceding types we have examined.

Edit Character	Purpose
.	Special insertion -
Z	Suppression and replacement.
$	Currency sign – Simple or floating insertion.
,	Simple insertion – thousands separator.
*	Check protection – Zero suppression, replacement by '*'.
0	Zero - Simple insertion.
B	Blank - Simple insertion.
CR	Credit characters – Fixed insertion.
DB	Debit characters – Fixed insertion.
+	Plus sign – Fixed or floating insertion.
-	Minus sign – Fixed or floating insertion.
P	Scaling

Table 10.03   Numeric edit characters

Zero Suppression

Zero suppression replaces leading zeros by spaces and is thus replacement editing. A leading zero is a zero located to the left of the most significant digit. As an example, 00908 has two leading zeros. The 0 between the 9 and the 8 is not leading because it has a significant digit to its left. Zero suppression uses the 'z' in the edit picture. The 9 will be used to signify that a digit should print irrespective of its value. The '.' represents a decimal point, normally implied in the source but actual when it comes to editing the data. The decimal point is used for alignment and is a case of special insertion. (We are using '^' to indicate a space.)

	Source			Destination	
	Picture	**Data**		**Picture**	**Result**
1	S999V9	536V4		ZZ9.99	536.40
2	S999V999	632V453		ZZ9.99	632.45
3	S999V999	042V841		ZZ9.99	^42.84
4	S999V999	-253V440		ZZ9.99	253.44
5	S999V999	000V000		ZZ9.99	^^0.00
6	S9999V999	7654V463		ZZ9.99	654.46
7	S9999V99	0000V00		ZZZZ.ZZ	^^^^^^^

Table 10.04 – Zero suppression examples

Comments

1. A zero was inserted on the right because the source has only one decimal position whereas the picture has two.
2. The source has three decimal positions whereas the picture only has two.
3. We have zero suppression with the leading zero being suppressed.
4. The source is signed but the picture is not, thus causing the sign to be dropped.
5. Leading zeros replaced by spaces. The 9's force printing so suppression stops.
6. Truncation occurs on the left and on the right.
7. The whole picture demands zero suppression. The source is all zeros causing spaces to print. Notice that the decimal point is also suppressed because it would not make sense to have a decimal point and no data.

Note that when the decimal point is reached, and there is a decimal value, suppression stops, the decimal point will print and zero suppression ceases.

Comma Insertion

Commas help in the case of large numbers, making for improved legibility. The comma will be inserted every three digits and is sometimes described as the "thousands separator". Commas are a case of simple insertion.

	Source			Destination	
	Picture	**Data**		**Picture**	**Result**
1	S9999V99	036V45		Z,ZZ9.99	^^^36.45
2	S9999V99	5042V84		Z,ZZ9.99	5,042.84
3	S9999V99	0000V05		Z,ZZ9.99	^^^^0.05
4	S9999V99	0123V45		Z,ZZ9.99	^^123.45
5	S9999V99	2000V00		Z,ZZ9.99	2,000.00
6	S9999V99	0000V06		Z,ZZZ.ZZ	^^^^^.06

Table 10.05 – Comma insertion examples

Comments

1. The source did not contain a thousands value so the comma is suppressed along with the leading zeros.
2. The comma and the decimal point occupy print positions.
3. Zero suppression extends up to the tens so the units print, although the corresponding value is zero.
4. Because of zero suppression there will not be a digit to the left of the comma, so the comma is suppressed.
5. Comma and decimal point print.
6. If printing is required to the right of the decimal point, the decimal point will print and so will all positions to the right of the decimal point.

Inserting Blanks

Blanks may be placed anywhere in the picture. When doing numeric editing the most common need for a space is in the thousands position, where we might otherwise have used a comma. If you are printing and pre-printed stationery is being used it might be wise to use the space for the thousands position. This is a case of simple insertion.

	Source			Destination	
	Picture	**Data**		**Picture**	**Result**
1	S9999V99	036V45		ZBZZ9.99	^^^36.45
2	S9999V99	5042V84		ZBZZ9.99	5 042.84
3	S9999V99	0000V05		ZBZZ9.99	^^^^0.05
4	S9999V99	0123V45		ZBZZ9.99	^^123.45
5	S9999V99	2000V00		ZBZZ9.99	2 000.00
6	999999	040804		ZBZZBZZ	4 08 04

Table 10.06 – Inserting blanks example

Comments

1. The source does not contain a thousands value so the space is part of zero suppression.
2. The space is placed where it was requested, between the thousands and hundreds.
3. The space is part of zero suppression.
4. The value of the source was less than a thousand so the space is part of zero suppression.
5. The space placed between thousands and hundreds.
6. We used the spaces for what is possibly a date and not for the thousands position.

Signing an Edited Field

Sometimes a **sign** is not necessary because it is positive by default. A person's age does not carry a sign because it simply cannot be negative. There are numbers however, that need a sign. A bank account may have a positive or a negative balance. For this reason we have a facility for providing a **sign** for a numeric-edited field. Note the following points.

- If we sign the edited picture using the '+' sign, then a sign will always print.

  - If the source is positive a '+' sign will print.
  - If the source is negative a '-' sign will print.

- If the edit picture is signed using the '-' sign, then the sign will print only if the value is negative, otherwise a space will replace the sign.

  - If the source contains a negative value, a '-' sign will print.
  - If the source contains a positive value, a space will print.

Edited Fields with the Sign on the Right

If the **sign** is specified on the right then that is where it will appear when printed. As you will see, we may also specify the **sign** on the left. When the **sign** is on the right, there may be no **sign** on the left. The **sign** on the right always constitutes fixed insertion editing.

	Source			Destination	
	Picture	**Data**		**Picture**	**Result**
1	S9999V99	5025V23		Z,ZZ9.99-	5,025.23^
2	S9999V99	-5002V84		Z,ZZ9.99-	5,002.84-
3	S9999V99	0000V34		Z,ZZ9.99+	^^^^0.34+
4	S9999V99	12121V45		Z,ZZ9.99+	2,121.45+
5	S99999V99	-40001V27		ZBZZ9.99+	^^^^1.27-
	Table 10.07 – Sign on the right examples				

Comments.

1. The source value is positive and the picture has a '-' sign. The sign will be replaced by a space.
2. The source value is negative and the picture has a '-' sign. The sign will print.
3. The source value is positive and the picture has a '+' sign. The sign will print.
4. The source value is positive and the picture has a '+' sign. However, the picture does not cater for five integer positions and the value is truncated. The sign will print.
5. The source value is negative and the picture has a '-' sign. The sign will print and the value will be truncated on the left.

Edited Field with the Sign on the Left

If the **sign** is specified on the left, it will appear on the left of the number displayed. If only one sign is being used we have a case of fixed insertion editing. If more than one sign is present we will have a case of **floating insertion** editing. If there is a sign on the left, there will not be a sign on the right.

When there is a **floating sign**, more than one sign, the one sign printed will always lie adjacent and to the left of the first character to be printed. Note that the floating sign also prevents fraud because a character may not be inserted on the left.

Source			Destination	
Picture	**Data**		**Picture**	**Result**
1	S9999V99	00325V23	+ZZ,ZZ9.99	+^^^325.23
2	S9999V99	-15002V84	+ZZ,ZZ9.99	-15,002.84
3	S9999V99	00305V34	-ZZ,ZZ9.99	^^^^305.34
4	S99999V99	-02121V45	-ZZ,ZZ9.99	-^2,121.45
5	S99999V99	-47001V27	Z,ZZ9.99	7,001.27

Table 10.08 – Sign on the left examples

Comments.

1. The source value is positive but the '+' forces the sign to print. Two zeros and the comma are replaced by spaces.
2. Because the source value is negative, the '+' in the picture will be replaced by a '-'.
3. The '-' sign in the picture forces a sign to print only if the value is negative. In this case the value is positive so the sign will be replaced by a space.
4. The source value is negative and the '-' in the picture will cause the sign to print.
5. The value is truncated on the left and no sign prints because the edit picture is un-signed.

Floating '+' Sign

The **floating sign** is placed on the left of the picture. The sign specified will cause zero suppression. The rightmost leading zero will be replaced by the specified sign. Of course, the rules as to whether a sign should or should not print are as before. The **floating sign** constitutes floating insertion editing.

Source			Destination	
Picture	**Data**		**Picture**	**Result**
1	S9(5)V99	14325V23	+++,++9.99	+14,325.23
2	S9(5)V99	00302V84	+++,+++.99	^^^+302.84
3	S9(5)V99	-00000V34	+++,+++.99	^^^^^^-.34
4	S9(5)V99	00000V00	+++,+++.99	^^^^^^+.00
5	S9(5)V99	00000V00	+++,+++.++	^^^^^^^^^^
6	S9(6)V99	115325V17	+++,+++.++	+15,325.17
7	S9(6)V99	230325V34	+,+++,+++.++	^+230,325.34

Table 10.09 – Floating '+' sign examples

Comments

1. Because the edited result contains only one sign, it is not possible to determine from the result whether a floating sign was used. The '+' sign printed because a sign will always print.
2. The sign prints as '+' because that is the sign of the value.
3. The source contains negative values so a '-' will print. The decimals force the decimal point to print.
4. The '9' forces decimals to print and this forced the sign to print.
5. The value is zero, and since there is no '9', the output will be blanks.
6. The sign must print, so the value is truncated.
7. The picture accommodates the value in the source so there is no truncation. If we had '1230' instead of '230' there would have been truncation and the value that would have printed would have been the same as in the example. The leftmost '+' must never be in a thousands position '+' but should be in a 10 thousands position '+'. We would then have '++,+++,+++.++' rather than '+,+++,+++.++'.

Floating '-' Sign

The **floating sign** is placed on the left of the picture. The sign specified will replace leading spaces. The rightmost leading zero will be replaced by the specified sign. Of course, the rules as to whether a sign should or should not print are as before. The **floating sign** constitutes floating insertion editing.

	Source			Destination	
	Picture	**Data**		**Picture**	**Result**
1	S9(5)V99	14325V23		---,--9.99	^14,325.23
2	S9(5)V99	00302V84		---,---.99	^^^^302.84
3	S9(5)V99	-00000V34		---,---.99	^^^^^^-.34
4	S9(5)V99	00000V00		---,---.99	^^^^^^^.00
5	S9(5)V99	00000V00		---,---.--	^^^^^^^^^^
6	S9(6)V99	115325V17		---,---.--	^15,325.17
7	S9(6)V99	230325V34		-,---,---.--	^^230,325.34

Table 10.10 – Floating '-' sign examples

Comments:

1. Since a sign will only print if the value is negative, no sign prints.
2. No sign prints and four blanks will print on the left.
3. The decimal point must print so a sign will print immediately to the left of the decimal point.
4. The value is 0; there are 9's, so 0's print for the decimals.

5.   The value is 0; there are no 9's, so only blanks print.
6.   Although the sign does not print, the space it would occupy still has to be catered for. The edited value is truncated.
7.   The value is positive, no sign prints and the value does not need to be truncated. As indicated earlier, the picture '--,---,---.--' is the correct picture. Before the leftmost comma, if there is a sign, there should be at least two signs

The Cr and DB Symbols

Both **CR** and **DB** will print only when the source value is negative. If the value is positive, blanks will occupy the two positions. The symbols are a case of fixed insertion editing. The symbols are always on the right. It is usual to precede the symbols by a space.

	Source			Destination	
	Picture	**Data**		**Picture**	**Result**
1	S9(3)V99	-325V23		ZZ9.99BCR	325.23^CR
2	S9(3)V99	032V84		ZZ9.99BCR	^32.84^^^
3	S9(3)V99	-418V34		ZZ9.99BDB	418.34^DB
4	S9(3)V99	121V00		ZZ9.99BDB	121.00^^^
Table 10.11 – CR and DB symbols					

Comments:

1.   The negative value causes CR to print.
2.   Since the value is positive, spaces will replace the CR.
3.   Again the value is negative, so DB will print
4.   The value is now positive, so spaces will replace the DB

The Fixed '$' Sign

As the name implies, the fixed dollar sign does not float. It will be placed in the same position as a fixed '+' or '-' sign. The **fixed '$' sign** is an example of fixed insertion. Note that the fixed $ sign does not prevent the use of the '+', the '-', the **CR** and the **DB** on the right hand side.

	Source		Destination	
	Picture	**Data**	**Picture**	**Result**
1	S9(5)V99	05325V23	$Z,ZZ9.99	$5,325.23
2	S9(5)V99	-00132V84	$Z,ZZ9.99CR	$^^132.84CR
3	S9(5)V99	00008V34	$Z,ZZ9.99	$^^^^8.34
4	S9(5)V99	15121V00	$Z,ZZ9.99	$5,121.00
	Table 10.12 – Fixed $ sign examples			

Comments.

1. There is no truncation and all positions are occupied.
2. The value is negative so 'CR' prints. The thousands and comma positions are occupied by blanks.
3. Identical to 2 but 'CR' not part of the picture.
4. There is truncation on the left. The fixed $ sign does not yield to the digit.

The Floating '$' Sign

As the name implies, the **floating dollar sign** will float in a manner identical to the floating of the '+' or '-' signs. The floating '$' sign is an example of floating insertion.

Like the fixed $ sign, the floating dollar sign must always be present. If a position to be occupied by a digit needs to be occupied by the sign as well, the sign will prevail and the value will be truncated. Note that the floating '$' sign, like the fixed '$' sign, does not prevent the use of the '+', the '-', the 'CR' and the 'DB' on the right hand side.

	Source		Destination	
	Picture	**Data**	**Picture**	**Result**
1	S9(5)V99	15325V23	$$$,$$9.99	$15,325.23
2	S9(5)V99	-00132V84	$$$,$$9.99CR	^^^$132.84CR
3	S9(5)V99	00008V34	$$$,$$$.99	^^^^^$8.34
4	S9(5)V99	00000V00	$$$,$$$.99	^^^^^^$.00
5	S9(5)V99	00000V00	$$$,$$$.$$	^^^^^^^^^^
6	S9(6)V99	125755V00	$$$,$$9.99	$25,755.00
	Table 10.13 – Floating $ sign examples			

Comments.

1. There is no truncation and all positions are occupied.
2. The dollar sign floats. 'CR' prints because the value is negative.
3. The dollar sign floats.
4. The $.99 forces printing even if the value is zero

5.   Since there are no '9's the output will be all blanks.
6.   As indicated, the '$' sign must always print; the result is truncation.

We have already indicated that whenever you have a sign on the left, floating or otherwise, and there is conflict between the requirement to place a digit in the position and to place a sign in the same position, then the sign will prevail. The following is therefore good practice:

Example:	$,$$$,$$$.99	Incorrect
	$$,$$$,$$$.99	Correct

In the examples, if we have a value, say, '123,456.78' the '$' will float. If you have a value, say '1,234,567.89', the first digit will be truncated and the '$' sign will float one position to the right. The second solution will not lead to truncation and the '$' sign need not float.

Cheque Protection

Like the 'Z', the asterisk will cause zero suppression with replacement by the '*'. For obvious reasons the '*' is associated with **cheque protection**. Note that the '*' is not a floating character and truncation is normal as there never is conflict between the '*' and a digit to print in that position.

	Source			Destination	
	Picture	**Data**		**Picture**	**Result**
1	S9(4)V99	0000V00		*****.**	*****.**
2	S9(4)V99	9132V00		**,***.**	*9,132.00
3	S9(4)V99	0308V34		**,***.**	***308.34
4	S9(4)V99	0000V28		**,***.**	******.28
5	S9(5)V99	15121V00		**,***.99	15,121.00
6	S9(5)V99	25755V00		$*,***.99	$5,755.00

Table 10.14 – Floating $ sign examples

Comments.

1.   The value is zero. Note that the decimal point prints.
2.   The value fits and one '*' prints on the left.
3.   The ',' is replaced by an '*'.
4.   All positions to the left of the decimal point are replaced by '*'.
5.   The value occupies all positions, so no '*' prints.
6.   The '$' sign causes truncation.

163

Scaling

We have all seen, on occasion, columns indicating that the values in the column represent thousands. The heading might be '$000'. This is called **scaling**.

	Source			Destination	
	Picture	**Data**		**Picture**	**Result**
1	S9(6)V99	10000V00		ZZ9PPP	^10
2	S9(6)	123456		ZZ9PPP	123
3	S9(7)	1000000		ZZ9PPP	000

Table 10.15– Scaling examples, result is in thousands

Editing the Date

The **date**, with no editing, is difficult though not impossible to understand. We have to make an effort to understand it. Normally all that is necessary is to add some slashes. Examine the following code. We split the **date** because we need to isolate year, month and day.

Editing the Date

```
01   W10-date.
     05   W10-yy          pic 9(4).
     05   W10-mm          pic 9(2).
     05   W10-dd          pic 9(2).
01   W10-edit-date        pic xxxx/xx/xx.
     accept W10-date from date yyyymmdd
     move W10-date to W10-edit-date
     display "The edited date is: " W10-edit-date
```

Figure 10.03

The code seems reasonable but would here not achieve the desired result. The date that will print will not be edited. The code moves a group field to the edited field. You will recall that when the group field is moved the rules that apply are the rules applying to alphanumeric moves, namely, align on the left, move byte by byte from source to destination and bytes left unused are space filled. What is needed is to move an elementary field to the edited field or accept the date directly into the edited field. Remember, though, that we need to isolate year, month and day. The following code is a solution:

Editing the Date

```
01   W10-date.
     05   W10-yy          pic 9(4).
     05   W10-mm          pic 9(2).
     05   W10-dd          pic 9(2).
01   W20-date            pic 9(8).
01   W30-edit-date pic xxxx/xx/xx.
     accept W20-date from date yyyymmdd
     move W20-date to W30-edit-date
                      W10-date
     display "The edited date is: " W30-edit-date
```

Figure 10.04

We moved an elementary field to the edited date field. The date will be edited. We also moved the date in W20-date to the group field W10-date. Remember that when moving a group field, alphanumeric rules apply.

The Blank When Zero Clause

When the source contains a value of zero, the **blank when zero** clause, will cause blanks to print, irrespective of the picture. The clause may not be coded for a field for which cheque protection has been specified, in other words, a field whose picture contains '*'.

If the value in the source field contains 0, blanks will print.

```
05   W10-amount         pic $99,999.99 blank when zero.
05   W10-payment        pic 999        blank when zero.
```

Note that COBOL 74 did not allow the clause to be used for a picture containing zero suppression.

```
05   W10-amount         pic ZZ,ZZZ.99 blank when zero.
05   W10-payment        pic 999       blank when zero.
```

W10-amount would be rejected but W10-payment would be accepted according to COBOL 74 rules.

The Special-Names Paragraph

The **special-names** paragraph enables us to specify many of the aspects of the environment with which the program will interact. We will be looking at the most commonly used of these.

165

On mainframes printers had a number of channels, numbered **C01** to **C12**, to control the operation of the printer. One of these, **C01** indicated top of page. In the special-names paragraph we can provide a name for **C01** and later use this name to go to the top of the next page. Possible code for the purpose follows:

```
C01 is to-top-of-page
```

In some countries the decimal point is used to indicate a fraction. In other countries it is the comma that is used for the purpose. The dot for the decimal point is the default. The following line of code will enable the programmer to use a **comma** for the **decimal point**. The dot is then used to separate thousands.

```
decimal-point is comma
```

The default for the currency sign is the '$'. To deviate from the default, we have the currency sign clause. The **currency sign** must be a single upper case character. The following characters may not be used:

A, B, C, D, L, P, R, S, V, X, Z

Micro Focus allows us to use the C and the R and COBOL 85 allows the use of the L.

The following line of code specifies the 'R' as the **currency sign**.

```
currency sign is 'R'
```

The entries in the **special-names** paragraph end on a period.

The following program incorporates the clauses covered. Note that once we specify a **currency sign** character, we are precluded from using the '$' as the **currency sign**. Similarly, if we specify **decimal point is comma**, we will be precluded from using the dot (.) as the decimal point. The functions of the '.' and the ',' in a numeric edit picture, will be reversed.

Special-Names Paragraph

```
identification division.
program-id. chapter1010.
configuration section.
special-names.
    C01 is to-top-of-page
    decimal-point is comma
    currency sign is 'R'.
```

Listing 10.02 – 1 of 2

166

Special-Names Paragraph

```
data division.
working-storage section.
01  W10-numeric-edit.
    05  W10-edit        pic RZZ.ZZ9,99.
    05  W10-value       pic 9(5)V99    value 12345,67.
procedure division.
    move W10-value to W10-edit
    display "Edited value: " W10-edit
    stop run.
```

Listing 10.02 – 2 of 2

```
Command Prompt                              _ □ ×
Edited value: R12.345,67
```

We have commented out division and section headers. These are often referred to as red tape statements and, though not a huge burden in the programming effort, may be dispensed with no loss of clarity resulting. This is a Micro Focus facility.

Culturally Specific Editing

The 2002 COBOL standard takes into consideration editing requirements that overcome previous limitations. Instead of a single currency character we can now use more than one character. For this facility we require some additional coding, that belongs in the special-names paragraph. We will employ the currency-sign clause but in a new way. The program listing that follows illustrates the preceding points.

Culturally Specific Editing

```
$set sourceformat "free"
  Program-id. Chapter1001.
  environment division.
  special-names.
      currency-sign is 'Eur '
          with picture symbol 'U'.
  Working-Storage Section.
  01  W10-edit          pic UZZ9.99.
```

Figure 10.05 – 1 of 2

167

Culturally Specific Editing

```
Procedure Division.
A100-start.
    move 195.5 to W10-edit
    display 'Edited value is: ' W10-edit
    accept W10-edit
    stop run.
```

Figure 10.05 – 2 of 2

Comments.

1. The following would print: Eur 195.50.
2. Notice that the Eur following the currency-sign clause ends on a space. This is necessary. ('Eur ')
3. We have indicated that where the symbol 'u' appears in the edit picture string, the characters 'Eur ' should appear instead.

Summary

- The purpose of editing is to make the data, particularly numeric data, more readable.

- Editing is of two types, **insertion** and **suppression** with replacement.

- **Alphabetic editing** uses only two symbols, A and B. Each A in the picture will be replaced by a character from the source. The B will cause a space to be inserted.

- **Alphanumeric editing** uses the characters X, B, 9, 0, /. Each X in the picture will be replaced by a character from the source. The B is for space insertion. The 9 will be replaced by a digit and the '/' is an insertion character like the B - a '/' will be inserted at the point at which it is specified.

- The Z will cause leading zeros to be replaced by spaces.

- The ',' is used as the thousands separator.

- The B is a numeric insertion character as in alphabetic and alphanumeric editing.

- Edited fields are signed using the '+' and the '-'. The signs may appear on the right or on the left of the edit picture. When the sign is specified on the left, it may float if more than one sign is coded. One sign will come to occupy a position immediately to the left of the leftmost digit. Furthermore, the '+' will cause a sign to always print. The '-' causes a sign to print only when the sign is negative.

- CR and DB are placed on the right and print only when the value is negative.

- The '$' sign may be fixed or floating.

- The '*' is for cheque protection and will replace leading zeros.

- The **special-names** paragraph enables us to specify a name for top of page, the "decimal point is comma" clause and the "currency sign" clause. The latter is available to specify a character that will replace the '$' sign.

Complete

		Picture	Data	Edit Picture	Result
1.	Given:	9(4)V99	0025V75	$$$$9.99	_____
2.	Given:	9(4)V99	0045V62	$***9.99	_____
3.	Given:	9(4)V99	0125V75	ZZ.99	_____
4.	Given:	9(4)V99	0136V752	$Z,ZZZ.99	_____
5.	Given:	9(6)	000005	ZZZ.999	_____
6.	Given:	9(4)V99	0000V85	$$,$$9.99	_____
7.	Given:	9(4)V99	0005V25	$$,$$9.99	_____
8.	Given:	S9(6)	-000364	ZZZZ9BCR	_____
9.	Given:	S9(6)	+001234	++,+++,++9	_____
10.	Given:	9(3)V99	255V15	$ZZZ.99	_____
11.	Given:	S9(2)V99	00V13	$ZZ.99+	_____
12.	Given:	S9(2)V99	+00V29	$ZZ.99-	_____
13.	Given:	S9(4)V99	-0517V87	Z,ZZ9.99-	_____
14.	Given:	9(6)	132547	ZZZBZZ9	_____
15.	Given:	S9(6) `	-123456	----,--9	_____
16.	Given:	S9(3)	-321	$ZZZ.99BDB	_____
17.	Given:	S9(2)V99	-00V45	$ZZ.99BCR	_____
18.	Given:	9(3)	100	99 blank when zero	_____

19.   Given: 9(4)V999   0043V123 $ZBZZZ.99   _____

20.   Given: S9(4)V99   0035V67 $$$$.99   _____

True/False

	Picture	Data	Edit Picture	Result
1.	S9(3)V9(3)	000V000	ZZ9.99	^^0.00
2.	S9(4)V9(2)	0000V00	ZZZZ.ZZ	^^^^.^^
3.	S9(4)V9(2)	0000V55	Z,ZZZ.99	^^^^.55
4.	S9(4)V9(2)	2500V15	ZBZZ9.99	2^500.15
5.	S9(5)V9(2)	-12345V30	ZBZZ9.99+	12^345.30-
6.	S9(5)V9(2)	10000V00	ZBZZZ.ZZ	^^^^^^^^
7.	S9(5)V9(2)	15000V00	+Z,ZZZ.99	+5,000.00
8.	S9(6)V9(2)	123456V00	+,+++,+++.++	^+123456.00
9.	S9(6)V9(2)	123456V15	+++,+++.++	+123,456.15
10.	S9(5)V9(2)	10000V00	-,---.--	^^^^^^^^
11.	S9(4)V9(2)	5125V34	Z,ZZZ.99BDB	5,125.34^^
12.	S9(4)V9(2)	-6323V45	Z,ZZZ.99BCR	6,323.45CR
13.	S9(5)V9(2)	15545V56	$Z,ZZ9.99	15,545.56
14.	S9(5)V9(2)	5656V67	$,$$$.99	^$656.67
15.	S9(5)V9(2)	10000V00	Z,ZZZ.ZZ	
			Blank when zero	^^^^^^^^
16.	S9(4)V9(2)	5375V00	$$,$$$.$$	$5,375.00
17.	S9(4)V9(2)	0000V00	*B***.**	*****.**

18.   Should we wish to use a comma as the decimal point, we would code "decimal point is ',' " in the special names paragraph.

Exercises

1.   Write a program and in the special names paragraph code the clauses that will enable you to:

  a) Use the comma as the decimal indicator.
  b) Use the 'R' as the currency sign.
  c) Use the phrase "to-top-of-page" to advance to the next page.

1.1   For each of the following, supply a PICTURE clause that would produce the edited result from the given date.

	SENDING ITEM		RECEIVING ITEM	
	PICTURE	CONTENTS	PICTURE	EDITED RESULT
1.1.1	9(4)V99	1234.56	?	$234.56
1.1.2	9(4)V99	0069.72	?	$**69.72
1.1.3	9(4)V99	0000.05	?	$^^^^.05
1.1.4	S9(4)V999	4343.434+	?	4b343.43^
1.1.5	9(5)V99	12345.60	?	2,345.000

1.2.1   Fill in the edited result column for each of the following: (Spaces denoted by a ^)

1.2.1	S9(3)V99	123.45+	$9999.99CR	?
1.2.2	S9(3)V99	123.45-	$9999.99CR	?
1.2.3	S9(3)V99	123.45-	$9999.99DB	?
1.2.4	S9(3)V99	700.00-	99.99 blank when zero	?
1.2.5	9(5)	10203	XBXBX	?

Chapter 11
More on Files

Topics Covered

- ❏ More on File Processing
- ❏ Writing to Disk
- ❏ Printing
- ❏ Determining Bottom of Page
- ❏ Indexed Sequential Files
- ❏ Dynamic Access
- ❏ The Start Statement
- ❏ First and Last
- ❏ Relative Access
- ❏ Updating a Relative File
- ❏ Write, Rewrite and Delete
- ❏ Summary
- ❏ Complete
- ❏ True/False
- ❏ Exercises

More on File Processing

We have looked at basic file processing involving the reading of files. We looked at loop implementation to read until end of file. We will now add to our knowledge by looking at how we create a file on disk. We will also see what we have to do to create a report.

Writing to Disk

In the example we will be using, we read a file sequentially and write the records read to an output file. The input file has two fields and the output file has those same two fields plus an amount field into which we place a value. We will start by looking at the hierarchy chart.

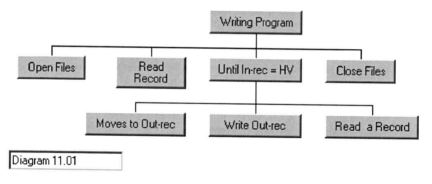

Diagram 11.01

Reading the hierarchy chart.

- We open files and read the first record. This is the preparatory step prior to entering the loop and uses the principle of reading ahead. Thus, when entering the loop we already have a record to process.

- The loop condition ensures that the input file is read to the end of the file.

- We update the amount field and move the data to the output area.

- The data are going to be written to disk and displayed on the screen.

- The record is ready for output and is written to disk.

- We have finished with the preceding record and are therefore ready to read the next record. Remember, we read the next record when we have finished with the preceding record.

- Once the record is read, since this is the last instruction in the loop, we go to the test condition. If it is not end of file, we re-enter the loop and process the record we now have.

Reading to EOF

```
program-id. Chapter1101 as "Chapter1101".

environment division.
input-output section.
file-control.
    select in-file assign  to 'C:\cob0\chap1101'.
    select out-file assign to 'C:\cob0\chap1102'.
data division.
file section.
fd  in-file.
01  in-rec          pic   X(05).
fd  out-file.
01  out-rec         pic   X(09).
working-storage section.
01  W20-data-in.
    05  W20-num     pic   9(02).
    05  W20-name    pic   X(03).
01  W30-data-out.
    05  W30-num     pic   9(02).
    05  W30-name    pic   X(03).
    05  W30-amt     pic S9(04) value 5000.
procedure division.
A100-start.
    open input  in-file
         output out-file
    perform Z100-read
    perform until W20-data-in = high-values
        move W20-num to W30-num
        move W20-name to W30-name
        add 100 to W30-amt
        display W30-num ' ' W30-name '  ' W30-amt
        perform Z200-write
        perform Z100-read
    end-perform
    stop run.
```

Listing 11.01 – 1 of 2

Reading to EOF

```
Z100-read.
    read in-file into W20-data-in
        at end move high-values to W20-data-in
    end-read.

Z200-write.
    write out-rec from W30-data-out
        invalid key display 'Invalid write'
    end-write.

end program Chapter1101.
```

Listing 11.01 – 2 of 2

We looked at the output file with the assistance of notepad.

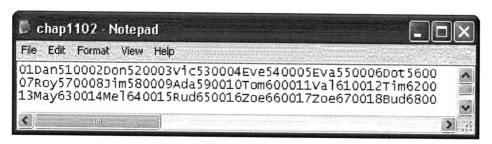

You should follow the code and see how it matches the hierarchy chart. Notice that the stop run is not at the physical end of the program rather, it is at the logical end of the program.

The first read precedes the perform that implements the loop. Notice also that the last instruction in the loop is the read, which immediately follows the write. The write, in turn, is the last instruction in the set of instructions that process the record retrieved by the preceding read.

Notice also that whereas in the read we read a **file**, in the write we write a **record**. The condition that detects an unsuccessful write is the invalid key. One reason an invalid key condition will be generated on a sequential write would be when a disk full condition is detected.

Printing

Printing is an essential requirement of a language, such as COBOL, which is intended to satisfy the requirements of business. One of the main requirements of a business environment is the printing of reports and we will now look at the points to be borne in mind when printing these.

Determining Bottom of Page

When printing, it is essential to be able to determine when it is that we need to go to the top of the next page. We might also have to do something at the bottom of the preceding page, like the printing of a running total. To determine whether we are at the bottom of a page we need to know two things: We need to know how many lines are on a page and how many lines have at any stage, been printed.

How many lines fit on a page is given, because we know what paper we are going to use. If we are printing invoices it is one thing, if we are printing statements it is another. On a standard page, on a mainframe, we are able to print a maximum of 66 lines. Bear in mind also that a report will require a heading and that some space needs to be left both at the top and bottom of the page. One thing we don't want to do is print on the perforation so we must leave some space at the bottom as well as at the top of the page.

We will assume that the paper allows for 66 lines on a page, that we leave five blank lines at the top and at the bottom. In addition, heading lines take up six lines. The following arithmetic needs to be carried out.

Number of lines on page:		66
Number of blank lines at top	5	
Number of blank lines at bottom	5	
Number of heading lines	6	16
Number of detail lines on a page:		50

We will derive the hierarchy chart to handle the information. We will start by looking at the Heading-Routine

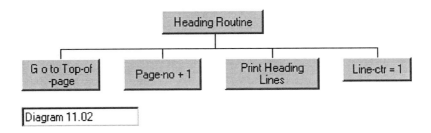

Diagram 11.02

We go to top of page, add 1 to the page number, print and lastly initialize the line counter to zero. Initially the page-no field should be set to zero. Next, we will derive the hierarchy chart that determines whether headings need to be printed.

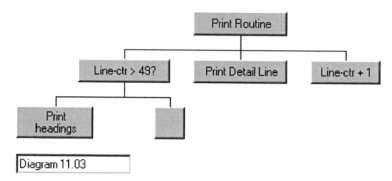

Diagram 11.03

When we enter the print routine, we do so because we have a detail line to print. However, before printing the detail line we must ensure that there is space on the page. There will be space if the line counter is not greater than 49, in which case we will go ahead, print the detail line and increment the line counter.

If, on the other hand, the line counter is greater than 49, we have to print the detail line on the next page, which means that we need to print headings first. When headings have been printed, we return, print the detail line we had ready and increment the line counter that now stands at zero.

Let us look at the format of a write to the printer.

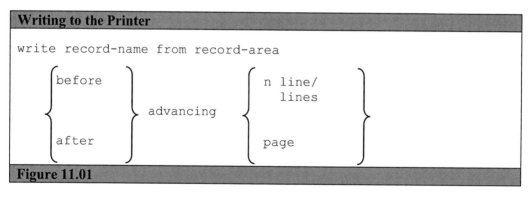

Writing to the Printer

```
write record-name from record-area

    ⎧ before ⎫              ⎧ n line/   ⎫
    ⎨        ⎬  advancing    ⎨   lines   ⎬
    ⎩ after  ⎭              ⎩ page      ⎭
```

Figure 11.01

In a write to the printer, as is usual with the write, it is the record defined under the FD that gets written. Notice, however, what it is that you have to write. You have to write the heading lines, of which there may be several, and you have to write the detail line. What this implies is that you will be using the **write from** version of the write. Notice that when you test to see if there is space on the page, to print a detail line, that detail line is ready for printing. This is because you are using the **write from**. If the detail line were on the print record, then printing a heading line would overwrite the assembled detail line. This is why when printing, and there is more than one type of record to be printed, we use the **write from**. When printing a detail line, you may choose to print and then advance, that implies using the **before advancing** option. Alternatively, you may advance and then print, which would entail using the **after advancing** option. You would also specify the number of lines you wish to advance, either using a literal or using a field, which must then be numeric.

Printing the Detail-line

```
B100-print-detail.
    if  W50-ln-ctr > 25
        perform B200-print-headings
    end-if
    write print-rec from W30-detail
        after advancing 1 line
    add 1 to W50-ln-ctr.
```

Figure 11.02

We start by checking whether the line counter exceeds the number of lines allowed on the page. If the test yields positive, a branch must be taken to print headings. On return from the branch, print-rec contains the last line printed in the headings routine. This does not disturb us because we are printing using the **write from** and our detail line is still intact. We coded: "after advancing 1 line". This is the default so we did not need to code the line. Next we have the heading routine. We simplified the headings. Normally the heading lines of a production report are considerably more complicated. A typical set of heading lines might contain the date and the time besides the company and report names.

Printing the Heading Lines

```
B200-print-headings.
    add 1 to W25-pg-no
    write print-rec from W25-heading-1
        after advancing page
    write print-rec from W25-heading-2
        after advancing 1 line
    write print-rec from W25-heading-3
        after advancing 1 line
    move 0 to W50-ln-ctr.
```

Figure 11.03

The listing that follows depicts the whole program. Notice that the first thing we do in the loop is to move spaces to the detail line. In the example it is not significant, but it is normally required because there are fields in the detail line that sometimes receive data and at other times do not. If we do not clear the detail line by moving spaces to it, fields that fail to receive data may have data from the preceding record.

Assume the detail line has the columns Account Number, Debit, Credit and Balance. Some records will be debits and the amount will print under debits. Other records will be credits and the amount will print under credits. It may happen that a credit record will follow a debit record. When the credit prints on the line, there will be a value for debits showing. Either before we move values to the detail line or after printing, we should move spaces to the detail line.

Printing Program

```
program-id. chapter1102.

    select in-file assign  to 'C:\cob0\chap1101'.
    select print-file assign to printer.

data division.
file section.
fd  in-file.
01  in-rec          pic  X(05).
fd  print-file.
01  print-rec       pic  X(80).
working-storage section.
01  W20-data-in.
    05  W20-num      pic  9(02).
    05  W20-name     pic  X(03).
01  W25-Heading-1.
    05              pic X(05) value spaces.
    05              pic X(06) value 'Emp-ID'.
    05              pic X(05) value spaces.
    05              pic X(04) value 'Name'.
    05              pic X(05) value spaces.
    05              pic X(06) value 'Amount'.
    05              pic X(05) value spaces.
    05              pic X(08) value 'Page No.'.
    05  W25-pg-no   pic 9     value 0.
01  W25-Heading-2.
    05              pic X(05) value spaces.
    05              pic X(40) value all '-'.
```

Listing 11.02 – 1 of 4

Printing Program

```
01  W25-Heading-3.
    05                  pic X(44) value all ' '.
01  W30-detail.
    05                  pic  X(05).
    05   W30-num   pic  9(02).
    05                  pic  X(09).
    05   W30-name  pic  X(03).
    05                  pic  X(07).
    05   W30-amt   pic Z,ZZ9.
01  W40-amt         pic S9(04) value 5000.
01  W50-ln-ctr      pic S9(02).
```

Listing 11.02 – 2 of 4

We did not initialize the line counter field. Instead, in the initialize routine, we moved a value greater than the number of lines on a page. This has the advantage that when examining the logic of the program, you see that you have done all that is required. If you initialize the field to 99 and remove the instruction to move 99 to the line counter, there will be no change in execution. But, when doing program maintenance, you will have to go back to the data division to see whether the field has been initialized. This will certainly cause some un- easiness.

Printing Program

```
procedure division.
A100-start.
    perform A200-initialize
    perform until W20-data-in = high-values
        perform B050-build-detail
        perform B100-print-detail
        perform Z100-read
    end-perform
    stop run.

A200-initialize.
    open input  in-file
         output print-file
    perform Z100-read
    move 99 to W50-ln-ctr.
              0-ln-ctr.
```

Listing 11.02 – 3 of 4

Printing Program

```
B050-build-detail.
    move spaces    to W30-detail
    add 100        to W40-amt
    move W20-num   to W30-num
    move W20-name  to W30-name
    move W40-amt   to W30-amt.

B100-print-detail.
    if  W50-ln-ctr > 25
        perform B200-print-headings
    end-if
    write print-rec from W30-detail
        after advancing 1 lines
    add 1 to W50-ln-ctr.

B200-print-headings.
    add 1 to W25-pg-no
    write print-rec from W25-heading-1
        after advancing page
    write print-rec from W25-heading-2
        after advancing 1 line
  write print-rec from W25-heading-3
            after advancing 1 line
        move 0 to W5  Z100-read.
    read in-file into W20-data-in
        at end move high-values to W20-data-in
    end-read.

end program Chapter1102.
```

Listing 11.02 – 4 of 4

Notice that we split the work that had to be done into separate routines thus increasing the cohesion of each routine. As you may recall, the initialize routine has what we call **temporal cohesion** or cohesion in time, because in it are done all things that, though apparently unrelated, need to be done at the same time. We open the file and read the first record. We get the time of day as well as the date. All of these steps must be executed at the same time, namely when the program starts running.

Indexed Sequential Files

So far we have looked at sequential access. **Sequential access** is suitable for some files and for some applications. For instance, a transaction file is normally accessed sequentially and batch applications use sequential access. However, as online applications came to predominate, random access came to be required more and more, and file organizations offering the facility became more significant. Notice, however, that applications needing **random access**, normally satisfy their requirements through the use of databases.

It must be said, though, that many applications function quite effectively with the aid of **indexed sequential** files bypassing database usage. Let us start by looking at the select for an indexed sequential file.

Indexed Sequential Files

```
    select file-name assign to 'mast001'
        organization is indexed
        access is sequential
        record key is mast-key
        file status is W50-status.
```

Figure 11.04 – Select Format

- **Organization is indexed** – The clause is required because all access to an indexed sequential file is done via the index, even when the file is being accessed sequentially.
- **Access** – The clause indicates how the file will be accessed in the program. Access may be any of the following:

Sequential	- This is the default.
Random	- Specifying random enables records to be retrieved randomly
Dynamic	- Dynamic access enables both random and sequential access in the same run.

- **Record key** – An index is based on a key and this key must be made known to the program. This is the difference between a sequential and an indexed file. You may see the records of a sequential file as having a key. This would be a logical key as no physical key could possibly be specified to the access method. In the **record key** clause we specify the field in the file on which the file is sequenced. The key named in the clause must be defined in the **file section**. In this way, the system will know which is the key field and where it is to be found in the file record.

Record key

```
fd  mast-file.
01  mast-rec.
    05  mast-key    pic X(06).
    05              pic X(84).
```

Figure 11.05

- **File status** – The **file status** returns a value that indicates the status of the read. The field in which the value is returned should be defined as a two-byte alphanumeric field. A two-digit value is returned, '00' standing for a successful result.

The following example depicts a query program using an indexed sequential file. The program prompts for a key. The key is then used to retrieve the record that is then displayed. The hierarchy chart below reflects the logic of the program:

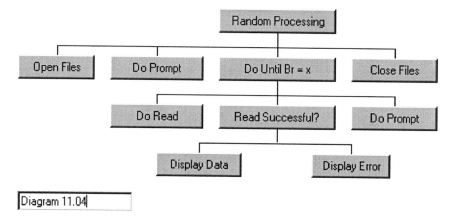

Diagram 11.04

- We start by opening all files required; in this case only one file is opened because we are using the screen for output.
- We branch to execute a routine that prompts the user for branch and account number.
- We iterate until the user enters a value of 'X' for the branch. Had the user entered 'X' to start off with, the loop would have been bypassed.
- We are inside the loop because we have data that enables us to read a record and we branch to read a record from the indexed sequential file.
- In the read routine, if the read is unsuccessful we move spaces to the branch.
- When we return from the read we test to see if the read was successful. If it was successful we display the data retrieved; alternately we display an error message.

- We are now at the bottom of the loop. If we were processing a transaction file we would read the next transaction because we would have finished processing the previous transaction. In this case the equivalent action would be to prompt once again.

Let us look at the program. Notice that we have left out most of the red tape statements. This feature has made COBOL less verbose:

Reading an Indexed Sequential File

```
program-id. chapter1104.
    select mast-file assign to 'C:\cob0\chap1102'
        organization is indexed
        access is random
        record key is mast-key.
fd  mast-file.
01  mast-rec.
    05  mast-key       pic 9(02).
    05                 pic X(07).
working-storage section.
01  W20-area.
    05  W20-key.
        10  W20-num    pic 9(02).
    05  W20-name       pic X(03).
    05  W20-bal        pic 9(04).
    open input mast-file
    perform A200-prompt
    perform until W20-br = 'X'
        perform Z100-read
        if  W20-key not = spaces
            display W20-num ' ' W20-num ' '
                    W20-name ' ' W20-bal
        end-if
        perform A200-prompt
    end-perform
    display 'Terminating'
    stop run.
A200-prompt.
    display 'Please enter account number: ' no advancing
    accept W20-num.
```

Listing 11.03 – 1 of 2

Reading an Indexed Sequential File

```
Z100-read.
    move W20-key to mast-key
    read mast-file into W20-area
        invalid key display 'record not found'
                      move ' ' to W20-key
    end-read.
```

Listing 11.03 – 1 of 2

```
Command Prompt                                    _ □ ✕
Please enter account number or 99 to end: 11
Val 6100
Please enter account number or 99 to end: 03
Vic 5300
Please enter account number or 99 to end: 15
Rud 6500
Please enter account number or 99 to end: _
```

In the preceding program we processed the master file randomly. We have previously processed similar files sequentially. What we sometimes need to do is process a master file in the same run, both sequentially and randomly.

Dynamic Access

When **access is dynamic** is specified we are able to flip flop between sequential and random processing as required by the application. When we specify that access is sequential, the pointer for the read is positioned at the beginning of the file. When **access is random** is requested, the pointer is not positioned until a valid key is specified. To position the pointer, when we move from random to sequential processing, would we like to always be positioned at the beginning of the file? Unlikely.

The Start Statement

The **start** statement enables us to position the pointer at a specified key in the file. We may want to process all records in a branch then stop. We could then be prompted for another branch to process sequentially. In this way, we would not need to go through the whole file, which might have 1000 000 records, when we only want to process two branches, one with 7000 records and the other with 15000 records.

Having seen the advantages of the start statement, note that we may also use the statement for **access is sequential**. If we do not specify the start statement when using

186

sequential access, the default will apply and the pointer will be positioned at the beginning of the file. If we do use a start statement the rules will be as for **access is dynamic**. Note that what we have said applies only when the file **organization is indexed** clause is used.

The Start Statement

```
start file-name

  First
              equal to         (=)
              greater than     (>)
              not less than (not <)
  Key         greater than or equal to (>=)        mast-key
              less than        (<)
              less than or equal to (<=)
  last

  invalid key imperative statement
  not invalid key imperative statement
end-start
```

Figure 11.06 – Start Format 1

If you use 'equal to' and the record is not there the program will terminate abnormally. It stands to reason that if you use 'equal to' you must be sure that the record is there. If you feel it is relatively safe to use the 'equal to' then include the **invalid key** exit. This will avoid the silent crash.

Dynamic Access

```
program-id. Chapter1104 as "Chapter1104".
environment division.
    select mast-file assign to 'C:\cob0\chap1104'
        organization is indexed
        access is dynamic
        record key is mast-key.
```

Listing 11.04 – 1 of 2

Dynamic Access

```
data division.
file section.
fd   mast-file.
01   mast-rec.
     05   mast-key        pic X(04).
     05                   pic X(07).
working-storage section.
01   W20-area.
     05   W20-key.
          10   W20-br     pic X.
          10   W20-num    pic 9(03).
     05   W20-name        pic X(03).
     05   W20-bal         pic 9(04).
01   start-key           pic X(04).
procedure division.
A100-start.
     open input mast-file.

A150-start.
     perform A200-prompt
     move start-key to mast-key
     start mast-file key is = mast-key
         invalid key
            display 'Invalid record key'
            go to A150-start
     end-start
     perform Z100-read
     perform until W20-key = high-values
         display W20-br   '  ' W20-num '  '
                 W20-name '  ' W20-bal
         perform Z100-read
     end-perform
     display 'Terminating'
     accept W20-bal
     stop run.

A200-prompt.
     display 'Please enter start key: ' no advancing
     accept start-key.
```

Listing 11.04 – 2 of 3

Dynamic Access

```
Z100-read.
    read mast-file next into W20-area
        at end move high-values to W20-key
    end-read.

end program Chapter1104.
```

Listing 11.04 – 3 of 3

```
C:\ Command Prompt                              _ □ X
Please enter start key: C200
C 200 May 6200
C 300 Mel 6300
C 400 Rud 6400
C 500 Zoe 6500
D 100 Bud 6600
D 200 Viv 6700
D 300 Pat 6800
D 400 Dot 6900
D 500 Rui 7000
```

Start-key will receive the desired starting point and must be moved to the key of the file to be processed.

Points to note:

- The **sequential read**, when **access is dynamic** has been specified, requires the **next** keyword.
- We use a forbidden instruction: the **go to**. The **go to** was banned many years ago and gotoless programming came into being. We have used the **go to** here, having adopted the constraints enforced in the C language. In C you are allowed to use a **go to** but you can only branch within the function. This is much what we have done. We created what I choose to call a pseudo paragraph, A150-start, which provides an entry point.
- The **go to**, with the assistance of the A150-start, enables us to implement a loop, which will be exited only when a valid key has been provided.
- We move **start-key** to **mast-key** and then issue the start instruction. The format is: start mast-file key is = mast-key. This means that you wish to start at the point specified in mast-key.

189

▪   Without modifying the rest of the code, we can change the condition in the **start** to cater for the other relational conditions.

```
move start-key to mast-key
start mast-file key is >= mast-key

move start-key to mast-key
start mast-file key is <= mast-key
```

When using this last relational expression the system will try to find an equal condition. If one cannot be found then the system will look for the first key that is less than the specified key.

   In the following example we flip flop between sequential and random access. You will notice that the **start** statement initiates sequential processing. You then use the **read next** form of the read. The **random read** needs no such introduction. The form of the read is enough to initiate random processing.

Access Is Dynamic

```
program-id. chapter1105.
    select mast-file assign to 'C:\Cob0\chap1104'
        organization is indexed
        access is dynamic
        record key is mast-key.
fd   mast-file.
01   mast-rec.
     05   mast-key        pic X(04).
     05                   pic X(07).
working-storage section.
01   W20-area.
     05   W20-key.
          10   W20-br     pic X.
          10   W20-num    pic 9(03).
     05   W20-name        pic X(03).
     05   W20-bal         pic 9(04).
01   start-key            pic X(04).
01   store-br             pic X.
```

Listing 11.05 – 1 of 5

   We use store-br to enable an iteration that will exhaust all records for a given branch. As preparation, we move W20-br to store-br and the loop condition is then until W20-br not = store-br.

Whenever we wish to process a group of records such as a branch or a department or books by a particular author, we always store the identifying field, say, author, and indicate in the condition that we wish to process the records until we read a record whose field author is not equal to the field store-author. In this way we are able to process groups.

Processing groups always involves a loop. Before the iteration we store and after the iteration we do those things associated with end of loop.

Access Is Dynamic

```
procedure division.
A100-start.
    open input mast-file.
A150-start.
    perform A200-prompt
    move start-key to mast-key
    start mast-file key is >= mast-key
        invalid key
            display 'Invalid record key'
            go to A150-start
    end-start
    perform Z100-read
    move W20-br to store-br
    perform until W20-br > store-br
        perform B100-display
        perform Z100-read
    end-perform
    perform 2 times
        perform A300-prompt
        perform Z200-read
        perform B100-display
    end-perform.
A175-start.
    perform A200-prompt
    move start-key to mast-key
```

Listing 11.05 – 2 of 5

Access Is Dynamic

```
    start mast-file key is >= mast-key
        invalid key
            display 'Invalid record key'
            go to A175-start
    end-start
    perform Z100-read
    perform until W20-key = high-values
        perform B100-display
        perform Z100-read
    end-perform
    display 'Terminating'
    stop run.
```

Listing 11.05 – 3 of 5

Because we initiate sequential processing twice, we need two start statements. As before, we used the **go to** to implement a loop. Because it is used in the same block of code it is not as sinful as it may at first appear. The first start statement initiates processing of the records for a branch, the second processes records till end of file.

Some points on the **go to**. Before good logic techniques were developed, programmers relied on their ability to produce good logic. Unfortunately, better or worse logic generally fell short of what one would wish for. Because programs often crashed, researchers set out to determine why this happened. What was found was that the more **go to**s a program had the more likely the program was to terminate abnormally, i.e. crash. In this way, the **go to** had to go.

Access Is Dynamic

```
A200-prompt.
    display 'Please enter key start key: ' no advancing
    accept start-key.
A300-prompt.
    display 'Please enter key: ' no advancing
    accept mast-key.
B100-display.
    display W20-br ' ' W20-num ' ' W20-name ' ' W20-bal.
Z100-read.
    read mast-file next into W20-area
        at end move high-values to W20-key
    end-read.
```

Listing 11.05 – 4 of 5

Access Is Dynamic

```
Z200-read.
    read mast-file into W20-area
        invalid key display 'Invalid key on read'
    end-read.
```

Listing 11.05 – 5 of 5

```
Command Prompt
Please enter start key: B100
B 100 Roy 5600
B 200 Jim 5700
B 300 Ada 5800
B 400 Tom 5900
Please enter key: C200
C 200 May 6200
Please enter key: D300
D 300 Pat 6800
Please enter key: D300
D 100 Bud 6600
D 200 Viv 6700
D 300 Pat 6800
D 400 Dot 6900
D 500 Rui 7000
Terminating
```

First and Last

These keywords may be used with both sequential and indexed sequential files. You would code:

```
start mast-file last
end-start
```

to position the pointer to the end of the file.

First, on the other hand, would reposition the pointer to point to the first record in the file.

```
start mast-file first
end-start
```

193

Relative Access

Relative access provides a random access facility based on the relative position of the record. A key of 15 returns the record in the 15th position in the file. Naturally, records must be fixed length. The field used as the key may be part of the record, in which case it is only for your guidance and is not used by the access method. The key must be numeric.

We will start by looking at the program that creates a relative file. Let us examine the select for a relative file:

Select for Relative Access

```
    select out-file assign to 'C:\cob0\chap1106'
        organization is relative
        access is sequential.
```

Figure 11.06

Points to note:

- We need to specify that the file organization is relative.
- Because we are going sequentially through the file we specify that access is sequential.
- Notice that there is no record key clause. This is because it is an output file and the record key clause is not allowed.
- The records will be placed one next to the other in storage.

Creating a Relative File

```
    program-id. chapter1106.

        select out-file assign to 'C:\cob0\chap1106'
            organization is relative
            access is sequential.
    data division.
    file section.
    fd  out-file.
    01  out-rec.
        05  out-key        pic 9(02).
        05                  pic X(07).
```

Listing 11.06 – 1 of 2

Creating a Relative File

```
working-storage section.
01   W10-area.
     05                        pic X(09) value '01Dan5000'.
     05                        pic X(09) value '02Don4000'.
     05                        pic X(09) value '          '.
     05                        pic X(09) value '04Roy3500'.
     05                        pic X(09) value '05Eve4700'.
     05                        pic X(09) value '06Vic9200'.
     05                        pic X(09) value '07Tim8600'.
     05                        pic X(09) value '08Viv3500'.
     05                        pic X(09) value '          '.
     05                        pic X(09) value '10Pat9300'.
     05                        pic X(09) value '11Val2200'.
     05                        pic X(09) value '12Tom8400'.
01   W20-sort-tab redefines W10-area.
     05   W20-entry               occurs 12.
          10   W20-key      pic 9(02).
          10   W20-name     pic X(03).
          10   W20-bal      pic 9(04).
01   ctr                    pic 9(02).
procedure division.
A100-start.
     open output out-file
     perform varying ctr from 1 by 1
         until ctr > 12
             display W20-key (ctr) '  ' W20-name (ctr) '  '
                     W20-bal (ctr)
             move W20-entry (ctr) to out-rec
             write out-rec
     end-perform
     stop run.
```

Listing 11.06 – 2 of 2

Points to note:

- The records are all written one next to the other because we have no way of communicating to the access method where the record is to go. As a result, it is placed in the next available position.

- Notice that those records that do not yet exist must still be 'created', so that records will occupy appropriate positions. If we had not created an empty record corresponding to record with key 3, record with key 4 would occupy the position corresponding to key 3.

- We have used a table and the redefines clause, topics with which you are not acquainted. We will be dealing with these in due course. For the time being, please accept both on trust.

Updating a Relative File

When updating a **relative** file we need to be able to specify a key. The compiler allows us to specify a key if the file is opened as input or I-O. Let us look at the select:

Select for Relative Access

```
select out-file assign to 'C:\cob0\chap1106'
    organization is relative
    access is random
    record key is W20-key.
```

Figure 11.07

196

We have defined W20-key in **working-storage**, it must not be defined in the file section.

Accessing a Relative File

```
program-id. chapter1102.
    select mast-file assign to 'C:\cob0\chap1106'
        organization is relative
        access is random
        relative key W20-key.
file section.
fd   mast-file.
01   mast-rec            pic X(09).
working-storage section.
01   W20-area.
     05   W20-key        pic 9(02).
     05   W20-name       pic X(03).
     05   W20-bal        pic 9(04).
01   store-key           pic 9(02).

procedure division.
A100-start.
    open i-o mast-file.
    perform A200-prompt
    perform until W20-key = 99
        perform Z100-read
        perform B100-display
        perform A200-prompt
    end-perform.
    perform 2 times
        perform A300-prompt
    end-perform
    display 'Terminating'
    stop run.
A200-prompt.
    display 'Please enter key start key: ' no advancing
    accept W20-key.
A300-prompt.
    display 'Please enter key : ' no advancing
    accept W20-key.
    move W20-key to store-key
    perform Z100-read
```

Listing 11.07 – 1 of 2

197

Accessing a Relative File

```
    if  W20-area = ' '
        move store-key to W20-key
        display 'Please enter name: ' no advancing
        accept W20-name
        display 'Please enter bal: ' no advancing
        accept W20-bal
        perform Z200-rewrite
    else
        display 'Record already exists'
    end-if.

B100-display.
    display W20-key ' '
            W20-name '  ' W20-bal.

Z100-read.
    read mast-file into W20-area
        invalid key display 'Invalid key'
    end-read.

Z200-rewrite.
    move W20-area to mast-rec
    rewrite mast-rec
        invalid key display 'Invalid rewrite'
    end-rewrite.
```

Listing 11.07 – 2 of 2

```
Command Prompt                                    _ □ ×
Please enter key start key: 1
01 Dan 5000
Please enter key start key: 99
Please enter key : 3
Please enter name: Ken
Please enter Bal: 5300
Please enter key : 9
Please enter name: Bev
Please enter Bal: 8300
Terminating
```

- Note that because a record is already there we must read it to see if a record exists. If the record contains spaces it does not logically exist. The number of keys only goes up to 12 - if we want to insert a record with key 13 we have to **write** it. To place a record with key 3, it already exists, although it only contains spaces, so we must use the **rewrite**. We rewrite it after changing it from spaces.

Write, Rewrite and Delete

We now look at the three statements **write**, **rewrite** and **delete**. The write is used when we are adding a new record to a relative or an indexed sequential file. At other times we might want to read a record, change it and then put it back where it came from. We call this operation a **rewrite**. So, when we are creating a new record and adding it to the file, this is a write operation. If we read a record, change it and then write it back, this is a re-write.

Note the following. When you reach a point in the execution of the program where an output operation to an **indexed sequential** file is required, you have to be able to ascertain whether it is a **write** or a **rewrite** operation that is required. The **delete** is used to remove a record from the file. The record is physically removed from the file.

The following is required of the program:

- There is an iteration in the body of the loop in which you select a record and then change its balance. The iteration will persist until you enter the code Z100. The record will be rewritten each time.
- The user is then asked to create two records. This operation will call for a **write**.
- Lastly the user is asked for the key of a record to be deleted.

Before looking at the program note that we:

- Write a **record**
- Rewrite a **record**
- Delete a **file-name** (Just as in the read, we read file-name but we get only one record, so with the delete, we delete a file but only the single record gets deleted).

Write, Rewrite and Delete

```
program-id. chapter1108.
    select mast-file assign to 'C:\cob0\chap1104'
        organization is indexed
        access is random
        record key is mast-key.
data division.
file section.
fd   mast-file.
01   mast-rec.
    05   mast-key        pic X(04).
    05                   pic X(07).
working-storage section.
01   W20-area.
    05   W20-key.
        10   W20-br      pic X.
        10   W20-num     pic 9(03).
    05   W20-name        pic X(03).
    05   W20-bal         pic 9(04).
procedure division.
A100-start.
    open i-o mast-file
    perform A200-prompt
    perform until mast-key = 'Z100'
        perform Z100-read
        if  W20-area not = spaces
            perform A300-display
            perform B100-change
        end-if
        perform A200-prompt
    end-perform

    perform 2 times
        perform B200-create
        perform Z300-write
    end-perform
    perform B300-delete
    display 'Terminating'
    close mast-file
    stop run.
```

Iteration catering for changes

Listing 11.08 – 1 of 2

Write, Rewrite and Delete

```
A200-prompt.
    display 'Please enter key: ' no advancing
    accept mast-key.
A300-display.
    display W20-br '  ' W20-num '  '
            W20-bal.
B100-change.
    display 'Please enter new balance: ' no advancing
    accept W20-bal
    perform Z200-rewrite.

 B200-create.
    display 'Enter key : ' no advancing
    accept W20-key
    display 'Enter name: ' no advancing
    accept W20-name
    display 'Enter bal : ' no advancing
    accept W20-bal.
B300-delete.
    display 'Please enter delete key: ' no advancing
    accept mast-key
    perform Z400-delete.
Z100-read.
    read mast-file  into W20-area
        invalid key display 'Record not found'
        move spaces to W20-area
    end-read.
Z200-rewrite.
    rewrite mast-rec  from W20-area
        invalid key display 'Record could not be rewritten'
    end-rewrite.
Z300-write.
    move W20-area to mast-rec
    write mast-rec
        invalid key display 'Record could not be written'
    end-write.
Z400-delete.
    delete mast-file
        invalid key display 'Unsuccessful deletion'
    end-delete.
```

Listing 11.08 – 3 of 3

We will now show you the result of execution in two steps. The second step confirms the results of the first execution.

Using a Sectionalized Procedure Division

For reasons of brevity none of the examples carry a sectionalized procedure division. Note however, that many, if not most, of the COBOL installations use sectionalization in their procedure divisions. When sectionalizing, a paragraph is inserted into a section, in this way when the paragraph is to be executed, it is the section that is invoked rather than the paragraph name.

When a section is invoked, all the paragraphs in the section will be executed. Note than when sectionalizing it is usual to end the section on an exit paragraph. In such cases the **exit** will be the only statement in the paragraph.

Whether as a practicing programmer you will sectionalize your procedure divisions is not so much a matter of preference as it is a matter of the standard being implemented at the company for which you are working. The following example depicts the structure of a section as we have been describing.

Sectionalization Example I

```
A100-Prompt Section.
A100-PromptPar.
    Display 'Please enter employee ID: '
    Accept empID.
A100-Exit.
    Exit.
```

Figure 11.08

Following you will find a number of sectionalized paragraphs extracted from the preceding program. You will notice that each section ends where the following section starts or, if no section follows, by the end of the program.

Sectionalization Example II

```
Z100-Read Section.
Z100-ReadPar.
    read mast-file  into W20-area
        invalid key display 'Record not found'
        move spaces to W20-area
    end-read.
Z100-Exit.
    Exit.

Z200-Rewrite Section.
Z200-RewritePar.
    rewrite mast-rec  from W20-area
        invalid key display 'Record could not be rewritten'
    end-rewrite.
Z200-Exit.
    Exit.
```

Figure 11.09 – 1 of 2

203

Sectionalization Example II

```
Z300-Write Section.
Z300-WritePar.
    move W20-area to mast-rec
    write mast-rec
        invalid key display 'Record could not be written'
    end-write.
Z300-Exit.
    Exit.

Z400-Delete Section.
Z400-DeletePar.
    delete mast-file
        invalid key display 'Unsuccessful deletion'
    end-delete.
Z400-Exit.
    Exit.
```

Figure 11.09 – 2 of 2

You see that sectionaliztion is very easy to implement.

Summary

- In reading files, we see the importance of the **read ahead** principle. The principle states that before embarking on a loop to process the records in a file we must read the first record in the file. The reason for this is that when we enter the loop we have a record to process. The last thing we do inside the loop is read the next record. In this way, at the top of the loop we have another record to process. If we did not read at the bottom of the loop, we would be processing the same record all the time.

- Furthermore, the **read ahead** principle states that we read the next record when we have finished with the preceding one.

- When printing a report we have to be in a position to ascertain whether it is necessary to go to the top of the next page. Notice that when we go to print we have a record ready for printing. Before we print, however, we must determine whether it is necessary to go to top of page. If it is not, we print the record and add one to line-ctr. If it is, we branch to print headings, set the line-ctr to 0 and only then, on return, do we print the record.

- When writing records it is the record defined under the FD that gets written.

- When printing, in the normal course of events, we need to write a number of records with differing formats, heading lines, total lines, and body lines, to name a few. For this reason we use the **write from**.

- Indexed sequential files may be processed sequentially or randomly. In addition, the file may be processed both sequentially and randomly, in which case the file is said to be processed dynamically.

- The start statement enables us to position the pointer to a suitable position in the file. The appropriate key value is moved to the record key. The read then retrieves the record satisfying the condition.

- When we have specified dynamic access and we are processing sequentially following a **start** statement, we should use not the usual **read** but a **read next**.

- It is also possible to have relative access, in which case a record with a key of 5 will be the fifth record in the file and so on.

Complete

1.   In reading ahead, the first read follows _____ open and precedes the _____.

2.   If we are applying the read ahead the _____ thing we do inside the loop is _____.

3.   In applying the read ahead we _____ the next record when we have finished processing the _____ record.

4.   We are reading randomly and we prompt the reader for the record key and will loop until the user enters 'xxx'. We should _____ before entering the loop.

5.   The detail line receives data _____ testing for end of page.

6.   You have paper that is 50 lines. You leave five lines at the top and five lines at the bottom. There are five heading lines. The body of the report is _____ lines.

7.   In writing to the printer we use the _____ _____.

8.   Write print-rec from detail-line _____ _____ .

9.   In the heading routine we move _____ to the line-ctr.

10.   When we are processing sequentially and have requested dynamic access, to retrieve a record we use _____ _____.

11.   Assume you have a field Start-key that has the point from which you want to start processing and that mast-file is sequenced on mast-key. Before using the start statement you would code 'move _____ to _____'.

12.   Assuming the information from the preceding question, your start statement would be: 'start _____ key is > _____.

13.   Records in a relative file must be _____ _____.

14.   In a relative file, records are all written _____ to each other.

15.   The delete requires a _____ name.

True/False

1.   The read requires the file name.

2.   The write requires the record name.

3.   The rewrite requires the file name.

4.   The after advancing clause has a default of 2 lines.

5.   When printing we can print either before or after advancing.

6.   We move 0 to the line-ctr after printing the last line on the page.

7.   If the page is able to hold 50 detail lines, moving 51 or 52 to line-ctr has the same effect.

8.   To delete a record we must first read it.

9.   The delete carries out logical deletion only.

10. The record key in an indexed sequential file must be defined in the record defined under the FD.

11. The file status field should be defined in working-storage as a pic xx field.

12. The values returned into the file status field are all numeric.

13. If we specify access is dynamic, we can specify read next or read prior.

14. Start statement calls for a key field that has the same length as the file key.

15. Relative access provides random access based on the relative position of the record, either from the beginning or the end of the file.

16. When processing a relative file to delete a record we should first read it.

17. The rewrite applies to the record retrieved by the immediately preceding read.

Exercises

1. Code the select statement for an ISAM file whose physical name is TestFile, which will be used randomly and whose key field is called TestKey. The file status field is W10-FileStat.

2. Code the read for an ISAM file called TestFile. The record key is TestKey. Test for the file status. If the file status is 0 display 'OK' otherwise display 'Error in Read'.

3. Create a file TestFile. It should have the following fields CustNo pic X(4), Cust-Name pic X(10) and Amount pic 9(5). Derive your own data. Specify access is dynamic and read the file sequentially and randomly. Perform the operations i) Add a record, ii) Change a record and iii) Delete a record.

Chapter 12
Program Design

Topics Covered

- Matching Files
- Matching Records
- The Match within a Control Break
- Defining Compound Keys
- Merging Files
- Summary
- Complete
- True/False
- Exercises

Matching Files

The problem we will look at next concerns the **matching** of two files, one a transaction file and the other a master file. To recapitulate, a master file is permanent it is there today and will be there tomorrow. If you have an account at the chemist, it will be there from one month to the next, in the chemist's debtors' master file. What you buy from the chemist, on credit, will give rise to transactions. Those transactions will be used to update the master and your record in the master, once your transactions have been processed, will end up with the new balance owing.

Matching Records

As indicated, the program will update the master records by applying the transactions to the matching master records. **Matching records** are records bearing identical keys. Because this is sequential processing we start off with a transaction file and what we will call the **old master file**. These will be the two input files. If a file is opened as input we cannot write to it. Writing is an output operation. The updated master is written out to produce a new version of the master. Graphically represented we have:

System Chart:

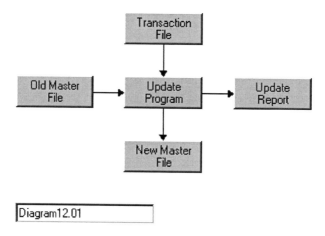

Diagram12.01

The report will have a starting account balance followed by the transactions and finally a new balance. At the end we will print the accumulated total of the transactions. There will be three types of transactions:

Additions   -   these will create a new master and carry a code of 'A'.

Changes   -   these will change a record and carry a code of 'C'.

Deletions   -   these will carry a code of 'D'.

The transactions are in sequence: Code within account number. Notice the following points:

- When we do sequential processing as depicted in the chart, we use what is called the grandfather-father-son method of file rotation. If we notice that something is wrong with the son we still have the father. If there is something wrong with the father, we still have the grandfather.

  - The old master was the son in the preceding run.
  - In the preceding run we overwrote the grandfather.
  - In this run, the son provides the input and the grandfather is overwritten. After the run the father becomes the grandfather, the son becomes the father and the file that received the output becomes the son.
  - In the next run, it is the grandfather that is overwritten and the father becomes the grandfather. The son, in turn, becomes the father.

- We keep the transaction files in case we should need to repeat any runs.

- When we create a new record, it will be created in the new master, the son. It will not be present in the old master, the father.

- When we delete a record from the old master we merely abstain from writing it to the new master. At the end of the run the deleted record will still be in the old master, the father, but will not be present in the new master, the son.

- We apply transactions to the master records. The old master will have the old balance and the new master will have the new balance.

Naturally, in structuring our program we will break it up into manageable modules, as we have been doing so far, so that we will respect the principles of good structure.

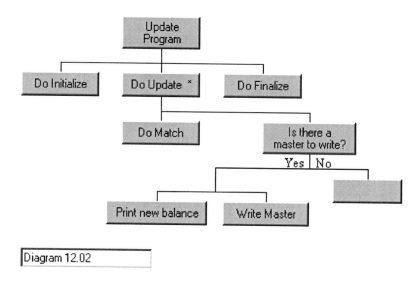

Diagram 12.02

Let us now examine the chart:

- In the Initialize routine we will do all that is necessary at the beginning of the program. An example would be opening files, reading a record or getting the date.
- The Update routine will do the bulk of the required processing.
- When all has been done we do the Finalize routine. It will include such things as closing files and printing totals, if these are required.
- At the next level, we see that each pass at this level processes a master record.
- We print the starting balance.
- In the match routine all transactions will be processed against the master.
- Finally we ask, did we process a master? If there were no transactions for this master we do not have a new balance to print. If the transactions were all invalid, we do not need to print a new balance. If the master was deleted we do not write a master record to the new master.

Let us see what we need to do in the Initialize routine:

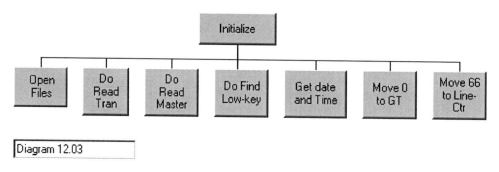

Diagram 12.03

The above structure is referred to as a **sequence**. Things are done one after the other. Sometimes the sequence in which things are done does not matter, but generally it matters. For instance, whether we get the data first or the time of day first, is of no significance. However, it is important that we open a file before we process a read against that file. Besides sequences we have two other constructs, namely iteration and selection. **Iterations** provide a looping facility and selection enables us to choose between different courses of action. The **if** statement and the **evaluate** satisfy the selection construct. Two individuals, Bohm and Jacopini, produced a famous paper in which they proved that the three constructs mentioned were sufficient to resolve any logic problem.

In the hierarchy chart, when we say 'Do' as in 'Do Read-Tran' it means that in COBOL we would use a perform to take us to a separate routine, after which we would return to the first instruction following the perform. **Selection** is shown as an 'o' in the top right hand corner and iterations appear as an '*' in the top right hand corner.

Let us see what we do in the Finalize routine:

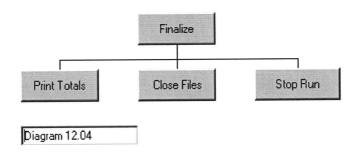

Diagram 12.04

The Finalize is also a sequence and in it we wrap up the job by doing those things that need to be done once we have processed all the records in both files.

In the Initialize routine we have a very important routine that needs to be executed only after we have read a record from both files. We call the routine **Find-Low-Key** because the routine determines which is the lowest key between master and transaction. The lowest of the two keys will be stored in a field we will call **Low-Key**.

To match two records, we match them based on the key in each of the records. In a debtors application the key is the account number. The key serves to identify the record just as a telephone number identifies a telephone account. Each call made returns a transaction and the transactions will be matched against a master based on the account number present in both records.

In our example, each account has an account number that is numeric and has five digits.

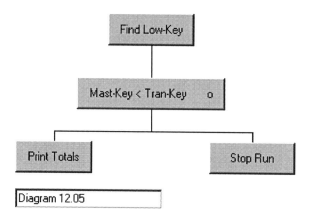

Diagram 12.05

Notice that at this stage we are not concerned with whether the keys are the same. What we know is that with this logic **Low-key** will always hold the lower of the two keys. If the keys are the same, then **Low-key** will hold a key that will be the same in both records.

Later, when we have to find out whether we have a master to process, we test the **Master-key** against **Low-key**. Similarly, to find out whether we have a transaction to process we test the **Transaction-key** against **Low-key**.

Next, we will look at the match. Note that because we read a master and a transaction at the beginning in Initialize, we are in a position to test the key of the master against the key of the transaction.

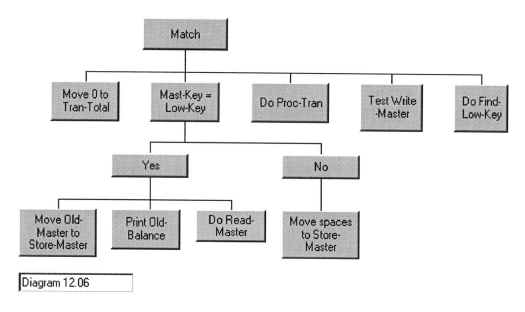

Diagram 12.06

- We will be accumulating the value of transactions so we move 0 to the transaction totals for this new set of transactions for this master.
- We test the **Master-key** against **Low-key**. If the **Master-key** is equal to **Low-key** we know that we have a master to process. We move it to store-master and read another master. This new-master will be in the input-area and the previous master will be in the store-area. It is in store-area that we process the current master.
- If the **Master-key** is not equal to **Low-key** there is no master to process so we move spaces to store-master. This is like turning on a switch to indicate that although we have transactions, there is no master for those transactions.

- We are now in a position to process the transactions so we branch to do this. When we have finished with one transaction, we read the next transaction. Eventually we will read a transaction where **Tran-key** is no longer equal to the **Low-key**. We exit the loop. Note that we have the next transaction in sequence.

- When we return we have both a transaction and a master so we can find **Low-key** once more. We have a master, either because we moved the master to store-area and read the next master or we already had a master because its key was higher than **Low-key** and we moved spaces to store-master.

- Note that when we are processing the transactions we have to know whether we have a master against which to process the transactions.

- In our solution we never ask two questions at a time and this reduces complexity. We either ask, do I have a master or do I have a transaction. Of course the question might take another form such as **Master-key** = **Low-key**, which means do I have a master?

- To find out whether we have transactions we use the loop condition, **until T-key not = Low-key**. If it is not equal we bypass the loop because there are no transactions to process against the master. If it is equal we enter the loop.

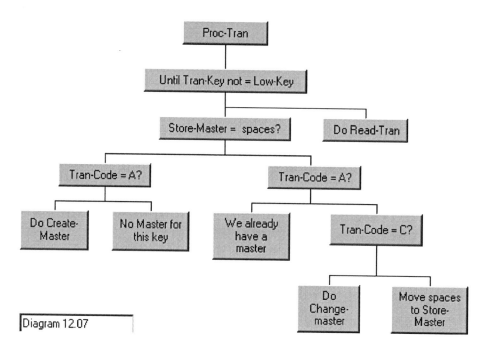

Diagram 12.07

Next we will examine the Proc-Tran routine. You will have noticed that the routine constitutes the heart of the program.

- We will iterate until we have exhausted all transactions for this **Low-key**. If there are no transactions for this Low-Key, this means that we have a master without transactions. We have already printed the balance for the master.

- If we go into the loop it is because we have a transaction. The first question we ask is, do we have a master? If store-master is spaces we do not have a master.

- If we do not have a master, is the transaction code an 'A'? If it is an 'A' we create a new master. Notice that the master is created in store-master. When the next transaction is processed, store-master will no longer be equal to spaces.

- If store-master is equal to spaces and the code is not 'A' there is the mistaken presumption that a master with that key is available. We output an error message.

- If store-master is not equal to spaces there is a master for this low-key. If the transaction code is an 'A' there is the mistaken impression that a master for the key does not exist. We output an error message.

- If the transaction code is not an 'A' is it a 'C'? If it is a C we update the master. If it is not a 'C' then it must be a 'D' and the relevant master is to be deleted. In sequential processing, to delete a master, we simply move spaces to store-master. If store-master is equal to spaces it will not be written out to disk.

- We have finished processing this transaction; it is time to retrieve the next transaction. Notice that this is the last thing we do in the loop. The purpose of the loop is to process a transaction. Once the transaction is processed the only thing left to do is to read the next record. Remember, we read the next record when we have finished with the preceding one.

- As we retrieve transactions, a time will come when the transaction we retrieved is for a different key. The loop condition will be satisfied and we will exit the loop.

Once we exit the loop, we go back up to the Match routine and determine whether there is a master to be written out. Note that if the master was deleted, there is no master to write out. Once the test-write-master routine has been executed, we will have finished all processing for the present **Low-Key** and it is time to find the new **Low-Key**.

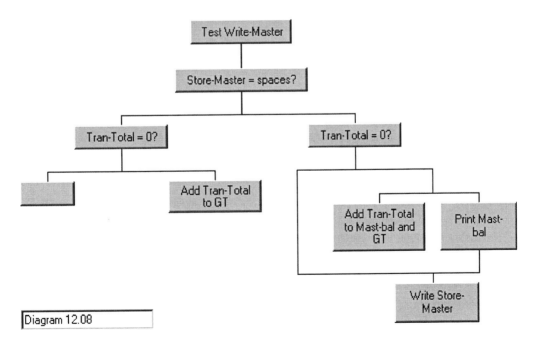

Diagram 12.08

- If store master is equal to spaces, then there is no master to write out. Maybe the master was deleted or there was no master for the low-key and the transactions were invalid.
- If store-master was deleted, there might have been transactions prior to the deletion. If tran-total is not equal to zero we must accumulate the value of the transactions processed.
- If store-master is not equal to spaces, we ask whether there were valid transactions. If there were, we update the balance in store-master and print the new balance in the master.
- Whether there were transactions or not we still need to write the master record out. That is the last thing we do in the routine.

We go up to the next level. If there are still transactions, we repeat the loop, otherwise we print the totals we have accumulated, close files and stop the run. Let us look at the program:

File Matching

```
program-id. Chapter1201 as "Chapter1201".
    select tran-file assign to 'C:\cob0\chap12b01'.
    select mast-file assign to 'C:\cob0\chap12b02'.
    select new-mast  assign to 'C:\cob0\chap12b03'.
file section.
fd   mast-file.
01   mast-rec.
     05   m-key                pic X(03).
     05   m-name               pic X(03).
     05   m-bal                pic 9(05).
fd   new-mast.
01   new-mast-rec             pic 9(11).
fd   tran-file.
01   tran-rec.
     05   t-code               pic X.
     05   t-key                pic X(03).
     05   t-deb-cred           pic X.
     05   t-amt                pic 9(04).
working-storage section.
01   W10-data.
     05   W10-low-key          pic X(03).
     05   W10-tran-total       pic S9(05).
     05   W10-grand-total      pic S9(05).
```

Listing 12.01 – 1 of 5

File Matching

```
      05   W10-GT              pic Z9(05)-.
      05   W10-store-master.
           10   sm-key         pic X(03).
           10   sm-name        pic X(03).
           10   sm-bal         pic S9(05).

  01   W20-heading.
      05                       pic X(20) value spaces.
      05                       pic X(20) value 'Update Report'.
      05   W20-date            pic ZZZZ/ZZ/ZZ.
      05                       pic X(05) value spaces.
      05   W20-time            pic ZZ/ZZ/ZZ.

  01   W30-detail.
      05   W30-code            pic 9(03).
      05                       pic X(02).
      05   W30-acc-no          pic 9(03).
      05                       pic X(02).
      05   W30-name            pic X(03).
      05                       pic X(02).
      05   W30-deb             pic Z,ZZ9.
      05                       pic X(02).
      05   W30-cred            pic Z,ZZ9.
      05                       pic X(05).
      05   W30-bal             pic Z,ZZ9.
      05                       pic X(02).
      05   W30-msg             pic X(21).

  procedure division.
  A100-start.
      perform B100-initialize
      perform until W10-low-key = high-values
          perform B200-match
          perform D500-test-write-master
      end-perform
      perform Y100-finalize.
  B100-initialize.
      open input  tran-file
                  mast-file
           output new-mast
      accept W20-date from date yyyymmdd
```

Listing 12.01 – 2 of 5

219

File Matching

```
       accept W20-time from time
       perform Z100-read-tran
       perform Z200-read-master
       perform B200-find-low-key
       display W20-heading
       move 0 to  W10-grand-total.

  B200-find-low-key.
     if  m-key < t-key
         move m-key to W10-low-key
     else
         move T-key to W10-low-key
     end-if.
  B200-match.
     move 0 to W10-tran-total
     if  m-key = W10-low-key
         move mast-rec to W10-store-master
         move spaces to w30-detail
         move W10-low-key to W30-acc-no
         move m-name       to W30-name
         move m-bal        to W30-bal
         display W30-detail
         perform Z200-read-master
     else
         move spaces to W10-store-master
     end-if
     perform C100-proc-tran
     perform B200-find-low-key.
  C100-proc-tran.
     perform until t-key not = W10-low-key
         move spaces to W30-detail
         if  W10-store-master = spaces
             if  t-code = 'A'
                 perform D100-create
             else
                 move t-key to W30-acc-no
                 move 'Master does not exist' to W30-msg
                 display W30-detail
             end-if
```

Listing 12.01 – 3 of 5

220

File Matching

```
            else
                if  t-code = 'A'
                    move t-key to W30-acc-no
                    move 'Master already exists' to W30-msg
                    display W30-detail
                else
                    if  t-code = 'C'
                        perform D200-change
                    else
                        perform D300-delete
                    end-if
                end-if
            end-if
        perform Z100-read-tran
    end-perform.

D100-create.
    move t-key to m-key
    move 'xxx' to m-name
    move t-amt to m-bal
    add  t-amt to W10-tran-total
    perform D400-put-tran.

D200-change.
    if  t-deb-cred = 'C'
        add  t-amt to W10-tran-total
        move t-amt to W30-deb
    else
        subtract t-amt from W10-tran-total
        move t-amt to W30-cred
    end-if
    perform D400-put-tran.

D300-delete.
    move t-key to W30-acc-no
    move 'Master deleted' to W30-msg
    display W30-detail
    move spaces to W10-store-master.

D400-put-tran.
    move t-key to W30-acc-no
    display W30-detail.
```

Listing 12.01 – 4 of 5

File Matching

```
D500-test-write-master.
    if  W10-store-master = spaces
        if  W10-tran-total = 0
            continue
        else
            add W10-tran-total to W10-grand-total
        end-if
    else
        if  W10-tran-total = 0
            continue

        else
            add W10-tran-total to sm-bal
                                  W10-grand-total
            move spaces to W30-detail
            move sm-bal to W30-bal
            display W30-detail
        end-if
    end-if
    perform Z300-write-master.

Y100-finalize.
    move W10-grand-total to W10-GT
    display 'Grand total: '  W10-GT
    stop run.

Z100-read-tran.
    read tran-file
        at end move high-values to t-key.
Z200-read-master.
    read mast-file
        at end move high-values to m-key
    end-read.

Z300-write-master.
    write new-mast-rec  from  W10-store-master
        invalid key display 'Cannot write'
    end-write.
```

Listing 12.01 – 5 of 5

```
 Command Prompt                                              _ □ ✕
   110                               Master does not exist   ▲
   110                               Master does not exist
   115 Don                    2,000
   120 Eve                    3,000
   120      6,400
   120              1,500
                              7,900
   125 Roy                    4,000
   130 Eva                    5,000
   130          5,000
   130                               Master deleted
   135 Vic                    6,000
   140 Tim                    7,000
   140      2,700
   140              1,800
                              7,900
   145 Viv                    8,000
   150 Tom                    9,000
   150      1,900
                                900
   160 Pat                    9,900
Grand total: 03800                                          ▼
```

The Match within a Control Break

Notice that the Match involves a transaction on the one hand, and a master on the other. **Control breaks**, you will notice, involve groups of records. This means that if we want a control break by branch, we will have to have the branch **control break** and subordinated to that we will have to have the match. If, in addition to the control break by branch, we also need a **control break** by department, then the Match will be subordinated to the innermost of these two **control breaks**.

Defining Compound Keys

We define **compound keys** to assist us in handling control breaks. In programming, it is easier to handle one question at a time rather than two questions at a time. In the match we did this. We determine whether we have a master, then we determine whether we have a transaction. We do not say: "Do we have a master and a transaction for this master?"

You have seen that when we are handling a control break we need to prepare for the condition. For instance, how are we going to know that we have processed all the records in a branch? If we are processing branch 'A100' we only know that we have processed all the records for the branch when we read a record and the record is for a new branch. To ascertain that the new record is for a new branch we need to ask a question and that question involves two variables because we have to compare the branch of this record to the branch we were processing.

In preparing for the condition that monitors the control break, we would have to code:

```
move W50-branch to W90-store-branch
```

The associated condition would be:

```
perform B200-process-branch
    until W50-branch not = W90-store-branch
```

In asking one question, our minds will be busy with two variables at the same time. If we are asking two questions, our minds will have to handle four variables simultaneously. Now, handling four variables is not twice as complicated as handling two variables; it is probably eight times as complicated and we need to keep things simple. What we do not want to do is this:

```
perform B200-process-branch
    until W50-branch not = W90-store-branch
        and W50-depart not = W90-depart
```

To ask only one question we would have to formulate the condition as follows:

```
perform B200-process-branch
    until W50-branch-dep not = W90-store-branch-dep
```

Let us see how we are going to construct our keys:

Compound Keys

```
01  W50-key.
    05  W50-branch-dep.
        10  W50-branch        pic X(03).
        10  W50-dep           pic X(02).
    05  W50-emp-no            pic 9(04).

01  W90-store-key.
    05  W90-store-branch-dep.
        10  W90-store-branch  pic X(03).
        10  W90-store-dep     pic X(02).
```

Figure 12.01

The level 01 field includes all subordinate fields. The level 05 includes all subordinate fields left over. Subordinate fields all have lower levels. The lower levels in this case are branch and department. We are able to address all elementary fields and all group fields. Let us now add region and company, so that we will have region within company.

Compound Keys with Four Levels

```
01   W50-key.
     05  W50-coy-reg-br-dep.
         10  W50-coy-reg-br.
             15  W50-coy-reg.
                 20  W50-coy        pic X(02).
                 20  W50-reg        pic X(02).
             15  W50-branch         pic X(03).
         10  W50-dep                pic X(02).
     05  W50-emp-no                 pic 9(04).

01   W90-store-key.
     05  W90-st-coy-reg-br-dep.
         10  W90-st-coy-reg-br.
             15  W90-st-coy-reg.
                 20  W90-st-coy     pic X(02).
                 20  W90-st-reg     pic X(02).
             15  W90-st-branch      pic X(03).
         10  W90-st-dep             pic X(02).
```

Figure 12.02

Notice that each group field contains one field less than its immediate superordinate. Eventually, the group field contains only elementary fields. That is where the elementary field definitions start. The store fields do not need the lowest level field because that comparison is at singular level. Let us look at the graphical representation of W50-key.

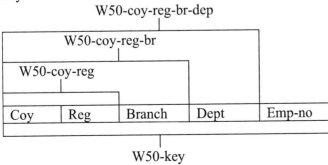

You will realize that it is the elementary fields subordinated to the group fields that contain data. We can see the group fields as templates that isolate some of the fields as required. W50-key, being the group field at the highest level, includes all the fields.

We will look at the hierarchy chart up to the level at which the match is invoked.

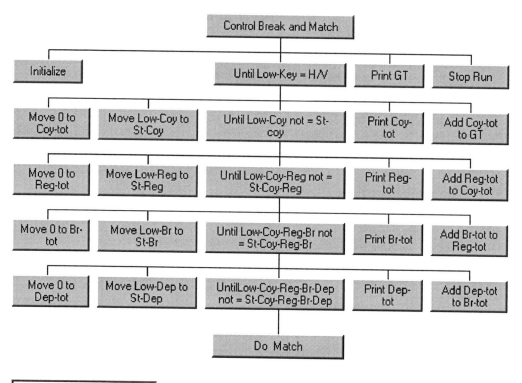

Diagram 12.09

Points to note:

- Remember that the logic we are using is based on **low-key**. It is not unusual that the first records in the master file will not have transactions. The key of the master will then be in **low-key** and, in that case, that is what must be stored.

- We must initialize the field in which we are going to accumulate. Once the iteration for the group terminates we must add the accumulation field to the accumulation field for the preceding iteration.

- Because we are comparing the group fields we restrict the comparison to two fields at a time, the group field in the master is compared to the group field in the transaction.

Merging Files

You have seen how useful the **low-key** technique can be. We call it **low-key** because the field contains the lowest key of all units participating. In our example we had two files, a transaction and a master file, but you could use the same technique, however large the number of files. To exemplify we will be merging three files. We will call the files T1, T2 and T3 and the keys will be respectively T1-key, T2-key and T3-key. The Find-Low-Key routine might then look as follows.

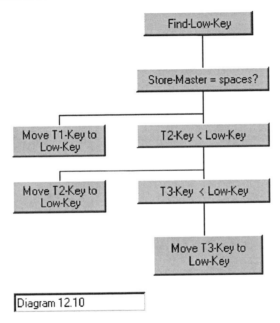

Diagram 12.10

From the preceding chart you see that irrespective of the number of files, low-key will always end up with the lowest key of all the files participating in the exercise.

In the next example we will merge three files to produce an output file containing the merged records. Furthermore, we will stipulate that if a record exists in file T1 and a record with the same key exists in file T2 or file T3, only the record from file T1 is to be accepted. The same principle applies between files T2 and T3. If a record with a given key is not present in file T1 but is present in file T2 and file T3, accept the record from file T2 and reject the record from file T3. In each file there is only one record per key. The hierarchy chart follows:

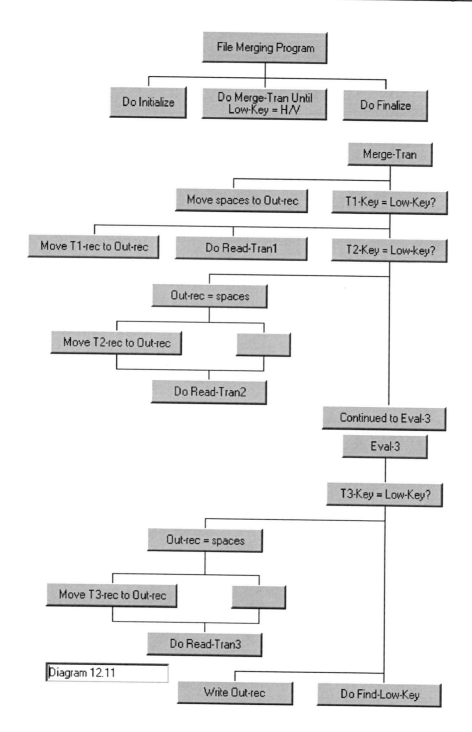

Diagram 12.11

Next, we will take a look at the operation of the chart:

- When we enter merge-tran we have one record from each of the files and we have found **low-key**.
- To determine whether there has already been a record for the key, we start by moving spaces to the field that will house the record to be processed further. We then test the field against spaces.
- If the area contains spaces we move the record to the area. If it already contains a record we don't do anything. In both cases we must read the next record from the file because in both cases we will have finished with the preceding record.
- When we have gone through the three files we will be ready to write the record.
- We find the **low-key** and repeat the loop until we have exhausted all records in the files.

In the initialize, we will do all those things that, as we have seen earlier, need to be done at the outset. When we read, we will read all three files.

Just as the match is subordinated to control breaks that involve groups of records, the groups of records from the transaction side must follow the match. Remember, we must exhaust all transactions for that master. So, where in the preceding chart we wrote the record, if the program had a match that is where the program would accept the next transaction.

Summary

- Master files are permanent and transaction files are temporary.

- In sequential processing, backups are obtained using the grandfather-father-son method of file rotation.

- In sequential processing, where we produce a new master, to delete a record we merely refrain from writing it to the new master.

- In sequential processing, where we produce a new master, to add a record we write it to the new master. The record is a new record - it will not be in the old master.

- What we can say about **Low-key** is that neither of the records can have a key which is lower than **Low-key**. **Low-key** will hold the lowest of the two keys or the key of both records if the keys are the same.

- When we ask: Is **Mast-key** = **Low-key**? - This is the same as saying 'Is there a master record to process?'. Similarly, the condition 'until **Tran-key** not = **Low-key**' implies a test for the presence of transaction records.

- When we are processing transactions we have to ask whether we have a master (store-master = spaces). If we are creating a new master then we must ascertain that there is not already a master for this **Low-key**. If however, we are changing or deleting a record, it is imperative that a record for that **Low-key** exists. If there is no record for the **Low-key**, we have an error situation.

- When we reach the stage where we have to write out the master, we have to determine whether there is a master to write out. Note that because we are totaling transactions, even though there is no master to write out, it is possible that there might have been transactions for the low-key.

- The match involves one record from each of the files. When dealing with control breaks we are working with groups of records. It follows that the match must follow the control break.

- Compound keys provide the programmer with a means of reducing the number of comparisons required in control breaks.

Complete

1.   Matching records have the same _____.

2.   If M-key is five and T-key is five, the value in low-key will be ____.

3.   When we are using the grandfather-father-son method of backup, the file that receives the output becomes the _____.

4.   When we are using the grandfather-father-son method of backup, the file that is providing the input is the _____ and becomes the _____.

5.   The file that is overwritten is always the _____.

6.   In a sequence it is not _____ important what we do first.

7.   The three logical constructs required to solve any logic problem are _____, _____ and _____.

8.   We read the next record once we have processed the _____ record.

9.   When creating a compound key, each level as we go up _____ one more field.

10. In the match, the test is _____ = _____.

11. In the match if there is a master we store the master and read the next master. We do this because if there is no master we already have the _____ master.

12. To find whether we have transactions to process we code until _____ not = _____.

13. If we are processing an addition store-master should have _____.

14. The match is _____ to the control break.

15. Any loop for transactions must be _____ to the match.

True/False

1. Master files are temporary and transaction files are permanent.
2. With sequential processing, we use the delete verb to delete a record.
3. The read ahead principle ensures that at the top of the loop we always have a new record to process.
4. In a sequence, the order in which the parts are executed is always important.
5. Low-key must be determined prior to entering the loop.
6. When Mast-key is not = Low-key, we have the next master.
7. When Mast-key is not = Low-key, we do not have a transaction.
8. To add a new record to the file, Mast-key must be = Low-key.
9. If Tran-key not = Low-key, we have a master without transactions.
10. If store-master = spaces we do not write out a master.
11. The match involves groups of records.
12. Compound keys enable the programmer to reduce the number of comparisons required in a condition.

13. If we have a match and control breaks, the match will be subordinated to the control breaks.
14. In merging, if a record from one of the files is equal to low-key we do not have to read the next record.

Exercises

1. A particular company has split its market into three areas: North, East and West. Customers may have accounts in all three areas. The company has now decided to consolidate all three areas into one area. You are to design the program that will carry out the consolidation bearing in mind the following additional information:

    a) Each customer record is always split into three records. You will produce one single record for each customer. The first record contains address information, the second contains historical information and the third contains balance owing information split into 30, 60, 90 days and current.

    b) If a record exists in file T1 and file T2 use the record from file T1 and discard the record from file T2. The same applies in respect of file T3.

    c) The resulting file must have one record per customer.

Chapter 13
Redefinition

Topics Covered

- Redefinition
- Redefinition in the File Section
- Implied Redefinition
- Renames
- Condition Names
- Multiple Literals in a Condition Name
- More About the Value Clause
- Continuing Literals
- The Concatenation Operator (&)
- Continuing Numeric Literals
- Qualification
- Summary
- Complete
- True/False
- Exercises

Redefinition

By **redefinition** we understand the possibility of two records, with different formats, occupying the same block of storage. Think of a restaurant; on weekdays it has the usual restaurant format, with tables occupying most of the available area. This is one format. On Sundays it caters for weddings and at such times, in the center of the hall, the tables have been removed and an area for dancing has been created. The tables have been spread around the sides and a place for a band has been created. This is a different format. We have the same area but two formats. At any time we have one format in operation or the other. We cannot have the two formats at the same time.

When we talk about **redefinition** in COBOL we have a similar idea in mind. We define two formats, of greater or lesser complexity, and using the **redefines** keyword, the two formats will be allocated the same area of storage. To understand the **redefines**, we have to understand how the compiler handles the problem of addressability. Consider the following definition:

Record Definition

```
01   W20-emp-rec.
     05 W20-emp-key.
        10   W20-emp-br        pic   X(02).
        10   W20-emp-no        pic   9(04).
     05 W20-emp-name           pic   X(16).
     05 W20-emp-salary         pic   S9(05)V99.
```

Figure 13.01

When the compiler comes across a data definition the compiler will store the following information.

- The name of the field.
- The length of the field.
- The address of the field's high order byte.
- The type of data the field will hold. If numeric, does it contain decimals and a sign.

We will assume that the compiler allocated hexadecimal address 4000 to the definition of the 01 level. The following table represents the information that would be kept by the compiler in respect of the definition:

Address	Field Name	Field Size	Data Type	Decimals
4000	W20-emp-rec	29	AN	
4000	W20-emp-key	06	AN	
4000	W20-emp-br	02	AN	
4002	W20-emp-no	04	AN	
4006	W20-emp-name	16	AN	
4016	W20-emp-salary	07	N	2
Table 13.01 Tabular representation of record area				

We see the first three definitions all start at the same address. Imagine three boxes, as shown below. Boxes, in real life have sides of some thickness; addresses however, have no thickness. Below, the boxes have close to no thickness. All three boxes start at the same point, equivalent to the same address, on the left.

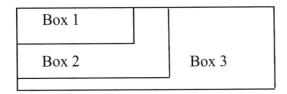

W20-emp-no is the first field that is displaced from the origin. Its displacement is two bytes. W20-emp-name is displaced six bytes from the origin, (2 + 4) and W20-emp-salary is displaced 22 bytes from the origin (2 + 4 + 16). The decimal value 22 is equivalent to 16 hexadecimal, the value of 10 being 16. Now, to the preceding definition we are going to add another one.

Using the Redefines

```
01 W20-emp-rec.
   05 W20-emp-key.
      10   W20-emp-br          pic   X(02).
      10   W20-emp-no          pic   9(04).
   05 W20-emp-name             pic   X(16).
   05 W20-emp-salary           pic   S9(05)V99.
01 W20-emp-rec-2 redefines W20-emp-rec.
   05 W20-emp-key-2.
      10   W20-emp-br-2        pic   X(02).
      10   W20-emp-no-2        pic   9(04).
   05 W20-emp-experience       pic   9(02)V9.
   05 W20-emp-qualification    pic   X(10).
   05                          pic   X(10).
```

Figure 13.02

The **redefines** indicates to the compiler that it should allocate to the 01 level, to which the redefines has been applied, the same address it allocated to the item redefined and named following the **redefines** keyword. The table for the redefining format is as follows:

Address	Field Name	Field Size	Data Type	Decimals
4000	W20-emp-rec-2	29	AN	
4000	W20-emp-key-2	06	AN	
4000	W20-emp-br-2	02	AN	
4002	W20-emp-no-2	04	AN	
4006	W20-emp-experience	03	N	1
4009	W20-emp-Qualification	10	AN	
4013	Filler	10	AN	

Table 13.02 Tabular representation of record area

If we had not used the redefines keyword, the two definitions would have occupied different areas and the starting address of the second definition would have been 401D. (4016 + 7)

Note the following points:

- At any point in time, the data in W20-emp-rec and in W20-emp-rec-2 will be the same, because they have the same storage address. What is important to note is that unless we use the appropriate format much of the data will make no sense.
- The data that will make sense is the data that obey one of the formats and that is used in accordance with that format. The key definition is common to both formats.
- It follows from the preceding point that if we say: Display W20-emp-br or display W20-emp-br-2, the same data would be displayed. The same applies to W20-emp-no and W20-emp-no-2.
- You should notice that the record definitions and the key definitions have the same addresses.
- When we use the redefines for two record definitions, as we did, we need some way of finding out which record type we are handling. For this reason, below we have added a code to identify the record type. We will assume that the code will be '1' for W20-emp-rec and '2' for W20-emp-rec-2.
- We used a 10 byte filler at the end of the redefining record to make both records the same length. When using the redefines this is recommended but not essential. The redefining item should never be longer than the redefined item.

Using an Identifying Code

```
01   W20-emp-rec.
     05   W20-emp-code          pic   x.
     05   W20-emp-key.
          10   W20-emp-br       pic   X(02).
          10   W20-emp-no       pic   9(04).
     05   W20-emp-name          pic   X(16).
     05   W20-emp-salary        pic   S9(05)V99.
01   W20-emp-rec-2 redefines W20-emp-rec.
     05   W20-emp-code-2        pic   X.
     05   W20-emp-key-2.
          10   W20-emp-br-2     pic   X(02).
          10   W20-emp-no-2     pic   9(04).
     05   W20-emp-experience    pic   9(02)V9.
     05   W20-emp-qualification pic   X(10).
     05                         pic   X(10).
```

Figure 13.03

The definitions that are common to both 01 levels may be dispensed with in one of the definitions and a **filler** used instead. We will repeat the definitions, but now using a **filler** for the first 05 level field defined in the redefining item.

Using a Filler for Common Fields

```
01   W20-emp-rec.
     05   W20-emp-code          pic   x.
     05   W20-emp-key.
          10   W20-emp-br       pic   X(02).
          10   W20-emp-no       pic   9(04).
     05   W20-emp-name          pic   X(16).
     05   W20-emp-salary        pic   S9(05)V99.
01   W20-emp-rec-2 redefines W20-emp-rec.
     05                         pic   X(07).
     05   W20-emp-experience    pic   9(02)V9.
     05   W20-emp-qualification pic   X(10).
     05                         pic   X(10).
```

Figure 13.04

237

You will recall that since COBOL 85, the word filler may be dispensed with at all levels, including the 01 level. The following code would therefore be valid:

Filler and the Redefines

```
01   W10-redefined.
     05   W10-num1              pic 9(5)V99.
01   redefines W10-redefined.  *> Redefining field not named
      05   W20-an              pic X(7).
```

Figure 13.05

We will now recapitulate as well as add some rules pertaining to the redefines statement.

- The redefines must refer to the immediately preceding field of the same level. The example below infringes this rule and would be rejected by the compiler:

Redefines Rule 1

```
01   W00-previous             pic A(7).
01   W10-redefined.
     05   W10-num1             pic 9(5)V99.
01   W20-redefining redefines W00-previous.
     05   W20-an              pic X(7).
```

Figure 13.06

- There may be lower levels between the redefined and the redefining items. The standard does not approve of this but I do not know of any compiler that objects to it.

Redefines Rule 2

```
01   W10-redefined.
     05   W10-num1             pic 9(5)V99.
01   W20-redefining redefines W10-redefined.
     05   W20-an              pic X(7).
```

Figure 13.07

- We may not have higher levels between the redefining and the redefined fields. In the example, W20-alfa-numeric is between redefining and redefined fields.

Redefines Rule 3

```
01   W10-numeric.
     05   W10-redefined      pic 9(5)V99.
01   W20-alfanumeric.
     05   W20-redefining redefines W10-redefined
                          pic X(7).
```

Figure 13.08

- The redefining field or a field subordinated to it may not have the value clause:

Redefines Rule 4

```
01   W10-redefined.
     05   W10-num1        pic 9(5)V99.
01   W20-redefining redefines W10-redefined.
     05   W20-an          pic X(7) value 12345.
```

Figure 13.09

- Note that although the above is invalid, the reverse is not. This follows the rule that although the host may decide on what food to present to her guests, it is improper for guests to bring their own food, although we might at times wish it were possible to do so.

Redefines Rule 5

```
01   W10-redefined.
     05   W10-num1        pic 9(5)V99 value 12345.67.
01   W20-redefining redefines W10-redefined.
     05   W20-an          pic X(7).
```

Figure 13.10

Redefinition in the File Section

For reasons that might not at first be obvious, redefinition in the file section is somewhat different from redefinition in working-storage, at which we have so far been looking. In the file section we are looking at the records held in the buffer. You will recall that when you issue a read command, the input output system makes the next record available to you. Consider the graphical representation of records in the buffer:

Rec 1	Rec 2	Rec 3	Rec 4	Rec 5

If two level 01 definitions follow one another, it does not mean that two record areas will be made available by the read command. Only one will be returned. In the graphical representation, the third record in the buffer would be returned. It could be a first 01 definition or a second. When we finished with Rec 2 we issued a read command and received the record occupying the area described as Rec 3. The area will hold a first 01 definition or a second, whichever is in the file. Note that redefinition asks that both definitions be of the same size.

In the file section redefinition is implied at 01 level. Two 01 level definitions following one another imply a redefinition of the first by the second. The following definitions reflect this situation:

Implied Redefinition in the File Section

```
01   emp-rec.
     05   emp-code            pic   x.
     05   emp-key.
          10   emp-br         pic   X(02).
          10   emp-no         pic   9(04).
     05   emp-name            pic   X(16).
     05   emp-salary          pic   S9(05)V99.
01   emp-rec-2.
     05                       pic   X(07).
     05   emp-experience      pic   9(02)V9.
     05   emp-qualification   pic   X(10).
     05                       pic   X(10).
```

Figure 13.11

We use the code to determine which type of record has been made available to the program by the input output system. The following code would be appropriate:

```
if  W10-emp-code = 1
        perform A200-process-type1
```

Note that at levels subordinated to level 01 redefinition in the file section is in no way different from redefinition in **working-storage**.

Redefinition in the File Section

```
01   emp-rec.
     05   emp-key.
          10   emp-br              pic   X(02).
          10   emp-no              pic   9(04).
     05   emp-name                 pic   X(16).
     05   emp-data redefines emp-name.
          10   emp-hire-date       pic   X(06).
          10   emp-qualification   pic   X(10).
     05   emp-salary               pic   S9(05)V99.
```

Figure 13.12

Implied Redefinition

You may specify the value clause at group level. The subordinates of that group level will occupy the same storage as the value specified. You know that a group field is defined by its subordinates with regard to size and is implicitly alphanumeric. When we specify a value for a group field the data will be placed starting at the address of the group field and extending the length of the group field. As indicated, this storage is the storage obtained by defining the subordinates. In fact, we have secured **implied redefinition**.

Implied Redefinition

```
01   W20-interest-rates value "10203040".
     05   W20-rate1            pic 9(02).
     05   W20-rate2            pic 9(02).
     05   W20-rate3            pic 9(02).
     05   W20-rate4            pic 9(02).
```

Figure 13.13

The length of the constant, specified following the value clause, is eight bytes. The eight bytes start at the first byte of W20-interest-rates and extend over the definitions subordinated to the group-level. Were you to display W20-rate2, the value 20 would be displayed.

Renames

The **renames** may be seen as a variation on the redefines. The **renames** uses level 66. The following snippet of code illustrates the use of the **renames**.

```
Renames

  01  W10-year-results.
      05  W10-1st-quart              pic S9(07) packed-decimal.
      05  W10-2nd-quart              pic S9(07) packed-decimal.
      05  W10-3rd-quart              pic S9(07) packed-decimal.
      05  W10-4th-quart              pic S9(07) packed-decimal.

      66  W10-yearly-sales   renames  W10-year-results.
      66  W10-first-quarter  renames  W10-1st-quart.

Figure 13.14
```

What the **renames** has done, as the name indicates, is to give the two fields, one a group field and the other an elementary field, new names. Note that the old names remain applicable. We are also able to create group fields that did not previously exist. In the following example, we have grouped two quarters giving a group for the first semester.

```
      66  W10-first-semester renames      W10-1st-quart thru
                                          W10-2nd-quart.
```

The level 66 must follow the 01 level to which it applies.

Condition Names

A **condition name** consists of a name we give, not to a field, but to the contents of the field. Condition names use the level number 88 to distinguish them from normal fields. A condition name has to be associated with a field so that it can give a name to a particular value in that field. The field with which the condition name is associated is called the **conditional variable**. Consider the following example:

Condition Names

```
01  W10-marital-status    pic 9.   *> Conditional variable
    88  W10-single              value 1.
    88  W10-married             value 2.
    88  W10-divorced            value 3.
```

Figure 13.15

Condition names make the code easier to understand. This concern with making the language easier to understand is unfortunately not common amongst the writers of other languages. Consider the two solutions that follow, one using the value in W10-marital-status and the other using condition names, and see the clarity gained:

Not Using Condition Names

```
if  W10-marital-status = 1
    display "single"
else
    if  W10-marital-status = 2
        display "Married"
    else
        display "Divorced"
    end-if
end-if
```

Figure 13.16

Now comes the condition name solution:

Using Condition Names

```
if  W10-single
    display "single"
else
    if  W10-married
        display "Married"
    else
        display "Divorced"
    end-if
  end-if
```

Figure 13.17

We coded 'W10-single' rather than 'single' so as to make it easier to know with what conditional variable the **condition name** is associated. Is it very important to know with what conditional variable the **condition name** is associated? At present it does not seem to be. In COBOL 74 we could not change the value in the **conditional variable** without using it. For W10-married to evaluate true, we would have had to code 'move 2 to W10-marital-status'. With COBOL 85 the **set** verb, which has other functions, was given the power to work with the **condition name**. We can now use the code:

```
Set W10-single to true
```

The code will move the value 1 to the **conditional variable** W10-marital-status. We need never use the conditional variable, so there is no longer any marked advantage in associating the **condition name** with the **conditional variable**. Our code would then change as follows:

Condition Names and the Set

```
01   W10-marital-status    pic 9.
     88  single                value 1.
     88  married               value 2.
     88  divorced              value 3.
01   W20-sum               pic S9(3) value 0.

procedure division.
    move 2 to W10-marital-status
    if  single
        add 100 to W20-sum
    else
        if  married
            add 200 to W20-sum
        else
            add 300 to W20-sum
        end-if
    end-if
    display "Value in W20-sum is: " W20-sum
    set single to true
        display "Single value  : " W10-marital-status
    set married to true
        display "Married value : " W10-marital-status
    set divorced to true
        display "Divorced value: " W10-marital-status
```

Figure 13.18

```
Command Prompt                                    _ □ ×
Value in W20-sum is: 200+
Single value   : 1
Married value  : 2
Divorced value: 3
```

Consider the following code under COBOL 74:

Condition Name Under COBOL 74

```
01  W10-end-of-file      pic 9.
    88  eof                      value 1.

    move 1 to W10-end-of-file
    if  eof
        display "eof is true."
    end-if
```

Figure 13.19

Because the code in the example is all seen together there does not seem to be a problem, but when the lines of code are separated by hundreds of lines it is difficult to ascertain the association between **eof** and **W10-end-of-file**. You can see that the **set** verb has brought a marked improvement to the clarity of the code.

Multiple Literals in a Condition Name

So far we have only considered a single value associated with a **condition name**. In fact we may have multiple values associated with a **condition name**. Consider the example:

```
    88  eof                      value 1, 3, 5.
```

We have separated the list of possible values by commas whereas the elements of a list of values are normally separated by spaces. If the company does not have a standard you can use whichever method you choose. Although unusual, you may also use the ';' as a list element separator, as shown below:

```
    88  eof                      value 1; 3; 5.
```

245

If you have a list, as in the preceding lines of code, what happens when you have the following code?

```
set eof to true
```

What is the value in the **conditional variable**? Is it 1, 3 or 5? The answer is, the **conditional variable** will be set to the first element in the list, in this case 1. If you had wanted the value 3 to be placed in the **conditional variable** with the preceding instruction, you would have had to code:

```
88   eof                    value 3 1 5.
```

Suppose you had the following line of code:

```
88   valid-code             value 1 2 3 4 5.
```

A better way of coding would be to establish a range of valid codes. The following code is the more elegant solution:

```
88   valid-code             value 1 thru 5.
```

Assume you have the following code for a file processing program:

Condition Names In File Processing

```
01   W10-rec-create    pic 9.
     88  record-create               value 1.
01   W10-rec-update    pic 9.
     88  record-update               value 1.
01   W10-rec-delete    pic 9.
     88  record-delete               value 1.
```

Figure 13.20

We can use a single **set** to set the three **condition names** to true. Unfortunately, we may not set the **condition names** to false. This feature would be convenient and not impossible if low-values were made equivalent to false. Low-values, of course, require an alphanumeric field:

```
set  record-create
     record-update
     record-delete to true
```

More about the Value Clause

Confusion sometimes arises as to where we are allowed to use the **value** clause. This confusion arises because the clause has to do with two somewhat different functions. Consider the code:

```
01   W10-rec-create      pic 9        value 0.
     88  record-create                value 1.
```

In the first statement, we are saying: Place a value in the field W10-rec-create. In the second statement we are saying: The value 1 in W10-rec-create is to be known as **record-create**.

The **value clause,** when associated with a condition name, may be used anywhere. When associated with placing a value in a field there are restrictions. When used in the latter sense it may not be used in the file section. Take the case of reading a record; the record data are coming in from disk and it is incorrect to say what the data should be by using the **value clause**.

Continuing Literals

An alphanumeric literal may be continued from one line to another. For this to happen the following conditions must be met:

- The literal will begin with opening single or double inverted commas.
- The literal must be continued to position 72 of any continued line.
- A '-' must be placed in column seven of the continuation line.
- A single or a double inverted comma must begin the continuation line.
- A single or double inverted comma must close the literal on the last continuation line.

The following lines of code demonstrate these requirements:

```
05   W10-msg1 pic X(80) value 'Whatever one's beliefs it
-                             'requires great courage to
-                             'willingly go to one's dea
-                             'th.'.
```

- The first line starts with single quotes.
- All continuation lines start with single quotes.
- Every continuation line has a '-' in column seven.
- The literal ends on closing single quotes.

We may use single or double quotes or we may mix them with no adverse effects, although for the sake of consistency we should opt for one or the other.

We may sometimes obviate the need for continuing a line by starting the literal on a new line, as we have done in the following example. You will notice that the literal occupies only one line and is therefore not continued.

```
05  W10-msg1              pic X(80)  value
      'Whatever one's beliefs it requires great courage.'.
```

The Concatenation Operator (&)

COBOL 2002 has introduced a **concatenation operator**. The **concatenation operator** enables us to concatenate two alphanumeric literals. Furthermore, the two operands **must** be literals and may not be alphanumeric fields. For fields there is the 'string' verb that will do the job. The **concatenation operator** is a binary operator, so concatenating three alphanumeric literals is out of the question.

```
05  W10-msg1              pic X(80)  value
      'Whatever one's beliefs it requires great ' &
    'courage to willingly go to one's death.'.
```

The **concatenation operator** satisfies most of the continuation requirements but may be used to advantage elsewhere.

```
05  W10-msg1              pic X(80).
procedure division.
    move  'Whatever one's beliefs it requires great ' &
        'courage  to  willingly  go  to  one's  death.'
        to W10-msg1 display W10-msg1
```

The message would have been successfully displayed

Continuing Numeric Literals

We may also **continue numeric literals** although, because of being an unreasonable continuation, it is not normally used. The only requirement in the case of numeric literal continuation is that there should be an '-' in column seven. There are no quotes, because these are not required in the case of numeric literals and the continued literal does not need to extend to column 72.

```
05  W10-num          pic 9(10)  value 12345
  -                                    67890.
```

Qualification

Qualification enables a group field to have subordinate fields that have the same names as subordinate fields in another group field. What is essential is that the group field names be unique for qualification to be possible. To qualify we use the key word **in** or **of**, in conjunction with the name of the applicable group field. There is no difference between using **in** or using **of**. I suggest you use the one with which you feel most comfortable.

The program that follows illustrates the implementation of **qualification**. As you will see, qualification entails a great deal more keystrokes and becomes very cumbersome. It is suggested that you keep away from **qualification** and if you do use it, see that you justify it very strongly.

Qualification

```
program-id. chapter1302.

 data division.
 working-storage section.
 01   book-area1.
      05   book-number        pic 9(04).
      05   book-name          pic X(20).
 01   book-area2.
      05   book-number        pic 9(04).
      05   book-name          pic X(20).

 procedure division.
 A100-start.
      move 5000 to book-number in book-area1
      move 'The Power of COBOL' to book-name of book-area1
      display "Book number is: " book-number of book-area1
      display "Book name is  : " book-name    of book-area1
      move 6000 to book-number in book-area2
      move 'Understanding C++'  to book-name of book-area2
      display "Book number is: " book-number of book-area2
      display "Book name is  : " book-name    of book-area2
      stop run.
```

Listing 13.01

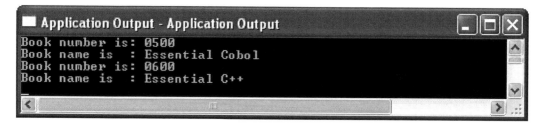

For demonstration purposes we have sometimes used **in** and at other times **of**.

Summary

- Redefinition refers to the possibility of having two field definitions sharing the same storage. The field redefined is the immediately preceding item of the same level. The compiler will assign to the redefining field the same address as had been allocated to the redefined field.

- Redefinition in the file section, for level 01, is implied. For level 01 we may not use the word **redefines** in the file section. For other levels, the redefines operates in the same way in the file section and in the working-storage section.

- At any time in storage, you will have either the redefined item or the redefining item but not both.

- When two definitions occupy the same storage without the **redefines** keyword being used, we will have implied redefinition.

- The **renames** is defined at level 66 and enables the programmer to ascribe a new name to some area of storage. The old names remain in effect. When we wish to ascribe a new name to a group of fields we may use the renames ... thru.

- Condition names enable the programmer to ascribe a name to a value in a field. We may use the set verb on a **condition name** by saying set W10-cond to true. We may not set to false

- To **continue an alphanumeric literal** we open inverted commas complete to column 72, place a '-' in column seven and start anywhere in area B by opening inverted commas. Closing inverted commas will end the literal.

- To **continue a numeric literal** place a '-' in column seven and continue the literal anywhere in area B.

- The **concatenation operator** is the '&'. It will concatenate two literals.

- Subordinate fields in two group fields may have the same names as long as the group fields have different names. We use **in** or **of** to refer to the subordinate fields.

Complete

1.   The redefined and the redefining items _____ _____ be in storage at the _____ time.

2.   The redefined and the redefining items will have the same _____.

3.   The redefined and the redefining items must be the same _____.

4.   If the redefined and the redefining items share a format such as a key field, we may address either _____ or the _____.

5.   Redefinition at 01 level in the file section is _____.

6.   Redefinition at level 05 in the file section must be _____.

7.   If we apply the **value** clause at group level we will have _____ redefinition.

8.   The **renames** uses level ____ and applies to the _____ _____ level 01.

9.   The **renames** enables the programmer to ascribe a new name to a field. The old name _____ in effect.

10. A condition name enables the programmer to allocate a _____ to a _____ in a field.

11. To place a value in the conditional variable we may use the _____ verb.

12. To place the value 1 in the conditional variable associated with condition name EOF we would code _____ EOF to _____.

13. When a list follows the value clause, the items in the list may be separated by ____ or _____ or a _____.

14. When a list follows the value clause, the set verb will use the _____ item in the list.

15. The concatenation operator _____ concatenates two _____.

True/False

1.   The redefined and redefining items occupy the same storage.

2.   The redefined and redefining fields may be in storage at the same time.

3.   The redefined and redefining fields have the same address.

4.   Redefinition in the file section, at level 05 is implied.

5.   The redefined and redefining fields should be of the same length.

6.   We may have implied redefinition at level 05 using the value clause.

7.   The renames clause applies to the immediately preceding 01 level.

8.   The original renamed name may no longer be used.

9.   A condition name names a value associated with a conditional variable.

10.   The set verb may be used to set a condition name to false.

11.   When the set verb must select from a list it will always select the first item in the list.

12.   When setting the conditional variable to multiple values with the value clause we may use the 'thru' if the values are in succession.

13.   The value clause may be used in the file section as long as it is used to set a value.

14.   When continuing an alphanumeric literal we must open and close inverted commas on every continued line.

15.   The concatenation operator may be used to concatenate up to three literals.

16.   The concatenation operator is able to concatenate a literal and a string.

17.   For qualification to operate, the group fields must be unique.

Exercises

1. A programmer defined the following fields.

    ```
        05  Br-dep                  pic 9(5)      comp-3.
     01  Br-key redefines Br-dep.
        10 Branch                   pic 9(2)      comp-3.
        10 Dep                      pic 9(3)      comp-3.
    ```

    At some stage in the procedure division this code was found:

    ```
        Move   st-br   to Branch
        Move   st-dep  to Dep
    ```

    The code did not seem to work correctly and you have been asked to correct the code.

2. Given the following fields:

    ```
     01    FIELD-1           PIC X(7)     VALUE  'FEB2002'.
     01    FIELD-2 REDEFINES FIELD-1.
           05    MONTH       PIC X(3).
           05    YEAR        PIC 9(4).
     01    FIELD-3           PIC 9(7).    VALUE 1234567.
    ```

    What would the contents of FIELD-1 be after the following move statements? If any command is illegal indicate this by writing: "INVALID".

    ```
     2.1    MOVE ALL '12' TO FIELD-1.
     2.2    MOVE FIELD-3 TO MONTH.
     2.3    MOVE 'JAN'TO MONTH.
     2.4    MOVE FIELD-3 TO YEAR.
     2.5    MOVE 82 TO YEAR.
     2.6    MOVE '82' TO YEAR.
     2.7    MOVE 'JAN' TO FIELD-3
            MOVE FIELD-3 TO FIELD-2.
     2.8    MOVE 'JANUARY' TO MONTH.
     2.9    MOVE YEAR TO FIELD-3.
            MOVE FIELD-3 TO FIELD-1.
     2.10   MOVE YEAR TO MONTH.
    ```

3. A transaction file Tran-File consists of the following two record formats:

Order record

Trans-Ac-tion-code 1	Cus-tomer Name	Item Code (nu-meric)	Qty ordered (nu-meric)	Cost per item (0.00)	Additional charges		Date	
					Tax (%)	Charges (Dollars and cents)	mth	year

```
1       5 6        20 21     25 26      28 29            34 35   36 37          40 41   42 43      44
```

Trans Action-code 2	Amount of Payment (Dollars and cents)	Date		Payment reference	Not Used	Customer Name
		mth	Year			

```
1       5 6          11 12   13 14    15 16            20 21          29 30           44
```

3.1   Write a complete FD entry for this file.

3.2   Assuming that an Order record has been read, and that the transaction code is 1, write only the procedure division code necessary to:

Display Customer Name and the Order Date if the date of the order is prior to January 85. The display must have the format:

Customer: xxxxxxxxxxxxxxxx Date: MM YY

Chapter 14
Tables - 1

Topics Covered

- Tables
- Processing Lists
- Defining Tables
- Iterating Through a Table
- Table Search with Not Found
- Tables with Subordinate Entries
- Condition Names and Tables
- Indexing
- Relative Indexing and Relative Subscripting
- Writing a Table to Disk
- Reading a File into a Table
- Initializing Tables
- Variable Length Tables
- Summary
- Complete
- True/False
- Exercises

Tables

Tables are fundamental to programming and for this reason there isn't a single computer language that does not offer the facility. The reason for the facility being so common is that they simplify so many tasks that it is inconceivable to program without using **tables**. We are all acquainted with **tables** in one form or another. We can have a bus or train timetable. We can also have a table, which most of us have seen at one time or another, which is simply a list of names or a list of numbers. Basically a table is a list of identical items. In storage each of these items will lie one adjoining the other.

Processing Lists

We will consider an example involving a very simple application where we have data coming in from the console. The data will consist of a number, between 1 and 12 for the month, and a monetary value reflecting the sales for the month. We will add the sales for the month to the existing value as each branch provides similar figures.

```
01   W20-mth-sales.
     05   W20-mth                    pic S9(02).
     05   W20-mth-sales              pic S9(05).
```

Because the programmer does not know how to use tables, his solution bypasses the use of **tables**. His definition for the fields to be updated is:

A List of Fields

```
01   W30-yearly-sales.
     05   W30-jan               pic S9(05).
     05   W30-feb               pic S9(05).
     05   W30-mar               pic S9(05).
     05   W30-apr               pic S9(05).
     05   W30-may               pic S9(05).
     05   W30-jun               pic S9(05).
     05   W30-jul               pic S9(05).
     05   W30-aug               pic S9(05).
     05   W30-sep               pic S9(05).
     05   W30-oct               pic S9(05).
     05   W30-nov               pic S9(05).
     05   W30-dec               pic S9(05).
```

Figure 14.01

We then need a string of **if** statements to determine the month that needs to be updated.

A List of Ifs

```
if  W20-mth = "jan"
    add W20-mth-sales to W30-jan
else if  W20-mth = "feb"
    add W20-mth-sales to W30-feb
else if  W20-mth = "mar"
    add W20-mth-sales to W30-mar
else if  W20-mth = "apr"
    add W20-mth-sales to W30-apr
else if  W20-mth = "may"
    add W20-mth-sales to W30-may
else if  W20-mth = "jun"
    add W20-mth-sales to W30-jun
else if  W20-mth = "jul"
    add W20-mth-sales to W30-jul
else if  W20-mth = "aug"
    add W20-mth-sales to W30-aug
else if  W20-mth = "sep"
    add W20-mth-sales to W30-sep
else if  W20-mth = "oct"
    add W20-mth-sales to W30-oct
else if  W20-mth = "nov"
    add W20-mth-sales to W30-nov
else if  W20-mth = "dec"
    add W20-mth-sales to W30-dec.
```

Figure 14.02

Defining Tables

The preceding solution is tiresome programming to say the least. It may be deduced then, that if **tables** did not exist they would have to be invented. We are going to solve the preceding problem using **tables**. One thing that makes **tables** so easy to use is that every element in the **table** has the same name. We then use what we call a subscript, which is just a number indicating which of the elements in the **table** we want. If the subscript contains five, we want the fifth element in the **table**. If it contains one, we want the first element in the table. Note that you apply the subscript to the field for which the **occurs** clause was specified or to a field subordinated to the field for which the **occurs** clause was specified. A graphical representation of the preceding **table** follows:

1	2	3	4	5	6	7	8	9	10	11	12
100	150	225	345	220	158	275	412	355	287	314	875

To define a table in COBOL we use the **occurs** clause. The **occurs** will tell the compiler how many times the element occurs in the table. The **occurs** may not be specified at level 01 although the Micro Focus compiler will allow it. For the sake of portability it is suggested that you adhere to the standard. Note that the word **times** is optional, being there for readability.

```
01    W30-yearly-sales.
      05   W30-mth          pic S9(05) occurs 12 times.
```

It is convenient to keep information about the table together. We suggest you incorporate the following definitions into the group:

```
01    W30-yearly-sales.
      05   W30-len          pic S9(02) value 12.
      05   W30-cur          pic S9(02) value 0.
      05   W30-mth          pic S9(05) occurs 12 times.
```

W30-len, of course, contains the length of the table and W30-cur contains the value of the element being currently addressed. If we wish to retrieve the value for June, either of the following lines of code will do this:

```
      display W30-mth (6)
```

or

```
      move 6 to W30-cur
      display W30-mth (W30-cur)
```

We describe the first line as being hard-coded. To change the value 6 to, say, 5, we would have to recompile the program. As can be seen, the **subscript** may be a constant or a field name.

Iterating Through a Table

We will create a loop that will take us through the table. Each time through the loop we will display the contents of one of the table elements and add them to a total field. Table elements are also referred to as table entries. The logic is depicted diagrammatically in the hierarchy chart below:

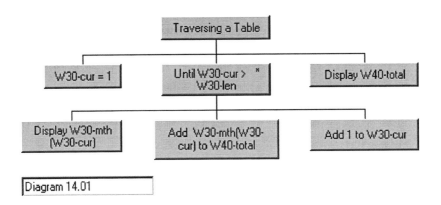

Diagram 14.01

Points to note.

- Before we embark on the loop we have to prepare for it. What should the initial value of the subscript be, if we are to start at the beginning?

- If we are to get an accurate value for the total we need to set the value of the total field appropriately.

- When do we display the final total? When we have completed the loop.

- The loop, you will notice, consists of all that is subordinated to the condition.

- What is the last thing we do in the loop? We add 1 to the subscript so that we may progress to the next entry. We only do this when we have fully processed the current entry. You will no doubt have noticed that the approach is the same as the read ahead approach we adopted when processing files.

- Processing the current entry entails displaying the data and accumulating the value of the current entry by adding it to the total field. The code follows:

Looping Through a Table

```
identification division.
program-id. Chapter1401.

data division.
working-storage section.
```

Listing 14.01 – 1 of 2

Looping Through a Table

```
01  W10-sales-tab.
    05  W10-len               pic S99    value 12.
    05  W10-cur               pic S99    value 0.
    05  W10-sales             pic S9(5)  occurs 12.
01  W20-total                 pic S9(5).
procedure division.
    move 0 to W20-total
    move 1 to W10-cur
    perform until W10-cur > W10-len
        display "Sales for the month: " W10-sales (W10-cur)
        add W10-sales (W10-cur) to W20-total
        add 1 to W10-cur
    end-perform
    display "Total sales for the year: " W20-total
    stop run.
```

Listing 14.01 – 2 of 2

I think you will agree that the condition > W10-len has more meaning than > 12. The constant appears very much like an arbitrary number. The preferred manner is to opt for the solution shown. You will see that the code follows the design in detail. In the design, what we do before entering the loop is on the left of the loop. What we do when execution of the loop has ended is on the right of the loop. What is done inside the loop is the layer beneath the loop. Note also that in each layer things are done starting on the left and proceeding to the right.

Next, we will be considering a table look up. You can imagine a motel with 10 rooms. One person occupies each of the rooms. The rooms are numbered one to 10 and each room has the name of the occupant on the door. The data are as follows. You have a card with the name of the person you are to contact. What would you do? Go randomly, say to room seven, then if not the right room you go to say, room three? This is a possible solution if you enjoy walking and rely on luck to help you.

Another solution would be to start in room one and see if it's the right room. If it is not, advance to the next room and so on until you locate the person you are looking for. Let us look at the design. It is very much like the preceding design except that we now have to ask a question. The question is part of the condition. After the lookup, display the room number. Notice from the design that all we do inside the loop is increment the subscript. Note that the range of values a subscript may take goes from **1 to table size**.

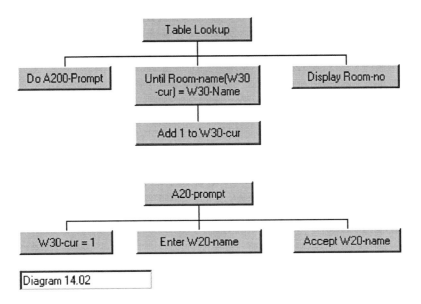

Diagram 14.02

Let us see the code. We will have to have a separate routine for the prompt. There is another problem; we don't know how the data got into the table. So far it seems to be a mystery. Let's see how it happens.

At level 05, i.e. at group level, we specify the value clause followed by the data. This, as you will recall, is implied redefinition. The table defined as a subordinate will occupy the same storage, 30 bytes, as the 30 bytes of data specified at the group level. Remember that the size of a group field is determined by the size of its subordinates

Loading a Table

```
program-id. Chapter1402.

data division.
working-storage section.
01   W10-names.
     05   W10-len              pic S99   value 10.
     05   W10-cur              pic S99   value 0.
     05   W10-names-tab values
          "TomValEveRoyDanDotVicMacEveZoe".
          10   W10-guests      pic X(3)   occurs 10.
01   W20-name                  pic X(3).
```

Listing 14.02 – 1 of 2

Loading a Table

```
procedure division.
A100-start.
    perform A200-prompt
    perform until W20-name = W10-guests(W10-cur)
        add 1 to W10-cur
    end-perform
    display  "Room number is : " W10-cur
    stop run.

A200-prompt.
    display  "Please enter guest name: " no advancing
    accept W20-name
    move 1 to W10-cur.
```

Listing 14.02 – 2 of 2

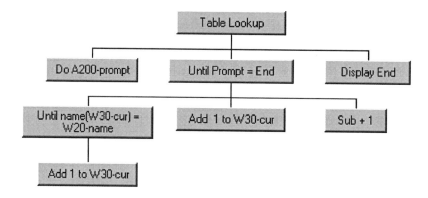

Let us modify the specification of the problem so that you enter names repeatedly to ascertain what room they are occupying in the motel. To terminate execution the user should enter 'End'. You will notice that we now have two loops, one for the prompts and another for the table lookup. Let us see how we do it.

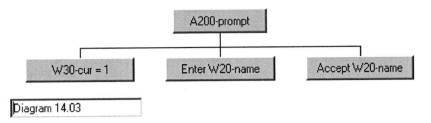

Diagram 14.03

Notice that we start the search at the beginning of the table each time we go through the loop. In the main loop we first do the look-up loop. Because we will always find it, once we exit the look-up loop we display the room number and prompt again. If a name is entered, we go back into the loop otherwise the terminating message is displayed. In the subordinate loop we increment the subscript by one.

Table Search

```
program-id. Chapter1403.
data division.
working-storage section.
01  num         pic 99.
01  W10-names.
    05  W10-len            pic S99  value 10.
    05  W10-cur            pic S99  value 0.
    05  W10-names-tab values "TomValEveRoyDanDotVicMacEveZoe".
        10  W10-guests     pic X(3)  occurs 10.
01  W20-name               pic X(3).
procedure division.
A100-start.
    perform A200-prompt
    perform until W20-name = "end"
        perform A300-lookup until W20-name =
                                    W10-guests (W10-cur)
            display "Room number is: " W10-cur
            perform A200-prompt
    end-perform
    display  "Terminating Application"
    stop run.
A200-prompt.
    display  "Please enter guest name: " no advancing
    accept W20-name
    move 1 to W10-cur.
A300-lookup.
    add 1 to W10-cur.
```

Listing 14.03

```
☰ Command Prompt                                    _ □ ✕
Please enter guest name: Dot
Room number is : 06+
Please enter guest name: Mac
Room number is : 08+
Please enter guest name: Zoe
Room number is : 10+
Please enter guest name: End
```

Table Search with Not Found

It does not often happen that we are able to establish with certainty that we will find the entry we are looking for in the table. We need to modify our design to cater for the possibility that the data will not be found. Notice that there are now two conditions for exiting the loop. We must either exit the loop because we have found the entry we are looking for or because we have gone beyond the end of the table. If we have gone beyond the end of the table then the lookup was unsuccessful.

Notice that we are precluded from accessing beyond the end of the table. If we do, the program will terminate abnormally, with a message signifying an invalid reference to the table. Our condition is going to be a compound condition connected by an **or**. We don't like compound conditions because they are more difficult to handle, from the standpoint of logic. However, in this case the situation can't be helped and we have to use a compound condition.

In addition, bear in mind that after the lookup loop we have to determine the reason for exiting the loop. Did we exit the loop because the search was successful or because we went through the whole table and did not find what we were looking for? To determine the answer to the question we check to see if the subscript has a value exceeding the table size. If the answer to this question is positive, the search was unsuccessful. Let us look at the code. The only thing that has changed is the procedure division, so we will restrict our display to the procedure division.

Look-up with Not Found

```
procedure division.
A100-start.
    perform A200-prompt
    perform until W20-name = "End"
```

Listing 14.04 – 1 of 2

264

Look-up with Not Found

```
            perform A300-lookup
                until W10-cur > W10-len or
                    W20-name = W10-guests (W10-cur)
            if  W10-cur > W10-len
                display "Not residing at motel."
            else
                display "Room number is: " W10-cur
            end-if
            perform A200-prompt
        end-perform
        display  "Terminating Application"
        stop run.

    A200-prompt.
        display  "Please enter guest name: " no advancing
        accept W20-name
        move 1 to W10-cur.
    A300-lookup.
        add 1 to W10-cur.
```

Listing 14.04 – 2 of 2

Note that, in the condition, the test for the subscript greater than table size must precede the test for the presence of the name in the table. This is because if the subscript is greater than table size there is no table look-up, only a comparison between two numbers. If we put the table look-up first, we will be accessing a position that is beyond the end of the table.

Tables with Subordinate Entries

In the tables we have been looking at, the **occurs** clause is applied to an elementary field. The example we will now look at has the **occurs** clause applied to a group level. Data is entered from the keyboard and the table updated.

Note that tables with subordinate entries are the norm and that you may also find that one of these subordinates will contain an **occurs** clause. We may then subscript:

- An item containing an **occurs** clause.
- An item subordinated to an item containing the **occurs** clause.

265

Sometimes we will subscript a group field that has a subordinate containing an **occurs** clause. The superordinate group field does not have multiple occurrences so it may not be subscripted. Its subordinate containing the **occurs** or any subordinate of this latter field may be subscripted.

Tables with Subordinate Entries

```
identification division.
program-id. Chapter1405.
data division.
working-storage section.

working-storage section.
01  W20-tab.
    05  W20-len             pic 9(02) value 10.
    05  W20-cur             pic 9(02).
    05  W20-marks                     occurs 10.
        10  W20-name        pic x(3).
        10  W20-average     pic S9(3).

procedure division.
A100-start.
    perform varying W20-cur
        from 1 by 1 until W20-cur > W20-len
            display "Please enter student name: " no advancing
            accept W20-name (W20-cur)
            display "Please enter student aver: " no advancing
            accept W20-average (W20-cur)
    end-perform
    display "Displaying from the table."
    perform varying W20-cur
        from 1 by 1 until W20-cur > W20-len
            display W20-name (W20-cur) "  "
                    W20-average (W20-cur)
    end-perform
    stop run.
```

Listing 14.05

```
Command Prompt                                          _ □ ×
Please enter student name: Eve
Please enter student aver: 98
Please enter student name: Eva
Please enter student aver: 87
Please enter student name: Vic
Please enter student aver: 93
Please enter student name: Mac
Please enter student aver: 89
Please enter student name: Roy
Please enter student aver: 95
Please enter student name: Tim
Please enter student aver: 86
Please enter student name: Mel
Please enter student aver: 91
Please enter student name: Zoe
Please enter student aver: 98
```

Condition Names and Tables

We have seen that **condition names** can be very useful by enhancing readability. You will be glad to know that we may use condition names in tables and you will also see how to use condition names in an **if** statement. You will notice that we subscript the condition name.

Condition Names and Tables

```
identification division.
program-id. chapter1406.

data division.
working-storage section.
01   W20-tab.
     05   W20-len              pic 9(02) value 10.
     05   W20-cur              pic 9(02).
     05   W20-marks-data value
          "DonEng RoyEconTomHistEveHistDotEcon" &
          "DanMathTimGeogVivHistVicEng ValHist".
          10   W20-marks                    occurs 10.
               15   W20-name        pic x(3).
               15   W20-major       pic X(4).
                    88   W20-hist              value "Hist".
```

Listing 14.06 – 1 of 2

267

Condition Names and Tables

```
procedure division.
A100-start.
    perform varying W20-cur
        from 1 by 1 until W20-cur > W20-len
            if W20-hist (W20-cur)
                display "Students with History major: "
                                W20-name (W20-cur)
            end-if
    end-perform
    stop run.
```

Listing 14.06 – 2 of 2

```
c:\ Command Prompt                                        _ □ ×
Students with History major: Tom
Students with History major: Eve
Students with History major: Viv
Students with History major: Val
```

Indexing

There are two kinds of subscripting; one uses **subscripts** and this is the kind of subscripting we have been using, and the other uses **indexing**. On mainframes, indexing used to be faster. I don't know if this situation still prevails. On Net Express **indexing** is approximately 40% slower than **subscripting**. I personally prefer **subscripting** but this is merely a personal preference. You may check which is faster on your system and opt for the fasteroption. If the difference is not significant you are free to choose. To obtain an index we use the indexed by clause with the **occurs** clause. Let us see how our preceding code would change. As far as the definitions are concerned we have:

Indexing

```
01  W10-names.
    05  W10-len                pic S99  value 10.
    05  W10-names-tab values
        "TomValEveRoyDanDotVicDoEveZoe".
        10  W10-guests         pic X(3)  occurs 10
                                    indexed by W10-cur.
```

Figure 14.03

The compiler will obtain a full word of storage for the named index. You do not define W10-cur, the definition is obtained for you by the system. **Indexes** store an address rather than an occurrence number.

Whereas with a subscript we code:

```
move 1 to W10-cur
```

With an index we code:

```
set W10-cur to 1
```

Similarly, to increment a subscript we would code:

```
add 1 to W10-cur
```
or
```
subtract 1 from W10-cur
```

For an index the code would be:

```
set W10-cur up by 1
```
or
```
set W10-cur down by 1
```

Sometimes we need to convert the address in the index to the corresponding occurrence number. The following code will do this for us:

```
01   W00-num                    pic 99.
     set W00-num to W10-cur
```

If the address in W10-cur were pointing to the fifth occurrence, the value in W00-num would be five after execution of the set. It is also possible to compare the index to a numeric field-name:

```
perform A300-lookup
     until W10-cur > W10-len or
           W20-name = W10-guests (W10-cur)
```

We may also use the index field in a perform varying:

```
perform A300-lookup
     varying W10-cur from 1 by 1
             until W10-cur > W10-len
```

269

The procedure division from the preceding program adapted to cater for indexing is as follows:

Using Indexes

```
procedure division.
A100-start.
    perform A200-prompt
    perform until W20-name = "end"
        perform A300-lookup
            until W10-cur > W10-len or
                W20-name = W10-guests (W10-cur)
        if  W10-cur > W10-len
            display "Not residing at the motel."
        else
            set W00-num to W10-cur
            display "Room number is: " W00-num
        end-if
        perform A200-prompt
    end-perform
    display  "Terminating Application"
    stop run.
A200-prompt.
    display  "Please enter guest name: " no advancing
    accept W20-name
    set W10-cur to 1.
A300-lookup.
    set W10-cur up by 1.
```

Figure 14.04

If we need to **store an index** it would perhaps be advisable to store it in an index field rather than in a numeric field that would entail conversion from an address to an occurrence number and later conversion in the reverse direction. The following code creates three index fields. We specified the usage at group level, thus making it applicable to all the subordinates:

```
01   W10-index-group            index.
     05  W10-ind-1.
     05  W10-ind-2.
     05  W10-ind-3.
```

We might code:

```
set W10-ind-1 to W10-cur and
set W10-cur to W10-ind-1
```

Relative Indexing and Relative Subscripting

COBOL 85 introduced **relative indexing** and **relative subscripting**. The relative comes from **relative addressing**. In relative addressing, which is how storage is addressed in the computer, there is a base address, kept in a register, and relative displacement from that base address. When the displacement is added to the base address we will have the address of the item we are processing.

In subscripting we have the address given by the subscript or index and the displacement is provided by a numeric literal. The displacement may be positive or negative. The following line of code illustrates relative indexing. **Relative subscripting** is indistinguishable from **relative indexing** .

```
if  W10-guests (W10-cur) = W10-guests (W10-cur + 2)
```

The preceding line is extracted from the program that follows. In the program we use displacement on both an index and on a subscript.

Relative Addressing

```
program-id. Chapter1407.

working-storage section.
01  W10-names.
    05  W10-len             pic S99  value 9.
    05  W10-names-tab values "TomValTomRoyDanDotVicDotEve".
        10  W10-guests      pic X(3) occurs 9
                                     indexed by W10-cur.
01  W20-names.
    05  W20-len             pic S99  value 9.
    05  W20-cur             pic S99.
    05  W20-names-tab values "TomValTomRoyDanDotVicDotEve".
        10  W20-guests      pic X(3)  occurs 9.
```

Listing 14.07 – 1 of 2

Relative Addressing

```
procedure division.
A100-start.
    set W10-cur to 1
    if  W10-guests (W10-cur) = W10-guests (W10-cur + 2)
        display "Two residents with same name."
    else
        display "Error"
    end-if
    move 3 to W20-cur
    if  W20-guests (W20-cur) = W20-guests (W20-cur - 2)
        display "Two residents with same name."
    else
        display "Error"
    end-if
    stop run.
```

Listing 14.07 – 2 of 2

```
Command Prompt
Two residents with same name.
Two residents with same name.
```

In the example, the index uses positive displacement and the subscript uses negative displacement. The COBOL 85 standard did not allow the displacement to be specified as a field name; it had to be a literal. The 2002 standard stipulates only that the displacement must be an integer. Micro Focus allows both a literal and a field name. Furthermore, the standard says "the subscript may be represented by an arithmetic expression that produces an integer result…". The first two lines of code below were rejected but the third was accepted.

```
display W10-guests ((W20-cur * W00-num) + 1)
display W10-guests (W20-cur * W00-num + 1)
display W10-guests (W20-cur * W00-num)
```

Net Express 4 is not happy with an arithmetic expression with more than two variables. However, under Net Express with .NET there is no problem whatever the number of variables in the expression. The following code compiled and executed successfully:

```
display W20-entry((num1 * 2) + (num2 * 2) + 2)
```

Writing a Table to Disk

Very often, we need to keep data in a table, and we would like to keep this data between executions. Before terminating the program, or perhaps at regular intervals during execution, we would write the table to disk. At the following execution, as part of the things we do in the beginning, we would read the file from disk and update the table in the normal course of events. The design depicting the logical requirements for the program is as follows:

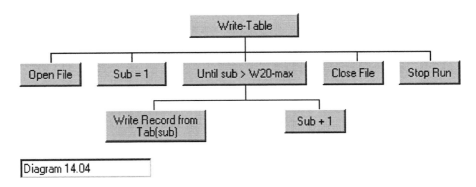

Diagram 14.04

      The preparation for the iteration, in this case, entails opening the file and setting the subscript to point to the first position in the table. In a way, both actions are similar; one makes the file available to the program, the other makes the table available to the routine. In the loop, we write the record from the table and increment the subscript. If the table were empty W20-max would be zero, the condition would be satisfied and the iteration would be bypassed. We have highlighted the loop. The asterisk indicates that the rectangle signifies an iteration.

Writing a Table to Disk

```
program-id. chapter1408.
input-output section.
file-control.
    select tab-file assign to "c:\cob0\tabfile.dat".
file section.
fd  tab-file.
01  tab-rec                      pic X(07).
working-storage section.
01  W20-major-tab.
    05  W20-cur                  pic S9(02).
```

Listing 14.08 – 1 of 2

273

Writing a Table to Disk

```
       05   W20-len                    pic S9(02) value 10.
       05   W20-max                    pic S9(02) value 10.
       05                                         value
            "DonEng RoyEconTomHistEveHistDotEcon" &
            "DanMathTimGeogVivHistVicEng ValHist".
            10   W20-marks                   occurs 10.
                 15   W20-name        pic x(3).
                 15   W20-major       pic X(4).

   procedure division.
   A100-start.
       open output tab-file
       perform varying W20-cur
           from 1 by 1 until W20-cur > W20-len
               display W20-name (W20-cur) "    "
                       W20-major (W20-cur)
                   write tab-rec from W20-marks (W20-cur)
           end-perform
       close tab-file
       stop run.
```

Listing 14.08 – 2 of 2

We have reduced the size of the program by concentrating on what it is that we wish to illustrate. In a normal situation, we would have grouped the things we need to do at the beginning into one routine, and the things we need to do at the end into another routine. The two routines could have been named A100-init and Z900-finalize.

Reading a File into a Table

The program that would read the file into the table is shown next. The program reads the file into a table. An iteration through the table then displays the entries in the table. The design of the program follows:

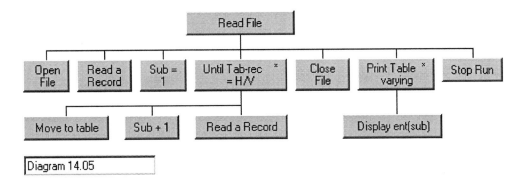

Diagram 14.05

In the preparation for the first loop, we open the file, read the first record, and move 1 to the subscript. Inside the loop, we come with the record read and the subscript is pointing to a vacant position in the table so we update the table. This process is repeated until all records have been exhausted. Note that if the file is empty, high-values will be immediately returned and the loop will be bypassed.

We close the file and proceed to the second loop, where we iterate through the table, transferring the data to the screen. Again, if the table is empty the condition will be satisfied, subscript > table-length, and the program will terminate uneventfully.

Let us look at the code. We have highlighted the two iterations.

Reading a File Into a Table

```
program-id. Chapter1409.
input-output section.
file-control.
    select tab-file assign to "c:\cob0\tabfile.dat".
file section.
fd  tab-file.
01  tab-rec                          pic X(07).
```

Listing 14.09 – 1 of 2

Reading a File Into a Table

```
working-storage section.
01  W20-major-tab.
    05  W20-cur                     pic S9(02).
    05  W20-len                     pic S9(02) value 10.
    05  W20-marks                     occurs 10.
        10  W20-name        pic x(3).
        10  W20-major       pic X(4).
procedure division.
A100-start.
    open input tab-file
    perform read-tab-file
    move 1 to W20-cur
    perform until tab-rec = high-value
        move tab-rec to W20-marks (W20-cur)
        perform read-tab-file
        add 1 to W20-cur
    end-perform
    close tab-file
    perform varying W20-cur from 1 by 1
        until W20-cur > W20-len
            display W20-name (W20-cur) "    "
                    W20-major(W20-cur)
    end-perform
    stop run.
read-tab-file.
    read tab-file
        at end move high-values to tab-rec.
```

Listing 14.09 – 2 of 2

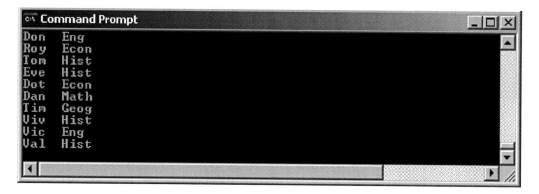

```
Don  Eng
Roy  Econ
Tom  Hist
Eve  Hist
Dot  Econ
Dan  Math
Tim  Geog
Viv  Hist
Vic  Eng
Val  Hist
```

Initializing Tables

There are a number of ways of **initializing tables**. By initializing a table we mean allocating values to the table entries at compile time. So far we have looked at placing data in a table through implied redefinition. Explicit redefinition may also be used, as we will show next.

Initializing Tables

```
program-id. Chapter1410.

working-storage section.
01.
    05  W10-cur                     pic S9(02).
    05  W10-len                     pic S9(02) value 5.
    05  W10-data.
        10                          pic X(07) value 'DonEng '.
        10                          pic X(07) value 'RoyHist'.
        10                          pic X(07) value 'VicMath'.
        10                          pic X(07) value 'DanEng '.
        10                          pic X(07) value 'DotHist'.
    05  W20-major-tab redefines W10-data.
        10  W20-marks                       occurs 5.
            15  W20-name            pic x(3).
            15  W20-major           pic X(4).

procedure division.
A100-start.
    perform varying W10-cur from 1 by 1
        until W10-cur > W10-len
            display W20-name (W10-cur) "    "
                    W20-major(W10-cur)
    end-perform
    stop run.
```

Listing 14.10

```
Command Prompt                                    _ □ ×
Don   Eng
Roy   Hist
Vic   Math
Dan   Eng
Dot   Hist
```

Through redefinition, the table will come to occupy the same storage as the redefined data. We had to define the subscript and the field containing the table length separately so as to respect the requirement that the redefining field not be longer than the redefined field.

In the following example we placed a value at the group level. By using all 'literal' we repeat the value so that all entries would contain the same value.

Initializing Using All 'Literal'

```
program-id. chapter1411.

working-storage section.
01  W20-major-tab.
    05  W20-cur               pic S9(02).
    05  W20-len               pic S9(02) value 5.
    05  W20-marks             occurs 5 value all "   Econ".
        10  W20-name          pic x(3).
        10  W20-major         pic X(4).

procedure division.
A100-start.
    perform varying W20-cur from 1 by 1
        until W20-cur > W20-len
            display W20-name (W20-cur) "    "
                    W20-major(W20-cur)
    end-perform
    stop run.
```

Listing 14.11

The same value would be repeated in each entry. The repeated value would be ' Econ'. The following table definition would result in all entries containing the value '100.00'. Of course, the decimal point would be implied. An actual decimal point would be illegal in a numeric field.

Initializing Tables I

```
01  W20-numbers-tab.
    05  W20-cur               pic S9(02).
    05  W20-len               pic S9(02) value 5.
    05  W20-marks             occurs 5 value all "10000".
        10  W20-amount        pic S9(03)v99.
```

Figure 14.05

We can also mix alphanumeric and numeric, as is shown in the following table definition:

Initializing Tables II

```
01  W20-numbers-tab.
    05  W20-cur              pic S9(02).
    05  W20-len              pic S9(02) value 5.
    05  W20-marks            occurs 5 value all "Yes10000".
        10  W20-msg          pic X(03).
        10  W20-amount       pic S9(03)v99.
```

Figure 14.06

What I imagine you might be wondering is, don't we have a more useful initialization that would cater for different values in a table? Of course, COBOL would not allow any primitive forms of initialization to stand in the way of progress, as the next example will show. The table has been initialized to the months of the year.

Initialzing Tables III

```
01  W10-calendar.
    05  W10-cur          pic S9(02).
    05  W10-len          pic S9(02) value 6.
    05  W10-month        pic X(9) occurs 6 value
                             "January  " from (1)
                             "February " from (2)
                             "March    " from (3)
                             "April    " from (4)
                             "May      " from (5)
                             "June     " from (6).
```

Figure 14.07

Variable Length Tables

COBOL offers the possibility of having tables of **variable length**. When constructing a variable length table, we have to specify the envisaged maximum length of the table. Note that storage is reserved at compile time, so even if the program does not use the maximum requested, the storage still has to be acquired in case it is needed.

279

The following program has a temperatures table that will keep a minimum of 10 and a maximum of 31 temperatures. The minimum is more for documentation purposes than anything else because if you keep only, say, five temperatures no harm will come of it. The **depending on** clause is used to secure a variable length table.

Depending On Clause

```
01   W20-temperature-tab.
     05   W20-cur      pic S9(02).
     05   W20-max      pic S9(02).
     05   W20-temp     pic S9(03) occurs 10 to 31
                                  depending on W20-cur.
```

Figure 14.08

You should have three fields associated with a table. One field will contain the current position, the one with which you are busy, another should have the last position occupied by data and another one should have the size of the table. Say the table has 50 entries; of those only 34 have data, then in a loop where you will process the data in the table we should not go beyond position 34. Similarly, when adding data to the table we must not go beyond position 50.

One advantage of keeping these fields is that in a condition, a field makes sense, whereas a literal does not. If you code:

```
if  W20-temp-sub > 25
```

it seems as if it may be the temperature that is being tested. If, instead, we put a field name it will make sense and automatically provide documentation.

```
if  W20-temp-sub > W20-no-of-entries
```

280

Summary

- A table is a list of repeating elements of the same format. The elements may be elementary or group. A subscript is used to reference table elements. The **subscript** has a numeric value. A value of five will reference the fifth element in the table. A table element is also referred to as a table entry.

- To define a table we use the **occurs** clause. If we say that the data name occurs 20 times, then the table will have 20 elements.

- The **subscript** must have a value in the range 1 to table size. If a value is placed in the **subscript** and the value does not lie within the specified range, as soon as it is used to reference the table the program will terminate abnormally. If it does not reference the table then, of course, there is no harm done.

- In iterating through a table we use the read ahead logic we used for sequentially reading files. Before the loop we set the subscript to 1. Inside the body of the loop, we increment the loop only after processing the preceding entry.

- For situations where an entry might not be found in the table, the loop condition must be a compound one. If the entry is not present in the table, we must traverse the whole table to determine this. The other condition deals with the entry we are looking for. Always specify the test for end of table first because the subscript will have a value greater than the table size and we must not reference a table entry using that value.

- Table entries may be subscripted using a subscript or using an index. To use an index we use the indexed by clause with the **occurs** clause. The **index** is a fullword defined by the system. To change the value in the index, where ind is the index, we would code set ind to num1 to place a value in the **index**, set ind up by 1 to increment the **index** and set ind down by 1 to decrement the **index**.

- **Relative indexing** and **relative subscripting** enable the programmer to specify a displacement that is added to the **index** or **subscript**.

- Variable length tables are specified using the depending on clause.

Complete

1.   The entries in a table must all have _____ format.

2.   The entries in a table must all be the same _____ .

3.   A subscript value must lie between ____ and the _____ _____.

4.   A table is defined using the _____ clause.

5.   To define a table with 25 entries you would code: 05 Tab _____ __.

6.   To reference a table entry we can use either a _____ or an _____.

7.   To subscript we may use either a _____ or a _____ _____.

8.   To define a variable length table we use the _____ ____ clause.

9.   The _____ ___ clause for a variable length table names a _____ field.

10.   When defining a variable length table we can specify _____ and _____ sizes.

11.   In looping through a table, in the body of the loop, we add one to the subscript at the _____ of the loop.

12.   An item containing the **occurs** clause may not be _____.

13.   To initialize a table we can use _____ _____ using the value clause.

14.   In preparing for an iteration we would move ____ to the subscript.

15.   Relative subscripting means that we are adding a _____ to the value in the _____.

16.   To increment an index by five you would code _____ ind ___ ___ 5.

True/False

1.   The entries in a table need not have the same format as long as they are all of the same size.
2.   The word 'times' which follows the length in the **occurs** clause is compulsory.
3.   In subscripting, if we use a literal, to change it we have to recompile the program.
4.   In looping through a table, we increment the subscript in the body of the loop.
5.   The space for a variable length table is reserved at _____ time.
6.   If you code occurs 50 depending on tab-size, and tab-size never has a value in excess of 25, then the space used up does not exceed the space required for 25 entries.
7.   A table is defined using the **occurs** clause.
8.   If we loop through a table, at the end of the loop the value in the subscript will be greater than the table size.
9.   If there is a possibility of a not found condition, the condition name(sub) = st-name must appear before the condition sub > tab-size.
10.   We may only subscript items for which the **occurs** clause has been coded.
11.   A condition name may be subscripted.
12.   We do not need to define an **index**. The compiler generates a fullword when we use the indexed by clause.
13.   To increment an **index** ind, we would code add 1 to ind.
14.   We may compare an **index** to a number as in if ind > 50.

Exercises

1.   Write a program that will do the following:

   a)   Display a message on the console requesting an amount.
   b)   Accept the amount. The amount should have the picture 9(5)V99.
   c)   Convert the integer part into words. Thus, 12345.67 should display as one two three four five 67 cents.
   d)   For the problem you will need to define a table with the values one to nine and the zero. You will need to redefine the field that accepts the value from the console so that you can go byte by byte, converting each digit into the corresponding word.

2.   Assume you are reading records from a file. The records have the following format.

Name	X(10)
Number	9(5)
Julian-date	9(5) (Packed)

(Julian date has a format of YYDDD)

Write a routine or routines to convert the Julian date from each record to the format dd/mmm/yy (mmm is a three character abbreviation for the month e.g. Jan for January)

3.   System chart

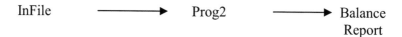

The sales manager of a company has asked the IT manager for a program to produce a weekly report formatted as follows:

Balance Report as at 99/99/99   Page ZZ9

      Cust. No. Name   Balance

      999999 * _____35_____ * RZZBZZ9,99
      999999 * _____35_____ * RZZBZZ9,99

The input file is on disk with a record of the following structure:

customer no.	9(6)
customer name and address	X(60)
not used	X(15)
balance	9(5)v99
not used	X(10)

The name is the first item in the name field. The length of the name is not known. It is known, however, that:

a)   It does not exceed 35 characters.
b)   The first character following the name is a "+"

You must make use of tables in your solution. All you are required to do in this exercise is to place the name in the field W10-pr-name, Customer-no in W10-pr-cust-no and Balance in W10-pr-bal.

4.   You have been asked by your manager to write a program that receives a record of the format below.

284

Record format:

Employee number	:	4 alphanumeric
Hourly rate	:	4 numeric, 2 decimals
Monday hours	:	"
Tuesday	:	"
Wednesday	:	"
Thursday	:	"
Friday	:	"

You should use a table in the record definition for the days of the week values. The fractional part of hours worked contains minutes. These must be converted to the fractional part of the hour (work to two decimal places rounded).

Compute total hours worked, which must be less than 100, and place the value arrived at in the field W10-total-hours. Test for the value arrived at with the on size error clause.

5.   A company pays its salesmen different commissions on their sales, depending on the amount of the sale.

5.1   Define the following table in working-storage. Use the data names shown and include the table element values in your definition.

W-sales-comm-table

W-sale-comm-element	
W-max-sale-amt (Dollars) PIC 9(6)	W-comm-amt (Dollars) PIC 9(4)
1 100	0
2 5000	30
3 10000	60
4 20000	125
5 50000	250
6 100000	525
7 250000	1500
8 999999	2500

Note: W-max-sale-amt is the maximum sale amount in the range, which applies to the corresponding commission amount. For example:

> No Commission is paid for sales equal to or less than $100.
> $30 Commission is paid for sales of $101 – $5000 inclusive.
> In addition to the commission, the sum of $10 is paid for every $1000 sold

5.2   Given a sales amount W-sale-amount (dollars), with a picture of 9(6), write the required COBOL code to determine what commission is payable and move it to a field W-commission, e.g. using the above table values, on a sale amount of $15 250. Commission will be $125 + $150.

5.3   The company pays double the standard amount of commission for all sales during during December each year. Define any necessary data fields and write the code necessary to:

- Establish what the current date is

- Double W-comm-amt for all elements of the table, (i.e. change the contents of the table) if the current month is December.

6.   Define a table to contain the names of students in a class of 10 and their latest test mark (out of 100). Accept 10 names and marks from the user. Once all ten names have been entered, **and only then,** display the name and the mark for each student and calculate and display the average mark for the class.

Once you have done this, progress through the table, now finding the highest and the lowest marks. Display these together with the corresponding names and end the run.

7.   Define a table that is able to contain the names of 10 people with their ages and load these names and ages into the table at compile time (i.e. hard-coded).

Repeatedly accept a name from the user and look up that name in the table. If not found, display 'Not in the table'. If the user wishes to stop, then they must be told that they may enter 'End' instead. When the name is found, display the message:

> name is now nn years old.

Sample data:

Sacha	24
Frans	19
Bernadette	25
Solomon	25
Michelle	35
Michael	26
Pascal	11
Werner	22
Charmaine	22
Helene	23

8.   W1-ACCT is a 17-digit unsigned numeric field. Display (unpacked) field containing an account number. The account number comprises 16 digits followed by a check digit (the 17th rightmost digit)

> i.e. nnnnnnnnnnnnnnnnnC where C is the check digit.

You are required to produce the following code:

8.1   Define field W1-acct

8.2   Using a table, redefine the field W1-acct so that you are able to address   each digit individually.

8.3   Write all necessary field definitions and procedure division code to validate the check digit of the account number as follows:

Find the sum of:

> the 1st digit of the account number multiplied by 1 plus
> the 2nd digit of the account number multiplied by 2 plus
> the 3rd digit of the account number multiplied by 3 plus
> the 4th digit of the account number multiplied by 4 plus
>
> …
> …
> the 14th digit of the account number multiplied by 14 plus
> the 15th digit of the account number multiplied by 15 plus
> the 16th digit of the account number multiplied by 16 plus
>
> (Note that the first digit is the leftmost digit of the account number).

Divide the sum of all the multiplication results by 10. The remainder of this division (or zero) must be equal to the check digit (17th digit).

If the check digit is not correct, display a meaningful message.

NOTE: You may assume that the content of field W1-acct is numeric and not = zeros. Your solution must contain one or more tables. You may <u>NOT</u> use repetitive coding.

9.   Write the code to calculate and store the squares of the numbers 1 – 30. Define a table as follows to hold the results, using indexing:

WS-square-table

	WS-square	
1st occurrence	1^2	Index name is
2nd occurrence	2^2	WS-square-index
30th occurrence	30^2	

Use the data shown above
Also define any additional working-storage fields required.

9.1   Define a table WS-check-table, with index WS-check-index, which has 10 elements. Each element consists of:

WS-check-square	:	3 digit number
WS-square-ind	:	May have a value of Yes or No
WS-square-root	:	2 digit number

WS-check-square occurrences need not be given initial values, but all WS-square-ind fields should contain No and all WS-square-root fields zero.

9.2   Assume the values for WS-check-square have been randomly loaded into each element of WS-check-table. Determine which of these are perfect squares by searching the table you set up in question 9. For each number that is a perfect square, set the corresponding WS-square-ind to Yes, and update WS-square-root. You must use only the table from question 9 to determine the square root (for example if a number matches with the 19th occurrence of WS-square-table, the WS-square-root will be 19).

9.3   Assume that WS-square-index has been set to five. Without changing the value of the index, or defining any new fields, code two different ways of moving the third occurrence of WS-square to a field called WS-third-square

10.   The following sequential transaction file contains records for the years 1990, 1992 and 1993:

```
data division.
file section.
    label records are standard
    data record is trans-rec
01  trans-rec.
    05  trans-agent pic x(4).
    05  trans-cust  pic x(8).
    05  trans-year  pic 9(4). (values 2000 through 2003)
    05  trans-month pic 9(2), (values 1 through 12).
    05  trans-value pic 9(5).
```

The following is a schematic representation of the transaction table defined in working-storage. Headings are shown for clarity only.

Year Month		No	Value	No	Value	No	Value	No	Value	Month Total No	Value
(1)	Jan	1	150	4	416						
(2)	Feb	5	240								
	.	.	.	.							
	.	.	.								
	.	.	.	.							
	.										
(11)	Nov	4	320			10	1200				
(12)	Dec	6	580								
(13)	Year-total	.									

10.1   Define the table in working-storage, using the names specified below:

w-no-recs (5 digits) and w-value (7 digits, packed), required per month (W-month) within year (w-year). Allow 13 months (January to December 13 for the total. Index name is m-idx). Allow five years (2000 through 2003, the 5th for the total. Index name is y-idx).

10.2   Code the procedure division statements required to do the following (You must use indexing):

10.3   Initialize the table without using the INITIALIZE verb.

10.4   Read the file (you may not assume records are in any logical sequence) and accumulate the number of records and value of records into the relevant fields of the transaction file. Assume that all year and month fields on the file contain valid values.

10.5   After doing the above, (i.e. once all records have been read), calculate the total for each year (months January to December) and place it into occurrence 13 of month; calculate the total for each month (years 2000 to 2003) and place it into occurrence 5 of year; calculate the totals for every month for every year and place it into occurrence 5 of year and 13 of month.

For each of the following, give the number of bytes occupied by W1-number:

```
10.6   01     w1-table                    pic 9(6).
       01     w1-number          redefines w1-table.
              02    w1-no1               pic 9(3).
              02    w1-no2               pic 9(3).

10.7   01     w1-number.
              05    w1-no1 occurs 5 pic 999.
              05    w1-no2               pic 99.

10.8   01     w1-number.
              05    w1-element   occurs 5.
                    10    w1-no1        pic 999.
                    10    w1-no2        pic 99.

10.9   01     w1-number.
              05    w1-element   occurs 5.
                    10    w1-no1        pic 999 comp-3.
                    10    w1-no2        pic 99  comp-3.
```

11.   The Florida Hills Golf Club has commissioned you to write a program that will update a golf scores file.

A transaction file containing the scores is used to update the master file, producing a new updated version of the old master file. The file names are: OldMast and NewMast. A report containing an entry for each of the members is also produced.

The transaction file is sorted in ascending sequence memberNo within tranCode. TranCodes are:

A – for additions
C – for changes
D – for deletions

There may be any number of transactions for a member. In the same run, for the same member, there may be an addition, changes and a deletion.

The record format is as follows:

	tranCode
	memberNo
Code A:	memberName
Code C:	number of scores
	1 to 5 scores
Code D:	Reason for deletion

The format for records in OldMast is as follows.

memberNo
memberName
noOfScores
16 latest scores

Men have codes 1 – 5000 and ladies have codes 5000 – 10000.

Processing:

There may be masters for which there are no transactions. These are to be written out unchanged.

If the code is C, replace the oldest scores by the new scores. The new scores are applied at the end of the table, on the right hand side. The oldest scores are on the right hand side, at the beginning of the table.

When scores are added, if space needs to be made available, the required number of scores must be shifted down so that the new scores come to occupy positions at the end of the table.

Your report, to be displayed on the screen, has the following format:

Member No.	Member Name	8 Oldest Scores
99999	xxxxxxxxxxxxxxxx	99
99999	xxxxxxxxxxxxxxxx	99

Required:

a) You are to design a solution to the problem. You must use tables where these will assist your solution.

b) If you feel up to it or when you feel up to it, create the files and test your solution.

Chapter 15
Tables - 2

Topics Covered

- Multidimensional Tables
- Fields in One Dimension
- The Search Verb
- The Search with Varying
- Two Dimensional Tables and the Search
- The Search All
- The Varying Revisited
- Varying an Index from Another Table
- The Sort Verb
- Summary
- Complete
- True/False
- Exercises

Multidimensional Tables

Most tables we are acquainted with are two-dimensional. We have bus, train or plane timetables and all these are two-dimensional. A two-dimensional table has columns and rows. The one-dimensional tables we have seen up to this point only have columns in a single row. When we say "occurs 10", we would be setting up a one-dimensional table with a single row and 10 columns. A two-dimensional table will have two occurs clauses. In fact, the number of occurs clauses will tell us how many dimensions the table has.

Assume that the elementary entry is 10 bytes in length. If we have a one-dimensional table with 10 entries, our table will be one hundred bytes long. For a two-dimensional table of 10 rows, our table would have been 1000 bytes long. If we now add a third dimension that also has a magnitude of 10, the table would now occupy 10 000 bytes. We see that for each dimension, with only 10 repetitions, the table grows by a factor of 10.

I think you will have seen that adding dimensions to a table may dramatically increase the storage requirements for the table. As in all things, as you increase the size of the object, the complexity involved in manipulating the object is also increased. Our advice to you is to bear these factors in mind when thinking of solutions involving multi-dimensional tables.

A graphic representation of a two-dimensional table for a school having three classes, each with five pupils would look like this:

Roy	Vic	Don	Eve	Dan
Dot	Eva	Ash	Tom	Gay
Tim	Viv	Ric	Jim	Mel

At the intersection of row two and column three we have located pupil Ash. In a two-dimensional table any entry will be located at the intersection of row X and column Y, where X will be greater than zero and not greater than the number of rows, and Y will also be greater than zero and not greater than the number of columns. We have seen above how we picture a two-dimensional table. In storage, however, everything is linear.

Addresses in memory start at zero and progress in linear fashion up to the highest memory location. Sometimes, in resolving problems associated with two-dimensional tables it is convenient to see them lying in a row, as shown next. The program sees a table of records; this is the first dimension, the rows. Each of these records then also contains a table, the columns. You see that this effectively corresponds to the two dimensional grid we picture when we speak of a two-dimensional table.

Row 1					Row 2					Row 3				
Roy	Vic	Don	Eve	Dan	Dot	Eva	Ash	Tom	Gay	Tim	Viv	Ric	Jim	Mel
1	2	3	4	5	1	2	3	4	5	1	2	3	4	5

Columns (1 - 5)

Let us see how we would define a table that would correspond to the preceding physical organization.

A Two Dimensional Table

```
   01   W10-school-tab.
        05   W10-class                    occurs 3
                                          indexed by W10-row.
             10   W10-st-name pic X(3) occurs 5
                                          indexed by W10-col.
```

Figure 15.01

Notice that by subordinating the columns to the classes we are in fact placing the columns within the rows. We used indexing in the example lest you forget all about indexing, but in succeeding examples we will use subscripting.

The definition of the two-dimensional table we will be using in the next example is as follows:

A Two Dimensional Table

```
   01   Temperature-table
        05   W20-days              occurs 31 times.
             10   W20-hours        occurs 24 times.
                  15   W20-temp    pic S9(02).
```

Figure 15.02

There are two occurs clauses and, as we have learnt, that means a two-dimensional table. Doing the arithmetic we see that the table would occupy 1448 bytes of storage. So far, we have used one loop to iterate through the table. Now we have a two-dimensional table so, not surprisingly, we need two loops.

Progressing Through a Two Dimensional Table

```
perform varying W20-cur-row from 1 by 1
    until W20-cur-row > W20-max-row
        perform varying W20-cur-col from 1 by 1
            until W20-cur-col > W20-max-col
                perform A200-compute-temp
        end-perform
end-perform
```

Figure 15.03

The outside loop takes us through the rows. The inside loop takes us through the columns. For each row we have to progress through all the columns. Once we have gone through all the columns in a row, we are ready to progress to the next row. Inside the loop, we calculate a number and assign it to the table entry being referenced. To calculate the number we used an intrinsic function 'random'. The word function is used, in some languages, to describe what we would in COBOL call a routine. To do some work, a C program will branch to a function. The function will do the work and return a value, if so required. **Intrinsic functions** are different from the functions just described, to the extent that no branch is involved. This is an advantage because a branch consumes resources. When we deal with an intrinsic function, we know that we do not need to branch because the required code will replace the function call. The code we created to invoke the function is:

```
Compute W20-temp(W20-cur-row, W20-cur-col) =
                        function random * 17
```

The function returns a pseudo random number with a magnitude of between zero and one. We then multiplied the value returned by 17 to get a number greater than one. Notice that the invoked function is preceded by the word **function**. We will be looking at intrinsic functions in the next chapter. The program follows:

Loading and Retrieving from a Two-dimensional Table

```
program-id. Chapter1501.
working-storage section.
01  W20-numbers-tab.
    05  W20-cur-row          pic S9(02).
```

Listing 15.01 – 1 of 2

Loading and Retrieving from a Two-dimensional Table

```
    05  W20-cur-col          pic S9(02).
    05  W20-max-row          pic S9(02) value 31.
    05  W20-max-col          pic S9(02) value 24.
    05  W20-days             occurs 31 times.
        10  W20-hours        occurs 24 times.
            15  W20-temp     pic S9(02)V99.
01  W50-temp                 pic 99.99.
procedure division.
A100-start.
    perform varying W20-cur-row from 1 by 1
        until W20-cur-row > W20-max-row
            perform varying W20-cur-col from 1 by 1
                until W20-cur-col > W20-max-col
                    perform A200-compute-temp
            end-perform
    end-perform
    perform varying W20-cur-row from 1 by 1
        until W20-cur-row > W20-max-row
            display " "
                perform varying W20-cur-col from 1 by 1
                    until W20-cur-col > W20-max-col
                        move W20-temp(W20-cur-row W20-cur-col)
                            to W50-temp
                        display W50-temp
                end-perform
    end-perform
    stop run.


A200-compute-temp.
    compute W20-temp(W20-cur-row, W20-cur-col) =
                            function random * 17
```

Listing 15.01 – 2 of 2

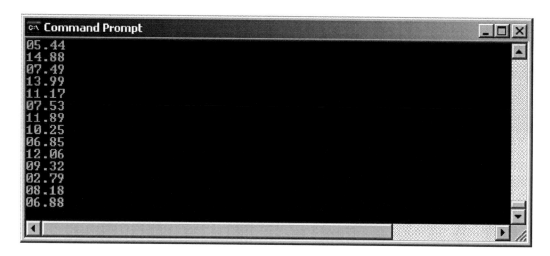

Fields In One Dimension

It is at times necessary to have some fields present in the rows but absent from the columns. The following graphical representation illustrates this situation.

COBOL.NET	Roy	Vic	Don	Eve	Dan
C++.NET	Dot	Eva	Ash	Tom	Gay
VB.NET	Tim	Viv	Ric	Jim	Mel

As illustrated, the subject of the class exists only in the rows. Following is the COBOL code corresponding to the graphical representation:

```
05  W20-school.
    10  W20-class          occurs 3 times.
        15  W20-subject  pic X(07).
        15  W20-st-name  pic X(03) occurs 5 times.
```

In tables, fields lie within the table or next to the table. In the preceding definition, we see that W20-subject lies within the rows because the row has level 10 and W20-subject has level 15. On the other hand, W20-subject does not lie within the columns because it exists side by side with the columns. Both W20-subject and W20-st-name are level 15 items, the latter repeating in the columns.

We have placed the names in a table with 15 occurrences and the subject in a table with three occurrences. We have a loop that places the subjects into the array.

Loading the First Dimension

```
perform varying W20-cur-row from 1 by 1
    until W20-cur-row > W20-max-row
        move W50-subject (W20-cur-row) to
            W20-subject(W20-cur-row)
end-perform
```

Figure 15.04

As can be seen, because we are using only one subscript, the subject names are only moved into the first dimension. The next iteration moves the names from the one-dimensional table to the second dimension of the two-dimensional table.

Loading the Second Dimension

```
perform varying W20-cur-row from 1 by 1
    until W20-cur-row > W20-max-row
        perform varying W20-cur-col from 1 by 1
            until W20-cur-col > W20-max-col
                move W40-name (W00-num) to
                    W20-st-name(W20-cur-row W20-cur-col)
                add 1 to W00-num
        end-perform
end-perform
```

Figure 15.05

Before looking at the whole program and how it fits together, let us do the design for the program.

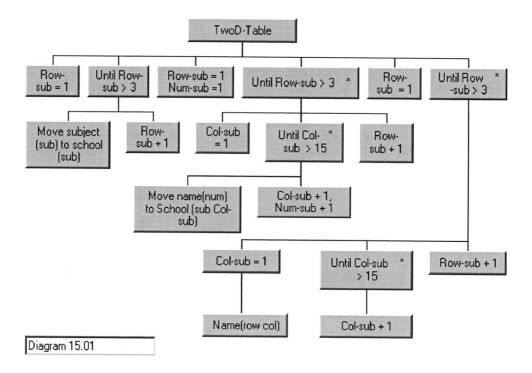

Diagram 15.01

Remember that reading of the chart proceeds from left to right. When you come to an iteration you will descend to the subordinates of the iteration. These provide the detail of what will be done in the loop. When you are finished with the iteration you will be back at the same level as the iteration and you will do what follows the iteration.

Because we are loading one table from another we have to look after all the subscripts. The program is as follows:

Loading and Displaying the Two-dimensional Table

```
program-id. Chapter1502.
working-storage section.
01  W00-num                   pic 9(02) value 2.
01  W20-numbers-tab.
    05  W20-cur-row            pic S9.
    05  W20-cur-col            pic S9.
    05  W20-max-row            pic S9 value 3.
    05  W20-max-col            pic S9 value 5.
```

Listing 15.02 – 1 of 2

Loading and Displaying the Two-dimensional Table

```
    05  W20-school.
        10  W20-class         occurs 3 times.
            15  W20-subject  pic X(07).
            15  W20-st-name  pic X(03) occurs 5 times.
01  W40-names                            value
    "RoyVicDonEveDanDotEvaAshTomGayTimVivRicJimMel".
    05  W40-name              pic X(03) occurs 15 times.
01  W50-subjects              value "COBOL  C++.NETVB.NET ".
    05  W50-subject           pic X(07) occurs 3.
procedure division.
A100-start.
    perform varying W20-cur-row from 1 by 1
        until W20-cur-row > W20-max-row
            move W50-subject (W20-cur-row) to
                W20-subject(W20-cur-row)
    end-perform
    move 1 to W00-num

    perform varying W20-cur-row from 1 by 1
        until W20-cur-row > W20-max-row
            perform varying W20-cur-col from 1 by 1
                until W20-cur-col > W20-max-col
                    move W40-name (W00-num) to
                        W20-st-name(W20-cur-row W20-cur-col)
                    add 1 to W00-num
            end-perform
    end-perform

    perform varying W20-cur-row from 1 by 1
        until W20-cur-row > W20-max-row
            perform varying W20-cur-col from 1 by 1
                until W20-cur-col > W20-max-col
                  display W20-st-name(W20-cur-row W20-cur-col) ' '
                        no advancing
                end-perform
                display " "
    end-perform
    stop run.
```

Listing 15.02 – 2 of 2

In the next example we will have a company that has branches in different European cities: In each city there will be a number of branches. There will be a maximum of 10 branches in a city. There will be a record for each city and the record will have sales values for each of the branches. The record will have the following format:

- City will be the first field
- The next field contains the number of branches in the city
- The sales figures for each of the branches follow.

The file contains variable length records because, as indicated, not all cities have the same number of branches. To indicate that the records are variable length we included the **record contains** clause. Notice also that the file record contains a table:

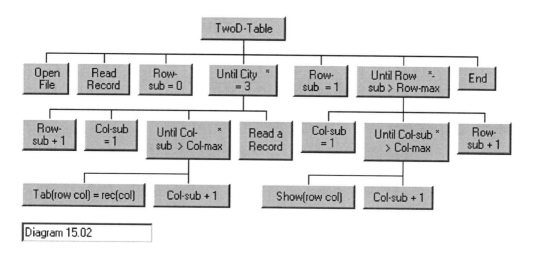

Diagram 15.02

The steps are:

- Open the file and read the first record.
- Set the row subscript, that must be incremented at the beginning of every row, to zero.
- Iterate until there are no more records.

- Increment the row and set the column subscript
- Iterate until all columns are processed.
- Move the value from the table in the record to the two dimensional table.
- Increment the column subscript.
- We have finished processing the record and read the next record.
- The file has no more records; we are going to read from the table. We set the row subscript to 1.
- We iterate through all columns
- We set the column subscript and iterate through all the columns in the row.
- Display the entry using row and column subscripts, then increment the subscript.
- Repeat until all columns are processed, then increment the row.

The program follows:

Records Containing Tables

```
program-id. Chapter1503.
input-output section.
file-control.
    Select sales-file assign to "C:\cob0\aaasales".
file section.
fd  sales-file
    record contains 30 to 66 characters.
01  sales-rec.
    05  city              pic X(06).
    05  num               pic S9.
    05  sales-tab.
        10  sales         pic S9(06) occurs 4 to 10
                                     depending on num.
working-storage section.
01  W20-numbers.
    05  W20-ctr           pic S9(03).
01  W30-tab.
    05  W30-row-sub       pic S9.
    05  W30-col-sub       pic S99.
    05  W30-row-max       pic S9.
    05  W30-col-max       pic S9.
    05  W30-sales-row               occurs 5.
        10  W30-city      pic X(06).
        10  W30-num       pic S9.
        10  W30-sales-col pic S9(06) occurs 10.
```

Listing 15.03 – 1 of 2

Records Containing Tables

```
procedure division.
A100-start.
    open input sales-file
    perform Z100-read-sales
    move 0 to W30-row-sub
    perform until city = high-values
        add 1 to W30-row-sub
        move city to W30-city (W30-row-sub)
        move num  to W30-col-max
                     W30-num (W30-row-sub)
        perform varying W20-ctr from 1 by 1
            until W20-ctr > W30-col-max
                move sales(W20-ctr)
                     to W30-sales-col(W30-row-sub W20-ctr)
        end-perform
        perform Z100-read-sales
    end-perform.

    move W30-row-sub to W30-row-max
    perform varying W30-row-sub from 1 by 1
        until W30-row-sub > W30-row-max
            move W30-num(W30-row-sub) to W30-col-max
            display " "
            display W30-city(W30-row-sub) "  " no advancing
            perform varying W30-col-sub from 1 by 1
                until W30-col-sub > W30-col-max
                    display
                        W30-sales-col(W30-row-sub W30-col-sub)
                                no advancing
            end-perform
    end-perform
    close sales-file
    stop run.

Z100-read-sales.
    read sales-file
        at end
            move high-values to city
    end-read.
```

Listing 15.03 – 2 of 2

```
Command Prompt
Paris   183058+845293+103295+728913+825394+720954+825319+
London  720578+489145+396201+865902+909289+839785
Lisbon  390720+582879+421073+675926
Madrid  672890+678518+567023+578692+892218+718418+
Rome    890672+815518+576230+875296+829216+753414+821833+
```

The Search Verb

The **search** verb will carry out a sequential search of a table. The advantage is that it replaces your own logic and the coding effort is thereby reduced. We will use a sequential
search when the number of look-ups is small. In addition, you should start the table with
the most frequently required items so as to reduce the number of look-ups. The alternative
to a **sequential search** is a **binary search,** which we will be looking at shortly. Let us see
what is eliminated by the **search** verb:

-       perform until
-       perform varying
-       adding to a subscript
-       the if statement used to test for a found condition

Let us see what is required:

-       The table must carry the indexed by clause.
-       The index will be set to the value corresponding to the position from which the
        search is to start. Setting the index to one will cause the search to start from the be-
        ginning of the table.
-       The **search** is specified at the level at which the **occurs** clause was specified.
-       When's are used to specify the conditions.
-       When a table has more than one dimension, the search verb may only be applied to
        one row at a time. The search will not conduct a search of the whole table.
-       The **at end** is used to exit from the search when a not found condition exists.

Search Verb – Format 1

```
search tab-name
     at end imperative statement
   when condition(1)
     imperative statement
   when condition(n)
     imperative statement
end-search
```

Figure 15.06

Multiple **when**s carry an implied **or** and there may not be an explicit **or**. The **and** is not allowed. Note, however, that a compound condition in a **when** may be linked by an **and**. **When** conditions are evaluated in sequence, going from top to bottom.

The Search Verb

```
program-id. Chapter1504.
working-storage section.
01  W30-numbers      value "10100020002020002500303000 2500" &
                           "40400045005050005500606000 6500".
      05   W30-accounts                     occurs 6
                                            indexed by ind.
           10   W30-acc-id    pic S9(02).
           10   W30-acc-amt   pic S9(04).
           10   W30-acc-lim   pic S9(04).
01  W30-sub          pic 9  value 1.

procedure division.
A100-start.
    set ind to 1
    search W30-accounts varying ind
        at end display "Not found."
      when W30-acc-lim (ind) = 2500
        display W30-acc-id (ind) " "
                W30-acc-amt (ind)
    end-search
    stop run.
```

Listing 15.04

We set the index to one, thus starting the search from the beginning of the table. The item W30-accounts carries the **occurs** clause so the search verb was applied to that field. The **end-search** terminates the scope of the search. In the following snippet of code we introduce an implied **or** by having more than one **when**.

Implied Or

```
search W30-accounts
    at end display "Not found."
        when W30-acc-lim (ind) = 2500
            display W30-acc-id (ind)  "  "
                    W30-acc-amt (ind)
        when W30-acc-id (ind) = 44
            display W30-acc-id (ind)  "  "
                    W30-acc-amt (ind)  "  "
end-search
```

Figure 15.07

The following code sample shows a compound condition using an **and**:

Compound Condition Using And

```
search W30-accounts
    at end display "Not found."
        when W30-acc-lim (ind) = 2500 and
             W30-acc-amt (ind) > 2300
            display W30-acc-id (ind)  "  "
                    W30-acc-amt (ind)  "  "
        end-search
```

Figure 15.08

The Search with Varying Option

The **varying** enables us to name a field. The field must be numeric and, as the search progresses, will have a value corresponding to the index value of the occurrence.

The Varying Clause – Format 2

```
search tab-name varying W30-number
     at end imperative statement
   when condition(1)
     imperative statement
   when condition(n)
     imperative statement
end-search
```

Figure 15.09

We do not do any arithmetic operation involving W30-number; the field being varied, the increment is automatically done for you. When the named index is incremented, the varied field will also be incremented. The following example not only uses the varying clause, but the search is also inside a loop.

You will have noticed that when the search condition is satisfied, the search is exited. This is not always satisfactory. When we have more than one item in the table, which might satisfy the condition, and we want to process each of these items, we need to change our approach. The effect of placing the search inside a loop is that we will be able to traverse the whole table instead of exiting the first time the condition is met. To utilize the loop, the following points should be borne in mind:

- We must use the **varying** clause. We will be varying W40-sub.

- Each time the condition is satisfied, the value of the index at that point will be in W40-sub.

- We set the index to the value in W40-sub; this will be the new starting position for the search.

- Before setting the index to W40-sub, we increment the value in W40-sub by one so that the condition will not be met again in respect of the same occurrence.

- The loop condition is until W20-cond = 9. Our not found, which will be true when the end of the table is reached, is used to move nine to W20-cond. When this happens, the loop is exited. The program incorporating the loop is as follows:

Incorporating the Varying

```
program-id. Chapter1505 as "Chapter1505".
environment division.

data division.
working-storage section.
01  W20-cond                 pic 9  value 0.
01  W30-numbers        value "10100020002020002500303000002500" &
                             "404000450050300025006060006500".

    05  W30-accounts             occurs 6
                                 indexed by ind.
        10  W30-acc-id    pic S9(02).
        10  W30-acc-amt   pic S9(04).
        10  W30-acc-lim   pic S9(04).
01  W40-sub                  pic 9 value 1.
procedure division.
A100-start.
    set ind to 1
    perform until W20-cond = 9
        search W30-accounts  varying W40-sub
            at end move 9 to W20-cond
          when W30-acc-lim (ind) = 2500
              display W30-acc-id (ind) " "
                      W30-acc-amt (ind) " " W40-sub
        end-search
        compute W40-sub = W40-sub + 1
        set ind to W40-sub
    end-perform
    stop run.
end program Chapter1505.
```

Listing 15.05

```
c:\ Command Prompt                        _ □ ✕
20+ 2000+ 2
30+ 3000+ 3
50+ 3000+ 5
```

Two-dimensional Tables and the Search

The **search** will only operate on a single dimension. Consequently, two-dimensional tables are out. The following program uses the search on a two-dimensional table. Notice, however, that the search is only applied to the second dimension, the innermost one. For the first dimension, the rows, we employ a loop. The following points should be borne in mind.

- We need a loop for the rows. In the example there are two rows, but the example would be equally valid for any number of rows greater than one.
- We also need to insert the search into a loop so that we may detect multiple occurrences of items that satisfy the search condition.
- For each row, before entering the inside loop, we must set the variable controlling the loop, W30-cond. We must set the varied field, W30-sub to one. We must initialize the counter W20-ctr to one, so that we get a count for each row.
- Inside the second loop we have to set the position from which the search will begin. The position is set from the value in W30-sub. The first time W30-sub will be one but subsequently it will be one more than the location of the preceding find.
- Each time the condition is met, the entry is displayed and one is added to W20-ctr.

Searching a Two Dimensional Table

```
program-id. Chapter1506.

working-storage section.
01  W20-numbers.
    05  W20-ctr            pic 99      value 0.
01  filler.
    05  W30-sub            pic S9.
    05  W30-cond           pic S9(2).
    05  W30-data           pic x(80)   value
        "44123410005515002500662500200077223425 00" &
        "88232125009920001800224200250033356740 00".
    05  W30-accounts redefines W30-data   occurs 2
                                          indexed by W30-ind1.
        10  W30-entry                     occurs 4
                                          indexed by W30-ind2.
            15  W30-acc-id    pic S9(02).
            15  W30-acc-amt   pic S9(04).
            15  W30-acc-lim   pic S9(04).
```

Listing 15.06 – 1 of 2

310

Searching a Two Dimensional Table

```
procedure division.
A100-start.
    perform varying W30-Ind1 from 1 by 1
        until W30-ind1 > 2
        move 1 to W30-sub
                  W30-cond
        move 0 to W20-ctr

        perform until W30-cond = 5
            set W30-ind2 to W30-sub
            search W30-entry varying W30-sub
                at end display W20-ctr
                    move 5 to W30-cond
                when W30-acc-lim (W30-ind1 W30-ind2) = 2500
                    display W30-acc-id (W30-ind1 W30-ind2) " "
                            W30-acc-amt (W30-ind1 W30-ind2)
                    add 1 to W30-sub W20-ctr
            end-search
        end-perform
    end-perform
    stop run.
```

Listing 15.06 – 2 of 2

```
Command Prompt                                    _ □ ✕
55+ 1500+
77+ 2234+
02
88+ 2321+
22+ 4200+
02
```

The Search All

The **search all** carries out a **binary search**. Note that for a **binary search** the entries in the table have to be in sequence, which means that the entries must have a key. In the preceding example, the key could have been W30-acc-id. In a binary search, the first lookup references the entry in the middle of the table. Thus, if the table contains 100 entries, we will look at the entry occupying position 50. If the lookup key is greater than 50 we will look at the entry in position 75, if it is less we will look at the entry in position 25 and so on. You can see that the part of the table we are considering is always split in two.

If the table contains 256 entries, it will take a maximum of eight lookups to locate the desired entry (2^8). This represents the maximum number of times we will have to split the table to find the required item. We count each lookup. For a table with 512 entries nine lookups would locate the entry (2^9). For a table with 256 entries, nine lookups means that the entry we are looking for is not there. For a table containing 200 entries a maximum of eight lookups would be required.

The Search All – Format 3

```
search all table-entry
     at end imperative statement/s
   when condition-1 and condition-2
      imperative statement/s
end-search
```

Figure 15.10

The following points should be borne in mind:

- The table must be in sequence by a key, the field on which the table has been sequenced. If the entries in the table have been sequenced based on the contents of the field age, then the field age would be the key.
- There may be only one **when**. For the **when**, the **and** is the only connector. The **or** may not be used.
- The key or a key element, in the case of a composite key, must appear either on the right or the left hand side of the relational operator in the condition.
- The test for equality is the only test authorized.

A table definition, catering for a binary search is shown:

The Search All

```
   05  W30-accounts redefines W30-data   occurs 8
                                         ascending key
                                         W30-acc-id
                                         indexed by W30-ind1.
       10  W30-acc-id    pic S9(02).
       10  W30-acc-amt   pic S9(04).
       10  W30-acc-lim   pic S9(04).
```

Figure 15.11

From the above definition you will observe the following.

- The sequence of the clauses following the **occurs** is not arbitrary. The **ascending/descending key** clause must precede the **indexed by** clause.
- Key elements are presented major to minor, i.e. most inclusive to least inclusive. In the key shown below, W10-br is the most inclusive and W10-emp-no is the least inclusive.

```
01   W10-key.
     05   W10-br...
     05   W10-emp-no...
```

The clause would then be: `ascending key W10-br W10-emp-no`

- The binary search requires a key because the ascending key clause is required.
- There is no need to set the key as the **search all** finds the mid points as required.

Here is a program illustrating the use the search all:

Binary search

```
program-id. Chapter1507.
working-storage section.
01   W10-num                 pic 9(02) value 2.
01   W20-numbers.
     05   W20-ctr            pic 99      value 0.
01   W30-numbers.
     05   W30-sub            pic S9.
     05   filler                              value "22446688".
          10  W30-cond       occurs 4     pic S9(2).
     05   W30-data           pic x(80)  value
          "11123410002215002500442500200005522342500" &
          "66232125007720001800884200250099356740000".
     05   W30-accounts redefines W30-data   occurs 8
                                            ascending key
                                            W30-acc-id
                                            indexed by W30-ind1.
          10   W30-acc-id    pic S9(02).
          10   W30-acc-amt   pic S9(04).
          10   W30-acc-lim   pic S9(04).
```

Listing 15.07 – 1 of 2

Binary search

```
procedure division.
A100-start.
    perform varying W30-sub from 1 by 1
        until W30-sub > 4
            search all W30-accounts
                at end display "Account not found"
              when W30-acc-id (W30-ind1) = W30-cond(W30-sub)
                    display W30-acc-id (W30-ind1) " "
                            W30-acc-amt (W30-ind1)
            end-search
        end-perform
        accept W10-num
        stop run.
```

Listing 15.07 – 2 of 2

Command Prompt
```
22+ 1500+
44+ 2500+
66+ 2321+
88+ 4200+
```

The Varying Revisited

We saw that we may use the **varying** to vary the value of a numeric field. Sometimes we may define a table with two indexes because we may want to reference more than one entry simultaneously. The first index defined in the table definition is the default index that will be used. To use the second index defined, use the varying clause naming the second index. The following program illustrates the point:

Varying

```
program-id. Chapter1508.
working-storage section.
01  filler.
    05  W30-data            pic x(80)  value
        "441234100055150025006625002000772342500" &
        "882321250099200018002242002500333567400".
```

Listing 15.08 – 1 of 2

Varying

```
      05  W30-accounts redefines W30-data  occurs 8
                                           indexed by ind1
                                           indexed by ind2.
          10  W30-acc-id     pic S9(02).
          10  W30-acc-amt    pic S9(04).
          10  W30-acc-lim    pic S9(04).

  procedure division.
  A100-start.
      set ind2 to 1
      search W30-accounts varying ind2
           at end display 'Entry not found'
          when W30-acc-lim (ind2) = 2500
              display W30-acc-id (ind2) " " W30-acc-amt (ind2)
      end-search
      stop run.
```

Listing 15.08 – 2 of 2

```
Command Prompt
55+ 1500+
```

Varying an Index from Another Table

When there is a one-to-one correspondence between two tables it is possible to search one table and vary the index from another table. The following program does this. We have a table with the countries of the world and another table with the currencies of the world. If we look at the United States in one table we should see US$ in the other table.

Varying an Index from Another Table

```
  program-id. Chapter1509 as "Chapter1509".
  01  filler.
      05  W30-data          pic X(12)  value
          "EUR US$ BSTG".
```

Listing 15.09 – 1 of 2

Varying an Index from Another Table

```
    05  W30-currency redefines W30-data occurs 3
                                indexed by Currency-ind.
        10  W30-money      pic X(4).
    05  W40-data    pic X(42)  value
        "Europe          United States United Kingdom".
    05  W40-country  redefines W40-data occurs 3
                                indexed by Country-ind.
        10  W40-nation      pic X(14).

procedure division.
A100-start.
    set Currency-ind, Country-ind to 1
    search W40-country varying Currency-ind
        at end display 'Entry not found'
            when W40-nation (Country-ind) = 'United States'
                display W40-nation (Country-ind) " "
                        W30-money (Currency-ind)
    end-search
    stop run.
    end program Chapter1509.
```

Listing 15.09 – 2 of 2

```
c:\ Command Prompt                                    _ □ ✕
United States US$
```

The Sort Verb

Previously, sorting a table when using COBOL, meant that the programmer had to undertake the **sort** because the language did not offer the facility. This is no longer the case. Furthermore, you are able to **sort** on a number of keys, in **ascending** or **descending** sequence, or a mixture of both. The standard does not stipulate the number of keys on which the sort will take place but, because these limits are generally theoretical, this is of no significance. You may rest assured that your requirements will always fall short of the offering.

The facility is particularly significant where the data coming into the table is not sequenced and a binary search is recommended. The sort verb, which may accept multiple keys, will come in very useful in these situations.

When a **sequential search** is envisaged you should place those elements that are most frequently required at the beginning of the table to reduce the number of look-ups. If, in general, the number of look-ups does not exceed say five, there is no need for a binary search. For a table with 32 elements, on the assumption that the element will be found, a maximum of five look-ups will be required. This makes a binary search a very inviting solution. The **sort** facility is now a powerful ally.

The Sort Verb

```
sort table-name

         ⎧ ascending  ⎫
   on    ⎨            ⎬ key
         ⎩ descending ⎭

with duplicates in order
```

Figure 15.12

Points to note:

- The level to which the **sort** applies is the level at which the occurs clause is specified.
- Key refers to the key elements. Keys will be specified in the sequence major to minor key. Some keys may be in ascending sequence, whilst others may be in descending sequence.
- Duplicates in order means that after the sort operation, records bearing the same key will retain their original sequence.

The following program illustrates the use of the sort as applied to a table:

The Sort In Action

```
program-id. Chapter1510.
working-storage section.
01  W10-area.
    05                      pic X(100) value
    '56Dan14Don07Vic11Eve35Eva21Dot18Roy02Jim43Ada25Tom' &
    '25Val17Tim12May06Mel01Rud13Zoe13Zoe23Bud28Viv22Pat'.
```

Listing 15.10 – 1 of 2

The Sort In Action

```
01   W20-sort-tab redefines W10-area.
     05   W20-entry                 occurs 20.
          10   W20-num    pic 9(02).
          10   W20-name   pic X(03).
01   ctr                  pic 9(02).

procedure division.
A100-start.
    sort W20-entry
         on ascending key W20-num
      with duplicates in order
    perform varying ctr from 1 by 1 until ctr > 20
        display W20-num (ctr) '  ' W20-name (ctr)
    end-perform
    stop run.
```

Listing 15.10 – 2 of 2

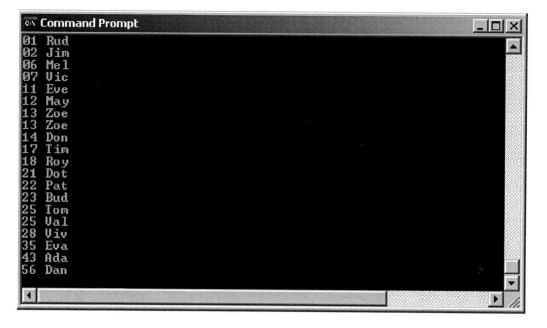

```
Command Prompt

01 Rud
02 Jim
06 Mel
07 Vic
11 Eve
12 May
13 Zoe
13 Zoe
14 Don
17 Tim
18 Roy
21 Dot
22 Pat
23 Bud
25 Tom
25 Val
28 Viv
35 Eva
43 Ada
56 Dan
```

Summary

- The use of two-dimensional tables is not infrequent. The more the dimensions the greater the complexity of the program and the more storage is used.

- Since storage is linear, the compiler sees a two-dimensional table as a one-dimensional table containing records that contain a one-dimensional table.

- COBOL has introduced functions into the language. In particular, it offers intrinsic functions. An **intrinsic function** does not branch to a routine, instead, the instructions replace the call to the function.

- Assuming we have a two-dimensional table, we may have fields that occur only in the rows as well as the fields that occur in the columns. For the fields that occur only in the rows we need only one subscript. For fields that occur in the columns, two subscripts are required.

- The **search** verb will do a sequential search of a one-dimensional table. The search will stop as soon as the entry is located. If you want to find out how many Vics are in the row, you need to insert the **search** inside a loop. As soon as the first Vic is found the search will exit. Because the **search** is now inside a loop, it will start at the position where the first Vic was located + 1.

- In a **search**, the search condition is specified using a **when**. Multiple whens are implicitly connected by **or**. An explicit **or** is not allowed. Similarly **and** is not acceptable.

- We may use the **varying** clause in a search to name a field that will be incremented every time the index is incremented.

- The **search all** enables us to perform a **binary search** on a table. The table must be in sequence and only one when is permitted. The only connector allowed with the **when** is the **and**. Only the key elements may be used in the comparison because those are the fields on which the table is sequenced.

Complete

1. Two-dimensional tables have _____ and _____.

2. A table has 100 byte entries and there are 10 rows each with 10 columns. The table would occupy _____ bytes in storage.

3. A two-dimensional table has one _____ _____ per dimension.

4. In a two-dimensional table we have a field that exists only in the rows, the field will occupy a position to the _____ of the columns table.

5. In a two-dimensional table we have a field that exists only in the rows, to reference that field we would need only one _____.

6. The **search** verb is applied to the item at the level where the _____ is coded.

7. In the **when**, the ___ is implied for _____ conditions.

8. In the **when**, the _____ is not a _____ connector.

9. When using the **search** verb the at end exit is taken for a ____ _____ condition.

10. The **search** requires that the _____ ___ clause be used.

11. We may vary a _____ field or an _____ field.

12. We may vary an index from _____ table.

13. The **search all** carries out a _____ search.

14. In the **search all**, in the when the _____ is the only connector allowed.

15. When using the **search all**, the table must be in _____ by a ____ field.

True/False

1.   In referring to a two-dimensional table, we would code entry (row, column).

2.   A two-dimensional table requires one occurs clause and two indexes.

3.   In a two-dimensional table we have a field that occurs only in the rows. The field must be coded so that it will be on the left of the columns.

4.   In a two-dimensional table, if the row is coded at level 15 then the columns would be coded at level 20.

5.   The varying clause causes a change in the index to be reflected in the field being varied.

6.   If you vary an index you will vary an index other than the first index specified for the dimension.

7.   In a two-dimensional table, the second dimension lies inside the first dimension.

8.   When sequential searches are involved we place the most frequently referenced items at the end of the table.

9.   When using the **search all**, we should place the most frequently referenced items at the beginning of the table.

10.   When using the **search**, multiple whens are explicitly connected by or.

11.   When using the **search**, in a when, multiple conditions may be connected by and.

12.   When using the **search all**, multiple whens must be connected by and.

13.   The **sort** verb enables us to sort the entries in a table in ascending sequence on one field and in descending field on another field.

14.   The table to be sorted must be indexed.

Exercises

1. Write a program that will read a file into a table. Use the search verb to locate all the accounts in which the balance exceeds the limit. The records have the following structure:

ID	X(2)
Balance	9(5)
Limit	9(5)

2. A company stocks material that they distribute to shops. The materials have two codes. One code identifies the colour and is in the range one to 20. The other identifies the type of material and the codes are in the range one to 50.

    The information is kept in a file and read into a two dimensional table at the start of business. At the end of the day the table is written back to disk. There are 20 rows for colours and each row has a maximum of 50 columns. During the day, as sales are made, the values in the table are updated.

    You are to write a program to read the file into the table and to write the table to disk. In addition, you will read a file containing transactions to update the table.

    The master records have the format:

Colour	9(2)
Material	9(2)
Sales	9(7)

    The transactions have identical format.

    The update merely adds the transaction value of sales to the table value of sales.

3. The SoftMicro company is a software company employing 100 employees. In a program, an array contains a unique employee code of format pic XXXXX. In addition, the table element has a field for name (pic X(20)) and a field for salary where values will not exceed $250 000. Define the table.

    Assuming that the table contains valid data you are to use a **search** statement to locate an employee whose code is XY543. The employee is to receive an increase of 10%. If the code is not found, display the message "Invalid code" followed by the code.

    Define all fields that you might need to implement the solution.

Chapter 16

Reference Modifitation &
Intrinsic Functions

Topics Covered

Reference Modification

Reference modification is a facility introduced into COBOL by the 1985 standard. It brings to the programmer the possibility of addressing not the whole field but rather a selected byte or group of bytes. For this to happen and make sense, note that **reference modification** acts on data with usage display or, put differently, where a character does not occupy half a byte, as happens with packed data.

Reference Modification – Format 1

```
Move cust-name(Starting-position : length) to surname
```

Figure 16.01

Starting-position would indicate where to start moving in cust-name, the source. If starting-position were 12, then the first byte moved would be in position 12. The value in length represents the number of bytes to be moved.

Reference Modification – Numeric to Alphanumeric

```
01   num                      pic 9(05)   value 12345.
01   alpha-num                pic X(05)   value 'ABCDE'.
     move num(2:3) to alpha-num
     display "After the move: " alpha-num
```

Figure 16.02

After execution: `After the move: 234`

Because the destination is alphanumeric, the data are aligned on the left and positions left vacant are space filled.

Reference Modification – Numeric to Numeric

```
01   num1                     pic 9(05)   value 12345.
01   num2                     pic 9(05)   value 67890 comp-3.
     move num1(2:3) to num2
     display "After the move: " num2
```

Figure 16.03

After execution: `After the move: 00234`

Because the destination is numeric, the data are aligned on the right and positions left vacant are zero filled. The destination field is not reference modified so it can be a packed field.

Reference Modification - Number of Bytes Unspecified

```
01   num1                    pic 9(06)   value 123456.
01   alpha-num               pic X(05)   value 'ABCDE'.

     move num1(2:) to alpha-num
     display "After the move: " alpha-num
```

Figure 16.04

After execution: `After the move: 23456`

Because the destination is alphanumeric, the data are aligned on the left. The data completely fill the destination field. Because we did not specify the number of bytes to be moved, all the bytes from the starting position to the end of the field were moved. This would be so, of course, if the destination could contain all the data to be transferred, as it did in this case.

Reference Modification – Format 2

```
Move surname to cust-name(Starting-position : Length)
```

Figure 16.05

If **reference modification** is acting on the destination field, the move always follows alphanumeric rules. The reason for this is that any numeric, numeric edited or alphanumeric edited field (receiving or sending) having **reference modification** applied to it will be treated as if the field had been redefined as alphanumeric. The following example illustrates this point:

Reference Modification - Number of Bytes Unspecified

```
01   num1                    pic 9(06)   value 12345.
01   num2                    pic 9(05)   value 88888.
     move num1 to num2 (2:3)
     display "After the move: " num2
```

Figure 16.06

After execution: `After the move: 80128`

The data were moved from the source, starting in position one on the left, to position two on the left, in the destination and for the specified number of bytes. Notice that the source field is six bytes long and therefore contains 012345. The three digits moved were 012 and placed in the destination in positions 2:3, i.e. 012.

Reference Modification – Format 3

```
Move surname    (Starting-position : number-of-bytes) to
     cust-name  (Starting-position : number-of-bytes)
```

Figure 16.07

In the example that follows, reference modification has been applied both to the source and to the destination. The number of bytes transferred and received is the same.

Reference Modification Applied to Source and to Destination

```
01  date1                pic 9(06)   value 850818.
01  date2                pic 9(06)   value 981125.

    move date1 (3:3) to date2 (3:3)
    display "After the move: " date2
```

Figure 16.08

After execution: `After the move: 980815`

Three bytes were moved, starting in position three:

Before	98**112**5
changed to	98**081**5
Source	85**081**8

Reference Modification – Using Fields in Place of Literals

```
01  date1                pic 9(06)   value 850818.
01  date2                pic 9(06)   value 981125.
01  start1               pic 9       value 3.
01  len1                 pic 9       value 3.

    move date1 (start1:len1) to date2 (start1:len1)
    display "After the move: " date2
```

Figure 16.09

We used fields to specify starting position and length. In general, where you specify a numeric literal you may specify a field name. The effect of the code would be identical to that produced by the preceding example. The following example depicts referenced modification being applied to table items. Notice the sequence of the subscript and the reference modification specification.

Using Reference Modification on Table Items

```
program-id. Chapter1601.
working-storage section.
01   Tables.
     05   nums1              pic 9(04)   occurs 3
                                         value 3456 from (1)
                                               4567 from (2)
                                               5678 from (3).

     05   nums2              pic 9(04)   occurs 3
                                         value 1111 from (1)
                                               2222 from (2)
                                               3333 from (3).

procedure division.
A100-start.
     move nums1 (1) (2:3) to nums2 (1)
     move nums1 (2) (2:3) to nums2 (2)
     move nums1 (3) (2:3) to nums2 (3)
     display  nums1 (1) ' '  nums1 (2) ' 'nums1 (3)
     display  nums2 (1) ' '  nums2 (2) ' 'nums2 (3)
     stop run.
```

Listing 16.01

```
3456 4567 5678
0456 0567 0678
```

You will have noticed that the subscript comes before **reference modification**. Because we did not specify **reference modification** for the destination fields and they were numeric, alignment was on the right.

It stands to reason that we cannot do arithmetic on reference modified fields because, as you will recall, once we apply **reference modification** to a field it is as if it had been redefined as alphanumeric.

Where to Use Reference Modification

We will use **reference modification** when we want to extract part of a field. Typically, an alphanumeric field will contain data and the data in which we are interested will start at a particular position. We will isolate the data using **reference modification** and process it as required.

We may use **reference modification** wherever we would use an alphanumeric field.

Extracting a Substring

```
01  Data1.
    05  string1              pic X(40)   value
    'We must defend the truth at all costs.'
    if  string1 (20:5) = 'truth'
        display 'Right string'
```

Figure 16.10

After execution: `Right string`

Intrinsic Functions

As indicated earlier and recapitulating now, **function** is just another name for routine. We invoke a routine, using the perform verb, because the routine contains coding that will do the work we need done. Maybe the routine gets the system date that we can then use. In C we may have an equivalent function that gets the date from the system. We see that in COBOL the equivalent to a function in C, is a routine.

When we call a COBOL routine or a C function, a branch is taken to the code that will execute. A branch requires computer cycles. In the case of an intrinsic function the code to be executed replaces the call statement and no branch is taken. The function code is said to be included inline, i.e. embedded into the code at the point at which it was specified. To invoke an **intrinsic function** we need to do the following:

- The keyword **function** must be used.
- Following the keyword **function** comes the name of the function.
- Following the function name and, enclosed in curved brackets, we enter any arguments required by the function.
- The function will return data and the type of the data returned determines the type of function invoked.

Types of Intrinsic Functions

Intrinsic functions fall into any one of the following categories based on the value returned.

- **Alphanumeric functions** – These return data of class alphanumeric and consequently return data of usage display. The receiving field may be alphabetic or alphanumeric. The type selected depends on the data being returned. We use alphanumeric functions with the **move** verb.
- **Numeric functions** – Numeric functions return a numeric value, signed and of type floating point.
- **Integer functions** – These functions return a numeric value that does not contain a fractional component.
- **Date conversion functions** – These functions manipulate dates in different ways.
- **Boolean functions** – There are two types of **boolean** functions; one converts a **boolean** value to a numeric value and the other operates in the reverse direction. Net Express, at the time of writing, does not implement the **boolean** type.

- **National functions** – There is one function only, **national-of,** and it will not be covered here.

We will cover some of the many, **intrinsic functions** of the first four types.

Date Conversion Functions

We have five **intrinsic functions** to handle dates. The following table depicts the functions in question and the types returned.

Function	Type
Current-date	Alphanumeric
Integer-of-date	Integer
Integer-of-day	Integer
Date-of-integer	Integer
Day-of-integer	Integer
Table 16.01 Date conversion functions	

Current-Date

Current-date is an alphanumeric function because it returns alphanumeric data. You know that, in COBOL, when you want to place data in a field you will use the **move**

statement. In the example that follows, we will use the **move** verb in assigning the value returned by the function. The **current-date** function is the only one returning the time. Let us look at the field we need to define to receive the data returned by the function. The field is 23 bytes long.

The Field Returned by Current-Date

```
01  W10-date-time.
    05  W10-date.
        10  W10-yyyy      pic 9(4).
        10  W10-mm        pic 9(2).
        10  W10-dd        pic 9(2).
    05  W10-time.
        10  W10-hh        pic 9(4).
        10  W10-min       pic 9(2).
        10  W10-ss        pic 9(2).
        10  W10-ff        pic 9(2).

    05  W10-gmt.
        10  W10-gmt-sign  pic x.
        10  W10-gmt-hh    pic 9(2).
        10  W10-gmt-min   pic 9(2).
```

Figure 16.11

W10-gmt has data indicating whether the location is ahead or behind Coordinated Universal Time. W10-gmt-sign will contain a '+' if local time is ahead and a '-' if local time is behind Coordinated Universal Time. If W10-gmt-sign has the value zero, zero will be returned for hours and minutes. The following statements will retrieve and display the data returned.

Using the Current-Date Function

```
move function current-date to W10-date-time
display "Date is: " W10-yyyy '/' W10-mm '/' W10-dd
display "Time is: " W10-hh ':' W10-min ':' W10-ss ':' W10-ff
display "GMT  is: " W10-gmt-sign ' ' W10-gmt-hh ':'
                                     W10-gmt-min
```

Figure 16.12

```
┌─────────────────────────────────────────────────────────────┐
│ ▄ Command Prompt                                   _ □ X   ▲  │
│ Date  is:  2004/07/05                                         │
│ Time  is:  08:08:38:14                                        │
│ GMT   is:  08  00:00                                          │
│                                                           ▼  │
│ ◄                                                         ►   │
└─────────────────────────────────────────────────────────────┘
```

Integer-of-Date

The function returns the number of days that have elapsed since December 31, 1600 to the date submitted in the Gregorian calendar. The date must be an integer and needs to be numeric. The following definitions enable us to retrieve the date and to submit it to the **integer-of-date** function:

Fields for Integer-of-Date

```
    01   W10-date.
         05   W10-yyyy          pic 9(4).
         05   W10-mm            pic 9(2).
         05   W10-dd            pic 9(2).
    01   W10-days               pic 9(8) redefines W10-date.
    01   W20-no-of-days         pic Z(7).
```

Figure 16.13

The value for the year must follow 1600 and not exceed 9999. The month will be in the range one to 12. The value for days must be valid for the month. The function returns an integer. The following lines of code will obtain the date and return the number of days elapsed:

Using Integer-of-Date

```
    move function current-date to W10-date
    display "Date is: " W10-yyyy '/' W10-mm '/' W10-dd
    compute W20-no-of-days = function integer-of-date(W10-days)
    display "No of days: " W20-no-of-days
```

Figure 16.14

The function enables us to easily find the number of days that have elapsed between two dates. The maximum value that can be returned by the function is 3,067,659. The following example illustrates the use of the function to determine the number of days elapsed between two dates.

Number of Days Between Two Dates

```
01  W10-date1          pic 9(8)   value 20030625.
01  W10-date2          pic 9(8)   value 20040827.
01  W20-no-of-days     pic Z(7).

    compute  W20-no-of-days  =  function  integer-of-date(W10-
date1)
                            -  function  integer-of-date(W10-
date2)
    display "No of days: " W20-no-of-days
```

Figure 16.15

Integer-of-Day

This function takes an argument in the Julian date format of the Gregorian calendar and returns an integer reflecting the number of days that have elapsed between the date submitted and December 31, 1600. What was said in respect to the integer-of-date function applies equally to the present **integer-of-day** function. The following code will illustrate the use of the function:

Using Integer-of-Day

```
01  W10-date1             pic 9(8)   value 2004187.
01  W20-no-of-days        pic Z(7).

    compute W20-no-of-days =
                 function integer-of-day(W10-date1)
    display "No of days: " W20-no-of-days
```

Figure 16.16

```
Command Prompt                                    _ □ X
No of days:  147379
```

Date-of-Integer

The **date-of-integer** function receives an integer as an argument and returns a date in the Gregorian format, YYYYMMDD. The argument will provide the number of days since December 31, 1600 and the corresponding date will be returned. If we enter one, we will receive 16010101, two will return 16010102. The following code illustrates the use of the function:

Using Date-of-Integer

```
01  W10-date1             pic 9(8).
01  W20-days              pic 9(7)   value 147379.

    compute W10-date1 = function date-of-integer(W20-days)
    display "Date is: " W10-date1
```

Figure 16.17

```
Command Prompt                                    _ □ X
Date is: 20040705
```

Day-of-Integer

As in the preceding function, the **day-of-integer** function receives an integer and returns a date. This time, however, the Gregorian date returned is in the Julian format YYYY-YDDD. If you type in 1 you will receive 1601001. In the code that follows we will provide the same value as above:

Using Day-of-Integer

```
01  W10-date1          pic 9(7).
01  W20-days           pic 9(7)   value 147379.

    compute W10-date1 = function day-of-integer(W20-days)
    display "Date is: " W10-date1
```

Figure 16.18

```
Date is: 2004187
```

Random

The random function is one of several functions returning a floating point number. The value returned is greater than zero and less than one. The value returned by the function is a pseudo-random number. The argument passed to the function is the seed value. The same seed value will cause the same value to be returned each time, as happens with pseudo-random numbers.

We have used the time for seeding. You might choose to seed it with hundredths of a second, in which case you would, in one second, be provided with 100 seeds.

Random

```
01  W20-time           pic 9(8).
01  W20-random         pic Z(4)9.99999.

    accept W20-time from time
    compute W20-random = function random (W20-time) * 145
    display "Random number is: " W20-random
```

Figure 16.19

Year-to-yyyy

The **year-to-yyyy** function adds the century to the year figure. The first argument speci-fies the year (yy) and must be positive and less than 100, the second argument provides the century. If the second argument is not provided, a value that cannot belong to this century will belong to the previous century. The third argument must be greater than 1600 and less than 9999. Examine the following code:

Year-to-YYYY

```
01   W20-yy              pic 9(2)   value 95.
01   W20-year            pic 9(4).

     compute W20-year = function year-to-yyyy (W20-yy)
     display "Year is: " W20-year
     move 4 to W20-yy
     compute W20-year = function year-to-yyyy (W20-yy)
     display "Year is: " W20-year
     compute W20-year = function year-to-yyyy (W20-yy 300)
     display "Year is: " W20-year
```

Figure 16.20

In the first example the year is 95 and the value for century returned is 1900. Since the actual date is early 2005, 95 must belong to the previous century; hence the cen-tury is 1900. In the second example the year is 4 so the value for century returned was 2000. In the third example we provided a displacement of 300 years, giving us a figure of 2300 for the century. Observe the output:

```
Command Prompt
Year is: 1995
Year is: 2004
Year is: 2304
```

Test-date-yyyymmdd

The **test-date-yyyymmdd** function tests a date for validity. If the year is not within the range 1601 and 9999, the value one will be returned. If the date is valid 0 will be returned. The values returned for the different errors follow:

- If the year is not within the allowed range, one is returned
- If the month is not in the range one to 12, two is returned
- If the day is not valid for the month, three is returned

The following code illustrates the use of the function:

Test-Date-YYYYMMDD

```
01  W20-yy                   pic 9(8)    value 19950625.
01  W20-result               pic 9.

    compute W20-result = function test-date-yyyymmdd (W20-yy)
    display "Result of test: " W20-result
    move 19950631 to W20-yy
    compute W20-result = function test-date-yyyymmdd (W20-yy)
    display "Result of test: " W20-result
    move 19950031 to W20-yy
    compute W20-result = function test-date-yyyymmdd (W20-yy)
    display "Result of test: " W20-result
```

Figure 16.21

The first test would return zero because the field contains a valid date. The second test has day invalid and three would be returned. The third test has the month wrong and two would be returned.

There is an equivalent function for the date in the Julian format. The function is **test-day-yyyydddd**. If the year is not within the acceptable range one is returned. If the day is not in the range for that year, two is returned. Again, zero signifies a correct Julian date.

Note that these functions are specified in the standard but have not yet been implemented by Micro Focus at the time of writing.

Lower-Case and Upper-Case

The names of these functions indicate plainly the reason for their existence. The field passed as an argument to the function remains unchanged. It is the destination field that will receive the inverted data. The function is an alphanumeric function and it may be applied to alphabetic as well as alphanumeric data. In principle, source and destination fields should be the same size - if they are not, there will be truncation; if the destination is shorter or longer, vacant positions will be space filled. Consider the example covering the **upper-case** function.

Converting to Upper Case

```
01   string1            pic X(30) value 'Hello global village!'.
01   string2            pic X(30).

     move function upper-case (string1) to string2
     display string2
```

Figure 16.22

Only the data that needs to change will be changed. Data that are already incapitals will remain unchanged. The **lower-case** function is as follows:

Converting to Lower Case

```
01   string1            pic X(30) value 'HELLO GLOBAL VILLAGE!'.
01   string2            pic X(30).

     move function lower-case (string1) to string2
     display    string2
```

Figure 16.23

SUM

The type of the **sum** function depends on the type of data on which it is operating. If it operates on floating point data it is numeric. If it operates on integer data, it is of type in-

teger. The function returns the sum of the fields passed to it. The use of the function becomes particularly inviting when it is used to add the elements of a table. Note, however,
that although practical to use it is heavy on CPU usage. As such, it is recommended only
when its use is infrequent. If heavy usage is anticipated you should create your own routine.

Obtaining the Sum of Four Fields

```
01   num1             pic 9(05) value 1500.
01   num2             pic 9(05) value 2500.
01   num3             pic 9(05) value 3000.
01   num4             pic 9(05) value 3000.
01   num5             pic 9(05).

     compute num5 = function sum (num1 num2 num3 num4)
     display  "Result is: " num5
```

Figure 16.24

The fields to be added are passed as arguments.

The following example illustrates the use of the function where the argument is a
one-dimensional table. In the argument we name the table subscripted by the word **all**.

Obtaining the Sum of the Elements of a Table

```
01   Dat-table value "05101520253035404550".
     05   nums        pic 9(02) occurs 10.
01   result           pic 9(03).

     compute result = function sum (nums(all))
     display  "Result is: " result
```

Figure 16.25

If we only wanted some of the elements of the table we would code:

```
compute result = function sum (nums(1) nums(3) nums(5)
                                       nums(7) nums(9))
```

Sum of a Two-dimensional Table

```
01   Dat-table.
     05   nums1           occurs 10.
          10   nums2      pic 9(02)     occurs 10.
01   result          pic 9(03).

     compute result = function sum (nums2(all all))
     display  "Result is: " result
```

Figure 16.26

Note that, in the case of a two-dimensional table, it is the innermost level that is subscripted. In this case there are two subscripts, one for each dimension. For a three-dimensional table we again subscript the innermost level and supply three subscripts. We would code:

```
compute result = function sum(nums3(all all all))
```

Min and Max

These functions return the highest and lowest values found in the arguments provided. The type of the function depends on the type of the arguments. The arguments may be:

- Alphabetic
- Alphanumeric
- Numeric
- Integer

Specifying **all** causes the whole table to be examined.   When examining tables this is the norm. In the example we obtain minimum and maximum values in a table.

339

Minimum and Maximum Values in a Table.

```
01   Dat-table value "05101520253035404550".
     05  nums1           pic 9(02)      occurs 10.
01   result              pic 9(02).

     compute result = function min (nums1(all))
     display   "The smallest value is: " result
     compute result = function max (nums1(all))
     display   "The highest value  is: " result
```

Figure 16.27

```
Command Prompt                                    _ □ ×
The smallest value is: 05
The highest value  is: 50
```

Minimum and Maximum Values in an Alphabetic Table

```
01   Dat-table value "AXCJHLFNBIWQPTSLGKMP".
     05  chars1          pic X(02)      occurs 10.
01   result              pic X(02).

     move function max (chars1(all)) to result
     display   "The highest value  is: " result
     move function min (chars1(all)) to result
     display   "The smallest value is: " result
```

Figure 16.28

```
Command Prompt                                    _ □ ×
The highest value  is: XK
The smallest value is: AX
```

Sqrt

The **sqrt** function returns the square root of the argument. This function is of type numeric. The need to find the square root of a number is not an unusual requirement and it is fortunate that a function for the purpose is now available in COBOL. The following example illustrates the use of the function:

Extracting the Square Root of a Number

```
01   Data1.
     05   num1              pic 9(03)V99  value 144.25.
01   result                 pic 9(03).9(6).

     compute result =  function sqrt (num1)
     display  "The square root of 144.25 is: " result
```

Figure 16.29

```
Command Prompt                                    _ □ ×
The square root of 144.25 is: 012.010412
```

Integer

The **integer** function returns the greatest integer value possible from the argument submitted. The function is of type numeric. If we move 7.5 to a field defined without decimals, we get the largest integer value possible from the source, in this case 7. However, if we move –7.5 to a field defined without decimals, we get -7. What we would like to get is –8. This is what the function does for us, given -7.5, -8 will be returned. Consider the example:

Getting the Greatest Integer.

```
01   Data1.
     05   num1              pic S9(01)V9  value 7.5.
     05   num2              pic S9(01)V9  value -7.5.
01   result                 pic -9(01).9.

     compute result =  function integer (num1)
     display "Integer of 7.5 is: " result
     compute result = function integer (num2)
     display "Integer of -7.5 is: "  result
```

Figure 16.30

341

```
c:\ Command Prompt                                    _ □ ×
Integer of 7.5 is:   7.0
Integer of -7.5 is: -8.0
```

Integer-part

The integer-part function returns the integer component of the number. The function is of type numeric. This time the processing is equivalent to moving the source to a signed integer field, thereby dropping the fractional component.

Getting the Integer Part of the Number.

```
01   Data1.
     05   num1          pic S9(01)V9  value 7.5.
     05   num2          pic S9(01)V9  value -7.5.
01   result             pic -9(01).9.
     compute result =  function integer-part (num1)
     display  "Integer of 7.5 is: " result
     compute result = function integer-part (num2)
     display  "Integer of -7.5 is: "  result
```

Figure 16.31

```
c:\ Command Prompt                                    _ □ ×
Integer of 7.5 is:   7.0
Integer of -7.5 is: -7.0
```

Rem

The **rem** function returns the remainder of a division. The function is of type numeric. The function takes two arguments: The first is the divisor and the second is the dividend. As is to be expected, the second argument may not be zero.

Getting the Remainder

```
01  Data1.
    05  num1             pic S9(02)V99  value 37.53.
    05  num2             pic S9(01)V9   value 7.3.
01  result               pic 9(02).9(3).

    compute result =  function rem (num1 num2)
    display  "Remainder is: " result
```

Figure 16.32

The result is arrived at with recourse to the following arithmetic expression.

```
((arg1) - ((arg2) * function integer-part(arg1 / arg2)))
```

Mean

The **mean** function returns a value that is the average of the values submitted. The function is of type numeric. The value obtained by adding all the arguments is divided by the number of arguments. The example that follows uses a table:

Finding an Average.

```
01  Dat-table value "05101520253035404550".
    05  num1             pic S9(02)V99  occurs 10.
01  result               pic 9(02).99.

    compute result =  function mean(num1(all))
    display  "Average is: " result
```

Figure 16.33

343

Midrange

The **midrange** function returns the average of the highest and lowest values. The function is of type numeric.

Finding the Average of the Highest and the Lowest Values

```
01   Dat-table value "05101520253035404550".
     05   num1            pic S9(02)  occurs 10.
01   result              pic 9(02).99.

     compute result =  function midrange(num1(all))
     display  "Middle of the range is: " result
```

Figure 16.34

```
Command Prompt                                          _ □ ✕
Middle of the range is:  22.75
```

The result is arrived at using the following expression.

```
(function max(num1(all)) + function min(num1(all))) / 2
```

There are additional intrinsic functions that we have not covered. The complete list follows:

Intrinsic Function	Arguments	Type	Value Returned
abs	int1 or num1	Depends on argument	The absolute value of the argument
acos	Num1	Numeric	Arccosine of num1
annuity	Num1, int2	Numeric	Ratio of annuity paid for int2 periods at interest of num1 to initial investment of one.
asin	Num1	Numeric	Arcsine of num1
atan	Num1	Numeric	Arctangent of num1
boolean-of-integer	int1, int2	Boolean	A Boolean item representing the binary value equivalent to the numeric value in argument-1
byte-length	Alph1 or alphn1 or num or obj or ptr	Integer	Length of argument in number of bytes.
char	int1	Alphanum	Character in position int1 of the alphanumeric program collating sequence
char-national	int1	National	Character in position int1 of the national program collating sequence
cos	Num1	Numeric	Cosine of num1
current-date		Alphanum	Current date and time and local time differential.
date-of-integer	int1	Integer	Standard date equivalent (yyy-ymmdd) of integer date.
date-to-yyyymmdd	int1 int2 int3	Integer	Arg1 converted from yymmdd to yyyymmdd based on the values in arg2 and arg3.
day-of-integer	int1	Integer	Julian date equivalent (yyyymmdd) of integer date.
day-to-yyyyddd	int1 int2 int3	Integer	Arg1 converted from yyddd to yyy-yddd based on the values in arg2 and arg3.
display-of	nat1, Anum2	Alphanum	Usage display representation of arg. nat1
e		Numeric	The value of e, the natural base
exception-file		Alphanum	Information about the file exception that raised an exception.
exception-file-n		National	Information about the file exception that raised an exception.
exception-location		Alphanum	Location of statement causing an exception

Table 2 – List of intrinsic functions

Intrinsic Function	Arguments	Type	Value Returned
exception-location-n		National	Location of statement causing an exception
exception-statement		Alphanum	Name of statement causing an exception
exception-status		Alphanum	Exception-name identifying last exception
Exp	num1	Numeric	e raised to the power num1
exp10	num1	Numeric	10 raised to the power num1
factorial	int1	Integer	Factorial of int1
fraction-part	num1	Numeric	Fraction part of num1
highest-algebraic	Anum or int1 or nat1 or num1	Integer or numeric	Greatest algebraic vale that may be represented in the argument
Integer	num1	Integer	The greatest integer not greater than num1
Integer-of-boolean	bool1	Integer	The numeric value of a binary-double item whose bit configuration is the same as bool1 right justified
Integer-of-date	int1	Integer	Integer date equivalent to standard date of Yyyymmdd
Integer-of-day	int1	Integer	Integer date equivalent to Julian date yyyyddd
Integer-part	num1	Integer	Integer part of num1
Length	alph1 or alphn1 or num or obj or ptr	Integer	Length of argument in number of character positions or number of Boolean positions
Log	num1	Numeric	Natural logarithm of num1
log10	num1	Numeric	logarithm to base 10 of num1
lower-case	alph1 or alphanum1	Depends upon argument	Sets the string from upper to lower case
lowest-algebraic	Anum or int1 or nat1 or num1	Integer or numeric	Lowest algebraic value that may be represented in the argument
Max	alph1 or alphn1 or ind1 or int1 or num1 or nat1	Depends upon argument	Value of maximum argument
Mean	num1	Numeric	Arithmetic mean of arguments
Median	num1	Numeric	Median of arguments
midrange	num1	Numeric	Mean of minimum or maximum arguments

Table 2 – List of intrinsic functions

Intrinsic Function	Arguments	Type	Value Returned
min	alph1 or alphn1 or ind1 or int1 or num1 or nat1	Depends upon argument	Value of minimum argument
mod	int1 int2	Integer	Int1 modulo Int2
numval	Alphanum1 or nat1	Numeric	Numeric value of simple numeric string
numval-c	Alpanum1 or nat1	Numeric	Numeric value of simple numeric string with optional commas and currency sign
numval-f	Alphanum1 or nat1	Numeric	Numeric value of simple numeric string representing a floating-point number
ord	Alph1 or Alphanum1 or nat1	Integer	Ordinal position of the argument in collating sequence
ord-max	Alph1 or Alphanum1 or ind1 or nat1 or num1	Integer	Ordinal position of maximum argument
ord-min	Alph1 or Alphanum1 or ind1 or nat1 or num1	Integer	Ordinal position of minimum argument
pi		Numeric	The value of pi
present-value	num1 num2	Numeric	Present value of a series of future period end amounts, num2, at a discount rate of num1
random	int1	Numeric	Pseudo random number
range	int1 or num1	Depends upon argument	Value of maximum argument minus value of minimum argument
rem	num1, num2	Numeric	Remainder of num1/num2
reverse	Alph1 or Alphanum1 or nat1	Depends upon argument	Reverses the order of the characters of the argument
sign	num1	Integer	The sign of num1
sin	num1	Numeric	Sine of num1
sqrt	num1	Numeric	Square root of num1
standard-compare			

Table 2 - List of intrinsic functions

Intrinsic Function	Arguments	Type	Value Returned
standard-compare	alph1, alphn1, or nat1, alph2, alphn2, or nat2 ord3 int4	Alphanum	A character indicating the result of comparing arg1 to arg2 using the ordering specified by arg3 at the comparison level specified by arg4
standard-deviation	num1	Numeric	Standard deviation of arguments
Sum	int1... or num1...	Depends upon argument	Sum of arguments
Tan	num1	Numeric	Tangent of num1
test-date-yyyymmdd	int1	Integer	0 if int1 is a valid standard date otherwise the subfield in error is identified
test-day-yyyyddd	int1	Integer	0 if int1 is a valid Julian date otherwise the subfield in error is identified
test-numval	Anum1 or nat1	Integer	0 if arg1 conforms to the requirements of the numval function; otherwise identifies the character in error
test-numval-c	Anum1 or nat1, anum2 or nat2 or key2, loc2, key3	Integer	0 if arg1 conforms to the requirements of the numval-c function; otherwise identifies the character in error
test-numval-f	Anum1 or nat1	Integer	0 if arg1 conforms to the requirements of the numval-f function; otherwise identifies the character in error
Upper-case	alph1 or alphanum1 or nat1	Depends upon argument	Sets the string from lower case to upper case
variance	num1	Num	variance of argument
When-compiled		Alphanum	Date and time compilation unit was compiled
year-to-yyyy	int1, int2, int3	Integer	Arg1 converted from yy to yyyy based on the values of arg2 and arg3

Table 2 - List of intrinsic functions

Functions

The 2002 standard enables the programmer to create her own **functions**. The programmer-created functions resemble intrinsic functions but **are not** intrinsic functions per se.

In invoking an intrinsic function, we use the keyword **function**. For an intrinsic function we coded:

```
move function upper-case (string1) to string2
```

For a programmer-created **function** we would code:

```
move upper-case (string1) to string2
```

In invoking the function, we did not use the keyword **function**.

A programmer-created **function** is very much like a program. Below we contrast the two:

Program	Function

Program-id. Prog1.
 	
Working-storage section.
01 data2   pic x(20).
 	
Linkage section.
01 data1   pic X(10)
 	
Procedure division using data1
            returning data2.
Exit **program**
 	
End **program** prog1
	Function-id. function1.
	
	Working-storage section.
	01 data2 pic x(20).
	
	Linkage section.
	01 data1 pic X(10)
	
	Procedure division using data1
	              returning data2.
	Exit **function**
	
	End **function** function1.

Figure 16.32 Called Program	**Figure 16.33 Invoked Function**

The differences have been highlighted. As you see, the similarities prevail. Normally, we reserve functions for situations where the purpose is restricted. In the example below, we show a function that changes the format of the date:

Function Definition

```$set repository (update on)```
 	
``` function-id. ConvDate.```
``` working-storage section.```
``` linkage section.```
``` 01 l-date1   pic X(6).```

Listing 16.03 – 1 of 2

Function Definition

```
01   l-date-01   redefines l-date1.
     05  l-dd1              pic XX.
     05  l-mm1              pic XX.
     05  l-yy1              pic XX.
01   l-date2               pic X(6).

01   l-date02   redefines l-date2.
     05  l-mm2              pic XX.
     05  l-dd2              pic XX.
     05  l-yy2              pic XX.

 procedure division using l-date1
                    returning l-date2.
     move l-dd1 to l-dd2
     move l-mm1 to l-mm2
     move l-yy1 to l-yy2
     exit function
end function ConvDate.
```

Listing 16.03 – 2 of 2

Invoking a Function

```
program-id. Chapter1603.
repository.
    function ConvDate.
working-storage section.
01   dat1              pic X(6) value '210506'.
01   dat2              pic X(6).

procedure division.
    display 'Date in original format: ' dat1
    move ConvDate (dat1) to dat2
    display 'Date in new format    : ' dat2
    stop run.
end program Chapter1603.
```

Listing 16.04

The **returning** clause must be specified in the procedure division statement, the item returned must be defined in the linkage section.

Summary

- **Reference modification** enables us to access, not the whole field but part of a field, given the starting position and the number of bytes. The field to which **reference modification** is applied must be usage display. However, if we are applying **reference modification** to a numeric source the destination may be packed.
- If the number of bytes to be reference modified is not specified (2:), the bytes, starting at position two, to the end of the field will be transferred.
- A reference modified field will be treated as if it had been implicitly redefined as alphanumeric. For this reason, reference modified fields may not participate in arithmetic.
- We may use fields rather than literals when specifying starting position and number of bytes.
- We use **reference modification** to access a particular position in a record. Assume we are reading a file: If the code is 'xxx' we move field1 to the record(Start:Length:).
- **Intrinsic functions** are routines that when called will replace the call with the code to be executed; in this way the expense of a branch is saved.
- To invoke an **intrinsic function**, the name of the function immediately follows the word **function**. Curved brackets then follow the function name. If necessary, arguments to be passed to the function will be placed inside the brackets.
- There are four main types of **intrinsic functions**: Alphanumeric, numeric for floating point operations, integer and date conversion functions.
- The 2002 standard enables the programmer to create her own **functions**. Note that these are not intrinsic functions. As such, the call to the function is not preceded by the word function. Except for this detail, the syntax of the call does not differ from the call to an intrinsic function.
- A **function** is built in a way similar to the construction of a program, except that where we use the word program we would instead use the word function. We would then have **function-id** and **end function** rather than **program-id** and **end program**.

Complete

1. Reference modification enables the programmer to _____ a group of bytes in a field rather than the _____ field.

2. In reference modification, we must always specify the _____ _____.

3. In reference modification, we need not always specify the _____ of bytes to be transferred.

4. A reference modified field is implicitly _____.

5. Reference modified fields may not be used in _____ operations.

6. If reference modified data is moved to an alphanumeric destination, alignment will be on the _____.

7. If we have a reference modified numeric destination field, alignment will be on the _____.

8. When applying reference modification to a table entry, the reference modification comes _____ the subscript.

9. The data type to which we may apply reference modification is _____.

10. You have defined a field pic 9(6), with the value 54321. The first byte contains the value ____.

11. If the value 48.55 were being returned by an intrinsic function the function would be of type _____.

12. When using _____ intrinsic functions we generally use the move verb.

13. The integer-of-day intrinsic function is of type _____.

14. When invoking a programmer-created function, we do not use the keyword _____.

True/False

1. We may not move a reference modified source to a packed destination.

2. When data is moved to a reference modified numeric field it will align on the right.

3. We may not reference modify a packed field

4. A packed field may not serve as a destination for a reference modified source.

5. We may omit the starting position in **reference modification** as long as we do not omit the number of bytes.

6. We may omit the number of bytes in **reference modification**.

7. If the starting position is omitted in **reference modification**, it's as if a starting position of one had been specified.

8. If the field is eight bytes long, starting position is four and number of bytes has not been specified, four bytes would be transferred.

9. In a programmer-created **function** we do not code the word function.

10. The **function** must have the returning clause in the procedure division statement.

11. The item returned may be defined in the **working-storage** section.

12. The last line of code in the function is exit function.

13. When compiling the function we need a compiler directive to update the repository.

14. If the seed for the random function is always the same, the same random number will be returned each time.

15. Numeric functions return an integer variable.

Exercises

Given the following field definitions, provide the value of the receiving field after each move.

```
01  value-fields.
    05  W-Val1      pic X(5)     value 'ABCDE'.
    05  W-Val2      pic X(5)     value '12345'.
    05  W-Val3      pic 9(7)     value 7777777.
    05  W-Val4      pic 9(5)     value 12345.
```

1. move W-Val1(2:3) to W-Val2   _____

2. move W-Val1(3:2) to W-Val2   _____

3. move W-Val1(2:) to W-Val2   _____

4. move W-Val1(2:3) to W-Val2(2:3)   _____

5. move W-Val3(3:3) to W-Val2   _____

6. move W-Val3(3:3) to W-Val4   _____

7. move W-Val3(3:3) to W-Val4(2:3)   _____

8. move W-Val3(3:3) to W-Val4(2:)   _____

9. move W-Val1(2:4) to W-Val2   _____

10. move W-Val1(2:4) to W-Val2(1:4)   _____

11. move W-Val1(2:4) to W-Val2(1:)   _____

12. move W-Val1(2:2) to W-Val2(2:2)   _____

13. move W-Val1(2:2) to W-Val2(2:3)   _____

14. move W-Val3(1:3) to W-Val4(2:3)   _____

15. move W-Val3(1:3) to W-Val4   _____

16. move W-Val3(4:) to W-Val4   _____

Chapter 17
Program Calling

Topics Covered

- Program Calling
- Dynamic Calls
- Calling by Reference, by Content or by Value
- On Exception
- Size
- Initial Programs
- Cancel
- Returning
- The Entry Statement
- Summary
- Complete
- True/False
- Exercises

Program Calling

Programs may be large or small. What a program should not be is very large. Very large programs, as you can imagine, are difficult to maintain. Also when compiling they take longer to compile and although that may be the least of our worries, it is no advantage. As you will see, object orientation takes this a step further. We have seen that we try to create routines that are cohesive, meaning they satisfy only one function. We can then say that when we create a program that we will later call, we will group in it associated functions. Another advantage is that different programmers may each be given a program to code. This will speed up the coding process and the application may be finished earlier.

When we want to have recourse to a particular program, we call it. Like a faithful dog, it will generally respond to our call. As can be seen, invoking a program is not altogether different from invoking a routine. We can say that called programs and subroutines are related, say, like cousins. Let us see how we invoke a routine and a program respectively:

Invoking a subroutine: `perform B100-calcint`

Invoking a program: `call 'calcint'`

The **perform** will cause the named routine to be executed. When the last instruction in the routine has been executed, execution will return to the first instruction following the **perform**.

The **call** will cause the named program to be executed. When the program returns execution to the calling program, execution will be resumed at the first instruction following the call.

For a start, where the two differ, is in the way data are passed. For a **perform** no data need to be passed. When calling a program, if the called program needs to use data that are in the calling program, the data have to be passed. It follows that the called program is able to see only the data that it defines.

When you call a program:

- If you are naming the program, the name must be enclosed in inverted commas.
- For an IBM mainframe, the name must not be more than eight characters because of JCL constraints.
- The name of the program must follow the rules for program name formation. The name of the program in the call is the name in the **program-id** in the called program. For the sake of coherence, you should make the program name and the file name the same. Of course the program name does not have the extension.

Program Calling – Format 1

```
call 'progname' using ...
```

Figure 17.01

The following code calls a program and passes data to it:

Calling a Program and Passing Data

```
01  calc-data.
    05  W10-capital      pic S9(5).
    05  W10-period       pic S9(2).
    05  W10-rate         pic S9(2)V9
    05  W10-interest     pic S9(5).

    call 'calcint' using W10-capital
                         W10-period
                         W10-rate
                         W10-interest
```

Figure 17.02

We passed the data, and to do so we employed the **using** clause. Following the using clause, we name the fields we are going to send. Note that the called program does not know what names we gave to the fields it will be receiving. Remember, another programmer may be coding the called program and, most probably, she won't know what names you gave to the fields you are passing.

There is one thing the other programmer has to know, that is, in what sequence the fields are being passed. She knows what she needs from you, namely, capital, period, and rate. The information that needs to pass between you and the other programmer is the sequence in which the fields will be passed as well as the types to which the fields belong and length and format of the fields. Note that you also need to pass the field in which the called program will place the result.

It is obvious from the coding, that we decided to pass the fields in the sequence capital, period, rate and interest earned. Interest earned is the field that will receive the value calculated by the called program. Let us now see what our called program will look like.

In called programs, data that pass between programs must be defined in the **linkage section**. The **linkage section** follows the **working-storage** section. We see then, that in the **data division**, sections are defined in the sequence:

357

- File section
- Working-storage section
- Linkage section

In the preceding calling program we passed 05 fields. When received, 05 fields must be defined as level 01 or as level 77 fields. IBM mainframes are word machines and level 01 data are aligned on a double word. Subordinate 05 levels will start anywhere in the 01 level field to which they are subordinated. The receiving program will not know where 05 level fields start. Level 01 and level 77 all start on a double word, so we define our fields at level 01 or level 77, otherwise the program will not compile. The following code shows the code in the called program. Notice that we have not shown the whole program.

Called Program

```
Working-storage section.
linkage section.

01  LS10-capital     pic S9(5).
01  LS10-period      pic S9(2).
01  LS10-rate        pic S9(2).
01  LS10-interest    pic S9(5)V99.
procedure division   using LS10-capital
                           LS10-period
                           LS10-rate
                           LS10-interest.
A100-start.
    compute LS10-interest =
            LS10-capital * LS10-period * LS10-rate / 100
    exit program.
```

Figure 17.03

Notice that the fields have different names. The first field passed was W10-capital the field received was LS10-capital. The important thing is that they both refer to the same data. The procedure division is the point at which the program receives control and that is where we specified the **using** clause. From the names we can see that the fields are in the appropriate sequence.

To return control to the calling program we specified the **exit program** statement. If you had specified **stop run** both programs would have stopped running. You have a choice; you can either code **exit program** or **goback**. On execution the calling program would display:

```
The interest is: 15000.00
```

Normally we do not pass subordinate fields. In our example all the fields were together. This is possible but unusual; what is usual is that the data we need to pass are scattered over several 01 fields. Rather than pass a number of level 05 fields, we move the data to a level 01 field we have defined for the purpose and pass the 01.

Data Definitions

```
01   time-categ.
     05 cat               pic 9    occurs 5.

01   rates.
     05  disc             pic S9(2)V9.
     05  inter            pic S9(2)V9.
     05  spec             pic S9(2)V9.

01   cust-data.
     05   cust-no         pic 9(5).
     05   cust-name       pic x(35).
     05   cust-cap        pic S9(5).
     05   cust-cat        pic S9(2).

01   W10-calc-data.
     05  W10-capital      pic S9(5)        value 50000.
     05  W10-period       pic S9(2)        value 2.
     05  W10-rate         pic S9(2)V9      value 15.
     05  W10-interest     pic S9(5)V99.
```

Figure 17.04

This last level 01, W10-calc-data, is the item that we are going to pass across to the called program. Before we do this we need to move the data across. We will do that now:

Moving Data to Be Passed

```
move cust-cap to W10-capital
move cat (cust-cat) to W10-period
move inter to W10-rate
move 0 to W10-interest
call 'calcint' using W10-calc-data
```

Figure 17.05

Notice that we passed the 01 level. This means that in the called program we need to make similar adjustments.

Calling Program

```
program-id. Chapter1703.
working-storage section.
01   time-categ value '24689'.
     05 cat           pic 9 occurs 5.
01   cust-data.
     05  cust-no          pic 9(5).
     05  cust-name        pic x(35).
     05  cust-cap         pic S9(5) value 50000.
     05  cust-cat         pic S9(2) value 1.
01   rates.
     05  disc             pic S9(2)V9.
     05  inter            pic S9(2)V9    value 15.
     05  spec             pic S9(2)V9.
01   W10-calc-data.
     05  W10-capital      pic S9(5)    value 50000.
     05  W10-period       pic S9(2)    value 2.
     05  W10-rate         pic S9(2)V9 value 15.
     05  W10-interest     pic S9(5)V99.
01   result               pic Z(5).99.
procedure division.
A100-start.
     move cust-cap to W10-capital
     move cat (cust-cat) to W10-period
     move inter to W10-rate
     move 0 to W10-interest
     call 'c:\cobnet\calcint' using W10-calc-data
     move W10-interest to result
     display  "The interest is: " result
     stop run.
```

Listing 17.03

It often happens that difficulties arise when testing calling and called programs. The reason for this is that fields passed and fields received might not be in the same sequence. This is another advantage of passing a single 01 level. If necessary you can compare the two 01 levels from calling and called programs to ensure that the subordinate fields in both are in the same sequence. Another point to bear in mind is that the definitions in both must be the same. If a field has one decimal in one and two decimals in the other there will be a problem. Similarly, if on the one side a field is packed and on the other it is display, there will be difficulties. Fields defined in the linkage section and which precede these erroneous definitions will be correct, but those defined after will be in error because the displacements will be incorrect. For example, a field is defined 9(7) comp-3 and the other 9(7). Assuming the first one is correct, the definitions following the erroneous definition will be displaced three additional bytes.

Called Program

```
program-id. calcint.
linkage section.
01  LS10-calc.
    05  LS10-capital      pic S9(5).
    05  LS10-period       pic S9(2).
    05  LS10-rate         pic S9(2)V9.
    05  LS10-interest     pic S9(5)V99.
procedure division  using LS10-calc.
A100-start.
    compute LS10-interest =
            LS10-capital * LS10-period * LS10-rate / 100

    goback.
```

Listing 17.04

Dynamic Calls

The type of call we have been looking at is described as a static call. In this call, when the program is compiled we already know which is the program we wish to call. For this reason the programs will be link-edited together and loaded into storage as one unit.

Dynamic Calls – Format 2

```
display 'Enter path and program name: '
accept progname
call progname using ...
```

Figure 17.06

We will use the **dynamic call** when, at compile time, we do not know which program we will be calling. One of the advantages of **dynamic calls** is that storage will only be required when the program is called. The disadvantage is that the called program has to be loaded into storage when the calling program is running, thus slowing down execution at the time of the first call.

The following code shows only the relevant statements:

Dynamic Call

```
01   prog-name              pic X(17).

     display 'Please enter program name and path'
     accept prog-name
     call prog-name using W10-calc-data
```

Figure 17.07

Calling by Reference, by Content or by Value

When we pass data between programs the **stack** is used. The stack is an item of dynamic storage that grows and shrinks at execution time. When a program is called and data is passed, the calling program will obtain a **stack frame**. On the stack frame you will find the following:

- The address of the preceding stack frame
- The address of this frame
- Addresses of data that are being made available to the called program
- Data that are passed

When the called program returns control to the calling program, the stack frame is released. The stack pointer will now point to the preceding stack frame.

Passing by **reference** is the default. When we pass by reference, what is passed is the address of the field. Changes done to the field in the called program will be reflected in the field in the calling program, because the changes are being applied at the same address.

When we pass **by content,** we are implying that the changes done to the data in the field must not be reflected in the corresponding field in the calling program. Note that when we specify **by content** it is still the address of the data that are being placed on the stack.

We may also pass **by value**. When we specify **by value**, what is placed on the stack is the actual data. As in the case of passing by content, any changes to the data are not reflected in the corresponding fields in the called program.

Passing Data – Format 3

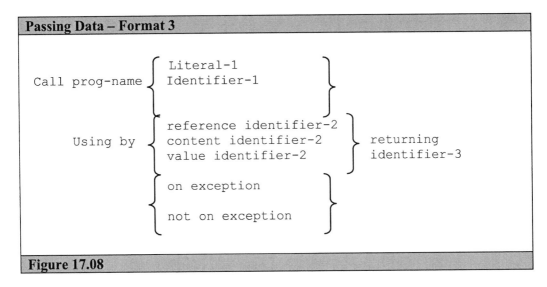

Figure 17.08

The listings that illustrate the use of the clauses follow. You will notice that what is passed by value or by content is not changed. The field passed by reference, did change as expected.

Ways of Calling

```
program-id. Chapter1705.

working-storage section.
01  W10-amt1       pic S9(5)    value 15000.
01  W10-amt2       pic S9(1)    value 2.
01  W10-result     pic S9(5)    value 19876.
procedure division.
A100-start.
    call 'c:\cobnet\passdata' using by value W10-amt1
                                    by content W10-amt2
                                    by reference W10-result
    display   "Amount1    is: " W10-amt1
    display   "Amount2    is: " W10-amt2
    display   "W10-result is: " W10-result
    stop run.
```

Listing 17.05

The called program follows:

Receiving Data

```
program-id. passdata.

linkage section.
01  LS10-amt1          pic S9(5).
01  LS10-amt2          pic S9(1).
01  LS10-result        pic S9(5).
procedure division  using by value LS10-amt1
                          by content LS10-amt2
                          by reference LS10-result.

A100-start.
    compute LS10-result = LS10-amt1 * LS10-amt2
    add 10000 to LS10-amt1
    add 5     to LS10-amt2
    goback.
```

Listing 17.06

Command Prompt
```
Amount1    is:  15000+
Amount2    is:  2+
W10-result is:  30000+
```

On Exception

If the call is unsuccessful the program will terminate abnormally unless we cater for it by coding an **on exception** clause. The programmer should always, to the extent possible, avoid abnormal termination. If the situation has a certain degree of unpredictability then the use of **on exception** is recommended.

To avoid abnormal termination there is also an **on overflow** clause that detects an exception. The **on overflow** does not have a matching **not on overflow** so we were forced to use the stop run. If we did not stop the run the program would have executed the code that should execute only if the call had been successful. It stands to reason that if **on exception** is considerably better, there is no reason to use **on overflow**; we show it simply because you may encounter it in earlier programs.

The following listing depicts the **procedure division** of the preceding calling program. In it we have incorporated the **on exception** condition.

On Exception

```
call 'c:\cobnet\passdat' using by value W10-amt1
                               by content W10-amt2
                               by reference W10-result
    on   exception
        display 'Call unsuccessful'
    not on exception
        display  "Amount1    is: " W10-amt1
        display  "Amount2    is: " W10-amt2
        display  "W10-result is: " W10-result
 end-call
```

Figure 17.09

Size

We may also pass a literal to a called program. To pass a literal across, we need to specify by value. We must then indicate how much storage the literal is to occupy. We do this by using the **size clause**. In the called program you need to specify a binary field of the appropriate size. We have changed the program and passed the value 15000 with a size of two. In the called program we defined a binary-short field to receive the data.

Using Size

```
    program-id. Chapter1707.
    working-storage section.
    01  W10-amt2         pic S9(1)    value 2.
    01  W10-result       pic S9(5)    value 19876.
    procedure division.
    A100-start.
        call 'c:\cobnet\passdata' using by value 15000 size 2
                                    by content  W10-amt2
                                    by reference W10-result
        display  "Amount2    is: " W10-amt2
        display  "W10-result is: " W10-result
        stop run.
```

Listing 17.07

The called program would be:

Receiving a Literal

```
program-id. passdata.
linkage section.
01   LS10-amt1                    binary-short.
01   LS10-amt2         pic S9(1).
01   LS10-result       pic S9(5).
procedure division   using by value LS10-amt1
                           by content LS10-amt2
                           by reference LS10-result.
A100-start.
    compute LS10-result = LS10-amt1 * LS10-amt2
    add 5      to LS10-amt2
    goback.
```

Listing 17.08

Initial Programs

An **initial** program is one so described by the attribute **initial** in the program-id paragraph of the identification division. An **initial** program has its **working-storage** fields that have been initialized, re-initialized each time the program is called.

Initial Program – Format

```
program-id. Init01 is initial.
```

Figure 17.10

Fields that have not been initialized using the value clause will be initialized to some arbitrary value.

The listings that follow illustrate the operation of the initial attribute. The result of execution provides proof that things happened as expected.

Calling Initial Program

```
program-id. Chapter1708.
working-storage section.
01  W10-name1          pic X(5)     value 'Kong'.
01  W10-name2          pic X(5)     value 'Levi'.


procedure division.
A100-start.
   call 'c:\cobnet\Init' using by reference W10-name1 W10-name2
   call 'c:\cobnet\Init' using by reference W10-name1 W10-name2
     stop run.
```

Listing 17.09

An Initial Program

```
program-id. Init is initial.
Working-storage section.
01  W10-name1          pic X(5) value 'King'.
01  W10-name2          pic X(5).
linkage section.
01  LS10-name1         pic X(5).
01  LS10-name2         pic X(5).


procedure division  using by reference LS10-name1 LS10-name2.
A100-start.
    display 'Name1 is: ' W10-name1
    move LS10-name1 to W10-name1
    display 'Name1 is: ' W10-name1
    display 'Name2 is: ' W10-name2
    move LS10-name2 to W10-name2
    display 'Name2 is: ' W10-name2
    goback.
```

Listing 17.10

367

```
Name1 is: King
Name1 is: Kong
Name2 is:
Name2 is: Levi
Name1 is: King
Name1 is: Kong
Name2 is:
Name2 is: Levi
```

Cancel

The **cancel** statement will terminate execution of the called program and release the storage it previously occupied. Any files open at the time of the **cancel** will be closed before termination. The next call will cause the program to be loaded once more.

The advantage that the **cancel** has over the **initial** is that the fields will only be reinitialized when the program is cancelled and not on every call. The disadvantage is that the program must be reloaded after every **cancel**. The **cancel** can only be issued on programs that have been dynamically called.

The listings that follow illustrate the use of the **cancel** statement:

Calling a Program That Uses Cancel

```
program-id. Chapter1711.
working-storage section.
01  W10-amt1            pic S9(3)    value 150.
01  prog-name          pic x(17)    value 'c:\cobnet\cancel1'.

procedure division.
A100-start.
    perform 3 times
        call prog-name using by reference W10-amt1
    end-perform
    cancel 'c:\cobnet\cancel1'
    call prog-name using by reference W10-amt1
    stop run.
```

Listing 17.11

Called Program – Uses Cancel

```
program-id. Cancel1.
Working-storage section.
01  W10-amt1          pic S9(3) value 0.
01  W10-ctr           pic S9(3) value 0.
linkage section.
01  LS10-amt1         pic S9(3).

procedure division  using by reference LS10-amt1.
A100-start.
    add LS10-amt1 to W10-amt1
    add 1 to W10-ctr
    display 'Call: ' W10-ctr '  W10-amt1 is: ' W10-amt1
    goback.
```

Listing 17.12

```
Command Prompt
Call: 001+ W10-amt1 is: 150+
Call: 002+ W10-amt1 is: 300+
Call: 003+ W10-amt1 is: 450+
Call: 004+ W10-amt1 is: 150+
```

Returning

We may use the **returning** clause to have the called program return a value. The returning clause must be specified in the call statement. Following the **returning** clause, you will specify the field that will receive the value returned. The field returned must be an elementary field.

```
call prog-name using by reference W10-amt1
                returning W10-amt2
```

In the called program, for the return to take effect, we specify the **returning** in the **goback** or **exit program** statement:

```
goback returning W10-amt2.
```

The listings that follow depict both calling and called programs.

369

The Returning Clause

```
program-id. Chapter1713.
working-storage section.
01  W10-amt1        pic S9(3)    value 150.
01  W10-amt2        pic S9(3)    value 750.
01  prog-name       pic X(17)    value 'c:\cobnet\Return1'.

procedure division.
A100-start.
    call prog-name using by reference W10-amt1
                            returning W10-amt2
    display 'W10-amt2  is: ' W10-amt2
    display 'New value is: ' W10-amt1
    stop run.
```

Listing 17.13

The Returning Clause

```
program-id. Return1.
working-storage section.
01  W10-amt2        pic S9(3).
linkage section.
01  LS10-amt1       pic S9(3).

procedure division  using by reference LS10-amt1.
A100-start.
    multiply 3 by LS10-amt1
    move 950 to W10-amt2
    exit program returning W10-amt2.
```

Listing 17.14

```
c:\ Command Prompt                                    _ □ ✕
W10-amt2  is: 950+
New value is: 450+
```

There is a register, the **return-code register,** that is generally used to return the status of execution. You could return zero to indicate that execution was successful or a

370

code of one to indicate that it was not. We will modify the preceding program to use the **return code**. We return a value of 64.

Return Code

```
program-id. Chapter1715.
working-storage section.
01  W10-amt1          pic S9(3)    value 150.
01  prog-name         pic X(17)    value 'c:\cobnet\Return2'.

procedure division.
A100-start.
    call prog-name using by reference W10-amt1
                          returning return-code
    display 'Value of return-code is: ' return-code
    if   return-code = 64
        display 'New value is: ' W10-amt1
    end-if
    stop run.
```

Listing 17.15

Returning the Return-code

```
program-id. Return2.
linkage section.
01  LS10-amt1         pic S9(3).

procedure division  using by reference LS10-amt1.
A100-start.
    multiply 3 by LS10-amt1
    move 64 to return-code
    goback returning return-code.
```

Listing 17.16

```
Command Prompt                                    _ □ ×
Value of return code is: +00000064
New value is: 450+
```

The Entry Statement

The **entry** statement enables us to provide more than one entry point into a called program. In the absence of an entry statement, execution always starts with the first instruction in the procedure division. We then need selection statements to determine the processing to be done. The following example does not use entry statements and instead uses if statements to select appropriate processing.

We need to pass across to the called program what we have called the op-code. The **op-code** determines what must be done.

- Op-code is 1 – load table.
- Op-code is 2 – buying operation.
- Op-code is 3 – selling operation.

Because there is only one **entry** point, the procedure division, we need to pass the same arguments irrespective of whether or not they are required by the operation. Thus, we pass the table every time, even though this is not required in the 'buy' and 'sell' operations.

Call Without Using Entry Statement

```
identification division.
program-id. Currency1.

working-storage section.
01   Conversion-rates value
     'BSTG12681215US$$08680823EURO08080752'.
     05   rates            occurs 3 times.
          10   cur-code  pic X(4).
          10   cur-buy   pic 99V99.
          10   cur-sell  pic 99V99.
01   tran-value           pic S9(4) value 1000.
01   tran-curr            pic  X(4) value 'EURO'.
01   op-code              pic  S9.

procedure division.
    display 'Loading conversion rates.'
    move 1 to op-code
    call 'convert1' using op-code
         conversion-rates tran-curr tran-value
    move 2 to op-code
```

Listing 17.17 – 1 of 2

Call Without Using Entry Statement

```
      call 'convert1' using op-code
            conversion-rates tran-curr tran-value
      display 'Value of purchase of 1000 Euros: ' tran-value
      move 3 to op-code
      move 1000 to tran-value
      call 'convert1' using op-code
            conversion-rates tran-curr tran-value
      display 'Value of sale of 1000 Euros: ' tran-value
      stop run.
```

Listing 17.17 – 2 of 2

Call Without Using Entry Statement

```
   identification division.
   program-id. Convert1.

   working-storage section.
   01  w-rates              occurs 3 times.
       05  w-cur-code       pic  X(4).
       05  w-cur-buy        pic  99V99.
       05  w-cur-sell       pic  99V99.
   01  w-sub                pic S9.
   linkage section.
   01  op-code              pic  S9.
   01  rates                pic  X(12) occurs 3 times.
   01  tran-curr            pic  X(4).
   01  tran-value           pic S9(4).

   procedure division using op-code rates tran-curr tran-value.
   A100-start.
       if  op-code = 1
           display 'Convert. Loading array'
           perform varying w-sub from 1 by 1
               until w-sub > 3
                   move rates(w-sub) to w-rates(w-sub)
           end-perform
```

Listing 17.18 – 1 of 2

Call Without Using Entry Statement

```
        else
            if   op-code = 2
                perform buy
            else
                perform sell
            end-if
        end-if
        exit program.

    buy.
        perform varying w-sub from 1 by 1
            until tran-curr = w-cur-code(w-sub)
        end-perform
        compute tran-value = tran-value * w-cur-buy (w-sub).

    sell.
        perform varying w-sub from 1 by 1
            until tran-curr = w-cur-code(w-sub)
        end-perform
        compute tran-value = tran-value * w-cur-sell (w-sub).
```

Listing 17.18 – 2 of 2

Every time we call we need to provide an appropriate op-code. In the first call, the called program will load the table. In subsequent calls it does nothing with the table that is passed because it already has the data.

What the **entry** statement does is to provide an **entry** point for each of the functions to be executed. You may ask how the system finds the entry points. If it looks in the library it will not find the entry points, but it will find them if the called program is already loaded.

Notice that the first call is to the program name and this will cause the program to be loaded. The subsequent calls will be successful because the system will look for the **entry** points in the loaded called program. In the next example we will be using the **entry** statement. You will see that a more elegant solution will result.

Entry Points

```
identification division.
program-id. Currency2.
working-storage section.
01   Conversion-rates value
     'BSTG12681215US$$08680823EURO08080752'.
     05   rates           occurs 3 times.
          10   cur-code   pic X(4).
          10   cur-buy    pic 99V99.
          10   cur-sell   pic 99V99.
01   tran-value           pic S9(4) value 1000.
01   tran-curr            pic X(4) value 'EURO'.
procedure division.
     display 'Loading conversion rates.'
     call 'convert2' using conversion-rates
     call 'buy' using tran-curr tran-value
     display 'Value of purchase of 1000 Euros: ' tran-value
     move 1000 to tran-value
     call 'sell' using tran-curr tran-value
     display 'Value of sale of 1000 Euros: ' tran-value
     stop run.
```

Listing 17.19

The calling program has been reduced in size. We no longer need an op-code, so there is no need to set it and to pass it when calling. In addition, we are only passing the arguments that are required by the particular function.

When calling the program we only pass the table. For the other **entry** points we pass the currency to be used in the transaction and the amount of the transaction.

Using the Entry Statement

```
identification division.
program-id. Convert2.
working-storage section.
01   w-rates              occurs 3 times.
     05   w-cur-code      pic X(4).
     05   w-cur-buy       pic 99V99.
     05   w-cur-sell      pic 99V99.
```

Listing 17.20 – 1 of 2

Using the Entry Statement

```
01   w-sub                pic S9.
linkage section.
01   rates                pic  X(12) occurs 3 times.
01   tran-curr            pic  X(4).
01   tran-value           pic S9(4).

procedure division using rates.
A100-start.
     display 'Convert2. Loading array'
     perform varying w-sub from 1 by 1
         until w-sub > 3
             move rates(w-sub) to w-rates(w-sub)
     end-perform
     exit program.

entry 'buy' using tran-curr tran-value.
     perform varying w-sub from 1 by 1
         until tran-curr = w-cur-code(w-sub)
     end-perform
     compute tran-value = tran-value * w-cur-buy (w-sub).
     exit program.

entry 'sell' using tran-curr tran-value.
     perform varying w-sub from 1 by 1
         until tran-curr = w-cur-code(w-sub)
     end-perform
     compute tran-value = tran-value * w-cur-sell (w-sub).
     exit program.
```

Listing 17.20 – 2 of 2

```
Command Prompt                                    _ □ ×
Loading conversion rates.
Convert2. Loading array
Value of purchase of 1000 Euros: 8080+
Value of sale of 1000 Euros: 7520+
```

You see that the **if** is no longer required, resulting in a simpler, more streamlined solution.

Summary

- We have learned to break our programs, through functional decomposition, into easy-to-handle cohesive routines. We now take things a step further and split the tasks so that each task may be handled by a separate program. In this scenario there will be a managerial program that calls on the services of other programs.

- The verb that is used to invoke a sub-program is the **call** verb. The verb is followed by the name of the program. If we need to pass variables, these are provided following the using clause. (Call 'subprog1' using field1 field2). In the called program, the data that is received is defined in the linkage section.

- The name of the program to be called may be specified using a literal. This will give rise to a **static call**. In static calls, the called program is link-edited together with the calling program; thus forming one unit for loading. If the name of the program to be called is specified using a field name, the call will be dynamic. In the case of a **dynamic call** the program will only be loaded when it is first called.

- To define data to be passed under a 01 level field, do the same as in the linkage section. In this way it is easy to compare passed and received fields and ensure that the definitions agree in all respects.

- Data may be passed by **reference**, by **content** or by **value**. When data are passed by reference it is the address of the data that is passed; a change to the variable by the called program will change the data in the source. When data are passed by content it is an address that is passed but the source data may not be changed. When data are passed by value, it is a copy of the data that is passed.

- To handle situations where the **call** is not successful we code the **on exception/not on exception** clauses. Subordinated to the clauses we place the statements that are appropriate for the required action.

- When passing a numeric literal we have to pass the size argument so that the receiving program may know what to expect.

- An **initial** program has its variables reset to the initializing values every time it is called. Variables that have not been initialized will be set to some arbitrary value. The initial keyword is used following the program name.

- The **cancel** statement will cause the called program to terminate. Before terminating, however, it will close all open files. The next call will cause the program to be loaded once more. The cancel can only be used on dynamically called programs.

- The **returning** clause enables the called program to return a field from its **working-storage**. The code will be: exit program returning work1. The call must also include the returning clause specifying the receiving field.

- The **entry** statement enables the creation of multiple entry points into the called program. For the entry points to be located the called program must be in storage when the entry point is called.

Complete

1.   Large programs are difficult to _____.

2.   The _____ clause is required to pass as well as to receive data.

3.   Data at the source are changed when the called program changes a field passed by _____.

4.   Data are not changed at the source when the called program changes a field passed by _____ or by _____.

5.   In passing a numeric literal we need to use the _____ keyword.

6.   In the static call, called and calling programs are _____ _____ together.

7.   In the case of a dynamically called program, the program is loaded when the program is _____ _____.

8.   We specify: call field-name using… in the case of a _____ _____.

9.   Received items are defined in the _____ _____.

10.   If the call to a program is not successful we should take the __ _____ exit.

11.   A program will be an initial program when the word initial follows the _____ _____.

12.   An initial program will have all initialized variables re-initialized every time the _____ is _____.

13.   The cancel will terminate a _____ _____ program.

14.   A cancelled program will be loaded once more when the program is _____.

15.   The returning clause in a called program is coded following _____ _____.

True/False

1.   A program is only able to see the data it defines.
2.   The data that pass between called and calling programs must have the same name in called and calling programs.
3.   Fields passed must be in the same sequence in called and calling programs.
4.   Unless data are returned they cannot be used by the calling program.
5.   If a level 05 field is passed it must be defined in the linkage section as a level 05.
6.   For control to revert to the calling program we code goback or exit-program.
7.   We use the dynamic call when at compile time we know the name of the program to be called.
8.   The default is passing by reference.
9.   **On exception** and **on overflow** do very much the same thing.
10.   The **initial** keyword causes data to be reinitialized on the first call.
11.   The **cancel** keyword causes data to be reinitialized on the first call.
12.   The files in a cancelled program will be closed before termination.
13.   A return code of zero generally indicates an error.
14.   The entry statement provides multiple entry points.
15.   For the entry to take effect the program must already be loaded.
16.   When there is only one entry point all the arguments are passed whether needed or not.
17.   We may not code the returning clause in the procedure division statement of a called program.

Exercises

1.   You are to write a program that will invoke a function that you have created. The function returns the date in the format YYYYMMDD. Prompt the user to enter a date in the same format. Pass the two dates to a program that returns the difference between the two dates.

2.   Write a program that passes two numeric variables by value. The program receiving the two variables multiplies them and returns the result. Also pass the literal 'Good One' and display it. Now pass the literal 'Good One!' by value and note the results.

Chapter 18

External

Topics Covered

- ❏ External Objects
- ❏ Run Unit
- ❏ The External Clause
- ❏ The External Clause in the File Section
- ❏ The External Clause and the Redefines
- ❏ Nested Programs
- ❏ Containing and Contained Programs
- ❏ Directly and Indirectly Contained Programs
- ❏ Common Programs
- ❏ The Global Clause
- ❏ The Global Clause and the Redefines
- ❏ Summary
- ❏ Complete
- ❏ True/False
- ❏ Exercises

External Objects

In a typical COBOL program data definitions are visible, and therefore available, to the whole program. The inconvenience of this situation is that if a data item becomes adulterated, it is difficult to ascertain which of the routines is the one at fault. C made it possible to define data that are local to the function or routine. If the data become adulterated, the function at fault could only be the function in which the data were defined. You can see that this feature would considerably enhance program maintenance. Object Orientation takes things even further along this route.

Run Unit

You will often come across the term **run unit**. For our purposes, a run unit consists of all the programs that will execute together in a job step. This means the root program and all called programs.

The External Clause

So far, all our storage definitions have resided in the program that uses those definitions. We may refer to these definitions as being internal. COBOL 85 introduced another level of storage, namely, storage that is **external** to the program. Such storage is associated with the run unit rather than with any particular program in the run unit.

This means that if we have a root program and a set of called programs, all these programs may access external storage. All the programs in the run unit have access to the storage but none of the programs owns the storage; it is external.

As indicated, all data defined in a COBOL program are visible to the whole program. This, as you know, makes program maintenance more difficult. In introducing external storage we have increased the maintenance load.

With external storage, if an item of data is adulterated, the culprit routine may be in any of the programs in the run unit. If we are not to increase complexity then, ideally, we should restrict the use of external storage to **read only** storage. If such storage is only used to obtain information but not to change it, then complexity is not increased.

Bearing in mind what has been said, we will look at ways of defining **external** storage. It stands to reason that if two programs have access to external storage they both need to know the format of the external data. This means that both programs must have definitions for the data. The definitions in the two programs must be identical in all respects.

External Data

```
program-id. Chapter1801.
working-storage section.
01  W10-ext-data is external.
    05  W10-ext-id              pic X(06).
    05  W10-ext-description     pic X(25).
program-id. Ext01.
working-storage section.
01  W10-ext-data is external.
    05  W10-ext-id              pic X(06).
    05  W10-ext-description     pic X(25).
```

Figure 18.01

We see that the names and pictures are identical and both definitions have been described as external. Note the following points:

- The **external** clause in **working-storage** may only be specified at 01 level.
- For two programs in the run unit to have access to external storage they need only have identical definitions and use the **external** clause at 01 level
- Data items subordinated to an item containing the **external** clause are themselves external.
- The value clause may not be specified for an item containing the external clause or for any item subordinated to it.
- Any item defined in the linkage section is always regarded as internal.

We have used a calling and a called program to illustrate the use of the external clause.

External Storage

```
program-id. Ext01.
working-storage section.
01  W10-ext-data is external.
    05  W10-ext-id              pic X(06).
    05  W10-ext-description     pic X(25).
```

Listing 18.01 – 1 of 2

External Storage

```
procedure division.
A100-start.
    move 'XK120' to W10-ext-id
    move 'Vintage sports car.' to W10-ext-description
    call 'Ext02'
    display 'Id is: ' W10-ext-id
    display 'Description is: ' W10-ext-description
    exit program.
```

Listing 18.01 – 2 of 2

Called Program

```
program-id. Ext02.
working-storage section.
01  W10-ext-data is external.
    05  W10-ext-id            pic X(06).
    05  W10-ext-description   pic X(25).
procedure division.
A100-start.
    display 'Id is: ' W10-ext-id
    display 'Description is: ' W10-ext-description
    move 'SLK320' to W10-ext-id
    move 'Mercedes Benz sports car.' to W10-ext-description
    exit program.
```

Listing 18.02

```
Command Prompt                                      _ □ ×
Id is: XK120
Description is: Vintage sports car.
Id is: SLK320
Description is: Mercedes Benz sports car.
```

The External Clause in the File Section

The **external** clause may also be applied to the **FD** in the file section. All the programs with identical definitions may access the record or records, defined under the FD. These programs do not need to open the file or to read it. In the examples you will notice that although the called programs close the file, the file record area remains available exactly because it is external.

External

```
program-id. Chapter1803.
    select ext-file assign to "extdata".
fd  ext-file is external.
01  ext-rec                pic X(11).
    perform  3 times
        call 'Ext03'
        call 'Ext04'
        display 'Chapter 16 calling: ' ext-rec
    end-perform
    stop run.
```

Listing 18.03

Called Program – File Is External

```
program-id. Ext03.
    select ext-file assign to "extdata".
fd  ext-file is external.
01  ext-rec                pic X(11).
working-storage section.
01  W10-time               pic 99/99/99/99.
    open output ext-file
    perform A200-get-time
    close ext-file
    goback.
A200-get-time.
    accept W10-time from time
    write ext-rec from W10-time.
```

Listing 18.04

Called Program – File Is External

```
program-id. Ext04.
    select ext-file assign to "extdata".
fd   ext-file is external.
01   ext-rec            pic X(11).
Procedure division.
    open input ext-file
    perform A200-get-time
    close ext-file
    exit program.

A200-get-time.
    read ext-file
    display "Time is: " ext-rec.
```

Listing 18.05

We have earlier indicated that we may, though not according to the standard, leave out statements described as red tape statements. In the preceding listing we left out all division headers and section headers. The **file-control** paragraph was also left out. COBOL has for many years been attacked for being very verbose. As can be seen, this need not be so. We will usually keep the red tape statements because they might be needed in certain environments.

If you have a **file section** and a **working-storage** section you will need the working-storage header, otherwise the working-storage definitions will fall under the file section, which is not what you would want.

The External Clause and the Redefines

The **external** clause may not be specified in the statement containing the **redefines** clause. If the external clause is applied to the field that is being redefined, then both definitions, redefined and redefining, will be external.

If the redefined item is not external, it stands to reason, that the redefining item, which occupies the same storage, may not be external either. The following examples illustrate the use of **external** and the **redefines**:

Both Level 01 are External

```
01   cust-area is external.
     05   cust-id          pic  X(05).
     05   cust-name        pic  X(35).
     05   cust-amt         pic S9(05)V99   comp-3.
01   cust-info redefines cust-area.
     05   cust-location    pic  X(25).
     05   cust-discount    pic S9(02)V9    comp-3.
     05   cust-phone       pic  X(11).
     05                    pic  X(06).
```

Figure 18.02

The redefined item is not **external,** therefore, the redefining item may not be **external**. The code is illegal.

External and the Redefines

```
01   cust-area.
     05   cust-id          pic  X(05).
     05   cust-name        pic  X(35).
     05   cust-amt         pic S9(05)V99   comp-3.
01   cust-info redefines cust-area is external.
     05   cust-location    pic  X(25).
     05   cust-discount    pic S9(02)V9    comp-3.
     05   cust-phone       pic  X(11).
     05                    pic  X(06).
```

Figure 18.03

Nested Programs

COBOL 85 introduced the possibility of having programs within programs. Such programs are described as nested programs. One important aspect of nested programs is that the nesting program cannot see into the nested program. You will recall that we said earlier that in COBOL data are **global**. Global data are data that are visible to the whole program. With nested programs we have data that are not visible to the nesting program. We can describe such data as **local**.

387

Containing and Contained Programs

A program having a nested program is a **containing** program. The nested program is referred to as a **contained** program. A **containing** program knows that it has a **contained** program. A **contained** program is not aware of being contained.

The implication of these statements is that the **containing** program may call on the services of the **contained** program. The **contained** program, however, is unable to call on the services of the **containing** program; it cannot see it. The following diagram depicts the relationship:

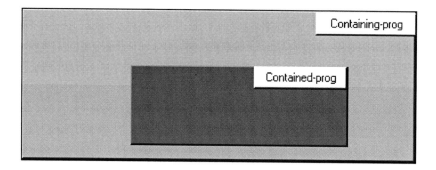

Directly and Indirectly Contained Programs

The fact that program B is a contained program does not mean that it may not benefit from having its own nested programs. Let us assume that program B is contained by program A and that it contains program C. We would then say that program A **directly contains** program B and **indirectly contains** program C. Program B, in turn, directly contains program C.

Graphically represented we have:

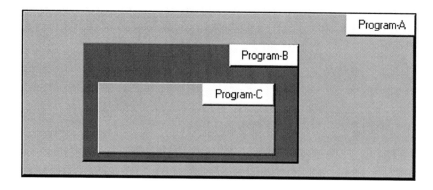

- Program-A directly contains Program-B.
- Program-A indirectly contains Program-C.
- Program-B directly contains Program-C.

Common Programs

The description of **common** does not carry any moral connotations but refers instead to its degree of visibility by other contained siblings. The following may then be said with respect to the visibility of a common program.

A common program is one that, being a contained program, may be called by:

- The program that directly contains it.
- Programs directly contained by the program directly containing it.
- Programs indirectly contained by the program directly containing it

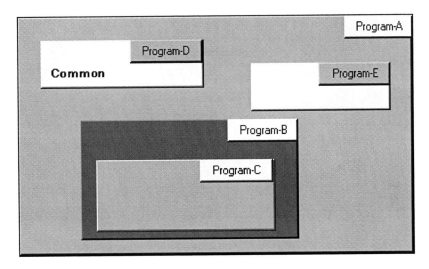

Program	May Call	Reason
Program-A	Program-B Program-D Program-E	Directly contained programs and besides Program-D is common
Program-D	May not call	Has no contained programs
Program-B	Program-C Program-D	Program-C is contained and Program-D is common
Program-C	Program-D	Because it is common
Program-E	Program-D	Because it is common
Table 16.01 – Possible calls of nested programs		

When calling **nested** programs the using clause needs to be specified unless you have specified the external clause and consequently have **external** data. In the example following, we do not pass any data but use the **external** clause:

Nested Program

```
program-id. Chapter1806.
01   temp-conversion is external.
     05   temp-sw          pic 9.
     05   temp-value       pic S9(5)V99.
01   temp                  pic Z(5).99.

procedure division.
A100-start.
    display 'To convert from Fahrenheit to Celsius enter 1'
    display 'To convert from Celsius to Fahrenheit enter 2'
    display 'Enter code: ' no advancing
    accept temp-sw
    display 'Enter temperature: ' no advancing
    accept temp-value
    call 'convert'
    move temp-value to temp
    if  temp-sw = 1
        display 'Temperature in Celsius: ' temp
    else
        display 'Temperature in Fahrenheit: ' temp
    end-if
    stop run.
* * * * * * * * * * * * * * * * * * * * * * * * * * * * * *
program-id. convert.
01   temp-conversion is external.
     05   temp-sw          pic 9.
     05   temp-value       pic S9(5)V99.
procedure division.
A100-start.
    if  temp-sw = 1
        compute temp-value = (temp-value - 32) * 5 / 9
    else
        compute temp-value = temp-value * 9 / 5 + 32
    goback.
end program convert.
* * * * * * * * * * * * * * * * * * * * * * * * * * * * * *
end program Chapter1801.
```

Listing 18.06

The program prompts for a code and a temperature. Depending on the code entered, the conversion will be from Celsius to Fahrenheit or in the reverse direction. Notice the following points:

- No fields are passed because they are defined as external.
- The program ends on the **end program** statement. The statement is the last statement in the program. It must end on a period.
- The last statement in the containing program is also an **end program** statement.
- We have enclosed the nested program convert, in rows of asterisks.
- We have removed most of the red tape statements, leaving only procedure division and the first paragraph.
- Notice that because there is no file section we did not need a working-storage header.
- The linkage section header is required if there are linkage section items. This is because there is no way of ensuring the item is a linkage section item rather than a working-storage item.
- Nested programs do not allow the use of the **returning** clause.
- If the **goback** or **exit program** is the last statement in the paragraph it must end on a period.

```
To convert from Fahrenheit to Celsius enter 1
To convert from Celsius to Fahrenheit enter 2
Enter code: 2
Enter temperature: 37
Temperature in Fahrenheit:      98.68
```

The following example has two levels of nesting. There is a 'getrec' nested program and, inside it, we have nested 'gettime':

Directly and Indirectly Contained Programs

```
program-id. Chapter1807.
01   cars.
     05   model            pic X(6).
     05   description      pic X(25).
01   ed-start-time         pic 99/99/99/99.
01   ed-end-time           pic 99/99/99/99.
```

Listing 18.07 – 1 of 3

Directly and Indirectly Contained Programs

```
procedure division.
A100-start.
    perform until model = high-values
        call 'getrec' using by reference cars
                                        ed-start-time
                                        ed-end-time
        if  model not =  high-values
            display 'Start time is: ' ed-start-time
            display model ' ' description
            display 'End time is  : ' ed-end-time
        end-if
    end-perform
    stop run.
**********************************
program-id. getrec.
    select cars-file assign to "c:\cob0\cardata".
fd  cars-file.
01  cars-rec            pic X(31).
working-storage section.
01  W10-sw             pic 9  value 0.
linkage section.
01  LS-cars.
    05  LS-model        pic X(6).
    05  LS-descrition   pic X(25).
01  LS-start-time       pic 99/99/99/99.
01  LS-end-time         pic 99/99/99/99.

procedure division using by reference LS-cars
                                      LS-start-time
                                      LS-end-time.

A100-start.
    if  W10-sw  = 0
        open input cars-file
        move 1 to W10-sw
    end-if
    call 'gettime'  using by reference LS-start-time
    perform Z100-read-rout
```

Listing 18.07 – 2 of 3

Directly and Indirectly Contained Programs

```
        if  cars-rec = high-values
            move high-values to LS-model
            close cars-file
        else
            move cars-rec to LS-cars
            call 'gettime' using by reference LS-end-time
        end-if.
        goback.

    Z100-read-rout.
        read cars-file
            at end move high-values to cars-rec.
    *++++++++++++++++++++++++++++++++++++
    program-id. gettime.
    linkage section.
    01  LS-Time              pic 99/99/99/99.
    procedure division using by reference LS-time.
        accept LS-time from time
        goback.
    end program gettime.
    *+++++++++++++++++++++++++++++++++++
    end program getrec.
    ***********************************
    end program Chapter1807.
```

Listing 18.07 – 3 of 3

The following points should be noted:

- In program Chapter1807 we iterate until the nested program signals that all records have been read. On return, the results are displayed. We need to place the display inside a test equivalent to a test for end of file. When the read detects end of file it moves high-values to cars-rec.

- In the nested program 'getrec' we need to ensure that we open the file only once, so a test is used.

- We call on the second level nested program 'gettime' to get the time before the read. The record is then read and 'gettime' is called once more to obtain the time after the read.

- In obedience to the principles of cohesion we have been following, we have created a paragraph to handle the read.

- The second level nested program 'gettime' merely gets the time into the linkage section field and returns.

393

- The end program statement for 'gettime' follows.
- The next statement is the end program header for the containing program 'getrec'. The program is also a contained program.
- The higher level containing program 'Chapter1807' now issues its own end program statement.

The execution follows:

```
Command Prompt

Start time is: 08/47/00/17
XK120    Jaguar vintage car.
End time is: 08/47/00/17
Start time is: 08/47/00/20
SLR320   Merceds Benz sports car.
End time is: 08/47/00/20
Start time is: 08/47/00/21
Z4       BMW sports car.
End time is: 08/47/00/21
Start time is: 08/47/00/21
Megane   Cabriolet
End time is: 08/47/00/21
Start time is: 08/47/00/21
S70      Volvo Tourer
End time is: 08/47/00/21
```

As indicated, an important advantage of nested programs is that the data defined in their **working-storage** are local to the program and cannot be changed by the enclosing program or programs. You will have noticed that by reducing the number of red tape statements COBOL's traditional verbosity is reduced to a very acceptable level.

In the next example we will be reading records from an employee file. The nested program that reads from the file also contains a program that returns the date. It also calls on the services of a common program 'getrate', which returns a rate. The rate is multiplied by the basic salary to produce a final salary, which is the value that is returned to the calling program Chapter1808 .

The first task undertaken by the containing program Chapter1808 is to invoke nested program 'putrate', which obtains rates from the console passing them to the common program 'getrate', which loads them into a table.

The graphic representation will look like this:

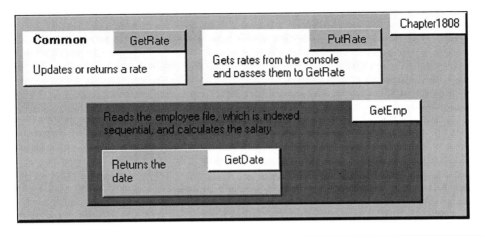

Using a Common Program

```
program-id. Chapter1808.
01   emps.
     05   emp-key              pic X(5).
     05   emp-name             pic X(15).
     05   emp-salary           pic ZZZ,ZZ9.99.
     05   emp-date             pic 9999/99/99.
01   W10-sw                    pic XX.
procedure division.
A100-start.
     call 'putrate'
     display 'Enter employee key: ' no advancing
     accept emp-key
     perform until emp-key = 'xxxxx'
         call 'getemp' using by reference emp-key
                                          emp-name
                                          emp-salary
                                          emp-date
                                          W10-sw
         if  W10-sw  =  '00'
             display 'Employee name is: ' emp-name
             display 'Employee salary: ' emp-salary ' 'emp-date
         end-if
         display 'Enter employee key: ' no advancing
         accept emp-key
     end-perform
     stop run.
```

Listing 18.08 – 1 of 4

Using a Common Program

```
* * * * * * * * * * * * * * * * * * * * * * * * * * * * * * * * * *
   program-id. putrate.
   01  W20-rate                pic 9V9 value 5.5.
   01  W20-code                pic 9 value 9.
       display 'Entering 5 codes.'
       perform 5 times
           display 'Enter code: ' no advancing
           accept W20-rate
           call 'getrate' using by content W20-code W20-rate
       end-perform
       goback.
   end program putrate.
* * * * * * * * * * * * * * * * * * * * * * * * * * * * * * * * * *
   program-id. getrate is common.
   01  rate-tab.
       05  rate        pic 9V9 occurs 5.
   01  ctr             pic 9 value 0.
   linkage section.
   01  LS-emp-code     pic 9.
   01  LS-rate         pic 9V9.
   procedure division using by reference LS-emp-code LS-rate.
       if  LS-emp-code = 9
           add 1 to ctr
           move LS-rate to rate (ctr)
       else
           move rate (LS-emp-code) to LS-rate
       goback.
   end program getrate.
* * * * * * * * * * * * * * * * * * * * * * * * * * * * * * * * * *
   program-id. getemp.
       select emp-file assign to "c:\cobnet\empdata"
           organization is indexed
           access is random
           record key is emp-key
           file status is W50-status.
   fd  emp-file.
   01  emp-rec.
       05  emp-key         pic X(05).
       05  emp-name        pic X(15).
       05  emp-code        pic 9.
       05  emp-basic       pic 9(4).
```

Listing 18.08 – 2 of 4

Using a Common Program

```
working-storage section.
01   W50-status              pic XX.
01   W10-sw                  pic 9 value 0.
01   W20-rate                pic 9V9.
linkage section.
01   LS-key                  pic X(05).
01   LS-name                 pic X(15).
01   LS-salary               pic ZZZ,ZZ9.99.
01   LS-date                 pic 9999/99/99.
01   LS-sw                   pic XX.


procedure division using by reference LS-key
                                      LS-name
                                      LS-salary
                                      LS-date
                                      LS-sw.

A100-start.
    if  W10-sw  = 0
        open input emp-file
        move 1 to W10-sw
    end-if
    call 'getdate'  using by reference LS-DATE
    move LS-key to emp-key
    perform Z100-read-rout
    move W50-status to LS-sw
    if  W50-status = '00'
        move emp-name to LS-name
        call 'getrate'  using by reference emp-code W20-rate
        compute LS-salary = W20-rate * emp-basic
        call 'getdate'  using by reference LS-date
    end-if.
    goback.


 Z100-read-rout.
    read emp-file
        invalid key
            display 'Read error, status is: ' W50-status
    end-read.
```

Listing 18.08 – 3 of 4

Using a Common Program

```
*++++++++++++++++++++++++++++++++++++
  program-id. getdate.
  Linkage section.
  01  LS-date            pic 9999/99/99.
  procedure division using by reference LS-date.
     accept LS-date from date yyyymmdd
     goback.
  end program getdate.
  *+++++++++++++++++++++++++++++++++++
  end program getemp.
  ********************************
  end program Chapter1808.
```

Listing 18.08 – 4 of 4

We used an indexed sequential file that we accessed randomly. As you will re-call, the key must be defined in the file section. We can only read once the key value of the desired record has been moved to the key in the file section. Access of an indexed sequential file is through the index, so in the select we indicate the organization as in-dexed.

Assuming the following relationship exists between the files, what programs have access to the common program Prog-E?

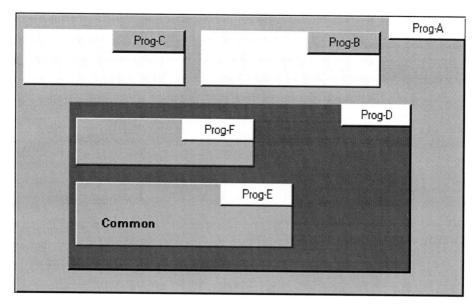

Because the program is directly contained by Prog-D, it is not visible to other programs with the exception of Prog-F, which is also contained by Prog-D, the program that also contains the common program.

The Global Clause

You may have fields that are needed by all, or nearly all, of the nested programs. In such a case you may define these fields attaching the global clause to them. **Global fields** must be defined in containing programs to be visible by all contained programs. Assume you have the following situation:

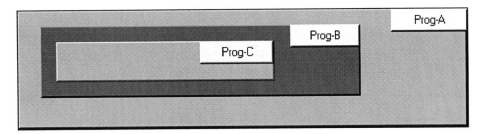

Visibility is as follows:

- If the **global** field is defined in Prog-A, it will be visible in Prog-B and Prog-C.
- If the **global** field is defined in Prog-B, it will be visible in Prog-C.
- It would be pointless to define a **global** field in Prog-C because it contains no nested programs.

We can then say that a **global** field will be visible in the program in which it is defined and all directly or indirectly contained programs. Definitions of **global** fields follow:

```
01  emp-area      is global.
    05  emp-id        pic X(3).
    05  emp-sal       pic 9(5).
```

If the group field is **global** its subordinates will also be global.

```
01  emp-area          pic X(3)    is global.
```

An elementary field may also be described as **global**.

```
01  emp-area          pic X(3) value 'X10'  is global.
```

The value clause may be applied to a **global** field.

399

In **working-storage** and in the linkage section, the **global** clause may only be applied at 01 level. In the file section it can be specified at 01 level or in the FD.

```
fd   emp-file is global.
```

or

```
01   emp-rec is global.
     05  emp-key               pic X(05).
     05  emp-name              pic X(15).
     05  emp-code              pic 9.
     05  emp-basic             pic 9(4).
```

If the **global** clause is specified at the FD level, I/O operations may be carried out in directly and in indirectly contained programs.

The Global Clause and the Redefines

The **global attribute** operates independently between object redefined and subject redefining. Thus, if you only want the object to be **global,** specify the **global** attribute for the object. If the property is required for the subject, specify it for the subject. If we want the property to apply to both, specify **global** at both levels. The following example illustrates this situation:

The Global Clause

```
01   car-make is global.                    (Object)
     05  make              pic X(15).
     05  model             pic X(10).
01   car-details  redefines car-make is global. (Subject)
     05  no-cyl            pic 99.
     05  registration      pic X(10).
     05  engine-no         pic X(10).
     05                    pic X(3).
```

Figure 18.04

Summary

- The run unit consists of all the programs, root and called programs, that together constitute an entity.

- The **external** clause enables us to specify storage that is not associated with a particular program but rather with all the programs in the run unit. By specifying that the data are **external** it may be referenced by any of the programs in the run unit.

- Every program needs to have a definition of the external storage to be able to reference it. The definitions must be identical in every program that references the storage.

- In **working-storage** the external keyword may only be used at level 01. Data defined in the linkage section are always internal.

- If **external** is specified for an FD all the programs with identical definitions will be able to access the record area without opening the file or reading the record.

- If a field is redefined and it contains the **external** clause, then both redefined and redefining fields will be external. Specifying **external** for the redefining field only is illegal.

- A **containing** program may call on the services of a directly **contained** program but not on the services of an indirectly **contained** program.

- A **common** program may be called by the program that directly contains it, or by any of the **common** program siblings, or by programs contained by any of its siblings.

- A **global** field is visible by any program lower in the containing hierarchy.

- The **global** clause may only be specified in the working-storage section and the file section at level 01. In the file section it may also be specified in the **FD**. If specified in the **FD**, directly and indirectly contained programs may perform I/O operations on the file.

Complete

1.   For the external clause to function, all programs must have _____ definitions of the external data.

2.   The external clause may only be specified at level___.

3.   The _____ clause may not be specified for a field bearing the external clause.

4.   An item defined in the linkage section is seen as _____.

5.   A 05 item subordinated to a 01 defined as external is also _____.

6.   An external item may be defined in the _____ section and the _____ section

7.   If the external clause is applied to a field that has been redefined, the redefining field is _____ **external**.

8.   A program which has a nested program is a _____ program.

9.   An indirectly contained program is not seen by the _____ _____ program.

10. A common program is accessible by its _____ and by any programs these may _____.

11. Nested programs are precluded from using the _____ clause.

12. If we want other programs lower in the containing hierarchy to see a variable we define it using the keyword _____.

13. The global keyword may be used in the _____ section and in the _____ section

14. If the global clause is specified in the FD, contained programs may _____I/O.

True/False

1. In the **linkage** section, the external clause may be specified at level 77.
2. To pass external fields to a contained program the **using** clause is required.
3. The **goback** or exit program must always end on a period.
4. We may use the **global** keyword at level 01 in the linkage section.
5. If a redefined field is **external**, the redefining field will also be **external**.
6. In the **working-storage** section the **external** clause may be specified at level 05 as well as level 01.
7. The **value** clause may not be specified for an **external** field.
8. If the **external** clause is specified in the FD, other programs may access the I/O area but we must first open the file.
9. A common program may only be accessed by its siblings and not by programs they contain.
10. When using the **returning** clause in a nested program, the clause must be specified in the procedure division header.
11. The fields to which the **global** clause is applied will be visible to all containing and contained programs.
12. The **global** clause must be defined at level 01 in the file section or in the FD.
13. The **global** clause may be specified in the working-storage section but not in the linkage section.
14. When using the global clause in the case of redefinition it applies independently to the item for which it is specified.
15. If the global clause is specified in the FD, directly and indirectly contained programs may perform I/O on the file.

Exercises

1. Write a program that processes a file that is defined as external. The program will call another program that writes to the file and also call a program that will read from the file.

2. Create a group field and then another group field that redefines the first one. Code the external so that both group fields will be **external**.

3. Code a nested program that returns the time of day. Every time the nested program is called it will add one to field Counter. Attempt to access the field Counter from the containing program.

Chapter 19
String and Unstring

Topics Covered

- The String Statement
- The Pointer Option
- The Overflow Option
- The Unstring Statement
- Delimiter In and Count In
- Pointer Option
- Tallying Option
- On Overflow
- Summary
- Complete
- True/False
- Exercises

The String Statement

The **string** verb enables us to concatenate a mixture of strings and literals. We earlier looked at the concatenation operator (&) that allows us to concatenate two strings. Furthermore, we can only concatenate literals. These limitations on the concatenation operator are overcome by the **string** verb, a powerful instruction not easily equaled by other languages.

String Verb – Format 1

```
string field-1
       literal-1
       field-2    delimited by '*'
       literal-2
       field-3    delimited by size
   into field-4
end-string
```

Figure 19.01

- Transfer starts on the left and proceeds byte by byte

- The source may be alphabetic, alphanumeric or numeric. If numeric, it must be of usage display because there must be one character per byte.

- We may transfer all or only some of the bytes in the field. The **delimited by** clause is used to control the transfer of characters to the concatenated destination.

- When we wish to transfer only part of a field, we use the **delimited by** clause to specify the character or characters that will control the transfer. Transfer will proceed until the specified character or characters are encountered.

- **Delimited by size** is the default. When using the default, spaces on the right will not be transferred. To transfer spaces on the right, delimited by size needs to be specified explicitly.

- The receiving field may be a group field or an elementary field.

- When a **delimiter** is specified, it will apply to the field for which it is specified as well as to all preceding fields in the list for which a delimiter was not specified. It is important to bear this point in mind because otherwise the results may sometimes appear to be inexplicable.

- If the receiving field is too small to receive the data, the data will be truncated.

- If the receiving field is longer than the data transferred, the bytes following the last byte transferred will remain unchanged.

- A numeric field may serve as a source field as long as it does not contain decimals.

Using the String Verb

```
program-id. Chapter1901.

01   emps.
     05   emp-key            pic X(5)      value 'AB010'.
     05   emp-name           pic X(15)     value 'Bertrand Russel'.
     05   emp-salary         pic 999,999.99 value 9312.55.
     05   emp-date-hire      pic X(10)     value '2004/09/25'.
01   out-string              pic X(50).

procedure division.
A100-start.
     string  emp-key  delimited by size
             " "
             emp-name delimited by ' '
             " "
             emp-salary delimited by '.'
             " "
             emp-date-hire delimited by '/'
     into    out-string
     display 'String is: ' out-string
     stop run.
```

Listing 19.01

We have transferred fields and interspersed literals containing spaces to produce the following output:

```
c:\ Command Prompt                              _ □ ×
String is: AB010Bertrand  009,312  2005
```

The following example illustrates two of the points to which you have been alerted:

- We see that, although we have a literal containing spaces following the emp-key field (the first field to be displayed), the spaces that follow are not displayed. The first delimited by clause encountered specifies delimited by spaces - this is the reason why the spaces following emp-key will not be displayed. When examining the literal, the **string** finds a space and stops - the space is the delimiter so the literal containing spaces is not displayed.

- As indicated, concatenation is secured by carrying out the transfer byte by byte, from source to destination until all data have been transferred or the destination field is full. The significant factor here is that data are transferred byte by byte until all data have been transferred, then the operation ends. This implies that bytes that did not receive data will remain as they were. If the receiving field is longer than the source data, the bytes that did not receive data will remain unchanged. For this reason it is suggested that spaces be moved to the destination field prior to the execution of the **string**.

Unused Bytes In the Receiving Field

```
program-id. Chapter1902.
01  emps.
    05  emp-key          pic X(7)     value 'AB010'.
    05  emp-name         pic X(15)    value 'Bertrand Russel'.
01  out-string           pic X(40)    value all '*'.
procedure division.
A100-start.
    string  emp-key
            " "
            emp-name delimited by ' '
    into    out-string
    display 'String is: ' out-string
    stop run.
```

Listing 19.02

Command Prompt

```
String is: AB010Bertrand*****************************
```

When does the concatenation operation of the **string** statement end? It ends when:

- All bytes to be transferred have been transferred; **or**
- The destination field has no more available bytes.

What if the specified delimiter is not present in the field? The default delimited by size is taken. If we specify a literal as the last element to be concatenated then the delimited by size clause will apply by default. Consider the following example:

Delimited by Size

```
program-id. Chapter1903.
01   W10-languages.
     05   W10-language-1     pic X(10)     value 'Chinese'.
     05   W10-language-2     pic X(10)     value 'English'.
     05   W10-language-3     pic X(10)     value 'Italian#'.
01   out-string             pic X(35)     value all ' '.

procedure division.
A100-start.
     string  W10-language-1 delimited by ' '
             "!"
             W10-language-2 delimited by size
             "!"
             W10-language-3 delimited by '#'
             "!"
     into    out-string
     end-string
     display 'String is: ' out-string
     stop run.
```

Listing 19.03

```
C:\ Command Prompt                                    _ □ ✕
String is: Chinese!English  !Italian!
```

The Pointer Option

The **pointer** option enables us to stipulate the position, in the destination field, at which the transfer should start. The field to be used as the **pointer** must be defined as an integer field able to contain a value equal to the size of the destination field plus one. Thus, if the destination field is 99 bytes long, the pointer field must be able to contain 100. The field used as the **pointer** is incremented by one every time a byte is placed in the destination. After the 99th byte is transferred the **pointer** will be incremented by one so, even if you only want to transfer 99 bytes you must cater for a counter able to hold three digits.

String Verb – Format 2

```
string field-1
       literal-1
       field-2    delimited by '*'
       literal-2
       field-3    delimited by size
into   field-4
       with pointer W10-pointer
```

Figure 19.02 – Pointer Option

The following example illustrates the use of the **pointer** option. We wish to centre the output in the destination field. From the length of the destination field we subtract the length of the data to be output. For centering we divide the value obtained by two.

Pointer Option

```
program-id. Chapter1904.

01  W10-heading.
    05  W10-data    pic X(23 value 'The Student Marks Report'.
    05  W10-pointer pic 9(2).
    05  W10-date    pic 9999/99/99.
    05  out-string  pic X(80)value all ' '.

procedure division.
```

Listing 19.04 – 1 of 2

Pointer Option

```
A100-start.
    accept W10-date from date yyyymmdd
    compute W10-pointer =(80 - (5 + function length (W10-date)
                            + function length (W10-data))) / 2
    string  W10-data delimited by size
            "     "
            W10-date
    into    out-string
        with pointer W10-pointer
    end-string
    display out-string
    stop run.
```

Listing 19.04 – 2 of 2

Points to note:

- If the programmer has specified the pointer option it is up to the programmer to initialize the pointer to the appropriate value prior to the execution of the **string** statement.

- Initialize the destination field to spaces before execution of the **string** statement.

- If there is **overflow** on the **pointer** field, transfer of data will stop. Assume the destination field is 120 bytes and the pointer has been defined as pic 99. When the value in the **pointer** is incremented from 99 to 100, the transfer of data will stop. Once transfer stops, execution will proceed with the first instruction following the **string**.

The Overflow Option

The **overflow** exit will be taken when the value in the **pointer** is greater than the size of the receiving field or becomes zero. If the destination field is filled and there is still data to transfer, the overflow exit will be taken if one is specified. If the **overflow** option is not specified, execution will proceed with the first instruction following the **string**.

411

On Overflow

```
string field-1
       literal-1
       field-2   delimited by '*'
       literal-2
       field-3   delimited by size
  into   field-4
  with pointer W10-pointer
  on overflow
     perform Z100-string-overflow
  not on overflow
     perform C100-execute
  end-string
```

Figure 19.03

We have doctored the example so as to produce overflow. You will notice that the destination field is smaller than the combined source fields. The on overflow condition will be triggered causing the appropriate action to be taken.

On Overflow

```
program-id. Chapter1905.
01  W10-heading.
    05  W10-data     pic X(23)value 'The Student Mark Report'.
    05  W10-pointer  pic 9(2).
    05  W10-date     pic 9999/99/99 value '20041025'.
    05  out-string   pic X(25).
procedure division.
    move 0 to W10-pointer
    move spaces to out-string
    string   W10-data delimited by size   "      "
             W10-date
       into out-string
       with pointer W10-pointer
       on   overflow      display 'Field too small.'
       not on overflow  display out-string
     end-string
     stop run.
```

Listing 19.05

The Unstring Statement

Whereas the string verb brings a number of separate strings together, the unstring verb breaks up a **string** into a number of separate strings. We see then that the **unstring** does the exact opposite of the string.

When coding the **string** statement we said: "Transfer data until a given delimiter is encountered then go on to another field and do the same'. We now say something not altogether different. We say: 'Transfer data from a given source to a specified destination until a given delimiter is found, then carry on transferring data from the same source but now to a new destination'. This process will be repeated until all the data have been transferred or there are no more fields to receive the data.

Unstring – Format 1
| ```
unstring source-field
        delimited by '*#' or '*' or '\n'
    into destination-1
        destination-2
        destination-3
end-unstring
``` |
| **Figure 19.04** |

Literals specified as delimiters must be alphanumeric and must therefore be enclosed in inverted commas. The delimiter may also be a figurative constant including **all 'literal'**. When we use **all 'literal'** multiple occurrences of the literal are treated as one, five spaces will be treated as a single delimiter rather than five delimiters each leading to a different destination. The following line of code uses figurative constants:

```
...delimited by zeros or spaces or all '*'
```

The following points regulate the operation of the **unstring**.

- All fields participating in the operation must be defined implicitly or explicitly, as **usage is display**.

- When a receiving field is numeric, it may contain decimals. Notice, however, that there is no way of specifying a decimal point in the source; the decimal positions in the destination will then contain zeros.
```

- The source field may be alphanumeric or numeric.

- The delimiter may be a literal or a field name.

- The **delimited by** clause may be omitted. If omitted, data will be transferred until the destination field is full, then proceed to the next destination field.

- **Delimited by** '   ' will treat two spaces as the delimiter. If we provide four spaces in succession in the date, this will mean two delimiters in succession.

- A maximum of 255 delimiters may be specified.

- As illustrated in the preceding line of code, the connector between delimiters is the **or**.

- Notice that the **delimited by size** option that is provided with the **string** is not available with the **unstring**. You will agree that in the case of the **unstring**, the clause would not make much sense.

The Unstring

```
program-id. Chapter1906.
01  W20-data              pic X(30) value '1234:2345:3456:4567:'.
01  W30-numbers.
     05  W30-num1         pic 9(4).
     05  W30-num2         pic 9(4)V99.
     05  W30-num3         pic 9(4)V99.
     05  W30-num4         pic 9(4).

procedure division.
A100-start.
     unstring W20-data delimited by ':'
        into W30-num1
             W30-num2
             W30-num3
             W30-num4
     end-unstring
     display W30-num1 '  ' W30-num2 '  ' W30-num3 '  ' W30-num4
     stop run.
```

Listing 19.06

414

Notice that the data end on the specified delimiter. If the data end on some other delimiter, the results will be unpredictable. If the last item in the data is alphanumeric, there is no problem because any bit configuration is alphanumeric. Two of the receiving fields have been defined with decimals. In the output the decimal positions will contain zeros. If the number of digits were greater than four, there would be truncation on the left.

```
Command Prompt                                          _ □ ×
1234   234500   345600   4567
◄                                                       ► 
```

The following example does not use delimiters. The decision to proceed with transfer to the following field is determined by the size of the receiving field. If the receiving field is full, transfer will proceed to the next field.

Absence of Delimiters

```
program-id. Chapter1907.
01  W20-data              pic X(30) value '1234234534564567'.
01  W30-numbers.
    05  W30-num1          pic 9(4).
    05  W30-num2          pic 9(4).
    05  W30-num3          pic 9(4).
    05  W30-num4          pic 9(4).
procedure division.
A100-start.
    unstring W20-data
      into W30-num1
           W30-num2
           W30-num3
           W30-num4
    end-unstring
    display W30-num1 '  ' W30-num2 '  ' W30-num3 '  ' W30-num4
    stop run.
```

Listing 19.07

```
Command Prompt                                          _ □ ×
1234   2345   3456   4567
◄                                                       ► 
```

The following lines of code illustrate the use of two spaces in succession as a delimiter. In such a situation we are precluded from using the figurative constant spaces.

Spaces as Delimiters

```
01  W20-data                 pic X(30) value'This is a   story'.
01  W30-numbers.
    05  W30-string1     pic X(10).
    05  W30-string2     pic X(10).
    unstring W20-data delimited by '  '
        into W30-string1
              W30-string2
    end-unstring
```

Figure 19.05

The **unstring** differs from the **string** in that bytes that do not receive data in the destination fields will be space filled. In the following example we will show multiple delimiters:

Unstring

```
program-id. Chapter1908.
01  W20-data        pic X(30) value 'Chinese*English#Italian!'.
01  W30-numbers.
    05  W30-lang1  pic X(10).
    05  W30-lang2  pic X(10).
    05  W30-lang3  pic X(10).
procedure division.
A100-start.
    unstring W20-data delimited by '*' or '#' or '!'
       into W30-lang1  W30-lang2 W30-lang3
    end-unstring
    display W30-lang1 display W30-lang2 display W30-lang3
    stop run.
```

Listing 19.08

```
Command Prompt                              _ □ ✕
Chinese
English
Italian
```

416

Delimiter in and Count in

Delimiters may be used to indicate the nature of the data they are delimiting. When this happens, it would be convenient to be able to isolate the delimiter and from it determine the data just transferred. The **delimiter in** clause enables us to name the field that is to receive the delimiter. Just as the delimiter must be alphanumeric so the field that receives the delimiter must be alphanumeric.

Sometimes it is also convenient to know how many bytes have been transferred into a field. The **count in** clause will do this and place the count into the named field. The field must be a numeric integer field. The two clauses must be specified in the sequence shown, namely **delimiter in** followed by **count in**. The listing depicts the use of both clauses:

Delimiter In and Count In

```
program-id. Chapter1909.
01  W20-data            pic X(30) value
                            'Chinese*English#Italian!'.
01  W30-numbers.
    05  W30-lang1        pic X(10).
    05  W30-lang2        pic X(10).
    05  W30-lang3        pic X(10).
01  W40-delimiters.
    05  W40-delim1       pic X.
    05  W40-delim2       pic X.
    05  W40-delim3       pic X.
01  W50-counts.
    05  W50-count1       binary-short.
    05  W50-count2       binary-short.
    05  W50-count3       binary-short.
procedure division.
A100-start.
    unstring W20-data delimited by '*' or
                                   '#' or
                                   '!'
        into W30-lang1 delimiter in W40-delim1
                       count in W50-count1
             W30-lang2 delimiter in W40-delim2
                       count in W50-count2
             W30-lang3 delimiter in W40-delim3
                       Count in W50-count3
    end-unstring
```

Listing 19.09 – 1 of 2

Delimiter In and Count In

```
display W30-lang1 '  ' W40-delim1 '  ' W50-count1
display W30-lang2 '  ' W40-delim2 '  ' W50-count2
display W30-lang3 '  ' W40-delim3 '  ' W50-count3
stop run.
```

Listing 19.09 – 2 of 2

```
Command Prompt                                    _ □ ✕
Chinese     *   +00007
English     #   +00007
Italian     !   +00007
```

Pointer Option

Although, in general, we will start the **unstring** from the beginning of the field, this is not always the case. Sometimes records contain header information in which we are not interested for purposes of the **unstring**. The **pointer** option enables us to specify where we should start in the field we are splitting. The default is that we start at the beginning of the field. If we want to override the default we have to use the **pointer** clause. Once we use the **pointer** clause, we have to set it to an appropriate value prior to execution of the **unstring**. The field that is to serve as a pointer is a programmer created field. As such, it is up to the programmer to ensure that when the field is used it will be in an appropriate state.

Using the Pointer Clause

```
program-id. Chapter1910.

01  W20-data            pic X(45) value
    'Time:1130,Date:040608Bugati*Ferrari#Maserati!'.
01  W30-numbers.
    05  W30-car1         pic X(10).
    05  W30-car2         pic X(10).
    05  W30-car3         pic X(10).
01  W40-pointer          pic 99.
```

Listing 19.10 – 1 of 2

Using the Pointer Clause

```
procedure division.
A100-start.
    move 22 to W40-pointer
    unstring W20-data delimited by '*' or '#' or '!'
        into W30-car1 W30-car2 W30-car3
            with pointer W40-pointer
    end-unstring
    display 'First car : ' W30-car1
    display 'Second car: ' W30-car2
    display 'Third car : ' W30-car3
    stop run.
```

Listing 19.10 – 1 of 2

```
Command Prompt                              _ □ ×
First car : Bugati
Second car: Ferrari
Third car : Maserati
```

The Tallying Option

After using the **unstring** you will have separated the data into a number of fields and pre-sumably will want to process them further. Sometimes the number of fields into which the data are split is always the same, but at other times it varies. When it varies, it would generally be convenient to know how many destination fields received data. The **tallying** option gives us the desired figure. In the following example we split the data into a variable length table. We then iterate through the table until we have exhausted the data in the table. You will have seen that to do this we need to know how many occurrences received data.

The Tallying Clause

```
program-id. Chapter1911.
01  W20-data                     pic X(52) value
    'Arabic$Bulgarian$Chinese$Dutch$English$French$German'.
01  W30-languages.
    05  W30-lang                 pic X(10) occurs 10
                                          depending on W30-count.
    05  W30-count                pic 99 value 0.
    05  W30-ctr                  pic 99 value 0.

procedure division.
A100-start.
    unstring W20-data delimited by '$'
        into W30-lang(1) W30-lang(2) W30-lang(3)
             W30-lang(4) W30-lang(5) W30-lang(6)
             W30-lang(7) W30-lang(8) W30-lang(9)
             W30-lang(10)
        tallying W30-count
    end-unstring
    perform varying W30-ctr from 1 by 1
        until W30-ctr > W30-count
            display 'Language is : ' W30-lang (W30-ctr)
    end-perform
    stop run.
```

Listing 19.11

```
Command Prompt
Language is: Arabic
Language is: Bulgarian
Language is: Chinese
Language is: Dutch
Language is: English
Language is: French
Language is: German
```

We can see that every time transfer to a field is initiated, the field named in the **tallying** clause is incremented by one.

On Overflow

As for the **string**, the **unstring** also has the **on overflow** facility, with the corresponding **not on overflow**. The exit specified will be taken when an exception condition is detected. The following situations will cause an exception condition to be detected.

- The **pointer** named in the **pointer** option contains a value less than one.

- The **pointer** contains a value that exceeds the length of the field named in the **unstring**.
- All fields have received data and not all data have been transferred

For an **on overflow** condition, there may be a **not on overflow** condition. If there is a **not on overflow** specified, then there must be an **on overflow** specified. Because **on overflow** is a condition, the unstring must end on **end-unstring**.

On Overflow

```
    program-id. Chapter1912 as "Chapter1912".

    data division.
    working-storage section.
    01  W20-data               pic X(52) value
        'Hungarian$Italian$Japanese$Korean$'.
    01  W30-languages.
        05  W30-lang1          pic X(10).
        05  W30-lang2          pic X(10).
        05  W30-lang3          pic X(10).

    procedure division.
    A100-start.
        unstring W20-data delimited by '$'
            into W30-lang1 W30-lang2 W30-lang3
                on  overflow
                    display "You should have been more careful."
                not on overflow
                    display 'Language is : ' W30-lang1
                    display 'Language is : ' W30-lang2
                    display 'Language is : ' W30-lang3
            end-unstring
            stop run.
```

Listing 19.12

Summary

- The **string** statement enables us to concatenate strings, literals and numeric fields. If the field is numeric it must be of type display because there must be one digit per byte. Furthermore, the numeric field must not contain decimals.

- We may concatenate part of a field by using the **delimited by** clause. Data will be transferred until the delimiter is found, then the **string** will progress to the next field.

- The **into** clause enables us to name the receiving field. Data will be transferred byte by byte from source fields to the destination. If, after all data have been transferred, there are still bytes in the destination that did not receive data, they will remain unchanged. For this reason it is advisable to move spaces to the destination field before execution of the **string**.

- The **string** is followed by a list of the fields to be concatenated. When the **delimited by** clause is coded for an item in the list, it is as if that **delimited by** clause had been coded for each of the preceding items in the list that did not carry the clause.

- The **pointer** option in the **string** statement enables us to specify where to start placing data in the destination field. The **pointer** field must be capable of holding the value for the position to which it will point plus one. It is up to the programmer to initialize the **pointer** field appropriately.

- The **overflow** option enables us to specify the action to be taken if the value in the **pointer** field exceeds the size of the receiving field or the receiving field is full and there is still data to be transferred.

- The **unstring** statement will transfer from a source field into one or more destinations. Transfer to one destination will proceed until a delimiter is encountered. Transfer will then continue, but on to a new destination. This process will continue until all data have been transferred.

422

■   The **pointer** option for the **unstring** statement will indicate the position in the source from which to start transferring data. It is up to the programmer to initialize the pointer field appropriately.

■   The **tallying** option provides a count of the number of fields that received data through the execution of the **unstring**.

■   Sometimes it is convenient to know which of the possible delimiters was involved. The **delimiter in** clause enables us to store the delimiter encountered.

■   The **count in** clause enables us to determine how many bytes were transferred into a field.

■   The **on overflow** clause enables us to specify what course of action to follow in the case of unsuccessful execution of the **unstring**. There is a corresponding **not on overflow** clause.

■   Overflow may be caused by one of the following:

   •   The pointer field contains a value less than one.
   •   The value in the pointer field exceeds the size of the source field.
   •   All fields have received data and there are still data to transfer.

Complete

1.   In the **string** statement transfer starts on the _____ and proceeds _____ by _____.

2.   If we string numeric data it must not contain _____.

3.   **Delimited by size** is the _____.

4.   If the field is too small to receive the data, the data will be _____.

5.   If the data to be transferred is 99 bytes, the pointer field must be able to hold the figure _____.

6.   It is up to the programmer to _____ the pointer field before using it.

7.   If there is _____ on the pointer field, transfer of data will stop.

8.   A value of _____ in the pointer field will cause overflow.

9.   If the pointer field has been defined as pic 99, a value of _____ will cause overflow.

10. All fields participating in the **string** or the **unstring** must have been defined implicitly or explicitly as usage is _____.

11. In the **unstring**, a receiving field may be numeric and contain _____.

12. If in the **unstring** a receiving field is numeric and contains decimals, the decimals will be _____.

13. **Count in** counts the _____ of _____ transferred.

14. In the **unstring**, the pointer option specifies the starting position in the _____ field.

15. The **tallying** option counts the _____ of _____ that received data.

16. A value of ____ in the pointer field will cause overflow.

True/False

1. The pointer option in the **string** enables us to stipulate from which point in the source field to start transferring.
2. A value of zero in the pointer field will cause overflow.
3. In the **unstring**, a receiving field may be numeric but may not contain decimals.
4. The **string** will accept a numeric field as long as it does not contain decimals.
5. In the **unstring** you may have one **delimited by** clause.
6. The **string** will concatenate a number of fields into a group or an elementary field.
7. In the **string** the delimited by applies only to the field for which it is specified.
8. The **overflow** exit will be taken for the string when the pointer field becomes one.
9. Literals specified as delimiters may be numeric or alphanumeric.
10. Delimited by '   ' will cause the **unstring** to treat two spaces as a delimiter.
11. Delimited by spaces will cause any number of spaces to be treated as a single space.
12. The **count in** clause is used to count the number of fields that received data.
13. The **tallying** option counts the number of characters transferred to a given field.
14. The pointer option in the **unstring** enables us to start transferring data from a point other than the first byte.
15. The **overflow** option will be taken in the **unstring**, if the pointer field contains zero.

Exercises

1. The print line contains 80 print positions. The program receives a string that is to be centered on the print line. The string has a maximum length of 60 characters. A space or a comma and a space separate the words in the string.

2. Assume the following fields are defined:

```
01   W30-STRING.
     05   STR-1          PIC X(10)    VALUE 'THIS IS YO'.
     05   STR-2          PIC X(15)    VALUE 'UR CAREER*'.
     05   STR-3          PIC X(12)    VALUE 'SO WORK HARD'.
     05   STR-4          PIC X(12)    VALUE ALL '*'.
01   W70 POINTER         PIC S99.
01   W90-NEW             PIC X(38).
01   W100-DISPLAY        PIC X        VALUE 'N'.
```

Using the above fields, code an instruction that will create the following string in W90-NEW (the three spaces before the inverted commas are part of the string).

```
‘   THIS IS YOUR CAREER!!SO WORK HARD!!’.
```

3.   What would the value in W100-DISPLAY be, after the following instruction?

a)

```
STRING    STR-1
          STR-2
          STR-3 DELIMITED BY SIZE
      INTO W90-NEW
      ON OVERFLOW
            MOVE ‘Y’ TO W100-DISPLAY
   END-STRING
```

b)

```
STRING    STR-1
          STR-2
          STR-3
          STR-4 DELIMITED BY SIZE
      INTO W90-NEW
      ON OVERFLOW
            MOVE ‘Y’ TO W-100-DISPLAY
   END-STRING
```

c)   Using b) above, coupled to the pointer option, what would happen if you initialized W70-POINTER to 0 or 39?

4.   Your program receives a string structured as follows:

```
XY156*James Joyce      *Renault Fuego      *001*015700
```

The contents of the data area are to be placed in the fields customerCode, customerName, productDescription, quantity and cost. The field for cost should be pic 9(6).

Create a function that will place the data in the appropriate fields and display the line.

Chapter 20

Inspect

Topics Covered

- The Inspect Statement
- Before and After Initial
- Inspect Replacing
- Inspect Converting
- Summary
- Complete
- True/False
- Exercises

The Inspect Statement

The purpose of the **inspect** is to determine whether a named field contains a particular character or string of characters. The field under inspection is examined from left to right, byte by byte, and the character or string of characters is counted or replaced as required.

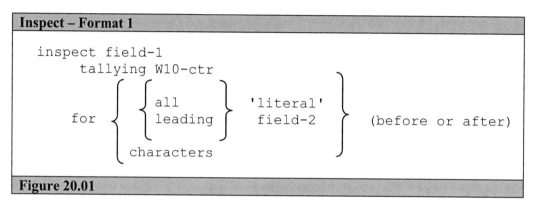

The following points should be borne in mind when coding the inspect statement:

- Field-1 is going to be examined and a count will be kept in W10-ctr of the number of times the selected character or set of characters occurs.
- Field-1 is the field that is going to be inspected.
- The **tallying** option indicates that we intend to have a count of the number of times the character or set of characters occurs in Field-1.
- The **for** enables us to specify additional options.
- **All** means all the occurrences of the character or characters.
- **Leading** means to the left of the first character that is different from the characters encountered up to that point. If you wish to count leading '*' and the string contains '***9**...', there would be three asterisks before the 9, the count would be three. The two asterisks following the 9 are not leading characters.
- **Characters** means any character in the collating sequence. This would include spaces. The **characters** option is generally used in conjunction with the **before** or **after** clauses. If not used with additional clauses, it will return the size of the field.
- We may name the characters we are looking for using a literal or a field name. In general we are able to specify a literal where we may specify a field name.

Inspect – Tallying

```
program-id. Chapter2001.

01  W20-product-code      pic X(20) value
    'XKXK120-1148-XX-01XX'.
01  W40-ctr               pic 9     value 0.
01  W50-input             pic XX.
procedure division.
A100-start.
    display 'Enter what to search for: ' no advancing.
    accept W50-input
    move 0 to W40-ctr
    inspect W20-product-code
        tallying W40-ctr for all W50-input
    display 'The characters occur ' W40-ctr ' times'
    stop run.
```

Listing 20.01

```
Command Prompt                                          _ □ ✕
Enter what to search for: XK
The characters occur 2 times
```

The following example depicts the use of leading:

Inspect – Leading

```
program-id. Chapter2002.

environment division.

data division.
working-storage section.
01  W20-product-code      pic X(20) value
    'XKXK120-1148-XX-01XX'.
01  W40-ctr               pic 9     value 0.
01  W50-input             pic XX.
```

Listing 20.02 – 1 of 2

429

Inspect – Leading

```
procedure division.
A100-start.
    display 'Enter what to search for: ' no advancing.
    accept W50-input
    move 0 to W40-ctr
    inspect W20-product-code
        tallying W40-ctr for leading W50-input
    display 'The characters occur ' W40-ctr ' times'
    stop run.
```

Listing 20.02 – 2 of 2

```
Command Prompt                                          _ □ ✕
Enter what to search for: XK
The characters occur 2 times
```

XK occurs twice before another set of two characters different from XK occurs. The first characters following XK are 12.

Before and After Initial

Before and **after** are used to set up a boundary somewhere in the string and examine that part of the string that occurs, either before or after the boundary you established. **Before** or **after** takes an identifier or a literal. The literal may be one or more characters. The following example illustrates the use of the clauses using characters and an identifier:

Before and After Initial

```
program-id. Chapter2003.

data division.
working-storage section.
01  W20-product-code    pic X(20) value
    'XKXK120-1148-XX-01XX'.
01  W40-ctr             pic 9      value 0.
01  W50-input           pic XX.
```

Listing 20.03 – 1 of 2

Before and After Initial

```
procedure division.
A100-start.
    display 'Enter what to search for: ' no advancing.
    accept W50-input
    move 0 to W40-ctr
    inspect W20-product-code
        tallying W40-ctr for all W50-input
                after initial '-0'
    display 'The characters occur ' W40-ctr ' times'
    move 0 to W40-ctr
    inspect W20-product-code
        tallying W40-ctr for characters before '12'
    display 'Leading characters : ' W40-ctr
    stop run.
```

Listing 20.03 – 2 of 2

When using tallying we have to use **all**, **leading** or **characters**. We have used **leading** in an earlier example. We are now using **before** and **after** with the **tallying** clause. We wanted to count the number of occurrences of the data in W50-input. For this, we need to specify **all**. If you do not specify **leading** or **character**, then you have to use the **all** option.

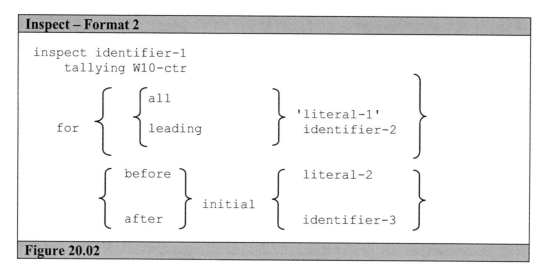

Inspect – Format 2

```
inspect identifier-1
    tallying W10-ctr

         ┌        ┌ all                ┐   ┌ 'literal-1'   ┐
    for  │        │                    │   │               │
         └        └ leading            ┘   └ identifier-2  ┘

    ┌ before ┐              ┌ literal-2     ┐
    │        │  initial     │               │
    └ after  ┘              └ identifier-3  ┘
```

Figure 20.02

The **initial** keyword is optional. Following we specify the character or characters that establish the boundary. In understanding the use of the word 'initial' we see that we could replace it by the word 'first'. For instance, if we want to say "Count all 'x' before the first '/' ", we would have coded "…all 'x' before initial '/'". It is also true that since **initial** is optional we may code "…all 'x' before '/'".

In the preceding listing, in one instance we used initial and in the other we did not. You are free to use **initial** or not. You will use it if you find that it adds clarity to your code or if the company establishes a standard that enforces the use of the keyword. Using initial adds to the clarity of the code and is a small price to pay for the benefit accrued. Remember, what is clear now may not be as clear in six months time. In addition, someone else may be maintaining the program and may welcome the additional clarity provided.

Inspect Replacing

The **replacing** option enables us to replace a character or set of characters in the string by another character or set of characters. When using replacing we have one additional option besides **leading** and **all**; we have **first**.

Inspect – Format 3

```
inspect identifier-1      ┌ 'literal-1'  ┐ (before /
   replacing characters by ┤ identifier-1 ├  after)
                          └              ┘

                          ┌ 'literal-1'  ┐
                          ┤              ├
                          └ identifier-1 ┘
```

Figure 20.03

The following example depicts the use of the keyword characters, which of course, means any possible characters.

Inspect Replacing

```
program-id. Chapter2004.
01  W20-product-code      pic X(20) value
    'XKXK120-1148-XX-01XX'.

procedure division.
A100-start.
    inspect W20-product-code
        replacing characters by '#' after initial '1'
    display 'New string: ' W20-product-code
    stop run.
```

Listing 20.04

```
C:\ Command Prompt                          _ □ ✕
New string: XKXK1################
```

Since we said "…after initial '1' " the data preceding the '1' as well as the '1' displayed.

Inspect – Format 4

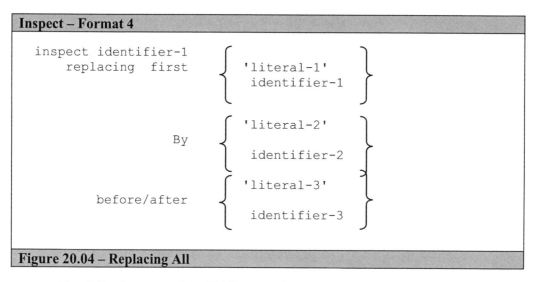

```
inspect identifier-1
     replacing  first        { 'literal-1'
                               identifier-1 }


                      By      { 'literal-2'
                               identifier-2 }

                             { 'literal-3'
     before/after             identifier-3 }
```

Figure 20.04 – Replacing All

The following example will illustrate the use of **first**. Unfortunately, there is no last. Of course we are free to create our own routine for the purpose.

Inspect – Replacing First

```
program-id. Chapter2005.

data division.
working-storage section.
01  W20-product-code     pic X(20) value
    'XKXK120-1148-XX-01XX'.

procedure division.
A100-start.
    inspect W20-product-code
        replacing first '11' by '22'
    display 'New string: ' W20-product-code
    stop run.
```

Listing 20.05

```
Command Prompt                                    _ □ ×
New string: XKXK120-2248-XX-01XX
```

1148 has been changed to 2248.

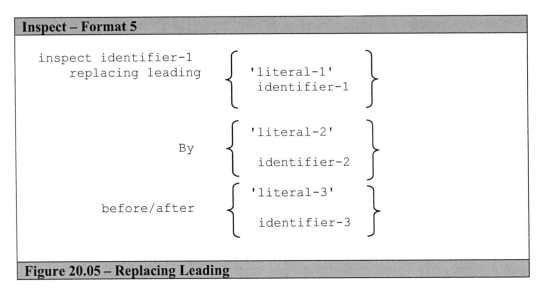

Inspect – Format 5

```
inspect identifier-1
     replacing leading        ⎧ 'literal-1'  ⎫
                              ⎨              ⎬
                              ⎩ identifier-1 ⎭

                      ⎧ 'literal-2'  ⎫
              By      ⎨              ⎬
                      ⎩ identifier-2 ⎭

                      ⎧ 'literal-3'  ⎫
     before/after     ⎨              ⎬
                      ⎩ identifier-3 ⎭
```

Figure 20.05 – Replacing Leading

Notice that in the **leading** option we have to specify which **leading** characters we wish replace. If we wish leading '*' to be replaced but the leading characters are '#', nothing will be replaced. In the following example we are replacing spaces by zeros.

We cannot say 'replacing leading characters' because characters are all possible characters in the collating sequence, so it would make no sense.

Inspect – Replacing Leading

```
program-id. Chapter2006.

working-storage section.
01  W20-amount      pic ZZZ,ZZZ,ZZ9.99 value 19.30.
procedure division.

A100-start.
    inspect W20-amount
        replacing leading spaces by zeros
    display 'New string: ' W20-amount
    stop run.
```

Listing 20.06

435

Inspect – Format 6

```
inspect identifier-1
    replacing   all          'literal-1'
                             identifier-1


                  By          'literal-2'

                             identifier-2

         before/after         'literal-3'

                             identifier-3
```

Figure 20.06 – Replacing All

In the example illustrating the **all** option we show two instances, one with the after clause and the other without a clause. The **all** goes through the whole field and replaces all instances of the named character or set of characters by the specified replacement.

The **before** and **after** introduce greater control in the operation of the **inspect**. It is not unusual that we want to change only part of the field.

Inspect Replacing All

```
program-id. Chapter2007.

data division.
working-storage section.
01  W20-product-code     pic X(20) value
    'XKXX120-1148-XX-01XX'.
01  W30-product-code     pic X(20) value
    'XKXX120-1148-XX-01XX'.
procedure division.
```

Listing 20.07 – 1 of 2

Inspect Replacing All

```
A100-start.
    inspect W20-product-code
        replacing all 'XX' by 'YY'
    display 'New string: ' W20-product-code
    inspect W30-product-code
        replacing all 'XX' by 'YY' after '48'
    display 'New string: ' W30-product-code
    stop run.
```

Listing 20.07 – 2 of 2

```
Command Prompt                                    _ □ ×
New string: XKYY120-1148-YY-01YY
New string: XKXX120-1148-YY-01YY
```

Inspect Converting

The **converting** was introduced with the COBOL 85 standard and you may find it quite useful. You will define two fields say, F1 containing 'ABC' and F2 containing 'XYZ'. F1 and F2 must have the same length. Using the converting you will be saying; "In the string under examination, if a position has a character present and the position is also present in F1, convert the character in F1 to the corresponding character in F2". Thus if the string contains an 'A' the 'A' will be converted to an 'X'. A 'B' in turn will be converted to a 'Y' and a 'C' will be converted to a 'Z'.

In the example constructed to illustrate a possible use of the **converting**, we convert a coded message that resides in a string. We have two additional strings; one contains the characters in code and the other contains the alphabet. Each character in the code string corresponds to a character in the alphabet. The space requires no conversion. The two strings follow:

```
01  W20-code     pic X(26) value
    '~!@#$%^&*()_+[]{};:<>?|\/`'.
01  W30-alfa     pic X(26) value
    'abcdefghijklmnopqrstuvwxyz'.
```

An 'a' corresponds to a '~' in the code, a 'b' corresponds to an '!' and so on.

Inspect – Format 7

```
inspect identifier-1
     converting                 {  'literal-1'
                                   identifier-1  }


                  To           {  'literal-2'

                                  identifier-2  }


                               {  'literal-3'
     before/after
                                  identifier-3  }
```

Figure 20.07 – Converting

The following example implements the **converting** to carry out the code translation.

Inspect Converting

```
program-id. Chapter2008.
01   W20-code                        pic X(26) value
     '~!@#$%^&*()_+[]{};:<>?|\/`'.
01   W30-alfa                        pic X(26) value
     'abcdefghijklmnopqrstuvwxyz'.
01   W40-string                      pic x(57) value
   '&>+~[ ;*^&<: ~;$ ~[ *+{];<~[< @][@$;[ ]% ~ &>+~[$ :]@*$</'.
procedure division.
A100-start.
     inspect W40-string
         converting W20-code TO W30-alfa
     display W40-string
     stop run.
```

Listing 20.08 – 1 of 2

```
Command Prompt                                    _ □ ×
human rights are an important concern of a humane society
```

Summary

- The **inspect** examines a field to determine how many times a character or set of characters is present in the field. If required, the occurrences of the given characters detected may be replaced by other characters.

- The **tallying** option enables us to count the number of times the character or set of characters was located.

- **All** means all occurrences of the specified characters in the string. It can be restricted by the use of the **before** and **after** clauses.

- **Leading** means all identical characters on the left of the field before a different character is encountered.

- **Before** and **after** provide a means of establishing a point in the string up to which or from which the **inspect** is to operate.

- **Characters** means any character in the collating sequence. If used with the **replacing** option then, whatever the character, it will be replaced.

- **First** is used with the **replacing** option. Furthermore, it can be used with the before and **after** keywords.

- When we use **replacing** with **leading** we need to specify which leading characters to replace. If the specified leading characters are not present no replacement takes place.

- **Converting** uses two fields of the same length and changes the character in the first field to the character in the same position in the second field.

Complete

1.   You wish to count all the occurrences of the characters 'th' in a field. The code would be: inspect field-1 _____ ctr for ____ 'th'.

2.   You wish to count the number of asterisks on the left of the field. You would code: inspect field-1 _____ ctr for _____ '*'.

3.   You wish to know how many bytes occur in the field before a '/' is encountered. Inspect field-1 _____ ctr for _____ _____ '/'.

4.   You wish to replace all characters preceding '/' by '0'. You would code: Inspect field-1 _____ _____ _____ '/' by ____.

5.   You wish to replace the first occurrence of 'XK' by 'SLR' following '...'. You would code: inspect field-1 _____ _____ 'XK' by 'SLR' _____ '...'.

6.   You wish to replace zeros on the left of the field by '#'. You would code   inspect field-1 _____ _____ zeros by '#'.

7.   You wish to change 'abc' to '123'. Assume that field-1 contains 'abc'.   Inspect _____ field-1 to _____.

True/False

1. **Before** and **after** call for either a literal or a field name but the literal must not be more than one character in length.

2. When using the **tallying** option we must use **all** or **leading** but not **characters**.

3. When using before or after, the **initial** keyword is optional.

4. The keyword **first** may be used with **tallying**.

5. When using **replacing** with **leading** we have to specify the leading character.

6. **Characters** means any character in the alphabet.

7. **Characters** and **leading** do not go together.

8. **Characters** may be used with **before** or **after**

Exercises

1. Your program contains an alphanumeric field that, at one stage, contains the following data: '   Ferrari'.
    Determine the number of spaces before the first alphabetic character.

2. Your program contains an alphanumeric field that, at one stage, contains the following data: 'ASP/5930/XK-932'
    Determine the number of characters following the first '/' and preceding the second '/'.

3. Using the **inspect**, determine the size of the alphanumeric field productDescription.

4. Your program contains an alphanumeric field that, at one stage, contains the following data: 'ASP/3930/XK-932'
    Count the number of 3's occurring in the data.

5. Your program contains an alphanumeric field that, at one stage, contains the following data: 'ASP/3930/XK-932'
    Using an inspect display the number of characters before the second '/' and following the second '/'.

6. Your program contains an alphanumeric field that at one stage contains the following data: 'XSP/39X0/XK-932'
    Change all Xs appearing in the field to 'Ys'.

7. Your program contains an alphanumeric field that, at one stage, contains the following data: 'XSP/39X0/XK-932'
    Change all Xs appearing in the field to 'Ys' following the first '/'

8. Your program contains an alphanumeric field that at one stage contains the following data: 'XSP/39X0/XS-932'
    Change all Xs appearing in the field to 'Ys'. All 'Ss' to 'Ts' and all 'Ps' to 'Qs'.

Chapter 21
Initialize

Topics Covered

- The Initialize Statement
- The Replacing Option
- Replacing Alphanumeric by Numeric
- Replacing Numeric-Edited by Numeric
- Summary
- Complete
- True/False
- Exercises

The Initialize Statement

The purpose of the **initialize** is to assign a value to a variable or values to multiple variables. Prior to having the **initialize** we used the move statement. Today we can use either the move or the **initialize**.

Initialize – Format 1

```
initialize field-1 field-2...
```

Figure 21.01

The following table depicts the result of using the **initialize** on the different types of data:

Picture	Before	After	Type
9(5)	45834	0000	Numeric
X(6)	XK-120	∇∇∇∇∇∇	Alphanumeric
99X99	04-12	∇∇∇∇∇	Alphanumeric edited
XXBX/XX	04 6/21	∇∇∇∇/∇∇	Alphanumeric edited
***99.9CR	*4567.8CR	***00.0∇∇	Numeric edited
A(7)	Michael	∇∇∇∇∇∇∇	Alphabetic
S9(3) comp-3	+456	0|0|0|C	Internal decimal

Table 21.01 – Results of the initialize

If you apply the **initialize** verb to a group field each of the elementary fields will be appropriately initialized. If you apply the move verb to a group field the elementary fields will all carry the same value. You can see the marked advantage that comes with the **initialize**. The following program illustrates the **initialize**:

Initialize

```
program-id. Chapter2101.
working-storage section.
01  W10-data.
    05  W10-number     pic S9(5)          value 12345.
    05  W10-code       pic  X(6)          value 'XK-120'.
    05  W10-ane        pic XXBX/XX        value '04 6/21'.
    05  W10-numed      pic ***99.9CR      value '4567.5'.
    05  W10-num        pic S9(3) comp-3 occurs 3 values
                       123 from (1) 123 from (2) 123 from (3).
```

Listing 21.01 – 1 of 2

444

Initialize

```
procedure division.
A100-start.
    display 'Unpacked:    ' W10-number
    display 'Code:        ' W10-code
    display 'AN edited :  ' W10-ane
    display 'Num edited:  ' W10-numed
    display 'Int numeric 1: ' W10-num(1)
    display 'Int numeric 2: ' W10-num(2)
    display 'Int numeric 3: ' W10-num(3)
    initialize W10-data
    display '   '
    display 'Unpacked:    ' W10-number
    display 'code:        ' W10-code
    display 'AN edited :  ' W10-ane
    display 'Num edited:  ' W10-numed
    display 'Int numeric 1: ' W10-num(1)
    display 'Int numeric 2: ' W10-num(2)
    display 'Int numeric 3: ' W10-num(3)
    stop run.
```

Listing 21.01 – 2 of 2

```
Command Prompt                                    _ □ ✕
Unpacked:       12345+
Code:           XK120
AN edited:      04 6/21
Num edited:     4567.5
Int numeric 1: +123
Int numeric 2: +234
Int numeric 3: +345

Unpacked:    00000+
Code:
AN edited:         /
Num edited: ***00.0
Int numeric 1: +000
Int numeric 2: +000
Int numeric 3: +000
```

W10-code is spaces so there is nothing to show. W10-ane is spaces with the '/' retained. In numeric edited, the value is positive so the CR does not show. Note that fillers are not initialized. All occurrences in the table were duly initialized. Since fillers are not addressable, it would be pointless to initialize them.

The Replacing Option

The **replacing** option enables us to use the **initialize** verb to initialize the field not only with the same type as the field type but also with any other type with which the target field is compatible.

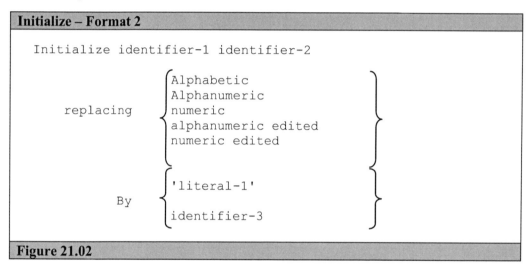

Initialize – Format 2

```
   Initialize identifier-1 identifier-2

                          ⎧ Alphabetic
                          ⎪ Alphanumeric
       replacing          ⎨ numeric
                          ⎪ alphanumeric edited
                          ⎩ numeric edited


                          ⎧ 'literal-1'
          By              ⎨
                          ⎩ identifier-3
```

Figure 21.02

Following **replacing** we specify the type of field that will be the target of the initialize. The **by** specifies the values that are to replace the data in the target field. The type of literal-1 or identifier-3 must be compatible with type of identifier-1 and identifier-2.

We cannot hope (programmers should not rely on hope) that the following item of code will execute successfully.

```
          ...replacing numeric by 'xyz'
```

Replacing Alphanumeric by Numeric

We indicated that the **replacing** required compatible types between source and target. A compatible type would be a type that would be acceptable in a move statement. If W10-num, a numeric field, contained decimals the type would be incompatible with an alphanumeric target type. Note, however, that Micro Focus Net Express 4, accepts a decimal field as the source for an alphanumeric target. It also accepts a move of a numeric field with decimals to an alphanumeric field but, in this case, provides a warning.

Initializing Alphanumeric By Numeric

```
program-id. chapter2102.

working-storage section.
01  W10-types.
    05  W10-code              pic X(05) justified.
    05  W10-num               pic 9(05) value 1991.
procedure division.
    initialize W10-code
        replacing alphanumeric by W10-num
    display 'Value after the initialize: ' W10-code
    stop run.
```

Listing 21.02

Command Prompt   _ □ ✕

```
Value after the initialize: 01991
```

Replacing Numeric-Edited by Numeric

When replacing numeric-edited by numeric the data will be edited.

Initializing Numeric Edited

```
program-id. chapter2103.
working-storage section.
01  W10-types.
    05  W10-edited           pic ZZZ,ZZ9.99   value 1234.
    05  W10-num              pic 9(05)V99      value 1364.99.

procedure division.
    initialize W10-edited
        replacing numeric-edited by W10-num
    display 'Value after the initialize: ' W10-edited
    stop run.
```

Listing 21.03

```
Command Prompt                                        _ ☐ ✕
Initializing numeric-edited:    1,364.99
```

We may also **initialize** more than one field at a time and each of the initialized fields may have its own type. Because we can only specify one field following the **initialize**, the fields must all belong to the same group field.

Initializing a Group Field

```
program-id. Chapter2104.
working-storage section.
01   W10-area.
     05   W10-type              pic 9(02) value 10.
     05   W10-description       pic X(05) value 'Fire'.
     05   W10-qty               pic 9(02) value 15.

procedure division.
     initialize W10-area
         replacing numeric by 95
                   alphanumeric by 'XK120'
     display 'Type : ' W10-type
     display 'Desc.: ' W10-description
     display 'Qty  : ' W10-qty
     stop run.
```

Listing 21.04

```
Command Prompt                                        _ ☐ ✕
Type : 95
Desc.: XK120
Qty  : 95
```

You will notice that both type and quantity, being numeric, were initialized to the same value.

The initialize is particularly advantageous when we have group fields. If we are initializing individual fields then the move statement will work just as well. Consider the following example:

Initializing a Group Field

```
program-id. Chapter2105.
working-storage section.
01   W10-area.
     05   W10-count1                    pic 9(04).
     05   W10-description1              pic X(10).
     05   W10-count2                    pic 9(04).
     05   W10-description2              pic X(10).
     05   W10-count3                    pic 9(04).
     05   W10-description3              pic X(10).
     05   W10-count4                    pic 9(04).
     05   W10-description4              pic X(10).

procedure division.
A100-start.
     initialize W10-area
         replacing numeric by 9999
                   alphanumeric by 'First prod'
     stop run.
```

Listing 21.05

Compare the **initialize** to the equivalent move statement where, besides all the extra work, the possibility of error is much greater. A common error of the past arose from moving spaces to the group field, resulting in numeric fields with spaces. Clearly, the **initialize** overcomes this problem.

Move vs Initialize

```
move 9999 to W10-count1
             W10-count2
             W10-count3
             W10-count4
move 'First prod' to W10-description1
                     W10-description2
                     W10-description3
                     W10-description4
```

Figure 21.03

We have covered the different aspects of the initialize and what will work successfully with the statement. Next we will show one situation that you might think should work but will not. The program that follows will compile successfully but will not work.

Remember what we said earlier: "A complete program is a program that works, meaning that it not only runs but produces the anticipated results."

Initialize Replacing

```
program-id. Chapter2106.
working-storage section.
01  W10-area.
    05  W10-edited1         pic Z,ZZ9.
    05  W10-edited2         pic Z,ZZ9.

procedure division.
A100-start.
    initialize W10-edited1
        replacing numeric by 9999
    initialize W10-edited2
        replacing numeric-edited by 8888
    display 'Numeric: ' W10-edited1
    display 'Edited : ' W10-edited2
    stop run.
```

Listing 21.06

The initialized field W10-edited1, was specified as **numeric** when it was, in fact, a **numeric-edited** field. The compiler issued no diagnostic but the execution was not as expected.

Summary

- The **initialize** is preeminently suited to the initialization of multiple variables, all to appropriate values.

- Numeric fields will be initialized to zeroes

- Alphabetic and alphanumeric fields will be initialized to spaces.

- Numeric edited will be initialized as if a value of zero had been moved to the field. The value will be edited in accordance with the picture.

- Alphanumeric edited will behave as if a value of spaces had been moved to it. The value will be edited. If the picture contains a '/' it will remain.

- A packed field will be set to zero packed.

- When the **initialize** is applied to a group field, each of the field types is appropriately initialized. If the group field contains fillers, these will not be initialized. This is because a filler is not addressable and what it contains is therefore not significant.

- The **replacing** option enables us to initialize a field, not with its default initialization but with any value with which it is compatible. The test for compatibility here is that if a move statement would function, then the initialization would function.

- We may use the **initialize** to move a fractional number to an alphanumeric field. A move, however, will not allow a fractional number to be moved to an alphanumeric field. We see that compatibility in the initialize goes beyond compatibility in the move statement.

- The **replacing** option enables us to initialize more than one type at a time. Note that if there are multiple values of a particular type, they will all be initialized to the same value.

- If a numeric-edited field is described as numeric in the **replacing** option, it might not give you a diagnostic but it will **not** work.

Complete

1.   The intention of the initialize is to permit a _____ or multiple _____ to be initialized.

2.   Using the initialize, a numeric field will be set to _____.

3.   Using the initialize, an alphanumeric field will be set to _____.

4.   Using the initialize, a numeric-edited field will be set in accordance with its _____.

5.   Using the initialize, an alphanumeric-edited field will be set in accordance with its _____.

6.   A field defined as pic S9(3) comp-3 is initialized; show the contents of the field: _____ .

7.   Using the initialize, an alphabetic field will be set to _____.

8.   Following the replacing, we specify the _____ of the target field.

9.   When using the replacing, the type of the source field must be _____ with the target field.

10. The target W10-data is alphanumeric and you are going to replace it with 1234. You would code: initialize _____ _____ _____ by 1234.

11. The target W10-edit is numeric-edited. You are going to replace it with 567.5. You would code: initialize _____ _____ _____ by 567.5.

12. The target W10-data is a group field containing an alphanumeric field and a numeric edited field. You are going to initialize W10-data with 'Good!' and W10-edited with 6543.75. You would code: initialize _____ _____ _____ by 'Good!' _____ by 6543.75.

True/False

1.   In the **initialize** you can only initialize group fields.

2.   Alphanumeric fields will be initialized to spaces.

3.   Numeric-edited fields will be initialized in accordance with the picture.

4.   Alphanumeric-edited fields will be initialized to spaces.

5.   Alphabetic fields will be initialized in the same way as alphanumeric fields.

6.   Following **replacing**, we code the name of the target field.

7.   **Fillers** are initialized to spaces.

8.   In the **initialize**, the source and the target need not be compatible.

9.   The type of data specified in the **replacing** must be the same type as the target.

10.   When using the **replacing** option, source and target fields must be of the same type.

11.   The replacing option enables us to initialize an alphanumeric field using a fractional number.

12.   When an alphanumeric field is initialized using a fractional number, say 123.45, the alphanumeric field will contain the value '123.45'.

13.   When we use a numeric value to initialize an alphanumeric field using the replacing, we would be coding: initialize W10-data replacing alphanumeric by '123.45'.

14.   Using ...replacing all numeric by 100 has the advantage of being explicit.

Exercises

1. Given the following definitions, give the value of GroupField after each of the following commands.

    ```
    01    GroupField.
          05  Field-1        pic S9(3)        value 123.
          05  Field-2        pic X(3)         value 'ABC'.
          05  Field-3        pic S9(5)        value 456.
          05  Field-4        pic X(4)         value 'DEF'.
          05  Field-5        pic S9(3)        value 789.
          05  Field-6        pic X(3)         value 'GHI'.
          05  Field-7        pic X(5)         value 'JKLMN'.
          05  Field-8        pic S9(4)        value 1011.
          05  Filler         pic S9(3)        value 444.
    ```

    a) initialize GroupField
    b) initialize GroupField replacing alphanumeric by '***'
    c) mumeric-edited by 0.
    d) initialize Field-5 Field-6 Field-8
        initialize GroupField replacing numeric by 999.

2. Write the code that initializes the field W10-header to zeros but not to spaces. W10-header contains all categories of numeric fields only.

Chapter 22
Sort

Topics Covered

- ❏ The Sort Statement
- ❏ The SD
- ❏ The Using Clause
- ❏ The Giving Clause
- ❏ With Duplicates in Order
- ❏ Input and Output Procedures
- ❏ The Input Procedure
- ❏ The Output Procedure
- ❏ Summary
- ❏ Complete
- ❏ True/False
- ❏ Exercises

The Sort Statement

The **sort** is more closely associated with batch applications that require transactions to be in an appropriate sequence, namely the same sequence as the master file. Generally, when salaries are paid the process involves a batched approach. Withdrawing cash from an automatic teller machine, on the other hand, calls for a random approach. In a random approach sequence is not important.

COBOL allows us to sequentially retrieve records from a file, sort them and then retrieve the sorted records, one at a time, and use them for further processing.

The sorting operation presumes the existence of a key. The key must be the same size and in the same position in every record in the file to be sorted. The key may be a simple or a compound key. A compound key consists of two or more fields.

The Sort – Format 1

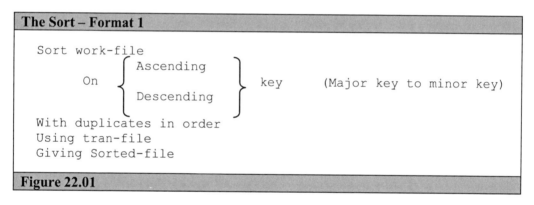

```
Sort work-file
            ┌  Ascending  ┐
       On   ┤             ├   key      (Major key to minor key)
            └  Descending ┘
With duplicates in order
Using tran-file
Giving Sorted-file
```

Figure 22.01

The file containing the records to be sorted is the source of the records for the sort. The records in this file remain unsorted. The sorted records will be in what we call the sort work file. This file is used in the sort statement. The file requires a **select** statement and, instead of an **FD**, file definition, it uses an **SD,** sort definition.

The Sort

```
input-output section.
    select sort-work-file assign to "C:\cob0\srtwork".
sd  sort-work-file.
01  sort-rec.
    05  sort-key      pic X(05).
    05  sort-rest     pic X(20).
procedure division.
    sort sort-work-file
```

Figure 22.02

The name sort-work-file is a name of your own creation. Because the sort uses it to carry out the sorting operation it seems an appropriate name.

In format 1 you see that we may specify keys in the sequence major to minor, sort-acc-no falling within sort-branch. We may specify up to 12 keys. In format 1, the simplest format, we are not doing anything with the sorted records except create an output file from them. The **sort** statement would then look as follows:

Coding the Sort Statement

```
sort sort-work-file
     on   ascending key sort-branch
          descending key sort-acc-no
     using in-file
     giving sorted-file
```

Figure 22.03

In-file would contain the records we want sorted and sorted-file would contain the sorted records. Note that it is only the sort that is able to work with the sort work file. The fact that the sort work file contains the sorted records is not of much use to us; we need to output the sorted records to a file that we can use later. In our coding, sorted-file is the file created by the sort to contain the sorted records.

The whole program follows:

Sort Program

```
 Program-id. Chapter2201.
     select in-file assign to "C:\cob0\srt001".
     select sort-work-file assign to "C:\cob0\srtwork".
     select sorted-file assign to "C:\cob0\srt002".
 file section.
 fd  in-file.
 01  in-rec           pic X(25).
 fd  sorted-file.
 01  sorted-rec       pic X(25).
 sd  sort-work-file.
 01  sort-rec.
     05   sort-branch   pic X(05).
     05   sort-acc-no   pic X(05).
     05   sort-name     pic X(15).
     05   sort-salary   pic 9(05).
```

Listing 22.01 – 1 of 2

Sort Program

```
procedure division.
    sort sort-work-file
        on  ascending key sort-branch
            descending key sort-acc-no
        using in-file
        giving sorted-file
    stop run.
```

Listing 22.01 – 2 of 2

The SD

The level 01 under the **SD** must contain the key definitions, because that is where the sort expects to find them. Although it is customary for the keys to be contiguous and arranged in the sequence major to minor, this need not necessarily be so. In our program the keys are sort-branch and sort-acc-no. As you can see from the example we may sort in ascending sequence on one field and on descending sequence on another. Note that there are no mandatory clauses in the SD.

The Using Clause

The **using** clause enables us to specify the file that the sort will use as the source of the records to be sorted. The **giving clause**, on the other hand, enables us to specify the output file in which the sort is to store the sorted records.

The **using** is employed when the program does no work on the input records prior to passing the records to the sort. The following applies when employing using:

- The program must not open the file containing the records to be sorted.
- The program must not close the file containing the records to be sorted.

It follows then that it is the responsibility of the **sort** to undertake the following:

- Open the file that will provide the input to the sort; the file may have sequential, indexed sequential or relative organization.
- Retrieve the records from the file one at a time.
- Make the records available to the sorting function.
- Close the input file.

Once the above has taken place, the sort operation starts, using the sort work file, and proceeds to completion.

The Giving Clause

The **giving** clause is used when the program containing the sort does not process the sorted records. Instead, the records are output to a file, namely the file associated with the **giving** clause. The following applies when the **giving** clause is being used:

- The program must not open the file to which the sort is to write the sorted records.

- The records are retrieved from the sort work file one at a time.

- The retrieved records are written to the output file one at a time.

- The sort closes the output file.

The **giving** clause enables us to write to a sequential file, an indexed sequential file or a relative file.

With Duplicates in Order

Assume you have, in the file to be sorted, more than one record with the same key. If you want the original sequence for records with the same key to be maintained, you should specify the **with duplicates in order** clause.

Input Key	Input Data	Output Key	Output Data
300	John Doe	100	Jack Russel
400	Jack Daniels	300	John Doe
100	Jack Russel	300	Tom Jones
300	Tom Jones	400	Jack Daniels
400	David Davies	400	David Davies
Table 22.01 – With duplicates in order			

After the **sort** the records are in sequence but in the case of those with the same key, those that were before are still before and those that were following are still following.

Input and Output Procedures

The advantage of the d**ynamic sort** is that it saves time on **input** and **output**. What we need to do is read a transaction file and validate it. Valid records are then sorted. The sorted file is then used to update a master file. If we use a **dynamic sort** the system chart would look like this:

System chart – Dynamic sort

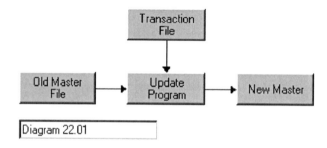

Diagram 22.01

System Chart – Independent Sort

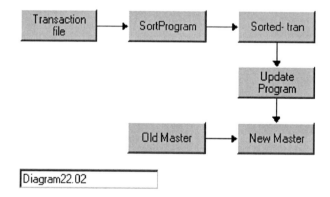

Diagram22.02

Assuming the transaction record contains 1000 records, the **dynamic sort** solution entails 1000 reads in respect of transactions. The **independent sort** solution entails 1000 reads for the sort and 1000 writes. In addition, 1000 reads are now required for the update program. The independent sort requires 1000 additional reads and maybe 1000 additional writes.

We are now going to process the records prior to passing them to the sort. We do this in the **input procedure**. A record that has been processed (assume a validation process) is ready to be passed to the sort. Once all the records have been passed to the sort, the sort process will begin. Once the records have been sorted they will be retrieved from the sort and used in the update of the master file. This is done in the **output procedure**:

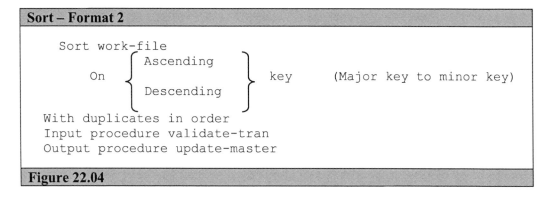

Figure 22.04

The Input Procedure

When we create an **input procedure** we are in full control of what is to be passed to the sort and what is not. In this case, the sort is not told from what file to get the records because it is not getting the records directly from a file. The input procedure will decide when to pass a record to the sort. We will now enumerate the responsibilities of the input procedure.

The input procedure will:

- Open the file because the sort has not been told which file to open.
- Read the records from the file.
- Decide which records to make available to the sort and pass these records to the sort.
- Close the file.

You must be curious to find out how it is that we pass a record to the sort. To do this we use the **release** statement, of which there must be at least one in the input procedure. The format of the statement is as follows:

Release

```
     Release sort-record
     or
     Release sort-record from input-area
```

Figure 22.05

461

Other important points:

- The release with the **from** option is similar to the write with the **from** option. It is therefore equivalent to a move followed by a release operation.

- Control must reach the **release** statement from within a **sort** statement because the statement only has meaning in association with a sort statement.

- The **input procedure** may consist of a number of paragraphs or a number of sections. None of the paragraphs may form part of the **output procedure**. The format of the sort statement then incorporates the **thru** or **through**. We would then have:

  - put procedure B100-validate-A thru B100-validate-Z
  - output procedure C100-update-A thru C100-update-Z

Points to bear in mind:

- The input procedure may not contain any sort verbs.

- A well-structured input procedure will not require you to branch outside the range of the input procedure. To keep things well organized, it is suggested that you put your input procedure inside a section.

- The point of return from the input procedure is placed by the compiler, as the last physical instruction in the input procedure. For this reason, the last instruction in the input routine is an exit instruction; the only instruction in the paragraph. When no further processing is required of the input procedure, we use a **go to** to branch to the exit paragraph.

The Output Procedure

The **output procedure** is able to obtain sorted records from the **sort**. To do this, it uses the **return** statement. You will notice the similarity between the **return** and the read. In a way you will be reading records from the sorted file. However, because the sort work file is no ordinary file, the read will not do and we have the **return** instead.

Return

```
return sort-file    [into sort-area]
    at end imperative statement
    not at end imperative statement
end-return
```

Figure 22.06

The following points apply to the output procedure:

- If an output file is being created it is not the function of the sort to open it; this is your responsibility.
- Retrieval of records from the sorted file is carried out using return.
- If required, write to a file.
- Close any output files.

Points to bear in mind:

- Control must reach the **return** statement from within a **sort** statement since the return only has meaning in association with a **sort** statement.
- Control passes to the output procedure from the sort statement.
- There must be at least one return statement.
- The **output procedure** must not contain any sort statements.
- Good structure implies that control will not branch to points outside the range of the **output procedure**. It is recommended that the **output procedure** be a section. You can visualize a section as a compartment into which everything to do with the **output procedure** will be slotted.

Next we will look at the hierarchy chart depicting the logic of the program. A brief description of the program follows:

- The records in the transaction file are to be validated.
- The validation is limited to ascertaining whether amount is numeric.
- Once the records are sorted, they will be used to update the master.
- There may be more than one transaction for a master so an iteration is needed for the sorted transactions.
- In the update, the amount in the transaction is added to the amount in the master.
- When all the transactions for a master have been exhausted, the master is re-written.

Hierarchy Chart 1 – File sort

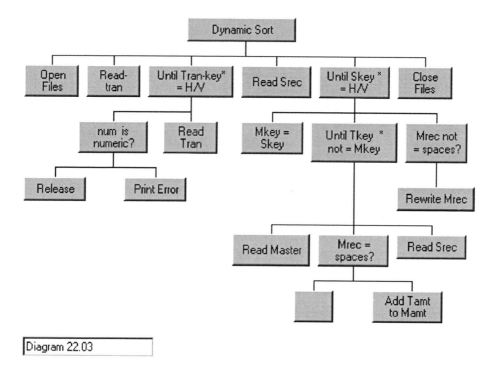

Diagram 22.03

The steps are as follows:

- We open files and do the first read. This is the preparatory stage that precedes the iteration.
- In the iteration we will process all transactions until end of file is reached.
- Inside the loop we test for a numeric value.
- If the value is numeric, the record is released to the sort; otherwise an error message is printed.
- The first loop is now over and we prepare for the next loop by returning the first sorted record.
- We will iterate until we have exhausted all sorted records.
- We prepare to read the master randomly by moving sort-key to mast-key.
- We will iterate until we have exhausted all records for this master.
- We test to see if the master was read successfully. If it was not, processing of the sorted transaction is bypassed; otherwise we add t-amt to m-amt.
- When the key of the transaction read is no longer equal to the key of the master, the loop is exited.

- We again test to see if we had retrieved a master record successfully. If we did, we rewrite the master.
- We go up to the top to test to see if there are still transactions to process. If there are, the loop is repeated.
- If all transactions have been exhausted, the files are closed and the run ends.

As for the input procedure, the point of return from the output procedure is a physical return instruction placed by the compiler as the last instruction in the output procedure. For this reason, we have created an exit paragraph containing a single exit instruction. When no further processing is required from the output procedure we use a **go to** to branch to this paragraph.

Sort with Random Update

```
program-id. Chapter2202.

environment division.
    select tran-file assign to "C:\cob0\tran01".
    select sort-file assign to "C:\cob0\sort01".
    select mast-file assign to "C:\cob0\mast01"
        organization is indexed
        access is random
        record key is mast-key
        file status is W10-stat.

data division.
file section.
fd  mast-file.
01  mast-rec.
    05  mast-key        pic X(03).
    05  mast-name       pic X(03).
    05  mast-amt        pic 9(05).
fd  tran-file.
01  tran-rec.
    05  tran-key        pic X(03).
    05  tran-amt        pic 9(03).
sd  sort-file.
01  sort-rec.
    05  sort-key        pic X(03).
    05  sort-rest       pic X(03).
```

Listing 22.02 – 1 of 3

Sort with Random Update

```
working-storage section.
01  W10-stat           PIC XX.

procedure division.
A100-start.
    open input tran-file
         i-o    mast-file
    sort sort-file
        ascending key sort-key
        input  procedure B100-validate-tran
        output procedure C100-update-master
    stop run.
********************Start of Input Procedure **************
B100-validate-tran section.
B100-validate.
    perform B900-read-tran
    perform until tran-key = high-values
        perform B200-test
        perform B900-read-tran
    end-perform
    close tran-file
    go to B999-exit.
B200-test.
B900-read-tran.
    read tran-file
        at end move high-values to tran-key.
B999-exit.
    exit.
******************End of Input Procedure ***************
C100-update-master section.
C100-update.
    perform C800-get-sorted-tran
    perform until sort-key = high-values
        perform C200-update-all
    end-perform
    go to C999-exit.
```

Listing 22.02 – 2 of 3

Sort with Random Update

```
C200-update-all.
    move sort-key to mast-key
    perform until sort-key not = mast-key
        perform C900-get-master
            if  mast-rec not = spaces
                add tran-amt to mast-amt
                perform C800-get-sorted-tran
         end-if.
    end-perform
    if  mast-rec not = spaces
        display mast-name '   ' mast-amt
        rewrite mast-rec
    end-if.
C800-get-sorted-tran.
    return sort-file
        at end move high-values to sort-key
    end-return.
C900-get-master.
    read mast-file
        invalid key move spaces to mast-rec
    end-read.
C999-exit.
    exit.
```

Listing 22.02 – 3 of 3

467

Summary

- The **sort** is more closely associated with batch applications because these require that the transaction file must be in the same sequence as the master file.

- The transactions to be sorted must have a key. The key fields must occupy the same position in every record. The key fields need not all be grouped together in the record, although they generally are.

- The **sort** requires a work file. The records are retrieved from the input transaction file passed to the **sort** and placed in the work file. When there are no more records to be passed to the sort, the sorting operation starts. The sorting operation is carried out in main storage. Eventually the work file will contain all the sorted records, at which stage the **sort** would pass control back to the program.

- The select for the work file is a normal select like any other. The file definition is absent and replaced by a sort definition, **SD**. Under the **SD**, as for an **FD**, there is a 01 level definition. Under the 01 will be the key definitions and a **filler** for the remaining bytes in the record.

- The **using** clause is employed when the input file is not processed before passing the records to the sort. The statement names the input file. The program does nothing with the input file. Note that this is rarely done.

- The **giving** clause is used when the sorted records are not processed; instead, a file containing the sorted records is created. The **giving** names the file to be created.

- Sometimes records come in sets, all with the same key, and it is important that the initial sequence be maintained. To secure this, we code the '**with duplicates in order**' clause.

- An **input procedure** names a section or group of paragraphs that will do the processing of the input records before passing them to the **sort**. Generally the input records are filtered or reformatted before being passed to the **sort**.

- The **output procedure** retrieves the sorted records from the sorted file. In this case the records are retrieved and processed further. If a file is further processed, this process will not be under the control of the **sort**.

Complete

1. In order for a **sort** to be possible, the records to be sorted must have a _____.

2. The actual **sort** operation is carried out in the _____ _____.

3. The **select** for the sort work file is a select for ____ _____ file.

4. The sort key must be defined in the _____.

5. The _____ clause is used if no processing is done prior to passing the records to the sort.

6. The _____ clause is used when no _____ is done on the sorted records.

7. The _____ _____ __ _____ clause is coded to maintain the sequence of records with the same key.

8. The **sort** is associated with _____ applications.

9. The using and the giving use _____ file organization.

10. When there are no more records to be passed to the sort, the _____ receives control.

11. When the **sort** has finished sorting, _____ reverts back to the _____.

12. Records are obtained from the **sort** by means of the _____ statement.

13. The **input** and the **output** procedure both have a _____ mechanism at the end of each procedure.

14. The invocation of the **sort** and the return of control to the program are _____.

15. Records are passed to the **sort** by means of the _____ statement.

True/False

1.   The sort keys are specified from minor to major key.
2.   The **input procedure** invokes the **sort** by means of a perform, but the sort returns control to the program automatically.
3.   When the **using** is employed, we do not use the **release** statement.
4.   When the **giving** is employed, we can only create a sequential file.
5.   The **using** only allows input of sequential files.
6.   When the **using** is employed, it is up to the programmer to open the file.
7.   When the **using** is employed, the program cannot read the file.
8.   When the **using** is employed, the program cannot release records to the sort.
9.   The file used by the **sort** must be given the name sort-work-file.
10.   The sort key must be defined in the file section.
11.   We may sort in ascending key on some fields and descending key on others.
12.   **With duplicates in order** means that records with the same key will remain in the sequence in which they were read.
13.   In an EBCDIC file that is sorted 123 will precede ABC.
14.   In an ASCII file that is sorted 123 will always precede ABC.
15.   The **input procedure** may not contain a sort verb.
16.   Control must reach the **return** statement from within a **sort** statement because **return** only has meaning in association with the sort.
17.   An **input procedure** need not contain a **release** statement.

Exercises

1.   Code the sort statement to sort Employee-file. The record name is employeeRec and contains the fields branchNo, employeeNo, totalHoursWorked and five values for hours worked during the week. The records are to be sorted in ascending sequence by branchNo and descending sequence of employeeNo. The sorted records are to be output to a file called SortedEmployees.

2.   The file EmployeeFile is to be sorted. The file record is called employeeRec. Code the statement that will pass the record to the sort.

3.   The file that contains the sorted records is called SortWork and the record is sort-Rec. Code the statement that will retrieve the sorted records.

Chapter 23
OO COBOL

Topics Covered

- Object Orientation
- Classes and Objects
- Encapsulation
- Inheritance
- Polymorphism
- Communication between classes
- Our First OO COBOL Program
- Class not Part of Program
- Self
- Factory and Super
- Memory Leaks
- Files in Object Orientation
- Summary
- Complete
- True/False
- Exercises

Object Orientation

Structured programming and object orientation both seek to reduce complexity in the programming arena. Structured programming seeks to reach this objective through **functional decomposition**. When using this paradigm we ask: "What do we need to do?" The answer might be, we need to read a record, we need to produce totals by branch, etc. The logic of the program then establishes relationships between the individual functions.

We have seen that we try to obtain modules that satisfy one function. Such modules we describe as cohesive modules. At times, we have to do a number of disparate things that have only one thing in common; they must be done at the same time. We describe these modules as being temporally cohesive.

The object oriented approach does not seek to determine the functions involved. rather than ask: "What needs to be done?" it asks: "What objects are involved?" A customer might be a possible object an employee might be another.

Classes and Objects

A customer is an **object**. All other customers have the same characteristics as this one customer. So, instead of treating each customer as if it were a unique object we say: "Let us group all customers together because they all have the same characteristics." We call this group we have created a **class**. All customers will have the same **attributes** and will all require the same functionality. An **attribute** is an item of data that is part of the nature of the object. For instance, a customer number, a customer address and customer balance all go to make a customer **object**, so they are attributes of customer. A function associated with all customer objects is one that would, say, make possible the addition of cost of purchases to amount-owing and the subtraction of payments from amount-owing.

All customer **objects**, also known as class **instances**, together constitute the **Customer class**, because they are all handled in identical fashion. Note that the class is an abstraction: What have physical existence are the objects of a class. Furthermore, an object is said to have **identity**, **state** and **behavior**. Without **identity** you would be unable to reach the object. **State** derives from an object's attributes. A change in the value of an **attribute** means a change in the **state** of the object. **Behavior** stems from the functions present in the object. In OO, functions are referred to as **methods**. In future we will not talk of routines but of **methods**.

One of the objectives of object orientation is to secure **reusability**. We have described situations where temporal cohesion exists. In such a situation we open all files in the same module; let us say we open three files. For this module to be reusable we would always need to open those three files. This would be an unlikely requirement.

Although there may be many thousands of customers when we process customer objects we normally process one customer at a time so we do not have to create thousands of customer objects. One customer object will generally be enough. Just as when we process a file containing thousands of customers we only need one customer area.

Encapsulation

One of the requirements of an object oriented language is that it should be able to provide a facility for **encapsulation**. The term signifies that we are going to construct a capsule. A capsule isolates its contents from the environment in which it exists. We will have a capsule in respect of every class needed by the application. The capsule will contain the **attributes** of the object as well as the functions required to manipulate the **attributes**.

The capsule is split into two parts, the **implementation** and the **interface**. The **interface** is described as **public** and is visible to the environment and enables us to communicate with the object. The **implementation** is described as **private** and is not visible except within the boundaries of the capsule. The **attributes** of the object reside within the implementation, as do methods that do not need to be visible to other classes.

Because all the **attributes** as well as all the functionality required by the class resides within the capsule, this makes for **reusability**. **Reusability** is important because it avoids duplication of code.

Inheritance

Another important facility afforded by an object oriented language is that a class should be able to inherit from another class. When a class inherits, it inherits all the functionality present in the class from which it inherits. Most object oriented languages also allow attributes to be inherited. However, COBOL does not. COBOL allows only the **interface** to be inherited.

You will recognize that inheritance is very valuable. If the **super-class**, the one from which we are inheriting, already calculates the distance between two points, then the sub-class does not need to duplicate the code to do the same calculation; it merely inherits that functionality. Another name for **super-class** is **base class** and for **sub-class** it is **derived class**. The COBOL compiler comes with a number of classes that do valuable work, all going to make life easier for the programmer.

One important point to note is that the **interface** of the derived class consists of the interface of the **base class** plus the methods of its own **interface**. If you know that class Manager is derived from class Employee, you will be able to use the methods that comprise the **interface** of class Employee when processing an object of class Manager. Net Express has all classes derive from class Base. In Net Express, with .Net all objects derive from class Object. In this way the functionality of class **base** or of class **Object** will be shared by all classes.

Polymorphism

Last, but not least, we have **polymorphism** as one of the facilities required of an object oriented language. It is closely associated with inheritance because it is only when used together with inheritance that we find runtime polymorphism.

In this respect let us point out one important aspect of **inheritance**. In **inheritance** we have 'a kind of' relationship. We say that a 'saloon car' is **a kind of** vehicle. We say that an 'employee' is **a kind of** person. The relationship holds only in one direction. It is not true to say that a 'vehicle' is a kind of 'saloon car'. What happens with **polymorphism** is that it allows us to treat an object of the derived class as if it were an object of the base class. We treat a 'saloon car' as if it were a 'vehicle' which it, in fact, is. We call this **upcasting**.

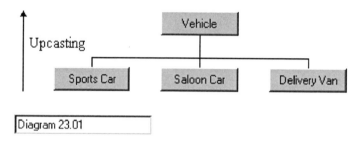

Diagram 23.01

The derived class may **override** the methods it inherits from the base class. When we override a method we are providing a different implementation from the method inherited. We have the same name but a different implementation. In this way we have the same interface but a different implementation.

Communication Between Classes

Bear in mind that COBOL is not a fully object oriented language; it is a **hybrid**. It is classed as a **hybrid** because you must always have a procedural program to receive control from the operating system. This procedural program may then pass control to class methods. This is also the situation with C++, which is also a hybrid.

Do not be discouraged by this. Java is reputed to be a fully object oriented language because everything must reside inside a **class**. However, its numeric data types are not **objects**. They are **objects** in C# and VB.Net. What matters is that it is just as easy to follow OO principles when structuring your program when you use Java as it is when you use COBOL or C++.

Classes communicate by sending **messages** to one another. Before a class can send a **message** to another class it needs to create a **reference** for the class. The **reference** will eventually contain the address of the class with which it needs to communicate. The **reference** needs to be created and then loaded with the address of the class. The following line of code creates a **reference**:

```
01  custRef      usage is reference CustomerClass.
```

The **reference** in this case is type specific, meaning that it can only point to objects of the named class. To load the reference, we create an object of the class and place its address in the **reference**. To create an object, we use the method 'New', a method from class **base**. **Class base**, as you know, is a class provided for you and from which all other classes implicitly inherit.

```
invoke CustomerClass "new" returning custRef
```

We use the **invoke** verb and name the class to which the desired object belongs. In addition, we name the **reference** that is going to receive the address of the object created. The address of the class object will be placed in custRef. The **invoke** is the verb used in COBOL to send a **message** to a method.

When an object is created, storage must be acquired for the **attributes** and the **methods** that comprise the **interface** must be accommodated. It is the address of this object that is returned, to be assigned to the **reference**.

Our First OO COBOL Program

We have created a program containing a class that has two methods. One of the methods converts temperatures from Celsius to Fahrenheit and the other converts temperatures from Fahrenheit to Celsius.

You will see that the entry point is provided by the program that uses the class.

Temperature Conversion

```
class-id. TempConversion  as "TempConversion"
          inherits from base.
repository.
object.
method-id. "celToFar".
linkage section.
01  temp                        pic S9(3)V9(2) comp-3.
```

Listing 23.01 – 1 of 3

475

Temperature Conversion

```
procedure division using temp.
    compute temp = temp * 9 / 5 + 32
    exit method
end method  "celToFar".

method-id. "farToCel".
linkage section.
01 temp                          pic S9(3)V9(2) comp-3.
procedure division using temp.
    compute temp = (temp - 32) / 9 * 5
    exit method
end method  "farToCel".
end object.
end class TempConversion.

program-id. Chapter2301.
repository.
    class base as "base"
    class TempConversion as "TempConversion".
working-storage section.
01  temp                   pic S9(3)V9(2) comp-3.
01  w-code                 pic 9 value 0.
01  temp-out               pic ZZ9.9(2)-.
01  convReference          object reference TempConversion.
procedure division.
A100-start.
    invoke TempConversion "new" returning convReference
    perform A110-prompt.
    perform until w-code = 3
        display "Please enter temperature: " no advancing
        accept temp
        perform A200-test
        perform A110-prompt
    end-perform.
    stop run.

A110-prompt.
    display "Enter 1 for Celsius to Fahrenheit else enter 2"
    display "Enter 3 to terminate: " no advancing
    accept w-code.
```

Listing 23.01 – 2 of 3

Temperature Conversion

```
A200-test.
    if  w-code = 1
        invoke convReference 'celToFar' using temp
        move temp to temp-out
        display 'Fahrenheit equivalent is ' temp-out
    else
        invoke convReference 'farToCel' using temp
        move temp to temp-out
        display 'Celsius equivalent is ' temp-out
    end-if.
```

Listing 23.01 – 2 of 3

- The **class-id** paragraph enables us to name the class and to stipulate from what classes it is inheriting. As indicated earlier, there is one class from which all classes inherit. The class is called 'base'. For programmers coming from other OO languages, 'base' corresponds to the class 'Object'.

- The AS clause is used to specify the external name of the class for the operating environment.

- The **repository** paragraph must be there even if it is an empty paragraph.

- **Object** is matched by **end object**. In the body of object you specify what constitutes an object of the class.

- Each method starts with **method-id** and ends with **end method**, followed by the method name. In the body of the method you specify all that is in the method.

- In the example, the methods do not have their own storage. As you will see, a method may define a **local-storage section**. We will look at this later. We do, however, have a **linkage section**. The section is used to pass data to the method and to return data from the method.

- We specified **inherits from base**, implying that we will be able to treat an object of this class as if it were an object of class **base**, thus sharing its **interface**. This is different from coding **class base** in the **repository** paragraph. The latter means that the class will be available for use.

- We have the following definition in the working-storage of the invoking program:

```
01 convReference object reference TempConversion.
```

To refer to a class instance, in other words an object of a class, we need to create a **reference** for that class. A **reference** is a pointer and a pointer or reference contains the address of an object. In the preceding definition, the **reference** is able to contain the address of an object of type TempConversion. We have made the **ref-**

erence specific to objects of the class by coding `object reference TempConversion`.

- To address any **object** we need to load the **reference** we have created with the address of an object of the class. We use 'new', a method of class 'base' that builds an object of the named class and then returns the address of the object. The address returned is placed in the **reference** field. The line of code below may be interpreted as: "Invoke method new found in TempConversion and place the reference obtained in convReference". Notice that the method **new** is found in TempConversion because it forms part of the **interface**. Remember, the methods of the base class become part of the **interface** of the derived class.

```
invoke TempConversion "new" returning convReference
```

- In addition, we have a prompt routine and a test routine to determine the type of conversion to carry out. Because we constructed a class for the conversion, the class would be catalogued and anybody needing a temperature conversion would be free to use it.

- Notice that to use any class we need to know what its interface looks like. How the **implementation** does the work is no business of ours; how we ask the object to do the work is our business. Situations like this are described as black boxes. You know what you put into the box, you know what you get out of the box but you do not know what happens inside the box. For most of us the TV unit is a black box to us, we know which buttons to press and that is about all.

Note that the code in the preceding example was run under Net Express 4. Most of the examples are run under Net Express 4 with .Net. The programs refer to the base class. When running under .Net you may not refer to the base class so remove all such references. The program Chapter2301 runs under .Net. The languages running under .Net implicitly inherit from the Object class that performs a similar function to class base.

478

Class Not Part of Program

In the preceding example the class TempConversion was part of the program but it may be a totally separate file. Using Net Express .Net the mechanism would be as follows:

- We create the project as we would normally do and we code program Chapter2302, which is like program Chapter2301. The solution explorer would be as shown following.

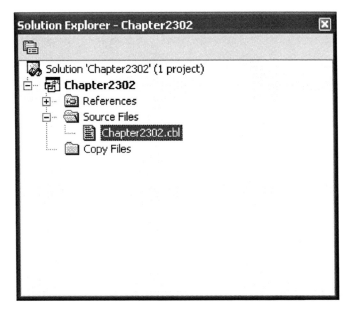

- We go to FILE|NEW|FILE and we will receive the following screen:

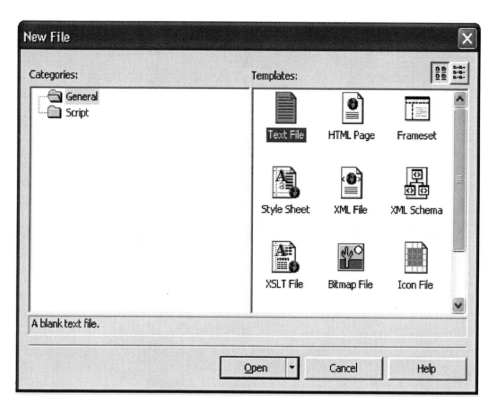

We select Text File and will receive a window that will allow us to enter the class TempConversion. We will save the file in project Chapter2302 as file TempConversion.cbl and close the solution.

- Open project Chapter2302 and you will receive the program that is to receive control. Select Project on the ToolBar to receive the following window. Since you have already created the file that you wish to add to the project, select Add Existing Item.

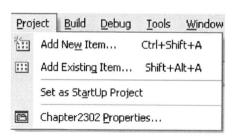

- You will receive a window reflecting the contents of project Chapter2302 and you will see an entry for a file labeled TempConversion, select the file. The Solution Explorer will now reflect the class file TempConversion.

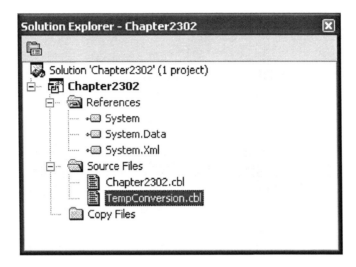

Because we used .Net we had to remove **inherits from class base**. As you will recall .Net programs implicitly inherit from class **Object**. Notice the reference to the class TempConversion in the repository.

Program Separate from Class

```
program-id. Chapter2302.
repository.
    class base as "base"
    class TempConversion as "TempConversion".
working-storage section.
01  temp                     pic S9(3)V9(2) comp-3.
01  w-code                   pic 9 value 0.
01  temp-out                 pic ZZ9.9(2)-.
01  convReference            object reference TempConversion.
```

Listing 23.02 – 1 of 2

Program Separate from Class

```
procedure division.
A100-start.
    invoke TempConversion "new" returning convReference
    perform A110-prompt.
    perform until w-code = 3
        display "Please enter temperature: " no advancing
        accept temp
        perform A200-test
        perform A110-prompt
    end-perform.
    stop run.

A110-prompt.
    display "Enter 1 for Celsius to Fahrenheit else enter 2"
    display "Enter 3 to terminate " no advancing
    accept w-code.

A200-test.
    if  w-code = 1
        invoke convReference 'celToFar' using temp
        move temp to temp-out
        display 'Fahrenheit equivalent is ' temp-out
    else
        invoke convReference 'farToCel' using temp
        move temp to temp-out
        display 'Celsius equivalent is ' temp-out
    end-if.
```

Listing 23.02 – 2 of 2

The procedural program is not as small as it might otherwise have been and CO-BOL bashers will have a field day. What we might do is to create a class to do what the procedural program is doing, namely prompting and evaluating. The Solution Explorer would now appear as follows:

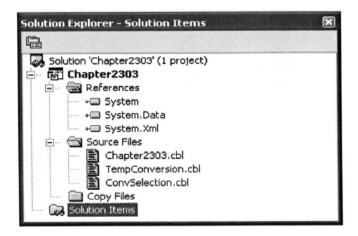

The three files follow:

Class TempConversion

```
class-id. TempConversion   as "TempConversion"

repository.
object.

method-id. "celToFar".
linkage section.
01  temp                        pic S9(3)V9(2) comp-3.
procedure division using temp.
    compute temp = temp * 9 / 5 + 32
    exit method
end method  "celToFar".

method-id. "farToCel".
linkage section.
01  temp                        pic S9(3)V9(2) comp-3.
procedure division using temp.
    compute temp = (temp - 32) / 9 * 5
    exit method
end method  "farToCel".

end object.
end class TempConversion.
```

Listing 23.03 – 1 of 3

Class ConvSelection

```cobol
class-id. ConvSelection  as "ConvSelection".
repository.
    class TempConversion as "TempConversion".
object.
working-storage section.
01  temp                    pic S9(3)V9(2) comp-3.
01  w-code                  pic 9 value 0.
01  temp-out                pic ZZ9.9(2)-.
01  convReference           object reference TempConversion.
procedure division.
method-id. convSelect.
procedure division.
    invoke TempConversion "new" returning convReference
    invoke self "convPrompt"
    perform until w-code = 3
        display "Please enter temperature: " no advancing
        accept temp
        invoke self "convTest"
        invoke self "convPrompt"
    end-perform
    exit method.
end method convSelect.
method-id. convPrompt.
procedure division.
    display "Enter 1 for Celsius to Fahrenheit else enter 2"
    display "Enter 3 to terminate " no advancing
    accept w-code
    exit method
end method convPrompt.
method-id. convTest.
procedure division.
    if  w-code = 1
        invoke convReference 'celToFar' using temp
        move temp to temp-out
        display 'Fahrenheit equivalent is ' temp-out
    else
        invoke convReference 'farToCel' using temp
        move temp to temp-out
        display 'Celsius equivalent is ' temp-out
    end-if
```

Listing 23.03 – 2 of 3

Class ConvSelection and Chapter2303

```
     exit method
 end method convTest.
 end object.
 end class ConvSelection.

 program-id. Chapter2303.
 repository.
     class ConvSelection as  "ConvSelection".
 working-storage section.
 01  selectRef                 object reference ConvSelection.
 procedure division.
 A100-start.
     invoke ConvSelection "new" returning selectRef
     invoke selectRef "convSelect"
     stop run.

 end program Chapter2303
```

Listing 23.03 – 3 of 3

Self

We have isolated the prompting and selection into a class and have also included some methods in the class invoking other methods in the same class. In this case we are already busy with the object so it does not make sense to use the reference because the **reference** identifies the **object**. When you talk to yourself you don't use your name. In OO CO-BOL, we use the word **self** where the reference would otherwise be to invoke a method in the same class as the invoking method. Note that **self** always refers to the **object** currently executing. The **object** currently executing is the **object** to which the **reference** is pointing and consequently the object that invoked the original method, the one now using **self**.

Notice also that the class has a working-storage section. What you define in the **working-storage** of the class will be visible to the whole class. Inside a method you may have **working-storage** or **local-storage**. The difference between the two is that values in the **working-storage** persist between invocations, whereas values in local-storage do not persist. You may use the **value** clause on items in local-storage and they will be initialized to the specified values each time. Fields whose values do not persist are described as **automatic**.

Notice that periods are required for repository, object and end object, method-id and end-method, Class-id and end-class. A period must follow the last entry in the **repository**. Remember that **end class** and **end method** carry the **class** and **method** names respectively.

Factory and Super

The function of a **factory** object is to create new instances where initialization is required. Another function is to have storage items that relate not to an instance in particular but to all instances of the class. If you are going to keep a count of the number of objects of the class that have been created, this storage cannot form part of the storage of the individual objects. To this extent, it is similar to static storage in other object oriented languages.

If no initialization code is necessary and global storage for the class is not used then the class need not have a **factory** object, as we saw earlier. Initialization code is only executed once, in a run, when the object is created.

A **factory** object has its own **working-storage** which is not visible to objects of the class. To this extent, it differs from **constructors** in other object oriented languages which have their own local storage and in addition use the object's storage. In other OO languages the **constructor** is not an object. The **factory** object must have all methods required to act on the data present in its **working-storage**. It must also have the code necessary to pass the data in its **working-storage** to objects of the class. This is done by having a **factory** method invoke a class method. In our example we have called this method 'initializeData'.

We have indicated that **factory** data is ideal for data that applies to the class rather than to class instances. The number of objects of the class created would be data of this type. If we are to be able to see the data, then the **factory** object must have a method that returns that data.

In the example that follows, we have a class Contestant which has a factory object. For every object created, one is added to cont-no and the date is retrieved. These fields are passed to the class instance when the object method 'initializeData' is invoked. We have the object method 'displayNo' which invokes the factory method 'showNo'.

Factory Object

```
   class-id. Contestant   as "Contestant" inherits from base.

   repository.

   factory.
   working-storage section.
   01  factory-data.
       05  cont-no    pic 99   value 0.
       05  cont-date  pic 9999/99/99.
```

Listing 23.04 – 1 of 3

Factory Object

```
    method-id. "new".
    linkage section.
    01   contReference        object reference active-class.
    procedure division returning contReference.
        invoke super "new" returning contReference
        add 1 to cont-no
        accept cont-date from date yyyymmdd
        invoke contReference 'initializeData'
            using by content factory-data
        exit method
    end method "new".

    method-id. "showNo".
    linkage section.
    01   lnkNo          pic 99.
    procedure division returning lnkNo.
        move cont-no to lnkNo
        exit method.
    end method "showNo".

    end factory.
    object.

    working-storage section.
    01   wk-data.
        05 wk-no      pic 99.
        05 wk-date    pic X(10).
    method-id. "initializeData".
    01   ctr          pic 9   value 5.
    linkage section.
    01   lnk-data.
        05   lnk-no       pic 99.
        05   lnk-date     pic X(10).
    procedure division using lnk-data.
        move lnk-data to wk-data
        display 'No is:    ' wk-no
        display 'Date is: ' wk-date
        display 'Ctr is: ' ctr
        exit method
    end method   "initializeData".
```

Listing 23.04 – 2 of 3

Class Object

```
method-id. "displayNo".
local-storage section.
01  loc-no          pic 99.
procedure division.
    invoke Contestant 'showNo'returning loc-no
    display 'Contestant no is: ' loc-no
    exit method
end method  "displayNo".
end object.
end class Contestant.
program-id. Chapter2304.
repository.
    class base as "base"
    class Contestant as "Contestant".
working-storage section.
01  contReference1              object reference Contestant.
01  contReference2              object reference Contestant.

procedure division.
A100-start.
    invoke Contestant "new" returning contReference1
    invoke contReference1 'displayNo'
    invoke Contestant "new" returning contReference2
    invoke contReference2 'displayNo'
    stop run.
```

Listing 23.04 – 3 of 3

- We used the keyword **super** when, in the factory object, we invoked the method 'new'. We use the word **super** to indicate that the method is in the class from which this class, the active class, inherits. The method in question is in class **base**.

- The **reference** returned points to the object created, as it usually does when we are not using a factory object. It is as if the compiler creates a **factory** object for us when we do not create one. The code in this hypothetical **factory** object would merely invoke **super**. Notice that the procedure division statement of the **factory** object has a **returning** clause and the **reference** is returned.

- We have made the **reference** point to **active-class**. This means that it can only point to the class in which it is coded. In the example the class is Contestant. It follows that had we coded Contestant instead of **active-class**, we would have secured the same effect.

- We use the **reference** to invoke a method in the object of the class and we pass data defined in the **factory** object. Remember that these fields are not otherwise accessible to the class object.

```
invoke contReference 'initializeData'
      using by content factory-data
```

- The other **factory** method is called 'showNo' and returns the number of contestants recorded. For this it needs a **linkage** section - the area for communication between methods.

- In the method 'initializeData', data are received from the **factory** object. This data will be in the linkage section. We transfer it to the object's **working-storage** after which it is displayed.

- We also wish to show that to access **factory working-storage** we need a **factory** method that will return the required data. The method we have created is 'showNo'. To invoke this method we created the class object method 'displayNo'.

- We invoke the method 'showNo' in class Contestant. Note that in invoking a **factory** object we may not use **self**.

```
invoke Contestant 'showNo' returning loc-no
```

- Let us now examine the procedural program used to invoke the class. We create two references to test the functioning of the **factory** object.

- In the method 'initializeData' we have a working-storage field Ctr that retains its value between calls. As you will recall, **Local-storage** fields do not retain values between calls.

```
Command Prompt                                    _ □ ×

No is:  01
Date is:  2005/06/08
ctr is: 5
Contestant no is:  01
No is:  02
Date is:  2005/06/08
ctr is: 5
Contestant no is:  02
No is:  03
Date is:  2005/06/08
ctr is: 5
Contestant no is:  03
No is:  04
Date is:  2005/06/08
ctr is: 5
Contestant no is:  04
```

Memory Leaks

When an object of a class comes into being, the **factory** object invoking 'new' must ensure that storage is acquired for the object's **working-storage** and local-storage. The address of this storage is then returned and assigned to the **reference**. The object created will, if not destroyed, live until the program terminates. When we no longer need an object we should destroy that object so as to free the storage with which it is associated. If we do not destroy it, it will be using storage and we may eventually run out of storage. This is what is called a **memory leak** and to avoid memory leaks some languages incorporate a **garbage collection** mechanism that releases memory to which no reference is pointing.

COBOL provides a **finalize** method which is implemented in the 'base' class and inherited by all classes. We have changed the invoking program from the preceding example. We placed the **invoke** inside a loop and at the bottom of the loop we use the 'finalize'. It is not absolutely necessary because the value in the **reference** would be overwritten.

Finalize

```
program-id. Chapter2305.

repository.
    class base as "base"
    class Contestant as "Contestant".
working-storage section.
01  contReference            object reference Contestant.
01  ctr                      pic 99.
procedure division.
A100-start.
    perform varying ctr from 1 by 1
        until ctr > 4
            invoke Contestant "new" returning contReference
            invoke contReference 'displayNo'
            invoke contReference 'finalize'
                    returning contReference
    end-perform
    stop run.
```

Listing 23.05

```
Command Prompt                                    _ □ ×
No is:  01
Date is:  2004/08/17
Contestant no is:  01
No is:  02
Date is:  2004/08/17
Contestant no is:  02
No is:  03
Date is:  2004/08/17
Contestant no is:  03
No is:  04
Date is:  2004/08/17
Contestant no is:  04
```

At first, for people acquainted with other object oriented languages, the factory object is a cumbersome form of constructor. With a bit of goodwill, however, it soon becomes acceptable.

The two preceding programs run under Net Express and not Net Express with .Net.

Files in Object Orientation

Files may be specified either in factory objects or in class instances. If the file is specified in the factory object, it may serve all instances of the class. Declared in class instances implies that each object will contain all the statements required for file definition and use.

The following example has the file declared in the **factory** object. The file is read in the beginning and loaded into a table. The table is then passed to the instance object.

File in the Factory Object

```
class-id. CustInfo   as "CustInfo"
         inherits from base.
repository.
factory.
file-control.
    select cust-in assign to 'C:\cob0\mast02'.
file section.
fd   cust-in.
01   cust-rec       pic X(11).
```

Listing 23.06 – 1 of 3

File in the Factory Object

```cobol
working-storage section.
01  cust-tab.
    05  cust-ent   pic X(11)   occurs 10.
01  ctr            pic 99.
method-id. "new".
linkage section.
01  custRef             object reference active-class.
procedure division returning custRef.
    invoke super "new" returning custRef
    open input cust-in
    read cust-in
    perform varying ctr from 1 by 1
        until ctr > 10
        move cust-rec to cust-ent (ctr)
        read cust-in
    end-perform
    close cust-in
    invoke custRef 'initializeData'
        using by content cust-tab
    exit method.
end method "new".
end factory.
object.
working-storage section.
01  cust-table.
    05  cust-ent                 occurs 10.
        10  cust-id    pic 9(3).
        10  cust-name  pic X(3).
        10  cust-sal   pic 9(5).
    05 wk-date         pic X(10).
01  ctr                pic 99.
01  cust-no            pic 999.
method-id. "initializeData".
linkage section.
01  lnk-data.
    05  cust-tab       pic X(110).
procedure division using lnk-data.
    move cust-tab to cust-table.
    exit method
end method  "initializeData".
```

Listing 23.06 – 2 of 3

File in the Factory Object

```
method-id. "interact".
procedure division.
interacting.
    perform getCustNo
    perform until cust-no = 999
        perform varying ctr from 1 by 1
            until ctr > 10  or cust-no = cust-id (ctr)
        end-perform
        if  ctr > 10
            display 'Invalid customer ID'
        else
            display cust-name(ctr) '  ' cust-sal(ctr)
        end-if
        perform getCustNo
    end-perform
    exit method.
getCustNo.
    display
        'Please enter customer number or 999 to terminate.'
    accept cust-no.
end method  "interact".
end object.
end class CustInfo.

program-id. Chapter2306.
repository.
    class base as "base"
    class CustInfo as "CustInfo".
working-storage section.
01  custRef              object reference CustInfo.
procedure division.
A100-start.
    invoke CustInfo "new" returning custRef
    invoke custRef 'interact'
    stop run.
```

Listing 23.06 – 3 of 3

Examine the preceding example. The only point that needs explaining is that method 'interact' consists of more than one function. In addition to the main function 'interacting', it has function 'getCustNo'.

You also see that the **factory** object has a **file-control** paragraph and a file section. In the **procedure division** of method 'new', we process the file and pass the array.

Note that we call the **factory** method 'new' by convention, because the name reflects its purpose, which is to create a new object.

The next example has the file in the class object. We have a **file-control** paragraph and a file section followed by the method 'getCust'. This time the class has a single method. You may add to the class by adding a method to change a record and another to add a record to the file.

File in Class Object

```
class-id. CustInfo  as "CustInfo"
             inherits from base.
repository.     *> Statement must be present

object.
file-control.
    select cust-in assign to 'C:\cobnet\mast01'
        organization is indexed
        access is random
        record key is cust-key.
file section.
fd   cust-in.
01   cust-rec.
     05   cust-key    pic X(03).
     05   cust-name   pic X(03).
     05   cust-sal    pic 9(05).

method-id. 'getCust'.
procedure division.
interacting.
    open input cust-in
    perform getCustNo
    perform until cust-key = 999
        read cust-in
            invalid key
                display 'Record not found'
            not invalid key
                display cust-name '  ' cust-sal
        end-read
        perform getCustNo
    end-perform
    exit method.
```

Listing 23.07 – 1 of 2

File in Class Object

```
getCustNo.
    display 'Please enter customer number or 999 to end.'
    accept cust-key.
end method "getCust".

end object.
end class CustInfo.

program-id. Chapter2306.
repository.
    class base as "base"
    class CustInfo as "CustInfo".
working-storage section.
01  custRef                 object reference CustInfo.
procedure division.
A100-start.
    invoke CustInfo "new" returning custRef
    invoke custRef 'getCust'
    stop run.
```

Listing 23.07 – 2 of 2

```
Command Prompt                                    _ □ ✕

Please enter customer number or 999 to end.
110
Dan 08430
Please enter customer number or 999 to end.
150
Val 08730
Please enter customer number or 999 to end.
225
Record not found
Please enter customer number or 999 to end.
999
```

Summary

- Procedural programming tackles complexity through functional decomposition. OO handles complexity through determination of the objects present in the problem domain. Notice that when we come to the determination of the functionality required by a class we enter a process akin to functional decomposition.
- If we establish that a customer is an **object** then the collection of all customers forms the Customer **class**. The members of the **class** all have the same **attributes** and the same **behaviour**, which is why we can assemble them into a group.
- An **attribute** is a feature of the object; therefore it is inherent to the object. An example for a Customer object would be CustomerNumber.
- **Encapsulation** entails the construction of a capsule that isolates the class from its environment. Of course we only want partial isolation. For this reason, we split the class into two parts. One part we call **implementation** and the other we call **interface**. The **implementation** is **private** meaning that it is not visible to other classes. The **interface**, on the other hand, is **public**, meaning that it is visible to other classes.
- **Attributes** and routines that we feel should not be visible to other classes we place in the **implementation**. The methods that are required for interaction with the class will be placed in the **interface**.
- Because the object comprises both **attributes** as well as the functionality associated with those **attributes**, it may be reused. If we made Customer a class, then any application where a customer object would be used could bring in that class, thus benefiting from the existing code. It is estimated that only 15% of code generated is new, 85% is already in existence. OO overcomes this problem.
- **Inheritance** enables a class to inherit from an existing class. In this way the functionality from the existing class may be inherited and therefore becomes available to the inheriting class without need to duplicate the code. The class from which we inherit is called the base class. The class that inherits is called the derived class.
- **Polymorphism** is closely associated with **inheritance**. Thus polymorphism enables us to, at runtime, treat an object of a derived class as if it were an object of the base class. Notice that if we have class Employee inheriting from class Person, it is legitimate to say "an Employee is a kind of Person". However, it is not legitimate to invert the direction of the relationship and say "A Person is a kind of Employee".
- Classes communicate by sending **messages** to methods in other classes. The method receiving the message may receive or return data. To send a message to a method in another class we must first create an object of that class. When we create the object, its address will be returned into a reference field able to point to the class. We then use this reference field in addressing the method in the class. We

use the invoke verb for the purpose. In the **invoke** we name the class and the method that is to be used and which is a member of the class.

- Whenever a program works with a class, it is the program (which is procedural) that invokes the class. This is also true of Net Express with .NET.

- The class starts with a **class-id** statement and ends on **end class**. Following class-id, we enter the name of the class followed by AS, enabling us to specify the external name of the class. The class explicitly inherits from class base. Class base contains the basic functionality that enables objects to be created. Rather than recreate this intricate functionality, we inherit from the class. In many OO languages the base class is known as the **Object** class and every class implicitly inherits from the class. This is also true of Net Express with .NET.

- Inside the class there is a **repository** paragraph. Following the paragraph we define the object. The definition of the object is inserted between **object** and **end object** statements.

- Each method may have a working-storage section that operates as a normal **working-storage**. In addition, we may also code a **local-storage** section. Fields in local-storage are not retained between calls. If fields in **local-storage** have been initialized, they will be reinitialized each time the method is invoked.

- If we need to invoke a method belonging to the same class as the invoking method we must use the keyword **self**. We would code: **invoke self** "**methodName**".

- When an object is created, storage needs to be acquired dynamically. This work is done for us by a default **factory** object. If, when an object is created we need to do some extra work, we need to create our own **factory** object.

- The **factory** object has its own **working-storage** that is not visible to objects of the class. **Factory** methods are accessible to objects of the class, therefore, **factory** methods must be available to **set** and **get factory** data. Factory data applies to the class rather than to individual instances of the class.

- When we use **super** we are referring to the class from which the present class derives. When the **factory** object creates a reference, we describe the reference as **active-class** in order to point to methods in the class to which it belongs.

- **Memory leaks** refer to references that point to objects that no longer exist. Although the objects no longer exist, the storage they occupied is still allocated. This is an example of a memory leak.

- Files may be specified in **factory** objects as well as in class objects. If specified in factory objects, the data retrieved will be available to all objects of the class.

Complete

1. Procedural programming uses _____ _____ as the mechanism for resolving complexity.

2. Encapsulation hides the _____.

3. Communication with a class is through the _____.

4. A class does not see another class until you create a _____ to the class and _____ it.

5. A class _____ must be loaded with the _____ of the class before it can be used.

6. In OO COBOL, _____ are inherited but _____ are not.

7. The relationship found in inheritance is the ___ _ _____ __ relationship.

8. The paradigm of polymorphism is reflected in the phrase one _____ many _____.

9. To call a method of another class we use the _____ verb.

10. To receive data from another class, the call to the method utilizes the _____ clause.

11. The factory object uses the returning verb to return the reference. The returning clause is coded in the _____ _____ statement.

12. The keyword _____ is used to refer to the class from which the current class inherits.

13. The reference that can only point to the class in which it is coded is the _____ reference.

14. Objects that are no longer used but are still using up memory give rise to _____ _____ reference.

True/False

1.   All class instances will have the same attributes and the same functions.

2.   A method can have only one paragraph.

3.   The most basic of classes is the Object class or the base class.

4.   A reference enables us to refer to a class.

5.   To use a class we need to know what its implementation looks like.

6.   Function overriding makes one form of polymorphism possible.

7.   We use **self** when we wish to refer to a method in the base class.

8.   Super is used to refer to a method in the same class.

9.   A method may not have working-storage, only local storage.

10. The factory object relies on the base class to create the object requested.

11. Initialization code present in the factory object may only be executed once the object is created.

12. Objects of a class may access the working-storage of the factory object of the containing class.

13. Factory data applies to the whole class rather than to particular objects of the class.

14   Memory leaks refer to memory usage that is no longer required but is not released.

15. The verb that releases storage that is no longer required is 'liquidate'.

16. The returning clause that in the factory object returns the reference may be coded in the procedure division or in the exit method statement.

17. The method 'new' in the factory object could be called by another name.

Exercises

1.   Create a Conversion class. The class converts inches to meters and pounds to kilo-grams. (1 in. = 2.542 cm, 1 pound = 452.6 gm).

     You are to iterate until the user enters a value 999. You should construct a class that will interact with the Conversion class. The invoking program should invoke the interacting class once only.

2.   Create a class CustomerCreate. When a new Customer is created a new customer number should be allocated. Start your customerNo at 5300. The methods should be invoked automatically, the customerNo should be updated and the time when the customer was created recorded. There should be methods that may be invoked to return the customerNo and the time.

Chapter 24

Finding Use Cases

Topics Covered

- ❑ Object Oriented Analysis - Introduction
- ❑ Preliminary Evaluation
- ❑ Elaboration
- ❑ Program Testing Software
- ❑ The Layered Approach
- ❑ The User Interface
- ❑ The Business Layer
- ❑ The Data Access Layer
- ❑ Use Cases
- ❑ Finding Actors
- ❑ Finding Use Cases
- ❑ Use Case Diagram
- ❑ The Include Relationship
- ❑ The Extends Relationship
- ❑ Rules
- ❑ When to use Use Cases
- ❑ Summary
- ❑ Complete
- ❑ True/False

Object Oriented Analysis

Introduction

When doing analysis, we gather information from different sources and try to extract meaning from the information we receive. We obtain the information from the domain experts. The domain experts are the people who are knowledgeable in the area under investigation.

Although these individuals are intimately acquainted with the subject of their expertise, this does not mean to say that there are no problems in communication and that other human flaws do not taint the communication between you and the domain expert. In addition, the analyst will receive conflicting information from different sources.

One thing is certain; we must provide the people who will be using the system with what they want. The Unified Modeling Language is a communication tool, generally referred to as **UML**, and was devised to facilitate the creation of object oriented systems and to ensure that the user will get what was asked for.

If the user wants a simple bottle opener, should we provide her with an all-purpose tool? The idea is that we should supply what the user wants, not what we think the user should want. This implies that as we progress with the analysis, we obtain confirmation from the user to the effect that we are on the right track.

This in turn implies is that we will not deliver the completed product at the end of the project. Instead, we will follow an iterative process delivering one component at a time. It is only when we are satisfied that each component operates to the satisfaction of the user that we progress to the next one.

Each iteration contains the usual steps found in the software life cycle and comprises analysis, design, implementation and testing.

Preliminary Evaluation

Creating a system costs money. It is not strange then that the people who are going to pay for the system would like to know the envisaged cost of the system and what it will provide. At this stage, estimates will be tentative and will cover not only costs but also expected benefits.

Elaboration

The next step is elaboration. In this step you will expand on your knowledge of what creating the proposed system will involve. An important issue to be tackled in this step is risk assessment. There are three types of risk.

- **Requirements risk** – Are we producing the required solution? We have seen above how we go about tackling this difficulty. One technique we use is covered below; we use '**Use Cases**' as shown further on. **Use Cases** assist us in ensuring that the requirements are met.
- **Technological risk** – Are the proposed software and hardware the most suitable for the job? Will the different items of software work together? What difficulty is associated with interoperability between programs written in different computer languages?
- **Skills risk** – Do we have the required skills available? If not, are they easy to procure? We must ensure that the skills will be available when required.

The approach to any risk item is that it should be tackled early. Do not postpone because it is unlikely that the problem will go away.

Once you have established the **Use Cases**, you are able to plan the steps in each **Use Case**, then estimate the time taken by each, and therefore the total time for the project.

How long should we spend on preliminary investigation elaboration and planning? Say the time envisaged for the project is six months, then spend at most one month in this step. In estimating total time allow a percentage, say, 10% for slippage.

Program Testing Software

Testing is extremely important. Remember that a program is not finished until it is tested and running. You should create your own software that will provide the test data in such a way that when the program to be tested is run, it will automatically invoke the program that generates the test data.

The Layered Approach

In today's world we can see that the creation of software can be seen as involving three layers. The layers are:

- The user interface - UI
- Business layer
- Data access layer

The User Interface

The function of the **User Interface** layer is to accept data from the screen and to make them available to the **business layer**. Similarly, it will present the data received from the business layer on the screen. By keeping the design of screens separate we may at any time redesign the screen without impacting on other layers. Where we place the information on the screen is of no concern to the other layers - rather, it is the sole responsibility of this layer.

The Business Layer

The **business layer** contains all the classes and objects that are concerned with the processing to be done. This layer passes data to the UI and the responsibility of placing it on the screen rests on the UI. The format of the screen may be changed but this is of no concern to the business layer.

Similarly, when the **business layer** needs data, it passes control to the **data access layer** telling it to get such and such items of data. It is not concerned with the database or file system being used. If tomorrow the database changes from Oracle to DB2 or vice versa, this should in no way affect any of the classes in the business layer.

In this way, the business layer is totally independent of communication with the outside world.

The Data Access Layer

The **data access layer** has to know how to translate requests coming from the **business layer** into a format appropriate to the database used. If the request is to write, it must do whatever is required to place the object in the database. If it is a request for data, the **data access layer** will do whatever is required to retrieve the data and return the object, now containing data, to the **business layer**.

Use Cases

Use cases were conceived by Ivor Jacobson and have today been incorporated into the UML where they play a prominent role.

What are **use cases**? **use cases** are defined in terms of scenarios. A group of related scenarios will be a **use case**. A scenario will be a possible interaction with a user. Note that any interaction with a **Use Case** is undertaken by an actor, always depicted as a stick figure. The actor need not be a person but may be a software unit – for arguments sake, the Accounting System.

Say you want to order a book through the Internet. The company is Nile.com. Notice the interaction between the user and the system. This basically, is what a **use case** is all about.

Buy book
1. From the options screen, the user selects Books;
2. The system presents a new screen to the user;
3. The user enters the name of the author;
4. The system presents a list of books by the author;
5. The user selects a book and clicks on check;
6. The system requests forwarding details;
7. The system requests credit card details;
8. The system authorizes payment;
9. The system confirms the deal immediately;
10. The system supplies details of delivery.

The above is one **use case** consisting of eight related scenarios. Note that we may have nested **use cases**. In the **use case** above, some of the items involve quite a complicated scenario and are themselves **use cases**. Let us see which would fall into the category.

1. Item one, book selection, is a good candidate. There is a reasonable degree of complexity.
2. Item six, filling in forwarding details
3. Items seven and eight would be considered jointly
4. Item nine and item 10 would be two **use cases** sharing much of the behaviour.

Another scenario is:

Authorization fails

1. Evaluate – insufficient funds - notify
2. Credit card details incorrect – request re-entry

Another scenario:

Existing Customer

System detects this is an existing customer and bypasses request for shipping information.

505

Finding Actors

The **actors** will be the likely users of the system. If the credit manager or the credit clerk use the system for the same purpose then they constitute a single **actor**. On the other hand, the same person may use the system for two purposes, in which case we have two **actors**.

Say the Credit manager looks at an account. In this case he is playing the role of the Accounts clerk. If he decides to change the credit limit he is acting as the Credit manager. We have two **actors**.

Remember that if in a particular **use case** the system interacts with another system, this will be a non-human **actor**.

Finding Use Cases

Once you have found the **actors** that interact with the system you are in a position to examine what it is that they want from the system. From the information you obtain you will eventually be able to derive roles and **responsibilities**.

Through examination, you have found the following requirements from the system.

- The customer wants to place an order
- The customer wants to look at an order
- The customer wants to determine the status of an order

Here we have three **use cases.** They are arrived at by ascertaining, in an order system what it is that the actor, in this case the customer, wants from the system.

Use Case Diagrams

Let us construct a **use case** diagram to reflect one of the three **use cases** depicted above, namely, placing an order. In the diagram the actor is the Customer. The system also needs to interact with the product database. This is another **actor**.

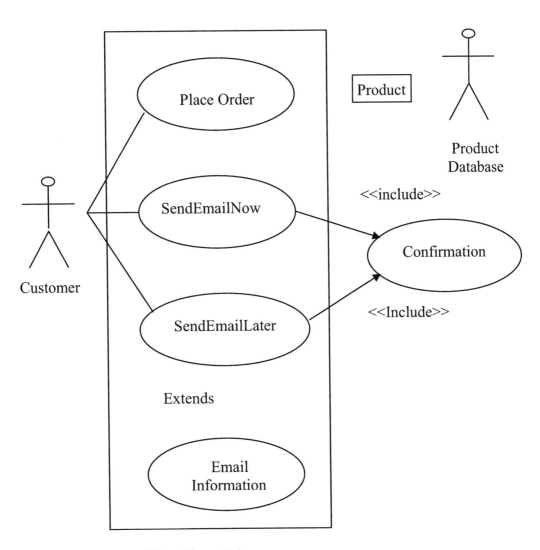

Use Case Diagram

When determining the **use cases** from the actors you should ensure that you ascertain the objectives to be met by the **use case**. In other words, make sure you will provide everything the user needs from the **use case**.

The Include Relationship

The **include** Relationship is used when there is a large unit of behavior that is common to one or more **use cases**. Rather than duplicate the code, we create a new **use case** that is available to the use cases sharing the behavior now isolated.

SendEmailNow and SendEmailLater share behavior that is now in the Confirmation **use case**.

The Extends Relationship

Extends is used with inheritance. Inheritance is graphically represented by the arrow pointing to the class from which inheritance takes place. In inheritance you are inheriting the attributes and the behavior from the more general class. In other words, the inheriting class is more specialized. Although inheritance may be viewed as generalization or specialization, inheritance is described as generalization.

We also describe the inherited class as the base class and the inheriting class as the derived class.

Extends signifies that we are not only inheriting but are also adding functionality. When retrieving e-mail information we have to iterate through the items, looking for the one in respect of which information is acquired.

Rules

What you should use:

- **Include** – use the include to avoid duplicating code common to two or more **use cases**.
- **Generalization** - use generalization when one class reflects a 'is a kind of' relationship. For instance, we would say "A savings account **is a kind of** account".
- **Extend** – extend is used to formalize the inheritance relationship. It is usual in such cases to have the extensions to the base class implemented in the derived class.

When to Use Use Cases

It is difficult to find a situation where we would not use **use cases**. What must be noted is that although you will start the analysis with x number of **use cases**, you will find that you will add **use cases** as your knowledge of the system progresses. Not surprisingly, it is also probable that you will eliminate some **use cases**.

Summary

- Communication between the domain expert and the analyst always contains some level of inaccuracy. In spite of this, we must ensure that the user is provided with the desired product and not some approximation. Rather than deliver the whole system and hope that it meets requirements, in OO an iterative process is followed.

- Because we follow an iterative process, when we are finished with the first unit we present it to the user for approval. Being finished with the first unit entails analysis, design, implementation and testing. If the user is not satisfied with the product we iterate through the indicated steps until the user is satisfied. Only then do we progress to the following unit.

- When the creation of a system is envisaged the people who are going to pay for it must be provided with a cost/benefit analysis to enable them to make a decision to abort or go forward.

- Risk assessment comprises three categories of risk, namely, requirements risk, technological risk and skills risk. When a risk is detected it should be immediately tackled. Waiting will not eliminate the risk.

- In testing, the programmer should create an appropriate testing program that will be automatically invoked when the program to be tested is run. Whenever changes are applied to the program the testing software will be automatically invoked. Note that a program is not complete until it has been tested.

- You know that OO breaks a problem into the objects in the domain. In addition, when using OO we group those objects based on where they are used. This approach is described as the layered approach. The objects will fall into one of the following groups: They occur in the user interface, or in the business layer or in the data access layer.

- If an object occurs in the user interface layer, then changes to the business layer will not impact either on the user interface layer or the data access layer.

- Basically, a use case reflects an interaction between a user and the system. Users are described as actors and an actor may be a person or a system. Actors are depicted as stick figures. Use cases are broken up into the steps required to obtain the required output that is returned, presumably, to the actor. The steps into which the use case is broken are referred to as a scenario. Use cases may be nested inside another use case.

- We create a diagram to reflect the relationships present in the use case. One relationship that stands out is the include relationship. The relationship reflects the presence of behavior that is common to two or more use cases. The extend relationship reflects the presence of inheritance where the derived class adds functionality.

Complete

1. When doing analysis, the analyst obtains information from the _____ _____.

2. Each iteration in the production of the system involves going through _____, _____, _____ and _____.

3. Risk assessment is of three types namely, _____, _____ and _____.

4. Program testing should be an integrated process where _____ of the program to be tested involves _____ of the testing program.

5. The layered approach involves the layers _____, _____ and _____.

6. When using the layered approach a change to the user interface will _____ _____ the other two layers.

7. A use case reflects the _____ between an actor and the system.

8. An actor is shown as a _____ _____.

9. An actor may be a _____ or another _____.

10. An include points to a possibility of reducing _____ of code.

11. The extend points to _____ of functionality in the _____ class.

True/False

1.   Before proceeding to the next module in the delivery of a system we obtain approval of the preceding module by the user. True/False

2.   The steps in a iteration in the system production process consists of the following steps: Analysis, design and implementation. True/False

3.   The preliminary evaluation seeks to produce a cost/benefit analysis. True/False

4.   Requirements risk refers to the possibility of providing the wrong solution to the user. True/False

5.   The business layer is concerned with the burden of securing the required results. True/False

6.   A way of finding the actors is through the presence of verbs in the description. True/False

7.   A way of finding scenarios is to locate the nouns in the requirements description. True/False

8.   The include relationship reflects the presence of a function that is required by only one scenario. True/False

9.   The extends relationship points to the need for additional functionality in the derived class. True/False

10.   In a base class/derived class relationship, the base class is the more generalized class. True/False

Chapter 25

Class Diagrams

Topics Covered

- ❏ Class Diagrams
- ❏ Perspectives
- ❏ Association
- ❏ Multiplicity
- ❏ Attributes
- ❏ Operations
- ❏ Generalization
- ❏ Constraints
- ❏ Summary
- ❏ Complete
- ❏ True/False

Class Diagrams

In the process of ascertaining user requirements via **use cases** you go on to **class diagrams**. **Class diagrams** are central to object oriented analysis and are generally used, although you don't have to, irrespective of the analysis method being used. In addition, **class diagrams** are central to the UML.

The class diagram will depict the relationships between the classes in the **use case** as well as the structure of each of the classes. The structure is provided by the **attributes** of the class as well as by its **behavior** components, the operations.

Perspectives

Martin Fowler categorizes **use cases** based on the viewpoint you take. You can take what he describes as the **conceptual** perspective, the **specification** perspective or the **implementation** perspective.

Conceptual – This is a high level view. You are concerned with the classes that reflect the domain under examination.

Specification – In this view you have determined the structure of the class, namely its methods. The class is split into two parts concerned with visibility. That part of the class that is visible to other classes is the interface and the part that is not visible is called the implementation.

The interface is what programming is directed to. All communication with a class is carried out via its interface. It follows that relationships between classes have to be established via the interfaces. The specification perspective is mainly concerned with the interface. Note that the interface reflects the **responsibilities** of the class. One responsibility might be to return the make of a car another might be to return the number of days between two dates.

This is not to say that all relationships between classes are established via the interfaces. **Generalization** involves a "**is a kind of**" relationship which is not established via the **interface**. Similarly, nested classes are related to the containing class via a "**has a**" relationship.

Implementation – You will notice that at each level we add more and more detail. At this level you should have a complete class that will include the implementation.

A class diagram follows. Following the diagram, we will examine its components.

Class Diagram

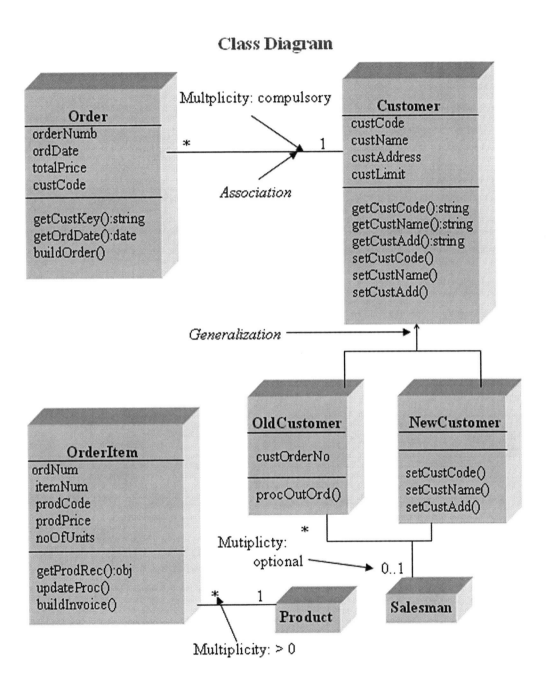

Association

An **Association** indicates that a relationship exists between the classes. **Associations** may be unidirectional or bi-directional. In the Customer/Order relationship, it is unidirectional because you can relate an order to a customer but you cannot relate a customer to an order.

Notice that the customer code is a foreign key in Order and this enables it to link back to Customer. A foreign key is a field or fields that enable a reference to another database file.

Multiplicity

Multiplicity specifies the type of relationship between the classes. Is it a one-to-one or one-to-many relationship. In the case of the relationship between the Customer and Order, for one customer there may be any number of orders.

A customer may have no orders or any number greater than zero. On the other hand, an Order may only be related to one Customer.

You will notice that when there is a lower bound and an upper bound, these are separated by two dots. A Customer may be serviced by one salesman but some customers will have no salesman servicing them.

For the relationship between Order and OrderItems we see that OrderItems are always related to only one order. On the other hand, an Order may have any number of OrderItems zero or greater. Generally there will be one or more OrderItems for an order. However, if you delete OrderItems an order may be left with no OrderItems.

Attributes

Attributes are the data items inherent to the class. We can say that **attributes** describe the class. The measurements that described Miss World might be 36-24-36. We would have been correct in saying that these were some of her **Attributes**, those that propelled her to prominence.

For a Customer class the **attributes** we had were customer code, name, address and limit. These **attributes** are inherent and describe a particular Customer object. You might have another data item, say date, as part of the class, to assist in the processing, but this data item would in no way describe the object so it is not an **attribute**.

In what we described as a conceptual perspective, we would say that a customer has a name. At a specification perspective, we would determine that we need to be able to see the customer name. At the implementation level, we would have the name as an instance variable or field and a method to return the variable or field or to change it, if necessary.

Operations

Operations consist of the methods that reflect the behaviour of the class. These methods are public because they are part of the interface, the interface being that part of the class that enables association between classes.

Some operations fall into categories. The main ones are:

- **Query** – An operation that gets data from the class but does not change the data.
- **Modifier** – These are operations that change the state of an object.
- **Getters** – These are operations that return a value
- **Setters** – These are operations that set an instance variable or field to the value passed.

We see that a query is a getter and a modifier is a setter.

Some clarification is perhaps warranted. We have mentioned operations and methods. More specifically, operations reflect procedure calls, whereas methods are the actual procedures. What we have referred to as a procedure call, in OO jargon, is referred to as a message. When a method requires work by another method it sends a message to the method. Sending the message translates into a call to the method.

UML syntax for depicting an operation.

```
visibility name (parameter list):return type{property string}
```

- visibility - + (public), - (private), # (protected).

- name – will be a string.

- parameter list – this is a comma-separated list. The syntax is:

```
direction name:type = default value
```

- direction shows whether this is an input parameter (in) or an output parameter (out) or an input/output parameter (inout). The default is in.

- return type – this is a comma-separated list of return types. Generally, only one variable is returned but more may be returned.

Generalization

In our class diagram we have a customer class from which we derived two classes New and Old Customers. The Customer class contains what is general to the other two classes. Each of the classes then has its own methods and variables and extends the characteristics found in the base class Customer.

The derived types share the base class's interface. Stemming from this feature of **generalization**, the derived objects may be treated as objects of the generalized class. A NewCustomer has the same **interface** as Customer although, as indicated, it will add its own methods.

Notice that although the derived classes share the **interface** with the base class, it may happen that a derived class implements an operation in a manner different from the way it is implemented in the base class. The derived class is then said to **override** the method of the base class.

Constraints

One of the concerns of class diagrams is the specification of **constraints**. We can see that an order can originate from only one customer. One customer may have any number of orders. Similarly, a Order-Item may be linked to one order only.

We also see that a Order-Item is for only one product.

Summary

- Class diagrams are very useful enabling us to reflect the relationships between classes as well as the structure of each of the classes involved. As with all other diagrams you might feel that you don't need them, in which case, you will not use them.

- You may choose the perspective you wish to adopt when looking at classes. The perspectives will vary with respect to the detail that is incorporated. The conceptual perspective views the relationships between classes. The specification perspective details the interface of each class and the implementation perspective looks at the implementation of each class.

- Associations describe the relationship between two classes. Associations may be unidirectional or bidirectional. In a unidirectional relationship we can go from one file to another but travel in the reverse direction is not possible. In a bidirectional relationship travel is possible in both directions.

- Multiplicity relationships establish relationships of the type one to one, one to many or many to many. In a one to one relationship, say marriage, a husband has one wife and a wife has one husband. Exemplifying a one to many relationship we have that a couple may have many children. We will have a many to many relationship when a driver may have many cars but it is also true that each car may have many drivers, not all at the same time of course.

- Attributes are the data items inherent to the class. If you create a variable to accumulate total hours worked this variable is not an attribute of the class. some of the attributes need to be accessible and visible in which case there must be a method that returns the variable.

- Operations fall into two categories, they are either queries or they are modifiers. If they are queries they return data without changing it. If they are modifiers, the content of the variable is changed.

Complete

1.   The class diagram will depict the _____ between two classes.

2.   The specification perspective enables us to specify the _____ of the class.

3.   The relationship between classes is established via the _____.

4.   A relationship established between classes which is not established via the interface is the _____ relationship.

5.   The specification perspective is mainly concerned with the _____.

6.   A _____ _____ enables an Orders file to link back to Customer.

7.   A method that returns data may be classified as a _____ or as a _____.

8.   A method that changes the value of an attribute may be described as a _____ or as a _____.

9.   If we have a base class Person and a derived class Student, the name would be in the _____ class.

10.   A base class shares its _____ with the derived class.

True/False

1.   Class diagrams must always be used when analysing a system. True/False
2.   The conceptual perspective provides the most detail. True/False
3.   All relationships between classes are established via the interface. True/False.
4.   The relationship between orders and line items is a one to many relationship. True/False
5.   An orders file must have at least one line item pending. True/False
6.   A getter operation is equivalent to a query operation. True/False
7.   If you were accumulating total amounts outstanding from customers, the variable used for the accumulation would be classified as an attribute. True/False
8.   A setter operation is equivalent to a modifier operation. True/False
9.   The interface of the base class may never be bigger than the interface of one of its derived classes. True/False
10.   An order may originate from only one customer. True/False

Chapter 26

Interaction Diagrams

Topics Covered

- ❑ Interaction Diagrams
- ❑ Sequence Diagrams
- ❑ Collaboration Diagrams
- ❑ Activity Diagrams
- ❑ Class, Responsibilities and Collaborations
- ❑ Extreme Programming
- ❑ Summary
- ❑ Complete
- ❑ True/False
- ❑ Exercise

Interaction Diagrams

As the name indicates, interaction diagrams depict the interaction between objects of different classes. There are two types of interaction diagrams, **sequence diagrams** and **collaboration diagrams**.

The example we will be using is based on an order entry system.

The requirements to be diagrammed are:

1. Enter customer number – There is a customer number entry window. Once we are ready to proceed the window will exit.
2. Validate customer number – if the customer number is not valid, i.e. it cannot be found in the Customer database, ask for re-entry. If it is again not found, this will be an error.
3. Create the order
4. Create line items - Ensure that the product is there and that the quantity is available.
5. Create delivery note
6. Create invoice

We will start with sequence diagrams

Sequence Diagrams

As the name implies, the **sequence diagram** depicts the sequence in which events take place. In so doing, it also depicts the interactions between classes.

When creating the sequence diagram, it will usually happen that you will find the need for new classes.

Sequence diagrams use a rectangle at the top, which reflects the entity, normally an object of the class. From the rectangle a line is dropped, the lifeline. The lifeline may be represented by a dashed line or by an elongated rectangle. We will use a dashed line.

The messages between objects are represented by arrows from the object sending the message to the receiving object. A return arrow may be shown, but is assumed.

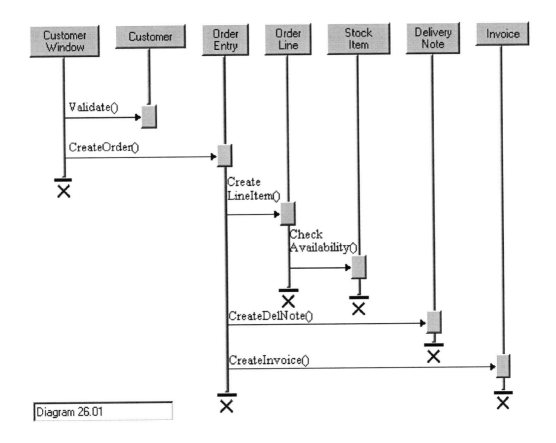

Diagram 26.01

Order Entry Sequence Diagram

Let us examine what is happening.

1. The CustomerWindow sends a message to see if the customer master exists. If the answer is negative, a re-try is allowed. If it is negative, an error is indicated once more.

2. If the customer number is valid, processing proceeds. A message is sent to Order-Entry. Note that a message translates into a function call.

3. An iteration now ensues. In each loop, a line item is processed.

4. For each line item the availability is checked.

5. Once the loop is exited, a message is sent by the OrderEntry object to create a delivery note.

6. The same happens in respect of Invoice.

We have created a use case in respect of the processing for each line item. The appropriate **sequence diagram** follows:

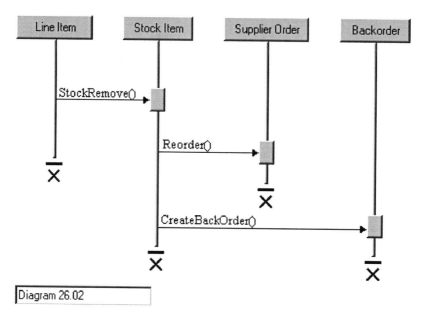

Diagram 26.02

Line Item Sequence Diagram

Let us examine the diagram:

1.   Line item needs to update stock so it sends a message to the stock object. Stock is updated.

2.   If necessary, a re-order process is initiated.

3.   If we have reordered, an appropriate back order must be created and a message is sent to the BackOrder object.

Collaboration Diagrams

Collaboration diagrams serve the same function as sequence diagrams. Some writers find collaboration diagrams easier to read. You should use the diagrams with which you feel most comfortable.

Collaboration diagrams lose clarity when more than one process needs to be reflected. Let us look at an example:

Collaboration Diagram

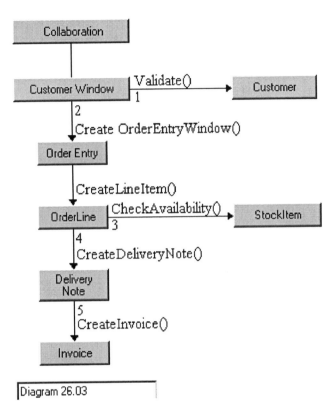

Diagram 26.03

Interaction diagrams are good at showing the associations between objects but they are not good at showing behaviour. For showing behaviour you should use **activity diagrams**.

Activity Diagrams

Activity diagrams are very much like flowcharts and, as such, are poor at showing dynamic behaviour as present in iterations. **Activity diagrams** differ from flowcharts in that they are able to represent parallel behaviour.

Activity diagrams are good at showing the sequence of operations.

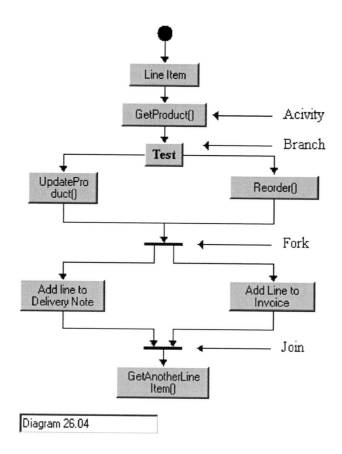

Diagram 26.04

Line Item Activity Diagram

We have assumed that there is always stock. If the stock level is below minimum stock, re-order. This means that if the stock is already below the minimum stock we will have to check against the existing backorder.

We have a decision block where we check for stock level. We will take one of the two courses of action.

We come to a fork. The fork does not denote a selection between two alternate courses of action. Rather, it reflects two courses of action to be executed concurrently. The join terminates simultaneity.

Class, Responsibilities, Collaboration

Towards the end of the 1980s two Smalltalk programmers, charged with the responsibility of passing on their knowledge of object oriented development, came up with the idea of using cards rather than diagrams to establish relationships between objects. These programmers were Ward Cunningham and Kent Beck.

They used index cards 10 by 15cm in which they specified the **class**, its **responsibilities** and the classes with which it interacts or **collaborates**. The cards are referred to as CRC cards. One of the advantages of using CRC cards is that their use encourages discussion between the members of the group.

The **class** is the class under examination.

The **responsibilities** reflect the purpose for the existence of the class. A responsibility may point to an attribute, to a method, or to a group of attributes or methods.

It is important to note the size of the **class**. The size does not allow for too many responsibilities. We want to capture the high-level responsibilities, not a multitude of low-level **responsibilities**.

The **collaborations** are the classes with which it interacts. If a class is unable to do something, it has to ask another class for assistance.

One thing you are likely to find is that once you look at **collaborations** you will find that classes will crop up and a thorough understanding of the system will develop.

An example of a CRC card follows:

Order	
Responsibility	Collaboration
Check availability of stock	LineItem
Compute price	
Get amount outstanding	Customer
Limit exceeded	

Use **CRC** cards to bring out interactions between classes. Once this has been done you can document it with interaction diagrams.

Extreme Programming (xp)

One approach to programming that has rapidly gained in popularity is that of **extreme programming**. It introduces a radical approach to programming that breaks with long standing tradition.

To find out more about **extreme programming** you can go to:

www.xprogramming.com

We will look at two aspects of extreme programming.

Program testing – Traditionally, program testing was always a second rate task done at the end of the job. This situation prevailed in spite of the known fact, that a program is not finished until it has been tested and found to be running satisfactorily.

Extreme programming changed the situation radically. The test data must be prepared before you start writing the program. Furthermore, there must be testing software such that when the program is compiled it will automatically be tested. In this way we will have compile, run and test all at the press of a button. Every time the program is changed and recompiled the test data must be automatically invoked.

Every change to the program implies that the test data must be reviewed to ensure that the changes introduced into the program are duly tested.

Paired programming – Traditionally, a programmer would be given a program to write. Once written and tested, it was his program and in a way he had ownership of it. People also saw the program as belonging to the person who wrote it.

Extreme programming says there is a better way. Two programmers will design the program and discuss pros and cons of different approaches. While one is still labouring with logic problems the other one will be entering the code on the machine. If one gets stuck, the other one will chip in and see what can be done. In this way programming is a collaborative effort and the program ownership problem disappears.

Summary

- Besides use case diagrams UML also uses interaction diagrams. The latter reflect the interaction between classes. The diagrams fall into two categories, sequence diagrams and collaboration diagrams.

- Sequence diagrams depict the sequence in which operations take place and also show when messages are sent to methods of other classes. A rectangle at the top reflects the class sending or receiving the message. The message is represented by an arrow pointing to the receiving object. A return arrow is assumed.

- Collaboration diagrams do much the same work as sequence diagrams so you may decide to dispense with either, or in fact, both. What happens is that, as you can imagine, because of the iterative process in which analysis is inserted, diagrams have to be changed or redone. For this reason, many analysts seek to reduce the number of diagrams involved.

- Activity diagrams resemble flowcharts, and to this extent, are poor at reflecting dynamic processes. One thing is true, and that is that we are able to depict simultaneity in activity diagrams. The beginning of the simultaneous processes is initiated by a fork and terminated by a join.

- CRC cards are frequently used to reflect collaboration between classes and the responsibilities of each. One of the advantages of CRC cards is that they stimulate discussion. In addition they are easy to modify and, in this respect, are much of an improvement on cards.

- Extreme programming has gained in popularity in recent times. One aspect of programming that it has brought into focus is program testing. What is advocated is that test data be created before the programming effort starts. The advantage is that in generating the test data a deeper insight into the problem is secured. In addition it envisages generation of test data, compile and run as being integrated into one process.

- Ownership of a program has always been associated with the writer of the program. To eliminate this bond, it was envisage that program creation be an associative process where two people collaborate. Through discussion, an improved solution will generally result.

Complete

1. Diagrams depicting interaction between classes are called _____ diagrams.

2. Sequence diagrams use an _____ to show the connection to another class.

3. In the sequence diagrams shown in the chapter an _____ was used to show a return point.

4. Some of the UML diagrams may be _____ with because they are difficult to update when changes are introduced.

5. Collaboration diagrams are not good at showing _____.

6. Activity diagrams are poor at showing _____ behavior.

7. Activity diagrams enable us to show _____ whereas flowcharts do not.

8. The _____ terminates the simultaneous process.

9. In a CRC card the class is the _____ under examination.

10. In a CRC card collaboration depicts the classes with which this class _____.

True/False

1. Interaction diagrams depict interaction between methods. True/False
2. Return arrows from the class instance that received control are always shown. True/False
3. In a sequence diagram, the lifeline may be a dashed line or an elongate rectangle. True/False
4. A collaboration diagram serves the same purpose as a sequence diagram. True/False
5. If we use sequence diagrams we must use collaboration diagrams. True/False
6. In a collaboration diagram, it is not easy to depict behavior. True/False
7. The fork initiates a simultaneous process. True/False
8. Responsibilities consist of what the class needs to do. True/False
9. Collaboration refers to what this class will do for others. True/False
10. CRC cards facilitate group interaction and discussion. True/False

Exercise

The Store Inc needs a system to manage its stock. The contract for the development of the financial modules has been farmed out to our main competitor, AMESoft.

Information about The Store:

1)   It has 1 000 different stock items in 10 retail outlets spread throughout the country.

2)   Sells $10 000 000 worth of merchandise direct to consumers every month.

3)   As company policy, a physical stock count takes place once every three months over a public holiday/weekend so as not to disrupt normal trading.

4)   The store has Pentium 1 machines and they are not keen to invest in new machines – so system performance is critical.

We are required to automate stock management, specifically ordering and replenishment.

Phase 1 (of our project)

-     Stock from The Store's many suppliers is received by the receiving clerk into the storeroom/warehouse.

-     Every morning the receiving clerk gets a schedule of deliveries for the day – our system must allow for this.

-     When the right delivery truck is allowed into the offloading bay, the driver will present the clerk with a delivery note which has an order number printed on it. The clerk will capture the order number to display the order details. The order details displayed will reflect each specific item ordered as one order line, and there can be as many order line items as may be necessary. An order line displayed will reflect the item code, item description, unit of measure and number of items ordered. The system should allow the clerk to then capture the items delivered against what has been ordered – on the same order screen described above.

-     There is no guarantee that the full order will always be delivered.

-     The system must not allow for over-deliveries but must allow for under-deliveries.

- If the partial order has been delivered the system must allow for the rest of the order to be delivered, else the order should be marked as closed. When the remainder of a partial delivery is received, only the outstanding items will be allowed. All order receiving will be done on the system.

- When stock is received, the system must update available stock on the system.

- When customers buy, the items bought will be taken off available stock values.

- When the available stock reaches a particular level, an order request will be generated, enabling the order clerk to authorize it – this will turn it into an actual order. Sometimes there may be a need to manually generate an order on the system.

- An item may be supplied by more than one supplier.

- All order information and processing takes place on a database.

- The point of sale system records sales information in a flat file. The file contains information reflecting item no, item description, unit of measure, number of items sold, date on which the items were sold. It holds information for the whole calendar month.

- We need to provide The Store with a system to query and update this file. At the end of each day, our new system must provide a facility to update the database with sales information – especially available stock and item sales per week, accumulating item sales history.

- The Store's supplier base is constantly growing/changing as they seek better prices and quality – the system must allow for this.

- When an invoice is received from a supplier, it must be validated against the right order before it is passed on to the AMESoft developed modules for payment.

- Create the database using MS Access.

The Store is still skeptical about the Internet, so the whole application will have Windows GUI presentation. For the final presentation, we will have to install the system on a computer at The Store – the installation and testing instructions must be clear and to the point, else we may lose the project to our competitors.

Chapter 27
Inheritance, Properties & Interfaces

Topics Covered

- Inheritance
- Properties
- Interfaces
- Inheriting an Interface
- Summary
- Complete
- True/False
- Exercises

Inheritance

Inheritance is one of the mechanisms contributing towards **reusability**. Any class that you build calls on the services of class 'base' If you go for increased independence do not inherit from 'base' and code your own functions and you will soon see that there is an advantage to not reinventing the wheel.

The class from which we inherit is the **base** class and the class that inherits is the **derived** class. You will recall that in encapsulation we split the class into two parts, the **interface** and the **implementation**. The interface is visible to objects of other classes and is referred to as **public**, and the implementation is visible only to members of the class and is generally referred to as **private**.

Because the **implementation** is **private**, we place in the **implementation** all those components we do not want other classes to see. In COBOL, only the data form part of the **implementation**. The methods are all part of the **interface**.

There is another important difference between the way COBOL implements OO and other OO languages. A method in a language like Java equates to a routine in CO-BOL, and routines may not have nested routines. In COBOL a method is much like a nested program and, consequently, may have any number of routines or functions. A method in COBOL may call one of its routines and not a routine from the implementation; in this way, the routine behaves as a private routine since it is not part of the **interface**.

We can then say that in COBOL data are private and methods are public. When it comes to inheritance **what is private is not inherited, what is public is always inherited**. What if there are data defined in the base class that the derived class needs? The base class must have methods that return those **private** fields. Similarly, if the derived class needs to change those fields, there must be methods in the base class that the derived class may invoke to accomplish this.

The next example uses **inheritance**. We have a CustAcc class, the base class and we have a CheckAcc class, the derived class. In the activating procedural program we create an instance of the derived class. If we create an instance of the base class, we can access data and methods of the base class only. By creating an instance of the derived class, we are able to access the methods of the derived class as well as methods inherited from the base class. You will recall that the interface of the derived class comprises the interface of the base class plus the methods that are in the derived class and not in the base class.

As we indicated earlier, from the derived class, we are unable to access the data fields defined in the base class. The only way to gain access to these fields is to provide a mechanism in the base class that will make the fields available to the derived class. We may create a method that returns the desired fields. After examining the program we will look at such a method.

The base class is a normal class, like the ones we have been looking at until now. For the derived class we need to include the code that follows and which differs slightly from the norm.

Inheriting a Class

```
class-id. CheckAcc  as "CheckAcc"
          inherits from CustAcc.
repository.
    class CustAcc as 'CustAcc'.
```

Figure 27.01

The base class inherits from **Base** or **Object**. The derived class will inherit from the base class as well as from all that the base class inherited. In the repository we have to include the class from which this class is inheriting.

Base Class

```
class-id. CustAcc  as "CustAcc"
          inherits from base.
repository.

object.

file-control.
    select mast-file assign to "C:\cob0\mast03"
        organization is indexed
        access is random
        record key is mast-key.
file section.
fd  mast-file.
01  mast-rec.
    05  mast-key          pic X(03).
    05  mast-rest         pic X(09).
working-storage section.
01  mast-area.
    05  w-mast-key        pic X(03).
    05  w-mast-code       pic X.
    05  w-mast-name       pic X(03).
    05  w-mast-bal        pic 9(05).
```

Listing 27.01 – 1 of 4

Base Class

```cobol
    method-id. 'custStart'.
    procedure division.
        open i-o mast-file
        exit method.
    end method "custStart".

    method-id. 'custEnd'.
    procedure division.
        close mast-file
        exit method.
    end method "custEnd".

    method-id. 'custSelect'.
    linkage section.
    01  acc-no                      pic 9(3).

    procedure division using acc-no.
        move acc-no to mast-key
        read mast-file into mast-area
            invalid key
                display 'Record not found'
                move 0 to acc-no
            not invalid key
                display 'Balance: ' w-mast-bal
                move 1 to acc-no
        end-read
        exit method.
    end method "custSelect".

    method-id. 'custDeposit'.
    linkage section.
    01  lnk-amount                  pic S9(5).

    procedure division using lnk-amount.
        add lnk-amount to w-mast-bal
        invoke self 'custRewrite'
        exit method.
    end method "custDeposit".
```

Listing 27.01 – 2 of 4

Base Class

```
method-id. 'custWithdraw'.
linkage section.
01  lnk-amount                    pic S9(5).
procedure division using lnk-amount.
    subtract lnk-amount from w-mast-bal
    invoke self 'custRewrite'
    exit method.
end method "custWithdraw".

method-id. 'custRewrite'.
linkage section.
procedure division.
    display 'Balance is: ' w-mast-bal
    rewrite mast-rec from mast-area
        invalid key
            display 'Cannot rewrite'
    end-rewrite
    exit method.
end method "custRewrite".

end object.

end class CustAcc.
class-id. CheckAcc  as "CheckAcc"
        inherits from CustAcc.
repository.
    class CustAcc as 'CustAcc'.
object.
working-storage section.
01  acc-no                    pic 999.
01  found-sw                  pic 9.
01  acc-amt                   pic S9(5).
01  tran-sw                   pic X.
01  custRef                   object reference CheckAcc.

procedure division.
method-id. 'custInterface'.
procedure division.
    invoke CheckAcc "new" returning custRef
    invoke custRef 'custStart'
    perform custPrompt
```

Listing 27.01 – 3 of 4

Derived Class

```
    perform until acc-no = 999
        invoke custRef 'custSelect' using acc-no
        if  acc-no = 1
            display 'Please enter amount: ' no advancing
            accept acc-amt
            display 'Enter D-deposit, W-Withdraw: '
                                            no advancing
            accept tran-sw
            if  tran-sw = 'D'
                invoke custRef 'custDeposit' using acc-amt
            else
                invoke custRef 'custWithdraw' using acc-amt
            end-if
        end-if
        perform custPrompt
    end-perform
    invoke custRef 'custEnd'
    exit method.
custPrompt.
    display  'Enter acc no or 999 to end: ' no advancing
    accept acc-no.
end method "custInterface".
end object.
end class CheckAcc.
program-id. Chapter2701.
repository.
    class base as "base"
    class CheckAcc as "CheckAcc".
working-storage section.
01  custRef                     object reference CheckAcc.
procedure division.
A100-start.
    invoke CheckAcc "new" returning custRef
    invoke custRef 'custInterface'
    stop run.
```

Listing 27.01 – 4 of 4

In examining the listing you should take note of the following:

- The base class accesses an indexed sequential file randomly. The file needs to be opened and needs to be closed. This should happen only once. There are methods for opening and for closing the file.
- There is a method 'custSelect' that reads the file. The method is invoked in the derived class so an indication is returned which enables the invoking method to determine whether the read was successful.
- There are methods for deposit and withdrawal and there is also a method that rewrites the record read.
- As you will recall, **self** is used when invoking a method in the same class as the invoking method.
- In the derived class there is only one method, one that interfaces with the user.
- We made an attempt to access w-mast-bal but the compiler did not allow the operation. Bear in mind that in OO COBOL only methods are inherited, not data members. We were attempting to reference a field from the base class using an object of the derived class and the compiler was not happy with this.

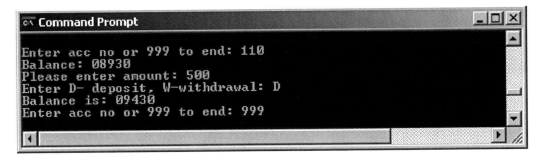

Properties

We saw that data in the base class are not accessible in the derived class. To get to the data we need to define **getter** and **setter** methods. A getter method returns a field and a setter method changes a field in the class. Object oriented languages provide a facility that is a modified form of a method. This facility is called a **property**. When you have defined a **property** you gain access to the field without going through a method.

Let us start by considering a **getter property**. If all you wish to do is get the field then you will use a simplified form where the compiler will generate a method to return the field to you. For this to happen you must specify the keyword 'property' to the definition of the field.

```
01  test-val              pic 9(3) value 500 property.
```

The compiler creates a method, with the same name as the field test-val that is invoked when the following reference is encountered:

```
display test-val of convReference
```

In the preceding line of code, convReference is a **reference** pointing to the class containing the **property**.

Properties

```
$set repository(update on)
class-id. TempConversion  as "TempConversion"
          inherits from base.
repository.

object.
working-storage section.
01  test-val                    pic 9(3) value 500 property.
method-id. "celToFar".
linkage section.
01  temp                        pic S9(3)V9(2) comp-3.
procedure division using temp.
    compute temp = temp * 9 / 5 + 32
    exit method
end method  "celToFar".
method-id. "farToCel".
linkage section.
01  temp                        pic S9(3)V9(2) comp-3.
procedure division using temp.
    compute temp = (temp - 32) / 9 * 5
    exit method
end method  "farToCel".
end object.

end class TempConversion.
program-id. Chapter2702.
repository.
    property test-val
    class base as "base"
    class TempConversion as "TempConversion".
```

Listing 27.02 – 1 of 2

540

Properties

```
working-storage section.
01  temp                      pic S9(3)V9(2) comp-3.
01  w-code                    pic 9 value 0.
01  temp-out                  pic ZZ9.9(2)-.
01  convReference             object reference TempConversion.
procedure division.
A100-start.
    invoke TempConversion "new" returning convReference
    move 37 to temp
    invoke convReference 'celToFar' using temp
    move temp to temp-out
    display 'Fahrenheit equivalent is ' temp-out
    move 98.6 to temp
    invoke convReference 'farToCel' using temp
    move temp to temp-out
    display 'Celsius equivalent is ' temp-out
    display 'Property returned: ' test-val of convReference
    stop run.
```

Listing 27.02 – 2 of 2

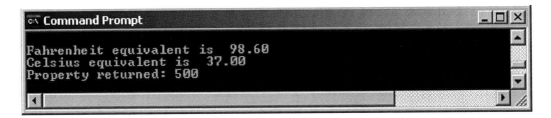

```
Fahrenheit equivalent is  98.60
Celsius equivalent is  37.00
Property returned: 500
```

Points to note:

- You must include a reference to the property in the repository paragraph.
- In addition, you have to register the property in the external repository. You do this with the first statement in the listing.

```
$set repository(update on)
```

The statement will register the property in the external repository. All the code required to implement the property has been included in bold.

If we need to do something with a variable, prior to returning it, we should code our own property method. The example shows the code of a property method:

Coding a Property

```
$set repository(update on)
class-id. TempConversion  as "TempConversion"
          inherits from base.

repository.

object.

working-storage section.
01  test-val                       pic 9(3) value 500.
method-id. "celToFar".
linkage section.
01  temp                           pic S9(3)V9(2) comp-3.
procedure division using temp.
    compute temp = temp * 9 / 5 + 32
    exit method
end method  "celToFar".

method-id. "farToCel".
linkage section.
01  temp                           pic S9(3)V9(2) comp-3.
procedure division using temp.
    compute temp = (temp - 32) / 9 * 5
    exit method
end method  "farToCel".

method-id. get property testVal.
linkage section.
01  lnk-val      pic 9(03).
procedure division returning lnk-val.
    move test-val to lnk-val
    exit method.
end method.

end object.

end class TempConversion.
```

Listing 27.03

If you move a property field, ensure that you move it to a field with the same picture, or there may be problems. Notice that the **property** ends on end method. There is no method name associated with the end method statement for a property.

542

Coding a Property

```
program-id. Chapter2703.
repository.

    property testVal
    class base as "base"
    class TempConversion as "TempConversion".

working-storage section.
01  temp                        pic S9(3)V9(2) comp-3.
01  w-code                      pic 9 value 0.
01  temp-out                    pic ZZ9.9(2)-.
01  convReference               object reference TempConversion.
procedure division.
A100-start.
    invoke TempConversion "new" returning convReference
    move 37 to temp
    invoke convReference 'celToFar' using temp
    move temp to temp-out
    display 'Fahrenheit equivalent is ' temp-out
    move 98.6 to temp
    invoke convReference 'farToCel' using temp
    move temp to temp-out
    display 'Celsius equivalent is ' temp-out
    display 'Value is: ' testVal of convReference
    stop run.
```

Listing 27.03

```
Command Prompt                                        _ □ ×

Fahrenheit equivalent is  98.60
Celsius equivalent is   37.00
Property returned: 600
```

The following points are to be noted:

- The method has any name you wish to allocate to it. We will generally provide a name that closely associates with the field name. We called the field 'test-val' and the method 'testVal'.

- The method is recorded in the **repository**.

- The field is no longer associated with the keyword **property**.

- We used the **$set repository** to record the **property** on the external repository.

Interfaces

You know that we split the class into **implementation** and **interface**. The implementation is private and the **interface** is public, meaning that it can be referenced from other classes. The **interfaces** we are now covering may be described as secondary **interfaces**. These **interfaces** may be seen as skeleton classes because they contain only the method **prototypes,** without the associated implementation. In other words, the method is empty. A method **prototype** consists of the following:

- The method name
- The variables passed to the method
- The variable returned

The class that implements an **interface** must implement the methods specified in the **interface**. If the **interface** specifies three method prototypes then the class that implements the interface must implement the three methods, one for each of the prototypes. It is not enough to implement only one or two of the method prototypes; all three must be implemented.

Using interfaces is also referred to as contract programming because all the users of an **interface** undertake to construct methods that all have the appropriate method signatures. By signature we mean that all implementations will have the same name, receive the same fields and return the same field as specified in the method **prototype**. The field names may be different but the data types must be the same.

Interfaces implement the polymorphism paradigm, which states: "One interface many implementations". To implement an **interface** all you need to know are the three components of the **prototype**.

The following example implements an **interface**:

An Interface and its Implementation

```
interface-id. Geometry.
repository.
procedure division.

method-id. 'areaOfCircle'.
linkage section.
01  lnk-radius              pic S9(3)      comp-3.
01  lnk-area                pic S9(5)V99  comp-3.
procedure division using lnk-radius
                 returning lnk-area.
end method 'areaOfCircle'.

method-id. 'areaOfSquare'.
linkage section.
01  lnk-side                pic S9(3)      comp-3.
01  lnk-area                pic S9(5)V99  comp-3.
procedure division using lnk-side
                 returning lnk-area.
end method 'areaOfSquare'.

end interface Geometry.

class-id. AreasCalc as "AreasCalc"
          inherits from base.
repository.
    interface Geometry as 'Geometry'.

object. implements Geometry.
procedure division.

method-id. 'areaOfCircle'.
linkage section.
01  lnk-radius              pic S9(3)      comp-3.
01  lnk-area                pic S9(5)V99 comp-3.
procedure division using lnk-radius
                 returning lnk-area.
    compute lnk-area = 3.1416 * lnk-radius * lnk-radius
    exit method
end method  'areaOfCircle'.
```

Listing 27.04 – 1 of 2

545

An Interface and its Implementation

```cobol
method-id. 'areaOfSquare'.
linkage section.
01  lnk-side                 pic S9(3)      comp-3.
01  lnk-area                 pic S9(5)V99  comp-3.
procedure division using lnk-side
                   returning lnk-area.
    compute lnk-area = lnk-side * lnk-side
    exit method
end method 'areaOfSquare'.
end object.
end class AreasCalc.
program-id. Chapter2704.
repository.
    class base as "base"
    class AreasCalc as "AreasCalc".
working-storage section.
01  temp                     pic S9(3)      comp-3.
01  w-code                   pic 9 value 0.
01  temp-out                 pic S9(5)V9(2) comp-3.
01  temp-edit                pic ZZ,ZZ9.99.
01  areaRef                  object reference AreasCalc.
procedure division.
A100-start.
    invoke AreasCalc "new" returning areaRef
    move 25 to temp
    invoke areaRef 'areaOfCircle' using temp
                                  returning temp-out
    move temp-out to temp-edit
    display 'Area of circle is: ' temp-edit
    move 25 to temp
    invoke areaRef 'areaOfSquare' using temp
                                  returning temp-out
    move temp-out to temp-edit
    display 'Area of square is: ' temp-edit
    stop run.
```

Listing 27.04 – 2 of 2

The following is to be noted:

- You will notice that the class that implements the **interface** implements both methods.
- The methods have the same names as the **interface** prototypes. The methods receive the same type of variable and return the same type of variable. If any of these do not match, results will be unpredictable.
- If results are not what you expect them to be, check the data types being passed. The field into which data are returned must be of the same type as the data returned by the method. If the method returns pic S9(5)V9(2) comp-3 the receiving field may not be S9(5)V9(2). In this case, both fields must be comp-3.
- The implements clause is specified at object level.

```
Area of circle is:   1963.50
Area of square is:    625.00
```

Inheriting an Interface

A class may inherit from more than one **interface** and an **interface** may inherit from another **interface** or **interfaces**. In the example that follows, the **interface** inherits from another **interface**. The class in turn inherits from one **interface** only. However, it needs to implement the methods from both **interfaces**. We highlight the changes to the program.

Inheriting Multiple Interfaces

```
    interface-id. AreaOfTri.
    repository.

    procedure division.
    method-id. 'areaOfTri'.
    linkage section.
    01  lnk-width           pic S9(3)    comp-3.
    01  lnk-height          pic S9(3)    comp-3.
    01  lnk-area            pic S9(5)V99 comp-3.
```

Listing 27.05 – 1 of 4

Inheriting Multiple Interfaces

```
       procedure division using lnk-width lnk-height
                          returning lnk-area.
       end method 'areaOfTri'.
       end interface  AreaOfTri.

       interface-id. Geometry
                     inherits from AreaOfTri.

       repository.
          interface areaOfTri as 'AOT'.

       procedure division.

       method-id. 'areaOfCircle'.
       linkage section.
       01   lnk-radius              pic S9(3)      comp-3.
       01   lnk-area                pic S9(5)V99  comp-3.
       procedure division using lnk-radius
                          returning lnk-area.
       end method 'areaOfCircle'.

       method-id. 'areaOfSquare'.
       linkage section.
       01   lnk-side                pic S9(3)      comp-3.
       01   lnk-area                pic S9(5)V99  comp-3.
       procedure division using lnk-side
                          returning lnk-area.
       end method 'areaOfSquare'.

       end interface Geometry.
```

Listing 27.05 – 2 of 4

In the interface-id we indicate that the **interface** is inheriting from another interface.

Inheriting Multiple Interfaces

```
class-id. AreasCalc as "AreasCalc"
          inherits from base.
repository.
    interface Geometry as 'Geometry'.
object. implements Geometry.
procedure division.

method-id. 'areaOfCircle'.
linkage section.
01  lnk-radius              pic S9(3)     comp-3.
01  lnk-area                pic S9(5)V99 comp-3.
procedure division using lnk-radius returning lnk-area.
    compute lnk-area = 3.1416 * lnk-radius * lnk-radius
    exit method
end method  'areaOfCircle'.

method-id. 'areaOfSquare'.
linkage section.
01  lnk-side                pic S9(3)     comp-3.
01  lnk-area                pic S9(5)V99  comp-3.
procedure division using lnk-side
                  returning lnk-area.
    compute lnk-area = lnk-side * lnk-side
    exit method
end method 'areaOfSquare'.

method-id. 'areaOfTri'.
linkage section.
01  lnk-width               pic S9(3)     comp-3.
01  lnk-height              pic S9(3)     comp-3.
01  lnk-area                pic S9(5)V99 comp-3.
procedure division using lnk-width lnk-height
                  returning lnk-area.
    compute lnk-area = lnk-width * lnk-height / 2
    exit method
end method  'areaOfTri'.

end object.

end class AreasCalc.
```

Listing 27.05 – 3 of 4

The method finds the area of a right-angled triangle.

Inheriting Multiple Interfaces

```
program-id. Chapter2705.
repository.
    class base as "base"
    class AreasCalc as "AreasCalc".
working-storage section.
01  temp              pic S9(3)      comp-3.
01  w-width           pic S9(3)      comp-3.
01  w-height          pic S9(3)      comp-3.
01  temp-out          pic S9(5)V99   comp-3.
01  temp-edit         pic ZZ,ZZ9.99.
01  areaRef           object reference AreasCalc.
procedure division.
A100-start.
    invoke AreasCalc "new" returning areaRef
    move 25 to temp
    invoke areaRef 'areaOfCircle' using temp
                                  returning temp-out
    move temp-out to temp-edit
    display 'Area of circle is: ' temp-edit
    move 25 to temp
    invoke areaRef 'areaOfSquare' using temp
                                  returning temp-out
    move temp-out to temp-edit
    display 'Area of square is: ' temp-edit
    move 10 to w-width
    move 15 to w-height
    invoke areaRef 'areaOfTri'    using w-width w-height
                                  returning temp-out
    move temp-out to temp-edit
    display 'Area of square is: ' temp-edit
    stop run.
```

Listing 27.05 – 4 of 4

```
Command Prompt                                    _ □ ×
Area of circle is:  1963.50
Area of square is:   625.00
Area of square is:    75.00
```

Summary

- **Inheritance** is closely associated with one of the main objectives of OO, namely, **reusability**. The class from which all classes inherit is class **base**. If you had to reproduce the functionality in class **base,** you would soon agree that **inheritance** is a blessing.

- In COBOL only **attributes** can be part of the **implementation**. Methods are all part of the **interface**. Therefore all **attributes** are **private** and inaccessible to other classes, whereas **methods** are part of the **interface** and therefore visible to other classes. Furthermore, in COBOL only the **interface** may be inherited. Consequently, if the derived class needs **attributes** from the base class, the base class must provide methods that will set and return those **attributes**.

- The base class inherits from **base** or from class **Object**. By inheriting from the base class, the derived class will also be inheriting from class **base**. In the **repository** we need to include the class from which the base class inherited.

- Object oriented languages have a facility, **Properties**, that resemble **setter** and **getter** methods. Properties enable us to indirectly address attributes. We address the **property** as if it were data.

  ```
  01  test-val        pic 9(3) value 500 property.
  ```

- When defining data we include the keyword **property**. This will cause the compiler to generate the required method with the same name as the field. Notice how we access the value in test-val:

  ```
  display test-val of convReference
  ```

- In the code where you will be calling on the services of the **property** you need to include a reference to the property in the **repository** paragraph. In addition, the class must register the **property** in the external **repository** with the following line of code:

  ```
  $set repository(update on)
  ```

- When naming a **property** in the method-id paragraph we have to say that this is a **get** property or a **set property**. The word property follows the get and is followed by the property name. The field with which the **property** is associated no longer carries the keyword **property**.

- We group interfaces into primary and secondary **interfaces**. A primary **interface** is an **interface** that enables other classes to communicate with the class in question. The secondary **interface** is inherited by the class.

- An **interface** of the secondary group contains only the method **prototype** and no **implementation**. The method prototype is specified in the procedure division statement and includes the arguments passed and the argument returned. The procedure division is empty because it is not followed by any code. It is up to the class that inherits the interface to provide the implementation. Secondary interfaces introduce the concept of contract programming. The class that inherits the interface undertakes to provide the implementation and the implementing method must comply with the **prototype** in the secondary interface.

- The paradigm of **polymorphism** states: "One interface, many implementations." Any class may inherit the secondary **interface** as long as it abides by the contract that states that the method prototype must be identical in the primary and secondary **interfaces**. All the methods contained in the secondary interface must be implemented by the inheriting class. If only some of these methods have been implemented, the program will not compile successfully. The advantage of interfaces is that anybody using the class knows how to invoke the methods and what to expect from the methods that form part of the inherited **interface**.

- An **interface** starts with the **interface-id** statement and ends with the **end interface** statement. The end interface carries the name of the interface. The **interface** contains a linkage section containing the fields that are to pass between the method and the invoking method. Note that what passes between the implementing method and the invoking method must have identical definitions. If one side is packed, the other side must be packed.

- The class that implements the **interface** specifies the implements clause at object level.

- A class may inherit from more than one interface and one **interface** may inherit from another **interface**. If a class inherits an **interface** that inherits another interface, it is up to the class to implement all the methods specified in the two **interfaces**.

Complete

1.   Inheritance is one of the mechanisms that contribute to _____.

2.   The class that inherits is the _____ class and the class from which inheritance takes place is the _____ class.

3.   The implementation contains _____ items and the interface contains _____ items.

4.   In COBOL the _____ is not inherited.

5.   A data item defined with the property clause causes the compiler to generate a _____ with the _____ name as the data item.

6.   A reference to the property must be included in the _____ paragraph.

7.   The reference to the property must be made in the _____ repository.

8.   The keyword property must be provided at the level of the _____.

9.   The keyword property must be preceded by the word _____ or _____.

10.   A property called finalValue would end on _____.

11.   A secondary interface contains the _____ for methods.

12.   When a class inherits an interface it must _____ all the methods contained in the interface.

13.   An interface B specifies three method prototypes. Interface B inherits interface A which specifies two method prototypes. If a class implements interface B, it must implement _____ methods.

14.   A class may inherit _____ interfaces.

15.   An interface definition starts with _____ and ends with _____.

True/False

1. The class from which all classes inherit is class Object

2. In COBOL, the data forms part of the implementation.

3. In COBOL, both data and methods are inherited.

4. To gain access to a field associated with a property, we need a reference to the class containing the property.

5. In the class containing the property a reference to the property must be included in the repository paragraph.

6. When a class inherits another class a reference to the base class must be included in the repository paragraph.

7. When a reference to the base class is included in the repository paragraph, the 'inherits from' in the class-id is no longer required.

8. When the **using** is employed, the program cannot release records to the sort.

9. When a class is inherited, the class must be registered in the external repository.

10. When coding your own property, the 'end method' does not take the property name.

11. When you code your own property, the definition of the field associated with the property must carry the keyword property.

12. When defining an interface, the interface ends on 'end interface'. The name of the interface is not required.

13. When a method inherits an interface, the interface must be reflected in the repository paragraph. In addition, at object level we must use the implements keyword followed by the name of the interface.

14. If interface B inherits from interface A, interface B must have 'inherits from A'.

Exercises

1.   Define a class Geometry that draws circles, squares and triangles. For circles pass the radius. For squares and triangles pass the side. Class StraightLines inherits from class Geometry and draws vertical lines and horizontal lines. The argument passed is in respect of the length of the line.

      You do not need to draw, just display a message indicating what would be drawn and the argument passed.

2.   Code a setter property that will update a table of makes of motor vehicles. Cater for a maximum of 10 makes. Code a getter property that returns the last car in the table. Once the car is returned it is removed from the table.

3.   Code an interface containing a method that receives an integer and returns a string. The string returned contains one of the capitals of the world obtained from a table of capitals. The integer will be used as a subscript.

      Another method receives a string containing a capital and updates the table.

Chapter 28
Collections

Topics Covered

- Collections
- The Array Class
- CobolComp5
- CharacterArray
- Loading an Array Instance with Strings
- Bags
- ValueSets
- OrderedCollection
- SortedCollection
- Dictionaries
- Queues
- Summary
- Complete
- True/False
- Exercises

Collections

Tables provided the original form of collection and we have seen how useful they can be. **Collections** have the advantage of being object oriented and therefore provide classes, with a wealth of methods, to assist the programmer. **Collections** are also known as containers in other languages. The **collections** available to the users of Net Express follow:

Collection	Description
Bag	Not indexed, automatic growth, allows duplicates.
Array	Indexed, manually growable, allows duplicates
CharacterArray	Indexed, manually growable, allows duplicates
OrderedCollection	Indexed according to insertion order, automatic growth, allows duplicates
SortedCollection	Indexed by sort order, grows automatically, allows duplicates.
ValueSet	Not indexed, grows automatically, duplicates not allowed.
Dictionary	Indexed by key, grows automatically, duplicate keys not allowed.
Table 28.01 – Collections	

In selecting a collection we would consider our requirements. Do we need indexed access, would we like the collection to grow automatically, would we like it to accept duplicates? In cases where growth is not automatic, methods are available in the class and these enable us to stipulate the desired size.

We will examine the different collection categories.

The Array Class

As we can see above, an **Array** instance is indexable, grows manually and may contain either objects or intrinsic data. Note that the index field may not be merely numeric but must be of type pic X(4) comp-5. It is advisable to code all fields associated with collections as pic X(4) comp-5. To grow manually we have two methods that we may use, **grow** and **grow to**.

In the example, we load an array into a collection of class **Array**. We have made the array also of type X(4) comp-5 so that the data loaded is of the same type. In this way we loaded maximum values enabled by the type.

We need to declare class **Array** in the repository. Because we inherited class base, it is not essential to declare class base in the repository. In the example we have three loops, one to load the array, a second one to transfer the data from the array to the collection and a third one to retrieve the data from the collection.

The Array Class

```
class-id. Arrays as 'Arrays' inherits base.
repository.
    class base as 'base'
    class Array as 'array'
    class COBOLComp5 as 'comp5'.
object.
working-storage section.
01  tab.
    05  numbers    pic X(4)  comp-5 occurs 7.
01  len           pic S9(9) comp-5 value 10.
01  ctr           pic 9(9)  comp-5.
01  num           pic X(4)  comp-5.
01  anArray       object reference.
01  aString       object reference.
01  st-num        pic X(4)  comp-5  value 4294967285.
01  picx4comp5    object reference.
method-id. 'ArrayColl'.
procedure division.
A-start.
    perform varying ctr from 1 by 1
        until ctr > 7
            add 1 to st-num
            move st-num to numbers(ctr)
    end-perform
    move 4 to ctr
    invoke CobolComp5 'newClass' using ctr
                               returning picx4comp5
    invoke Array "ofValues" using picx4comp5 len
                               returning anArray
    perform varying ctr from 1 by 1 until ctr > 7
        invoke anArray 'atPut' using ctr numbers(ctr)
    end-perform
    perform varying ctr from 1 by 1 until ctr > 7
        invoke anArray 'at' using ctr returning num
            display num
    end-perform
    invoke anArray 'size' using anArray returning ctr
    display 'Number of occurrences is: ' ctr.
 end method 'ArrayColl'.
end object.
end class Arrays.
```

Listing 28.01- 1 of 2

The Array Class

```
program-id. Chapter2801.
repository.
    class Arrays as 'Arrays'.
working-storage section.
01  ArrayRef          object reference Arrays.
procedure division.
A100-start.
    invoke Arrays 'new' returning ArrayRef
    invoke ArrayRef  'ArrayColl'
    stop run.
```

Listing 28.01- 2 of 2

CobolComp5

The **CobolComp5** class enables us to store COBOL intrinsic data as an object. In the preceding example we stored COBOL intrinsic data implicitly as an object. As you will see later when creating **dictionaries**, the present class is important in creating associations. **Associations** are necessary to associate key and data in a **dictionary** collection. The class converts an intrinsic item to an object by using a template. The template and the intrinsic item must have the same length.

The **newClass** method returns a template that may be used in creating collections. The template is used later when we create the Array collection using the **ofValues** method. Only data of the length of the template can be stored in the collection. The reference picx4comp5 points to the template. Notice that we moved four to ctr, because the length of the data must match the length of the template.

```
invoke CobolComp5 'newClass' using ctr
                             returning picx4comp5
```

The **ofValues** method returns an instance of the class. The method receives a field containing the envisaged length of the object, in other words, the length of the array; this is the second argument. The method expects the length field to be defined as pic S9(9) comp-5. The first argument is a reference to the template to be stored in the array. In addition, the method should return the object reference into the reference specified following the returning clause.

```
invoke Array "ofValues" using picx4comp5 len
                        returning anArray
```

560

To store an item in the Array instance we use the **atPut** method. The first parameter is an index item, ctr, specifying the position the item is to occupy in the array collection. The index field should again be defined as pic S9(9)   comp-5. The second argument is the item to be inserted. The line of code was inserted into a loop that traverses the array, each element being placed into the collection.

```
invoke anArray 'atPut' using ctr numbers(ctr)
```

The next line of code is also inserted into a loop. This time we traverse the collection retrieving each of the elements, we will use the **at** method.. We have to pass the index field defined as indicated previously. Num will be the field into which the item from the collection is returned.

```
invoke anArray 'at' using ctr
                    returning num
```

We have also used the **size** method. The method receives a reference to the collection and returns the number of occurrences.

```
invoke anArray 'size' using anArray
                    returning ctr
```

As indicated earlier, the instances of the Array class do not grow automatically. Rather, they require an intervention on the part of the programmer. We have changed the program to cater for growth and have used the method **grow** for the purpose.

```
invoke anArray 'grow'
```

You see from the result that follows that the collection has grown to 34.

CharacterArray

A CharacterArray is intended to store strings of any length as objects. Invoking the method **withBiteLengthValue** in CharacterArray returns an instance of CharacterArray. In the example that follows, we create an array of references and load each reference into the array. We then iterate through the array of references and display the contents.

CharacterArray

```
class-id. CharArrays as 'CharArrays'
        inherits base.

repository.
    class base as 'base'
    class CharacterArray as 'chararry'.

object.

working-storage section.
01  tab      value
    'Lancia FerrariBugati Alfa    BMW      RenaultCitroen'.
    05  cars       pic X(7)   occurs 7.
01  len            pic X(4)   comp-5.
01  ctr            pic S9(9)  comp-5.
01  Ref-Tab.
    05  aCharArray     object reference occurs 7.
01  aValue         pic X(10).

method-id. 'CharColl'.
```

Listing 28.03 – 1 of 2

562

CharacterArray

```
procedure division.
A-start.
    move 7 to len
    perform varying ctr from 1 by 1 until ctr > 7
        invoke CharacterArray 'withByteLengthValue'
                              using len cars(ctr)
                              returning aCharArray (ctr)
    end-perform
    perform varying ctr from 1 by 1 until ctr > 7
        invoke aCharArray(ctr) 'getValue' using ctr
                               returning aValue
        display 'The CharacterArray contains: ' aValue
    end-perform.
    move 5 to ctr
    invoke aCharArray(ctr) 'size' using aCharArray(ctr)
                           returning ctr
    display 'Length of character array is: ' ctr.
end method 'CharColl'.

end object.
end class CharArrays.

program-id. Chapter2803.
repository.
    class CharArrays as 'CharArrays'.

working-storage section.
01  CharArrayRef          object reference CharArrays.
procedure division.
A100-start.
    invoke CharArrays 'new' returning CharArrayRef
    invoke CharArrayRef  'CharColl'
    stop run.
```

Listing 28.03 – 2 of 2

The code that follows, extracted from the preceding program, creates a CharacterArray instance and loads it with the data passed as the second argument. The first argument provides the length of the data.

What is returned is a reference pointing to the CharacterArray instance. The reference is loaded into an array of references. The method used to accomplish this is the **withByteLengthValue** method.

563

```
invoke CharacterArray 'withByteLengthValue'
                      using len cars(ctr)
                      returning aCharArray (ctr)
```

The **getValue** method retrieves the data from the CharacterArray instance

```
invoke aCharArray(ctr) 'getValue' using ctr
                                  returning aValue
```

The execution follows:

```
Command Prompt                                                _ □ ×
The CharacterArray contains: Lancia
The CharacterArray contains: Ferrari
The CharacterArray contains: Bugati
The CharacterArray contains: Alfa
The CharacterArray contains: BMW
The CharacterArray contains: Renault
The CharacterArray contains: Citroen
Length of CharacterArray is: +0000000007
```

Loading an Array Instance with Strings

If we wish to load an Array instance with strings we need the assistance of the **CharacterArray** class in conjunction with the **ofReferences** method in class Array. The method enables us to store objects in the Array object. In the example we create a collection of class Array. In the loop we create a **CharacterArray** reference and load it into anArray as an element.

CharacterArray

```
class-id. Arrays as 'Arrays'
        inherits base.
repository.
    class Array as 'array'
    class CharacterArray as 'chararry'.

object.
```

Listing 28.04 - 1 of 3

CharacterArray

```
working-storage section.
01  tab     value
    'Lancia FerrariBugati Alfa    BMW     RenaultCitroen'.
    05  cars    pic X(7)  occurs 7.
01  len         pic X(4)  comp-5.
01  ctr         pic S9(9) comp-5.
01  anArray     object reference.
01  aString     object reference.

method-id. 'ArrayColl'.
procedure division.
A-start.
    move 7 to len
    invoke Array 'ofReferences' using len
                                 returning anArray
    perform varying ctr from 1 by 1 until ctr > 7
        invoke CharacterArray 'withByteLengthValue'
                              using len cars(ctr)
                              returning aString
        invoke anArray 'atPut' using ctr aString
                              returning aString
    end-perform
    perform varying ctr from 1 by 1 until ctr > 7
        invoke anArray 'at' using ctr
                            returning aString
        display 'The car make is: ' no advancing
        invoke aString 'display'
        display ' '
    end-perform.
end method 'ArrayColl'.

end object.
end class Arrays.
program-id. Chapter2804.
repository.
    class Arrays as 'Arrays'.
working-storage section.
01  ArrayRef          object reference Arrays.
```

Listing 28.04 - 1 of 2

CharacterArray

```
procedure division.
A100-start.
    invoke Arrays 'new' returning ArrayRef
    invoke ArrayRef  'ArrayColl'
    stop run.
```

Listing 28.04 - 2 of 2

In the super-class **base,** from which all other classes inherit, there is a method called **display.** In the example we used an object reference pointing to an anArray object. When the reference is used to invoke the **display** method, the string to which the reference is pointing will be displayed. The code that follows creates a **CharacterArray** instance and the reference to it is returned

```
invoke CharacterArray 'withByteLengthValue'
                        using len cars(ctr)
                        returning aString
```

The following line of code loads the reference into the Array instance:

```
invoke anArray 'atPut' using ctr aString
                        returning aString
```

```
Command Prompt                                        _ □ ×
The car make is: Lancia
The car make is: Ferrari
The car make is: Bugati
The car make is: Alfa
The car make is: BMW
The car make is: Renault
The car make is: Citroen
```

Bags

The **bag** collection derives its name from the way we keep items in a bag. Items are dumped in a bag in no particular sequence. In general it does not make sense, except to a magician, to ask for the third item in the bag and know beforehand what the third item is.

Thus, bags are not **indexable** and because items are not arranged in any particular sequence duplicates are allowed. One good thing about bags is that they grow automatically, no intervention being required on the part of the programmer. It is good to know that bags provide a more efficient storage mechanism than arrays by the way duplicate values are handled.

The elements of the **bag** may be objects or COBOL intrinsic data. Two class methods are available to create an instance of the **bag** class. If we want a bag to store objects we will use the **ofReferences** method. To store intrinsic values, we use the **ofValues** method.

Bag

```
class-id. Bags as 'Bags'
          inherits base.
repository.
     class base as 'base'
     class Bag as 'bag'
     class Array as 'array'
     class CharacterArray as 'chararry'.

object.

working-storage section.
01  tab      value
    'Lancia FerrariBugati Alfa    BMW     RenaultCitroen'.
    05  cars       pic X(7)  occurs 7.

01  len          pic X(4)   comp-5.
01  ctr          pic S9(9)  comp-5.
01  num          pic S9(9)  comp-5.
01  num1         pic ZZ9.
01  aBag         object reference.
01  anArray      object reference.
01  aString      object reference.

01  TrueOrFalse  pic 99     comp-5.
    88  isTrue                    value 1.
    88  isFalse                   value 0.

method-id. 'BagColl'.
```

Listing 28.05 – 1 of 2

567

Bag

```
procedure division.
A-start.
    move 7 to len
    invoke Array 'ofReferences' using len
                                returning anArray
    invoke Bag 'ofReferences' using len
                              returning aBag
    perform varying ctr from 1 by 1 until ctr > 7
        invoke CharacterArray 'withByteLengthValue'
                                using len cars(ctr)
                                returning aString
        invoke aBag 'add' using aString
                          returning aString
        invoke anArray 'atPut' using ctr aString
                               returning aString
    end-perform
    perform varying ctr from 1 by 1 until ctr > 7
        invoke anArray 'at' using ctr
                            returning aString
        invoke aBag 'includes' using aString
                               returning TrueOrFalse
        if  isTrue
            display 'Bag contains:  '  no advancing
            invoke aString 'display'
            display ' '
            if  ctr = 5
                invoke aBag 'remove' using aString
                display 'Item 5 containing BMW removed'
            end-if
        else
            display 'Bag does not contain indicated value.'
        end-if
    end-perform
    invoke aBag 'size' using aString
                       returning num
    move num to num1
    display 'The size of the bag is: ' num1
end method 'BagColl'.
end object.
end class Bags.
```

Listing 28.05 – 2 of 3

Bag

```
program-id. Chapter2805.
repository.
    class Bags as 'Bags'.

working-storage section.
01  BagRef           object reference Bags.
procedure division.
A100-start.
    invoke Bags 'new' returning BagRef
    invoke BagRef  'BagColl'
    stop run.
```

Listing 28.05 – 3 of 3

Notice that the **bag** class uses the **add** method to add an item to the object. This is the only method available to the programmer for inserting an item into the bag. In the example, as done earlier, we load a **CharacterArray** reference into the bag. The **CharacterArray** reference is in aString. The following line of code was used to insert an item into the bag:

```
            invoke aBag 'add' using aString
                      returning aString
```

The **bag** class does not allow us to retrieve items from the **bag** instance. Instead, we may interrogate the bag to find out whether a particular item is present in the list. We do this using the **includes** method. In the example we loaded the bag object and we loaded an **Array** object. We then traversed the array and each time, asked whether the item in the array was included among the items in the bag. The following code was used:

```
            invoke aBag 'includes' using aString
                              returning TrueOrFalse
```

The method returns a Boolean value. The value will be one for true. If the ctr is five, we remove the item from the bag using the **remove** method. The item removed will be the one to which the reference aString is pointing.

```
            invoke aBag 'remove' using aString
```

We know that we placed seven items in the **bag** - we removed one so there should now be six. When we ask for the size of the **bag** we get six. The result of execution follows:

```
Bag contains: Lancia
Bag contains: Ferrari
Bag contains: Bugati
Bag contains: Alfa
Bag contains: BMW
Item 5 containing BMW removed
Bag contains: Renault
Bag contains: Citroen
The size of the bag is:  6
```

ValueSets

A **ValueSet** is a collection of unordered strings or intrinsic data. Duplicates are not allowed but it will grow automatically. The user will be prevented from entering a duplicate item because the **equal** method is invoked for each of the elements.

To insert a new item into the **ValueSet** we must use the **add** method. As happened with the **bag** class, there is no method available to retrieve items from the collection. What we do have is again the **includes** method. We may also use the **occurrencesOf** method to determine the presence of an item. Because a **ValueSet** does not allow duplicates, the method returns either zero, if there isn't an item with the value, or one if an item with the value is present.

ValueSet

```
class-id. ValueSets as 'ValueSets'
          inherits base.
repository.
    class base as 'base'
    class ValueSet as 'valueset'
    class Array as 'array'
    class CharacterArray as 'chararry'.
object.
working-storage section.
01  tab      value
    'Lancia FerrariBu.gati Alfa    BMW      RenaultCitroen'.
    05  cars       pic X(7)  occurs 7.
01  len            pic X(4)  comp-5.
01  ctr            pic S9(9) comp-5.
```

Listing 28.06 – 1 of 3

570

ValueSet

```
01   num            pic S9(9) comp-5.
01   num1           pic ZZ9.
01   aSet           object reference.
01   anArray        object reference.
01   aString        object reference.
01   TrueOrFalse    pic 99    comp-5.
     88  isTrue                       value 1.
     88  isFalse                      value 0.

method-id. 'ValueSetColl'.
procedure division.
A-start.
    move 7 to len
    invoke Array 'ofReferences' using len returning anArray
    invoke ValueSet 'ofReferences' using len returning aSet

    perform varying ctr from 1 by 1 until ctr > 7
        invoke CharacterArray 'withByteLengthValue'
                            using len cars(ctr)
                            returning aString
        invoke aSet 'add' using aString returning aString
        invoke anArray 'atPut' using ctr aString
                            returning aString
    end-perform
    perform varying ctr from 1 by 1 until ctr > 7
        invoke anArray 'at' using ctr
                            returning aString
        invoke aSet 'includes' using aString
                            returning TrueOrFalse
        if  isTrue
            display 'ValueSet contains:  '  no advancing
            invoke aString 'display'
            display ' '
            if  ctr = 4
                invoke aSet 'remove' using aString
                display 'item 4 containing ' no advancing
                invoke aString 'display'
                display ' removed'
            end-if
```

Listing 28.06 – 2 of 3

ValueSet

```
            else
                display 'ValueSet does not contain the value.'
            end-if
            if  ctr = 5
                invoke aSet 'occurrencesOf' using aString
                                           returning TrueOrFalse
                if  isTrue
                    invoke aString 'display'
                    display ' is present.'
                else
                    display 'ValueSet does not contain the value.'
                end-if
        end-perform
        invoke aSet 'size' using aString returning num
        move num to num1
        display 'The size of the ValueSet is: ' num1
    end method 'ValueSetColl'.
    end object.
    end class ValueSets .
    program-id. Chapter2806.
    repository.
        class ValueSets as 'ValueSets'.
    working-storage section.
    01  SetRef          object reference ValueSets.
    procedure division.
    A100-start.
        invoke ValueSets 'new' returning SetRef
        invoke SetRef  'ValueSetColl'
        stop run.
```

Listing 28.06 – 3 of 3

For the strings to be acceptable we used the **CharacterArray** class and the **add** method for insertion into the value set.

The Add Method

```
    invoke ValueSet 'ofReferences' using len
                              returning aSet
    invoke aSet 'add' using aString
                    returning aString
```

Figure 28.01

The **includes** method was used to test for the presence of an item. We also used the **remove** method. You are already acquainted with both these methods. What is new is the **occurrencesOf** method. The method tests for the presence of a given value in the collection and returns the number of occurrences of the item. Because the **ValueSet** does not allow duplicates the value returned will be either zero or one.

```
        invoke aSet 'occurrencesOf' using aString
                              returning TrueOrFalse
```

```
Command Prompt
Bag contains: Lancia
Bag contains: Ferrari
Bag contains: Bugati
Bag contains: Alfa
Bag contains: BMW
Item 5 containing BMW removed
Bag contains: Renault
Bag contains: Citroen
The size of the bag is:  6
```

OrderedCollection

As the name indicates, an **OrderedCollection** holds its elements in the sequence in which they were received. Furthermore, duplicates are allowed and the **OrderedCollection** will grow automatically as required.

We will introduce two new methods that enable us to insert at the beginning of the collection or at the end of the collection. The two methods are **addFirst** and **addLast**.

These methods assist us in implementing **stacks** and **queues**. The stack implements a Last In First Out collection(LIFO). For a stack we will addLast. Queues on the other hand implement First In First Out collections (FIFO). For a queue we will **addFirst**. The next example incorporates these two methods:

573

OrderedCollection

```
class-id. OrdColl as 'OrdColl'
        inherits base.

repository.
    class OrderedCollection as 'ordrdcll'
    class CharacterArray as 'chararry'.

object.

working-storage section.
01  tab       value
    'Lancia  Ferrari Bugati  Alfa    BMW     Renault Citroen '.
    05  cars      pic X(8)  occurs 7.
01  first-car    pic X(8)  value 'Chrysler'.
01  last-car     pic X(8)  value 'Mercedes'.
01  len          pic X(4)  comp-5.
01  ctr          pic S9(9) comp-5.
01  anOrdColl    object reference.
01  aString      object reference.
method-id. 'OrderedColl'.
procedure division.
A-start.
    move 8 to len
    display 'Ordered Collection Example'
    invoke OrderedCollection 'ofReferences' using len
                             returning anOrdColl
    perform varying ctr from 1 by 1 until ctr > 7
        invoke CharacterArray 'withByteLengthValue'
                             using len cars(ctr)
                             returning aString
        invoke anOrdColl 'add' using aString returning aString
    end-perform
    display 'After Insertions'
    invoke CharacterArray 'withByteLengthValue'
                    using len first-car returning aString
    invoke anOrdColl 'addFirst' using aString

    invoke CharacterArray 'withByteLengthValue'
                    using len last-car returning aString
    invoke anOrdColl 'addLast' using aString
```

Listing 28.07 – 1 of 2

OrderedCollection

```
        perform varying ctr from 1 by 1 until ctr > 9
            invoke anOrdColl 'at' using ctr returning aString
            display 'The element is: ' no advancing
            invoke aString 'display'
            display ' '
        end-perform.
    end method 'OrderedColl'.
    end object.
    end class OrdColl.

    program-id. Chapter2807.
    repository.
        class OrdColl as 'ordcoll'.
    working-storage section.
    01  OrdCollRef          object reference OrdColl.
    procedure division.
    A100-start.
        invoke OrdColl 'new' returning OrdCollRef
        invoke OrdCollRef  'OrderedColl'
        stop run.
```

Listing 28.07 – 2 of 2

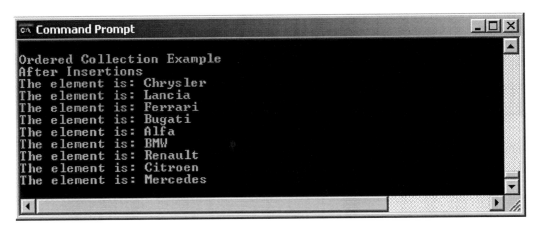

We used the **ofReferences** method to create an instance of the class.

```
        invoke OrderedCollection 'ofReferences' using len
                                 returning anOrdColl
```

To add the next element in sequence we used the **add** method with which you are already acquainted.

```
invoke anOrdColl 'add' using aString
                      returning aString
```

The **addFirst** and **addLast** follow the pattern. You will notice that we used the returning clause in the code following. This is not strictly necessary because we don't use what is returned.

The addFirst and the addLast
| ```
invoke anOrdColl 'addFirst' using aString
                            returning aString

invoke anOrdColl 'addLast'  using aString
                            returning aString
``` |
| **Figure 28.02** |

The next example depicts a **Stack** class. As indicated, a stack implements a last in first out. This situation is identical to the situation we have when we have a stack of plates. We add to the top of the stack and we remove from the top of the stack. The last plate placed on the stack will be the first plate to be removed.

In a stack we have two operations, adding to the stack. This is referred to as a push operation. When removing from the stack, we refer to this operation as a pop operation. To push we used **addFirst**. To pop we use a new method, **last**. **Last**, as the name indicates, will remove the item from the end or top of the stack. Notice that when processing the pop operation we must not remove from an empty stack. For this situation we use a counter field. The pop will operate when the counter is greater than zero.

Stacks
| ```
class-id. Stacks as 'Stacks'
        inherits base.
repository.
    class OrderedCollection as 'ordrdcll'
    class CharacterArray as 'chararry'.

object.
working-storage section.
``` |
| **Listing 28.08 – 1 of 4** |

Stacks

```
01  tab       value
    'Lancia  Ferrari Bugati  Alfa      BMW       Renault Citroen '.
    05  cars      pic X(8)  occurs 7.
01  len         pic X(4)  comp-5.
01  len1        pic X(4)  comp-5.
01  ctr         pic S9(9) comp-5.
01  ctr1        pic S9(9) comp-5.
01  anOrdColl   object reference.
01  aString     object reference.
method-id. 'init'.
procedure division.
A-start.
    move 8 to len
    display 'Stack Example'
    invoke OrderedCollection 'ofReferences' using len
                             returning anOrdColl
    perform varying ctr from 1 by 1 until ctr > 7
        invoke CharacterArray 'withByteLengthValue'
                             using len cars(ctr)
                             returning aString
        invoke anOrdColl 'add' using aString returning aString
    end-perform
    move 7 to ctr
    perform varying ctr1 from 1 by 1 until ctr1 > ctr
        invoke anOrdColl 'at' using ctr1
                             returning aString
        invoke aString 'display'
    end-perform.
    display ' '
    move 7 to ctr
end method 'init'.
method-id. 'push'.
linkage section.
01  make          pic X(20).
procedure division using make.
A-start.
    add 1 to ctr
```

Listing 28.08 – 2 of 4

Stacks

```
      invoke CharacterArray 'withByteLengthValue'
                          using len make returning aString
    invoke anOrdColl 'addLast' using aString returning aString
end method 'push'.
method-id. 'pop'.
procedure division.
A-start.
    if  ctr > 0
        display 'Popped car is: ' no advancing
        invoke anOrdColl 'at' using ctr
                            returning aString
        invoke aString 'display'
        invoke anOrdColl 'last' returning aString
        subtract 1 from ctr
    else
        display 'Collection is empty'
    end-if
end method 'Pop'.
end object.
end class Stack.

program-id. Chapter2808
repository.
    Class Stack as 'stack'.
working-storage section.
01  StackRef            object reference Stack.
01  selection           pic 9  value 0.
01  make                pic X(20).
01  redefines make.
    05                  pic X(5).
    05  new-make        pic X(15).
procedure division.
A100-start.
    display 'Push and Pop Example'
    invoke Stack 'new' returning StackRef
    invoke StackRef 'init'
    perform A100-prompt until selection = 3
    stop run.
```

Listing 28.08 – 3 of 4

Stacks

```
A100-prompt.
    display 'Enter 1 for push, 2 for pop, 3 to end'
    accept selection
    evaluate selection
        when 1 display
            'Please enter car name, maximum 15 characters'
            accept new-make
            invoke StackRef 'push' using new-make
        when 2 invoke StackRef 'pop' returning make
        when 3 display 'Terminating'
        when other display 'Invalid code re-enter'
    end-evaluate
```

Listing 28.08 – 4 of 4

```
Command Prompt                                    _ □ ×

Stack Example
Lancia  Ferrari Bugati  Alfa     BMW      Renault Citroen
Enter 1 for push, 2 for pop, 3 to end: 2
Popped car is: Citroen
Enter 1 for push, 2 for pop, 3 to end: 2
Popped car is: Renault
Enter 1 for push, 2 for pop, 3 to end: 2
Popped car is: BMW
Enter 1 for push, 2 for pop, 3 to end: 2
Popped car is: Alfa
Enter 1 for push, 2 for pop, 3 to end: 2
Popped car is: Bugati
Enter 1 for push, 2 for pop, 3 to end: 2
Popped car is: Ferrari
Enter 1 for push, 2 for pop, 3 to end: 2
Popped car is: Lancia
Enter 1 for push, 2 for pop, 3 to end: 2
Collection is empty
Enter 1 for push, 2 for pop, 3 to end: 3
Terminating
```

In the pop method, the collection item that is returned has two components, a pointer component, four bytes, and a data component, 15 bytes. The pop method retrieves the last item from the collection.

The push method uses a CharacterArray instance that receives a field containing the make of the car and returns a reference. The reference then goes on to the collection.

Every time we add to the collection we add one to ctr. In fact, ctr always has the number of elements in the collection.

Adding to the Collection

```
        invoke CharacterArray 'withByteLengthValue'
                              using len make
                              returning aString

     invoke anOrdColl 'addLast' using aString
                                returning aString
```

Figure 28.03

There is another interesting method, at which we looked earlier the **occurrencesOf** method. In our example, if we used the method and entered the same make of car twice, the method would return a number into a pic X(4) comp-5 field. Using a normal pic 99 would yield an error. The code to be used is:

Using OccurrencesOf

```
     if  ctr = 3
         invoke anOrdColl 'occurrencesOf' using aString
                                          returning num1
         move num1 to num2
         display 'Collection contains: ' num2 ' ' make
     end-if
```

Figure 28.04

As before, aString points to the last car entered and that is what will be counted.

Sorted Collection

The **SortedCollection** class provides indexed access to an automatically growable collection. The elements are by default organized in ascending sequence. The **atPut** method is not available to add records to the collection, we must instead use the **add** method. The other methods we have used so far are all available to the different collections we have dealt with and to this collection category as well.

The following example implements a **SortedCollection**:

SortedCollection

```
class-id. SortColl as 'sortcoll'
          inherits base.
repository.
    class base as 'base'
    class SortedCollection as 'srtdclln'
    class CharacterArray as 'chararry'.
object.
working-storage section.
01  tab       value
    'Lancia FerrariBugati Alfa    BMW      RenaultCitroen'.
    05  cars      pic X(7)   occurs 7.
01  len           pic X(4)   comp-5.
01  ctr           pic S9(9)  comp-5.
01  aSortColl     object reference.
01  aString       object reference.

method-id. 'SortedColl'.
procedure division.

A-start.
    move 7 to len
    invoke SortedCollection 'ofReferences' using len
                                      returning aSortColl
    perform varying ctr from 1 by 1 until ctr > 7
        invoke CharacterArray 'withByteLengthValue'
                              using len cars(ctr)
                              returning aString
        invoke aSortColl 'add' using aString
    end-perform
    perform varying ctr from 1 by 1 until ctr > 7
        invoke aSortColl 'at' using ctr
                              returning aString
        display 'The make is: ' no advancing
        invoke aString 'display'
        display ' '
    end-perform.
end method 'SortedColl'.

end object.
end class SortColl.
```

Listing 28.09 – 1 of 2

SortedCollection

```
program-id. Chapter2809.
repository.
    class SortColl as 'sortcoll'.
working-storage section.
01  sortRef          object reference SortColl.
procedure division.
A100-start.
    display '     Sorted Collection Example'
    display ' '
    invoke SortColl 'new' returning sortRef
    invoke sortRef  'SortedColl'
    display ' '
    display '     Terminating'
    stop run.
```

Listing 28.09 – 2 of 2

The **at** returns an aString object, which as we have had occasion to see, contains both a reference and the data pointed to. To use the data we have to consider the presence of the reference, this is what the **display** method does.

The **add** may be coded with the returning clause but this is not required. As you can see from the execution, the items are all sorted into ascending sequence.

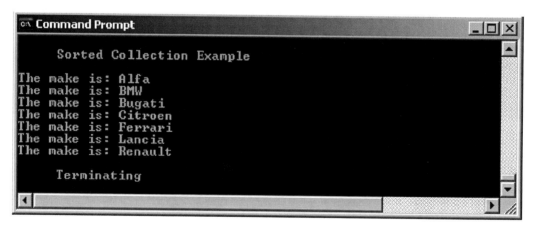

The next example recapitulates on collections bearing intrinsic data. As you will recall, we need the following class:

```
class COBOLComp5 as 'comp5'.
```

We will be using the **newClass** method.

```
invoke COBOLComp5 'newClass' using ctr
                       returning picx4comp5
```

To generate unsorted values to place into the collection, we used the intrinsic function **random.** We used system time for seeding.

SortedCollection Using Intrinsic Data

```
class-id. SortColl as 'sortcoll'
        inherits base.
repository.
    class SortedCollection as 'srtdclln'
    class COBOLComp5 as 'comp5'.
object.
working-storage section.
01  tab1.
    05  numbers    pic X(4) comp-5 occurs 7.
01  time-1         pic 9(8).
01  num            pic X(4)  comp-5.
01  ctr            pic S9(9) comp-5.
01  chara          pic X.
01  aSortColl      object reference.
01  aString        object reference.
01  picx4comp5     object reference.

method-id. 'SortedColl'.

procedure division.
A-start.
    perform varying ctr from 1 by 1 until ctr > 7
        accept time-1 from time
        accept chara
        compute numbers (ctr) =
                function random(time-1) * 1000000
        display 'Number loaded: 'numbers(ctr) no advancing
    end-perform
```

Listing 28.10 – 1 of 2

```
        display  ' '
        display  ' '
        display 'Numbers in the Sorted Collection'
        display  ' '
        move 4 to ctr

        invoke COBOLComp5 'newClass' using ctr
                                    returning picx4comp5
        move 7 to ctr
        invoke SortedCollection 'ofValues' using picx4comp5 ctr
                                    returning aSortColl
        perform varying ctr from 1 by 1 until ctr > 7
            invoke aSortColl 'add' using numbers(ctr)
        end-perform
        perform varying ctr from 1 by 1 until ctr > 7
            invoke aSortColl 'at' using ctr returning num
            display 'The number is: ' num
        end-perform.
    end method 'SortedColl'.
    end object.
    end class SortColl.

    program-id. Chapter2810.
    repository.
        class SortColl as 'sortcoll'.

    working-storage section.
    01  sortRef          object reference SortColl.
    procedure division.
    A100-start.
        display '    Sorted Collection Example'
        invoke SortColl 'new' returning sortRef
        invoke sortRef  'SortedColl'
        display ' '
        display '    Terminating'
        stop run.
```

Listing 28.10 – 2 of 2

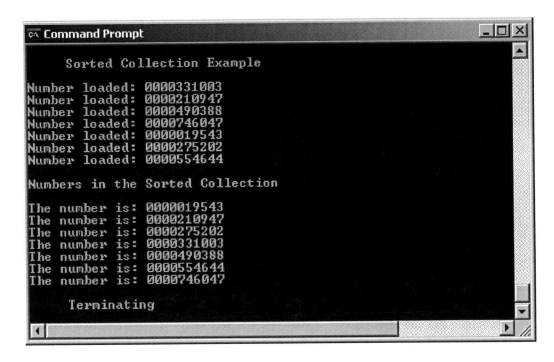

Dictionaries

A **dictionary** differs from other collections in that each element has two components, a key coupled to a data component. Dictionaries allow you to store both objects and intrinsic data. One thing that needs to be done is to associate the key with its relevant data. For this we need to create an object of the **Association** class. The **Association** object consists of two templates, one for the key and another one for the data. The templates describe to the association what the **key** and the **data** look like. Both **CobolCompX** and **CobolPicX** enable data of the types to be treated as objects. A **COBOLComp5** item is used to store the data.

Creating Templates
``
invoke CobolCompX 'newClass' using len
returning aKeyTemp
invoke CobolPicX   'newClass' using len
returning aDataTemp
``
Figure 28.05

The preceding code creates the two required **templates**; we now use them to create the **Association** object. We use the latter to create the **Dictionary** object:

Creating Association Objects

```
      invoke Association 'newClass' using aKeyTemp
                                          aDataTemp
                                 returning anAssocTemp

      invoke Dictionary  'ofValues' using anAssocTemp
                                          len
                                 returning aDictionary
```

Figure 28.06

We used the methods **atPut** and **at** to respectively store in and retrieve data from the dictionary. We stored both keys and data in two tables. The complete program is as follows.

Dictionaries

```
class-id. Dictionaries as 'dictionaries'
          inherits base.
repository.
    class CobolCompX  as 'compx'
    class CobolPicX   as 'picx'
    class Association as 'associtn'
    class Dictionary  as 'dictinry'.
object.
working-storage section.
01  tab1      value
    'Lancia FerrariBugati Alfa   BMW    RenaultCitroen'.
    05  cars      pic X(7)  occurs 7.
01  tab2      value '100200300400500600700'.
    05  keys      pic 9(3)  occurs 7.
01  len       pic X(4)  comp-5.
01  ctr       pic S9(9) comp-5.
01  dictData  pic X(7).
01  aKeyTemp      object reference.
01  aDataTemp     object reference.
01  anAssocTemp   object reference.
01  aDictionary   object Reference.
```

Listing 28.11 – 1 of 2

586

Dictionaries

```
method-id. 'DictColl'.
procedure division.
A-start.
    move 7 to len
    invoke CobolCompX  'newClass' using len
                                 returning aKeyTemp
    invoke CobolPicX   'newClass' using len
                                 returning aDataTemp
    invoke Association 'newClass' using aKeyTemp
                                       aDataTemp
                                 returning anAssocTemp
    invoke Dictionary  'ofValues' using anAssocTemp len
                                 returning aDictionary

    perform varying ctr from 1 by 1 until ctr > 7
        invoke aDictionary 'atPut' using keys (ctr)
                                         cars(ctr)
    end-perform
    perform varying ctr from 1 by 1 until ctr > 7
        invoke aDictionary 'at' using keys (ctr)
                                 returning dictData
        display 'The key is: ' Keys(ctr)
                ' The make is: ' dictData
    end-perform.
end method 'DictColl'.
end object.

end class Dictionaries.
program-id. CollProg7.
repository.
    class Dictionaries as 'dictionaries'.
working-storage section.
01  DictRef          object reference Dictionaries.
procedure division.
A100-start.
    invoke Dictionaries 'new' returning DictRef
    invoke DictRef  'DictColl'
    stop run.
```

Listing 28.11 – 2 of 2

```
 ▄▄ Command Prompt                                    _ □ ×

    Dictionary Example
The key is: 100 The make is: Lancia
The key is: 200 The make is: Ferrari
The key is: 300 The make is: Bugati
The key is: 400 The make is: Alfa
The key is: 500 The make is: BMW
The key is: 600 The make is: Renault
The key is: 700 The make is: Citroen

    Terminating
```

Queues

We saw that we could create a **stack** using an OrderedCollection. Because a stack uses Last In First Out (LIFO) organization we used the method **last** to retrieve the last element in the collection. A queue, on the other hand, uses First in First Out (FIFO) organization. To obtain a queue we must pop the first element in the collection. Not surprisingly, we use the method **first** to retrieve the first item in the collection. In addition, we need to use the **remove** method to get the second element to the beginning of the queue.

Queues

```cobol
    class-id. Queues as 'Queues' inherits base.
    repository.
        class OrderedCollection as 'ordrdcll'
        class CharacterArray as 'chararry'.
    object.
    working-storage section.
    01  tab      value
        'Lancia  Ferrari Bugati  Alfa     BMW      Renault Citroen '.
        05  cars      pic X(8)  occurs 7.
    01  len       pic X(4)  comp-5.
    01  len1      pic X(4)  comp-5.
    01  ctr       pic S9(9) comp-5.
    01  ctr1      pic S9(9) comp-5.
    01  ctr2      pic S9(9) comp-5.
    01  anOrdColl    object reference.
    01  aString      object reference.
```

Listing 28.12 – 1 of 4

588

Queues

```
method-id. 'init'.
procedure division.
A-start.
    move 8 to len
    display 'Queue Example'
    invoke OrderedCollection 'ofReferences' using len
                             returning anOrdColl
    perform varying ctr from 1 by 1 until ctr > 7
        invoke CharacterArray 'withByteLengthValue'
                             using len cars(ctr)
                             returning aString
        invoke anOrdColl 'add' using aString
                             returning aString
    end-perform
    move 7 to ctr
    perform varying ctr1 from 1 by 1 until ctr1 > ctr
        invoke anOrdColl 'at' using ctr1
                             returning aString
        invoke aString 'display'
    end-perform.
    display ' '
    move 7 to ctr
    move 1 to ctr1 ctr2
end method 'init'.

method-id. 'push'.
linkage section.
01  make            pic X(20).
procedure division using make.
A-start.
    add 1 to ctr
    invoke CharacterArray 'withByteLengthValue'
                             using len make returning aString
    invoke anOrdColl 'addFirst'
                             using aString returning aString
end method 'push'.

method-id. 'pop'.
working-storage section.
linkage section.
```

Listing 28.12 – 2 of 4

589

Queues

```
procedure division.
A-start.
    if  ctr1 <= ctr
        display 'Popped car is: ' no advancing
        invoke anOrdColl 'at' using ctr2
                              returning aString
        invoke aString 'display'
        invoke anOrdColl 'first' returning aString
        invoke anOrdColl 'remove' using aString
        add 1 to ctr1
    else
        display 'Collection is empty'
    end-if
    display ' '
end method 'Pop'.  end object.

end class Queues.

program-id. Chapter2812.
repository.
    class cls-string  as 'System.String'
    class Queues as 'Queues'.

working-storage section.
01  queueRef           object reference Queues.
01  obj-string         object reference cls-string.
01  selection          pic 9 value 0.

procedure division.
A100-start.
    invoke Queues 'new' returning queueRef
    invoke queueRef  'init'
    perform A100-prompt until selection = 3
    stop run.

A100-prompt.
    display 'Enter 1 for push, 2 for pop, 3 to end: '
                                        no advancing
    accept selection
```

Listing 28.12 – 3 of 4

Queues

```
    evaluate selection
        when 1 display
            'Please enter car name, maximum 15 characters: '
                                        no advancing
            accept new-make
            invoke queueRef 'push' using new-make
        when 2 invoke queueRef 'pop' returning make
        when 3 display 'Terminating'
        when other display 'Invalid code re-enter'
    end-evaluate.
```

Listing 28.12 – 4 of 4

```
Command Prompt                                          _ □ ×

Queue Example
Lancia    Ferrari Bugati  Alfa     BMW      Renault Citroen
Enter 1 for push, 2 for pop and 3 to end: 2
Popped car is: Lancia
Enter 1 for push, 2 for pop and 3 to end: 2
Popped car is: Ferrari
Enter 1 for push, 2 for pop and 3 to end: 2
Popped car is: Bugati
Enter 1 for push, 2 for pop and 3 to end: 2
Popped car is: Alfa
Enter 1 for push, 2 for pop and 3 to end: 2
Popped car is: BMW
Enter 1 for push, 2 for pop and 3 to end: 2
Popped car is: Renault
Enter 1 for push, 2 for pop and 3 to end: 2
Popped car is: Citroen
Enter 1 for push, 2 for pop and 3 to end: 2
Collection is empty
Enter 1 for push, 2 for pop and 3 to end: 3

     Terminating
```

Summary

- Up to this point arrays constituted the only collection available to us. Now **collections** have been introduced into Net Express. Because Collections are object oriented, they benefit from a wealth of methods all at the disposal of the programmer.

- A particular set of advantages is associated with each type of collection. Some collections are indexed, others grow automatically and others grow manually, yet others allow duplicates to be stored.

- **Array** collections are indexable and grow manually. Two methods are available to us when the size of the Array instance needs to be increased. The methods are **grow** and **grow to**. The index field **must** be of type Pic X(4) Comp-5. We use the **ofValues** method to create an Array object to store intrinsic data. To store objects such as strings, in an Array we use the **ofReferences** method. To add to the array we use **atPut** method and to retrieve from the array we use **at** method. The **newClass** method returns a template that can then be used to create the Array collection of intrinsic data. The reference returned by the method points to the template. A template looks like the object with which it is associated but is not the object.

- **CharacterArray** is another collection and it is able to store strings. The method **withByteLengthValue** returns an instance of the collection. The method **getValue** returns an instance of the collection. To load an Array object with strings we use CharacterArray instances and we load the references to the CharacterArray instances into the Array.

- **Bags** store elements in no particular sequence. For this reason they are not indexable and they allow duplicates. Bags will grow automatically. We may store objects or intrinsic data in a bag. To store objects we use the **ofReferences** method. To store COBOL intrinsic data we use the **ofValues** method in conjunction with the **newClass** method. To insert into the bag we use the **add** method. We cannot extract elements from the bag. However, we may determine if the item is present using the **includes** method. Similarly, we may eliminate an item from the bag using the **remove** method.

- **ValueSet** is an unordered collection of strings or of intrinsic data. The **ofReferences** method is used to create a ValueSet collection of objects. Duplicate items are not allowed. To insert into the ValueSet we use the **add** method. To determine whether an item is present, we may use the **occurrencesOf** method or the **includes** method. The **remove** method will remove the item from the collection.

- **OrderedCollection** contains items in the sequence in which they were provided. Duplicates are allowed and the collection grows automatically. To insert into the collection we have two methods **addFirst** and **addLast**. If we are implementing a stack we use **addLast** and retrieve using the method **last**. If we are implementing a queue we use **addFirst** and retrieve using the method **first**. When implementing a queue we need to use the **remove** method to remove the item from the queue.

- **SortedCollections** provide indexed access and the collection grows automatically. To insert into the collection we use the **add** method and to retrieve from the collection we use the **at** method. The collection can store both objects and intrinsic data.

- **Dictionaries** are unique in that they offer access by means of a key. Obviously the key needs to be associated with the data. To create an **Association** we need templates for the key and for the data. Once we have these templates we are in a position to establish the relationship. The relationship is then used to create the **Dictionary**.

- **Queues** utilize **First In First Out** organization. This implies that in retrieving elements from a queue we must pop the first element. Once we have the element, to get the next element in the queue we must first remove the first element so that the second now becomes the first.

Complete

1.   Collections are also known as _____ in other languages.

2.   Array class instances grow _____ .

3.   The index for Array class objects must be of type _____.

4.   The method _____ creates an instance of class CharacterArray.

5.   The getValue method of class CharacterArray receives a _____ to a string.

6.   The _____ method displays the string pointed to by the invoking reference.

7.   The _____ method is used to add elements to an Array class instance.

8.   In a bag, items are placed in the _____ in which they were _____.

9.   To store _____ in a bag we use the ofReferences method.

10.   To store intrinsic data in a bag we use the _____ method.

11.   The **remove** method from the **bag** class removes the item to which the _____ passed is _____.

12.   Bags grow _____ .

13.   ValueSets _____ allow duplicates.

14.   ValueSets _____ grow automatically.

15.   To insert an item into a ValueSet we use the _____ method.

16.   When testing for the presence of an item in a ValueSet we use the _____ method or the _____ method.

17.   An OrderedCollection will grow _____.

18.   To add at the beginning of an OrderedCollection we would use the _____ method.

19. To implement a stack using an OrderedCollection we would use the _____ method.

20. To implement a queue using an OrderedCollection we would use the _____ method.

21. To remove from a stack we use the method _____.

22. When retrieving from an OrderedCollection, the item returned has two components, a _____ component and a _____ component.

23. The value returned by the **occurrencesOf** method must be placed in a field defined as _____.

24. SortedCollections grow _____.

25. SortedCollections use the _____ method to insert an item in the collection.

26. If a SortedCollection is to contain strings it is created using the _____ method.

27. If a SortedCollection is to contain intrinsic data we will us the _____ method to create it.

28. Dictionaries have two components a _____ component and a _____ component.

29. An _____ relates the two components of a **Dictionary** instance.

True/False

1.   **Array** class objects are indexable.
2.   The Array class instances grow by using the **increase to** method.
3.   The **getValue** method of class **CharacterArray** returns a string.
4.   **Bags** are not indexable.
5.   In a bag, duplicates are not allowed.
6.   The **remove** method receives a reference.
7.   We may not retrieve an element from a bag.
8.   **Bags** require manual intervention to grow.
9.   To insert an item into a **ValueSet** we use the **atPut** method.
10.   If we want to know if there is more than one particular item in a **ValueSet**, we would use the **includes** method.
11.   In an **OrderedCollection**, duplicates are not allowed.
12.   To implement a stack using an **OrderedCollection**, we would use the **addLast** method.
13.   To implement a queue when using an **OrderedCollection**, we would use the addLast method.
14.   A **SortedCollection** provides indexed access.
15.   A **Dictionary** has both pointer and data components.
16.   To relate the two components of a **Dictionary** instance we use a Relation.

Exercises

1.   Construct a class that uses an object of an Array class to store speed of cars. Have another object of the Array class that stores makes of cars. Load the array objects and retrieve from them.

2.   Repeat the exercise for the remaining collections, namely:

             CharacterArray
             Bag
             ValueSet
             OrderedCollection
             SortedCollection
             Dictionary

Chapter 29
Data Normalization

Topics Covered

- Databases
- Properties of a Relation
- Data Normalization
- First Normal Form
- Insertion Anomaly in First Normal Form
- Deletion Anomaly in First Normal Form
- Update Anomaly in First Normal Form
- Reason for Anomalies in First Normal Form
- Functional Dependency
- Second Normal Form
- Transitive Dependency
- Third Normal Form
- Relationships Between Relations
- Registering the Database
- Using the Open Esql Assistant
- Summary
- Complete
- True/False
- Exercises

Databases

So far, we have looked at file systems and one of the file types that we found to be most versatile was the indexed sequential type. This was because indexed sequential files offer both sequential as well as random access. So, why do we have databases?

File systems have some drawbacks, one of them being the presence of **redundancy**. **Redundancy** gives rise to **inconsistencies** causing inaccurate results to be produced. Consider the following example:

Payroll File
EmployeeID
EmployeeName
EmployeeNoDependents
EmployeeSalary
EmployeeDeductions
Table 1

Personnel File
EmployeeID
EmployeeName
EmployeeNoDependents
EmployeeHireDate
EmployeeAppraisalDate
Table 2

You will notice that the first three fields are identical in the two files. Assume that employee Ann Smith gets married and her name changes to Ann Peabody. This information reaches the company on the 18th. The Payroll file is updated on the 17th and the Personnel file is updated on the 22nd. The result is that if on the 25th you ask the payroll department if there is an employee by the name of Ann Peabody they will say no. If you ask the personnel department the same question, they will reply yes.

A database is a centralized repository of non-redundant data accessible by multiple users. With the centralization of data comes centralized control which results in a uniform approach to the handling of data.

The database model we will be looking at is the **relational** model. The model derives its name from the fact that it consists of associated relations. For our purposes a relation is a file. A relation is also seen as and referred to as a table. Each row in the table is called a **tuple** and a column is called an **attribute**. You may have noticed the similarity between a **tuple** and a record and between an **attribute** and a field.

Properties of a Relation

We will now examine the features a file must possess to be a relation.

- Each column must pertain to the same attribute and must have a single value.

- Each column must have a name and the name must be unique.

- The key for a **tuple** must be unique.

- Sequence of rows is not material.

If a relation has the properties enunciated above it will be in the **first normal form**.

Data Normalization

For our current purposes we will assume that you have a running application using files and that you now wish to move these files on to a relational database. To do this you must first normalize each of the files. The process will result in additional files being created.

Data normalization will split a file into two or more files so as to remove insertion, and deletion and update anomalies. A given anomaly will prevent the operation from being executed. A file may be described as being in first, second or third normal form. Generally we will not go beyond third normal form because splitting the one file into a number of files signifies additional reads when processing against the database. Files, in a relational database are called **relations**.

First Normal Form

When a **relation** is in **first normal form** it may still experience insertion, deletion and update anomalies. Let us look at an un-normalized relation.

Stud No	Student Name	Major	Course No	Course Title	Instructor Name	Instructor Location	Grade
03218	Brenner	BIS	13750	Database	D. Codd	CB117	A
			13818	Sys.Anal	B. Date	CB105	A
03221	King	Datam	13422	Acc.Meth	D. Smith	CB122	B
			13075	Database	D. Codd	CB117	C
			13818	Sys.Anal	B. Date	CB105	A
03223	Jollivet	PM	13465	Prod.Mgt	B. Date	CB105	A
Table 3 - Student-Course Relation – Un-normalized							

We find that there are multiple values at the intersection of particular rows and columns. Course data is then a repeating item within a student **tuple**. Repeating groups of data are not allowed in a **relation** because it goes against the requirement that each item must have a unique name. When we have repeating items, all items have the same name. If we break up the **tuple** in such a way that there will be a **tuple** in respect of each of the repeating values, then a single **attribute** will not be sufficient to uniquely identify the record.

Stud No	Student Name	Major	Course No	Course Title	Instructor Name	Instructor Location	Grade
03218	Brenner	BIS	13750	Database	D. Codd	CB117	A
03218	Brenner	BIS	13818	Sys.Anal	B. Date	CB105	A
03221	King	Datam	13422	Acc.Meth	D. Smith	CB122	B
03221	King	Datam	13075	Database	D. Codd	CB117	C
03221	King	Datam	13818	Sys.Anal	B. Date	CB105	A
03223	Jollivet	PM	13465	Prod.Mgt	B. Date	CB105	A
Table 4 – Student-Course Relation – Repeating items eliminated							

The solution entails creating an additional **relation** for the repeating items. The key for the relation containing the repeating items must now be a compound key. The key of the original relation is carried across. Let us see the resulting **relations**:

Stud No	Student Name	Major
03218	Brenner	BIS
03221	King	Datam
03223	Jollivet	PM
Table 5 - Student-Course Relation		

Stud No	Course No	Course Title	Instructor Name	Instructor Location	Grade
03218	13750	Database	D. Codd	CB117	A
03218	13818	Sys.Anal	B. Date	CB105	A
03221	13422	Acc.Meth	D. Smith	CB122	B
03221	13075	Database	D. Codd	CB117	C
03221	13818	Sys.Anal	B. Date	CB105	A
03223	13465	Prod.Mgt	B. Date	CB105	A
Table 6 – Student-Subject Relation					

The primary key for the Subject relation is **student-no, course-no**. As you can see from the sample data there is considerable **redundancy** when the data are in the **first normal form**. You will notice that instructor names and locations are repeated throughout the relation.

Insertion Anomaly in First Normal Form

Because student-no is part of the key, we are unable to insert a tuple for a new course, 'Data Structures', until at least one student has enrolled on the course. A key field may not contain a null value, although non-key fields may. Obviously, since a key field must uniquely identify a **tuple**, the field must at all times contain a valid value.

Deletion Anomaly in First Normal Form

Assume that two students are enrolled for a course. One has to leave through illness and the other is forced to leave for financial reasons. The **tuples** in respect of these students must be deleted. Notice that the deletion will carry with it the removal of all course information. As you can imagine, this is most unsatisfactory because we never know whether we are able to accept an enrollment for a particular course.

Update Anomaly in First Normal Form

Let us assume that a course name has changed. The original course name was Sys Anl and the new name is Sys Anl & Des. Because **first normal form** has not totally eliminated **redundancy**, we have to do a full pass through the relation. Ir we don't do this, there will be inconsistencies because old and new names will be in the relation.

Reason for Anomalies in First Normal Form

The grade attribute is the only one that depends on the whole key. The remaining attributes are said to be partially dependent on the primary key.

Stud No	Course No	Course	Instruct. Name	Instruct Loc.	Grade
03218	13750	Database	C. Boyce	CB117	A
03218	13818	Sys.Anal	B. Date	CB105	A
03221	13422	Acc.Meth	D. Smith	CB122	B
03221	13075	Database	D. Codd	CB117	C
03221	13818	Sys.Anal	B. Date	CB105	A
03223	13465	Prod.Mgt	B. Date	CB105	A

Table 7 - Student-Subject Relation

Attributes depending only on Course-no and not on the whole key.

Functional Dependency

Item X is said to be functionally dependent on item Y if at any point in time there is only one value of X for a given value of Y. In the preceding relation we find Sys.Anal for different key values; therefore, Course-Title is not functionally dependent on the whole key. In fact, we see that it depends only on part of the key, namely Course-No.

Second Normal Form

A relation is in **second normal form** if it is in first normal form and does not contain any **partial dependencies**. It follows that in converting from first normal to second normal form we are in fact removing **partial dependencies**. Let us see how we implement **second normal form**, i.e. remove partial dependencies:

▪   We create one relation containing those **attributes** that were dependent on the whole key. The relation then contains the original key and the **attributes** that are fully dependent on it.

▪   We create another relation containing those **attributes** that depend only on part of the key.

▪   The key of this latter relation will be the key attribute on which the partially dependent attributes depended.

Let us look at the decomposed relations now in second normal form:

Stud No	Course No	Grade
03218	13750	A
03218	13818	A
03221	13422	B
03221	13075	C
03221	13818	A
03223	13465	A

Table 8– Student Relation

Course No	Course Title	Instructor Name	Instructor Location
13750	Database	D. Codd	CB117
13818	Sys.Anal	B. Date	CB105
13422	Acc.Meth	D. Smith	CB122
13465	Prod.Mgt	B. Date	CB105

Table 9- Course Relation

Cross reference key

You will notice that data **redundancy** has been reduced since each course appears only once in the relation. We will now look at the anomalies found in relations that are in second normal form.

Anomalies

- Insertion Anomaly

We are unable to insert instructor data until the instructor has been assigned to at least one course.

- Deletion Anomaly

Deleting data for a course that has been discontinued will cause instructor data to be lost.

- Update Anomaly

Instructor data occurs more than once in the relation. To change the data with respect to an instructor, we have to traverse the whole relation.

Transitive Dependency

We will find **transitive dependency** in a relation when a field is dependent on another field that is not part of the key. In the example there is an association between instructor name and instructor location and the latter is not part of the key.

Third Normal Form

A relation is said to be in **third normal form** if it is already in second normal form and does not contain any **transitive dependencies**. To remove **transitive dependencies**, remove **attributes** that are transitive dependent and place them in a new relation. One of the transitive dependent fields is left behind to provide a cross-referencing link to the new relation.

The field that is left behind is described as a **foreign key**. Foreign keys enable programs to navigate between relations.

The relations in third normal form are shown below:

Stud No	Course No	Grade
03218	13750	A
03218	13818	A
03221	13422	B
03221	13075	C
03221	13818	A
03223	13465	A

Table10–StudentRelation

Course No	Course Title	Instructor Name
13750	Database	D. Codd
13818	Sys.Anal	B. Date
13422	Acc.Meth	D. Smith
13465	Prod.Mgt	B. Date

Table 11- Course Relation

Instructor-Name	Instructor Location
D. Codd	CB117
B. Date	CB105
D. Smith	Cb122

Table 12 – Instructor Relation

The decomposition process from an unnormalized relation to a set of relations in third normal form is now complete. You have no doubt seen that a database system makes our lives considerably simpler. Naturally there is a price to pay; whereas previously you had only one record to read, you now need additional reads.

Relationships Between Relations

To describe the relationships between the relations constituting a relational database we will use the diagram provided by Microsoft with the access database. We will be using the Northwind database. Whenever we construct a database we need to elaborate a diagram of this type to ensure that we are able to adequately navigate the database at all times.

You will notice from the diagram that you can travel from one relation to another but generally navigation is in one direction. Thus, you can go from Order to Customer but not from Customer to Order. You are also able to find all the order details for a given Order and the Customer to which this order pertains. When preparing the Order we need to know the Shipper but there is no need to travel from Shipper to Order. Each Detail is for a Product so we need the product as a foreign key in Detail. Similarly, there is a Supplier for the product and supplier is a foreign key in Product.

In the Northwind database, for each product there is only one supplier. If we had any number of suppliers for a given product, the Supplier relation would need a compound key SupplierId, ProductID. In addition, it is likely that the supplier will supply more than one product. However, the Northwind database had to be kept within a reasonable degree of complexity.

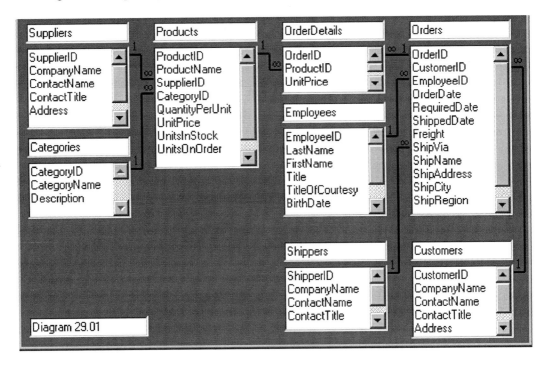

Diagram 29.01

Registering the Database

Suppliers of databases have found it necessary to establish a language independent mechanism that will interface between the program and the database. This interface method is called OPEN DATABASE CONNECTIVITY(**ODBC**). Furthermore, suppliers will provide appropriate ODBC drivers with which the program will communicate.

    The operating system will also have a database administration system that will enable you to register the database so that your program will be able to locate the database when required. The mechanism will be outlined below for Windows XP, for Windows 2000 the operation is only slightly different.

    Click Start/Control Panel and then select **Administrative tools**. Go to Data Sources(**ODBC**) and click. You will receive the **ODBC** Data Source Administration window. Through this window you may be able to add the database you plan to use. For this click on ADD.

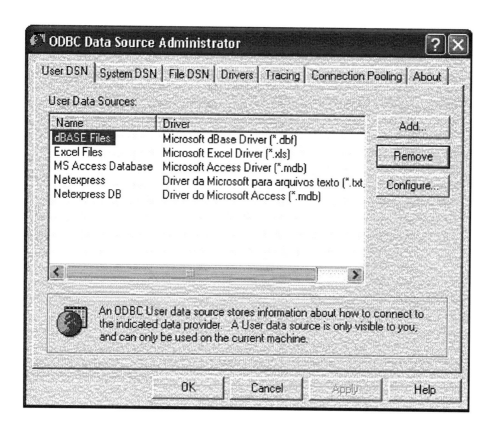

By clicking on add you will be taken to the next step. The window will have a number of available drivers. Because we will be using the Microsoft Access database, we will select accordingly and click on Finish.

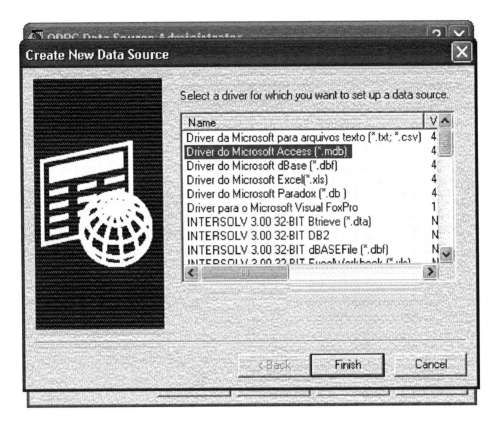

You will be presented with a setup window in which you will name the data source. Note that this is a meaningful and descriptive name, not the name of the database. Once you have entered the names, click on Select. You will receive a window that will enable you to specify the location of the database.

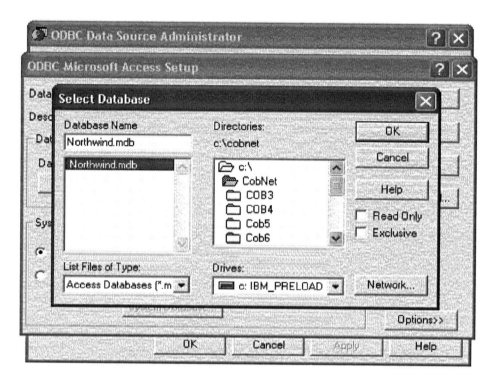

You will notice that we selected the Northwind database located in C:\Cobnet directory. You will be taken back to the first database administration screen, which now contains an entry for Customers in Northwind.

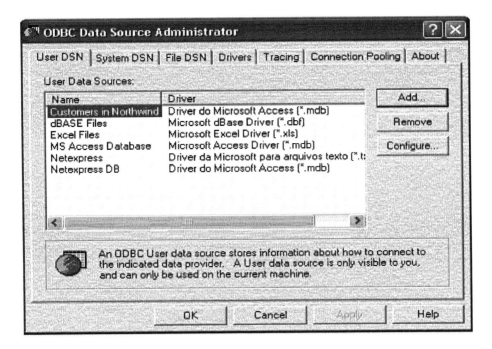

Using the OpenESQL Assistant

When accessing the database we will not be using COBOL commands; instead we will be using **SQL** commands. **Structured Query Language** is a language developed by the computer industry so as to standardize database access. The name is perhaps misleading because it does not provide only a query facility but rather a whole range of commands for manipulating the database. SQL may be pronounced **SQL** or **SEQUEL**. SQL commands may be used independently or they may be embedded in a host language, in our case, the COBOL program. We will become acquainted with **SQL** commands in the next chapter. Next you will be using the **select**, an **SQL** command that enables the program to retrieve selected records from the database, in your first database program.

To facilitate database programming, Micro Focus provides the OpenSQL Assistant, which enables the programmer to easily generate the required statements. You go to Tools in the Net Express IDE and there select **OpenESQL Assistant**. You will receive the following window that will enable you to select the appropriate database.

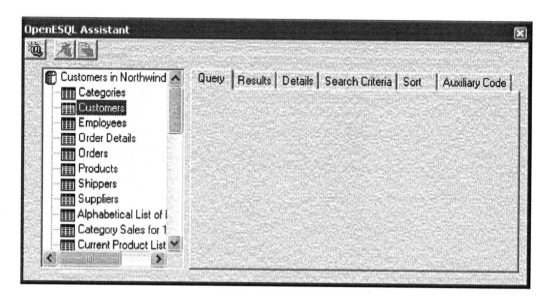

Because we registered the database, the Assistant is able to find it. When we select it we will be able to reference any of the files in the database, as you can see from the
next window.

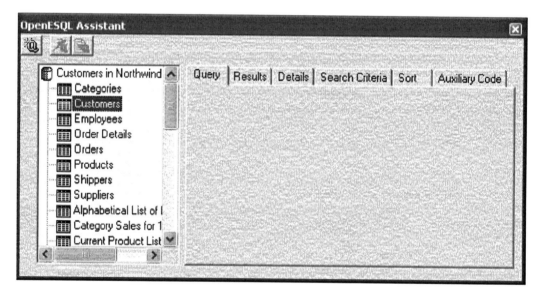

In our case we selected Customers. We will receive the following window in
which we will specify what we wish to do with the database. Our selection indicates that
we wish to retrieve particular records.

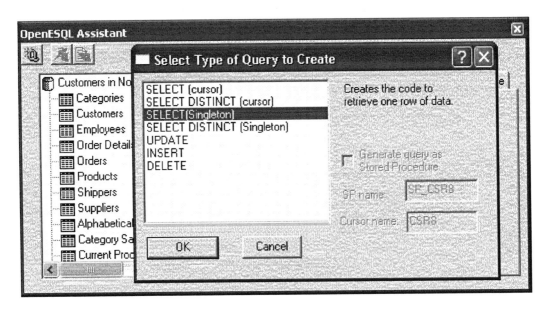

When we click on OK we will receive a screen containing a list of all the fields in the relation. The basic format of the select is shown next:

The Select

```
EXEC SQL
SELECT DBCOL1, DBCOL2, DBCOL3
    INTO
        :HOST1, :HOST2, :HOST3
    FROM RELATION1
END-EXEC
```

Figure 29.01

The host variables are your COBOL fields that will receive the data retrieved from the database and must each be preceded by a ':'. The list is comma separated. The variables are called host variables because they are variables that belong to the host program, the program that hosts the embedded SQL.

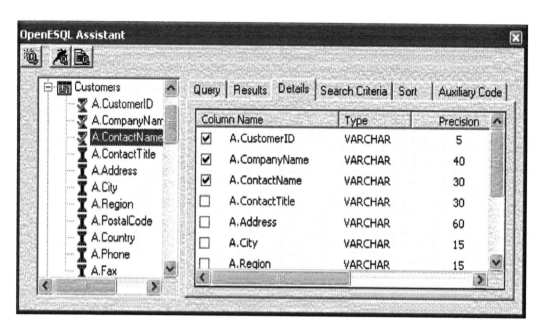

Notice that when a field is selected it acquires a tick to indicate that it has been selected. Next we clicked on details and saw that the fields were selected. We can now click on Query to see the SQL code generated.

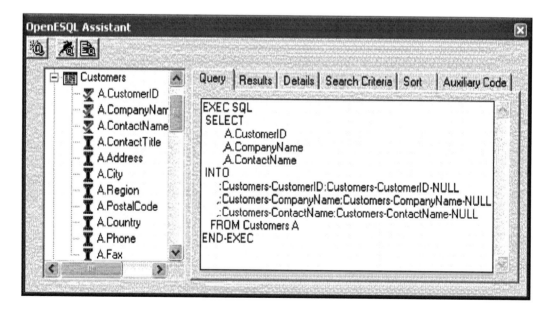

If we wish to test the program at this point, we will click on Results and then click on the run icon 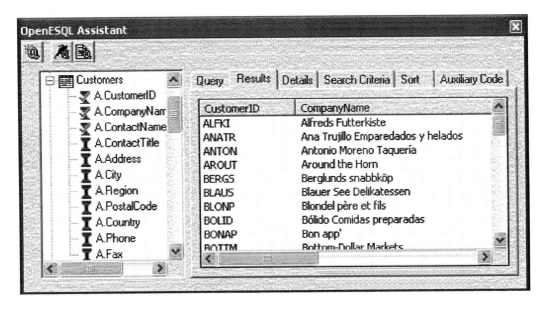.The following list will be produced:

An 'A.' has been inserted to identify the source. If we use another relation, its prefix will be 'B.'. We now click on **Auxiliary Code** and select the radio button for **Connect**.

You will recall that when we were using files we had to establish a connection between the program and the file, thus making the file available to the program. Similarly, when we no longer needed the file we would sever the connection by closing the file.

When operating with a database we need to do something similar. We will **connect** to the database and to sever the connection to the database we will **disconnect**. The following window connects to the database:

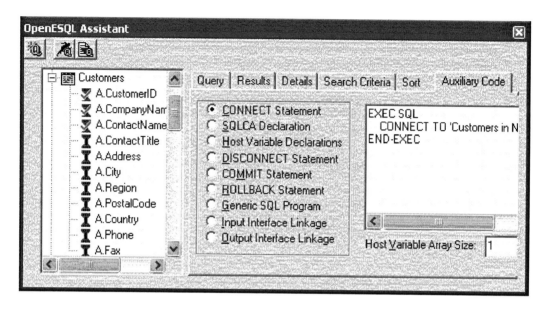

On the right you see the code generated. In the program you will position the cursor appropriately because we are going to insert the code generated into the program. You will click on the 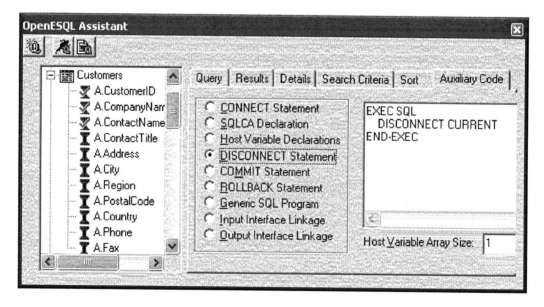 icon and the code will be appropriately positioned. Next we select the Disconnect radio button with the result depicted on the following window:

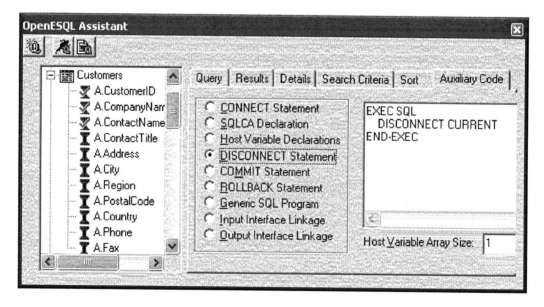

We again position the cursor at the point where we wish the code to be inserted and click on the same icon as before and the code will be incorporated into the program. It is also time to include the host variable declarations. We click on the **Host Variable Declarations** radio button with the result depicted in the following window:

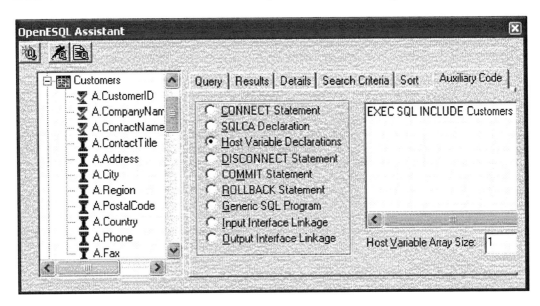

All operations on the database return a code. To gain access to the information returned you need to define the required fields. By selecting the **SQLCA** declaration radio button you will be able to incorporate the required fields. **SQLCA** is the **SQL** communication area.

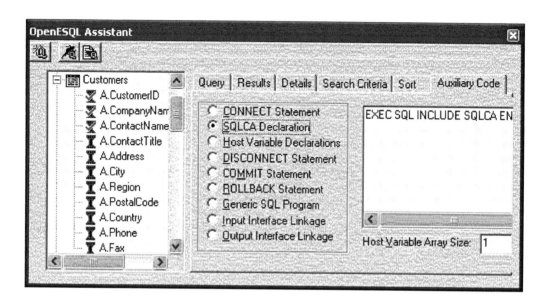

The program is not yet ready to run. We still need to specify the search criteria. You will recall that we wish to retrieve only selected records. Click on Search Criteria.

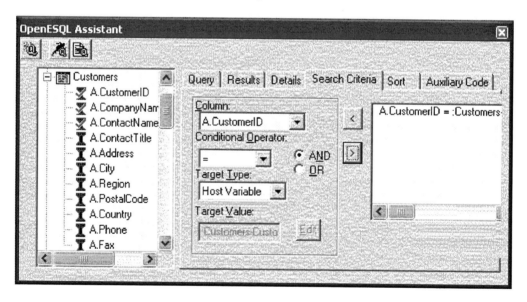

The condition we wish to specify and which was generated for us was that we wished to retrieve records where the column was A.CustomerID. The name of the column in the database was equal to the host variable Customers-CustomerID. The host variable is the corresponding variable in **working-storage** and has been incorporated into the program as Customers-CustomerID.

We clicked on the right arrow to place it in the box on the right. To apply it to the **Select**, we click the left arrow. You will notice that the **select** now incorporates a **where** clause.

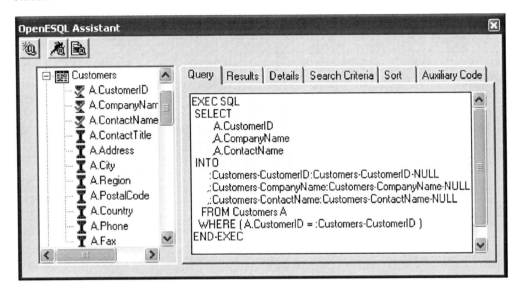

The program is now ready to run. Let us see what it looks like. Because we positioned the cursor immediately following the working-storage statement that is where the two includes for the data definitions were placed. Similarly, we placed the **Connect** before accessing the database and the **disconnect** following the access to the database.

Using OpenESQL Assistant - The Invoking Program

```
$set SQL(dbman=ODBC)
  identification division.
  program-id. DB1.
  repository.
      class DataInterface as "DataInterface".
  data division.
  working-storage section.
  01  data-rec.
      05  custID           pic   x(05).
      05  custName          pic   x(40).
      05  custContact       pic   x(30).
```

Listing 29.01 – 1 of 4

```
01   dataRef               object reference DataInterface.
procedure division.
A100-start.
    invoke DataInterface "new" returning dataRef
    invoke dataRef "openDB"
    perform A100-prompt
    perform until custID = 'finis'
        perform A200-get-data
        perform A300-display-data
        perform A100-prompt
    end-perform

    invoke dataRef "closeDB"
    stop run.
A100-prompt.
    display "Please enter Customer ID or 'finis' to end"
    accept custID.
A200-get-data.
    invoke dataRef "get-data" using data-rec.
A300-display-data.
    display custID  '  '
            custName  '  '
            custContact.
```

Listing 29.01 – 2 of 4

```
class-id. DataInterface as "DataInterface".
repository.
object.
working-storage section.
    EXEC SQL INCLUDE Customers END-EXEC
    EXEC SQL INCLUDE SQLCA END-EXEC
method-id. openDB.
```

Listing 29.01 – 3 of 4

```
procedure division.
    EXEC SQL
        CONNECT TO 'Customers in  Northwind' USER 'admin'
    END-EXEC.
    if  SQLCODE not = 0
        display SQLCODE " " SQLERRMC
    end-if
end method openDB.

method-id. closeDB.
procedure division.
    EXEC SQL
        DISCONNECT CURRENT
    END-EXEC
    if  SQLCODE not = 0
        display SQLCODE " " SQLERRMC
    end-if
end method closeDB.
method-id. get-data.
linkage section.
01  data-rec.
    05  custID         pic x(5).
    05  custName       pic x(40).
    05  custContact    pic x(30).
procedure division using data-rec.
    EXEC SQL
      SELECT DISTINCT
             A.CustomerID
            ,A.CompanyName
            ,A.ContactName
      INTO
            :Customers-CustomerID:Customers-CustomerID-NULL
           ,:Customers-CompanyName:Customers-CompanyName-NULL
           ,:Customers-ContactName:Customers-ContactName-NULL
        FROM Customers A
          WHERE ( A.CustomerID = :Customers-CustomerID )
    END-EXEC
    move Customers-CompanyName to custName
    move Customers-ContactName to custContact.
end method get-data.
end object.
end class DataInterface.
```

Listing 29.01 – 4 of 4

Look at the prompt. You see the field `Customers-CustomerID` being used but where is it defined? It is part of the **Include**. If you place the cursor over the **Include** and right click you will see an option 'Show CopyFile'. If you click on it, the file will be expanded. The following listing shows the expanded files:

Expanded Files

```
$set SQL(dbman=ODBC)
program-id. NW0101.
Working-storage section.
    EXEC SQL INCLUDE SQLCA END-EXEC
01  SQLCA.
    05  SQLCAID        PIC X(8)            VALUE "SQLCA    ".
    05  SQLCABC        PIC S9(9) COMP-5 VALUE 136.
    05  SQLCODE        PIC S9(9) COMP-5 VALUE 0.
    05  SQLERRM.
        49  SQLERRML   PIC S9(4) COMP-5.
        49  SQLERRMC   PIC X(70).
    05  SQLERRP        PIC X(8).
    05  SQLERRD        PIC S9(9) COMP-5 OCCURS 6 VALUE 0.
    05  SQLWARN.
        10  SQLWARN0   PIC X.
        10  SQLWARN1   PIC X.
        10  SQLWARN2   PIC X.
        10  SQLWARN3   PIC X.
        10  SQLWARN4   PIC X.
        10  SQLWARN5   PIC X.
        10  SQLWARN6   PIC X.
        10  SQLWARN7   PIC X.
        10  SQLWARN8   PIC X.
        10  SQLWARN9   PIC X.
        10  SQLWARN10  PIC X.
        10  SQLWARNA   PIC X REDEFINES SQLWARN10.
    05  SQLSTATE    PIC X(5).
    EXEC SQL INCLUDE Customers END-EXEC
    EXEC SQL DECLARE
    Customers TABLE
    ( CustomerID       VARCHAR(5)
    , CompanyName      VARCHAR(40)
    , ContactName      VARCHAR(30)
    , ContactTitle     VARCHAR(30)
```

Listing 29.02 – 1 of 3

Expanded Files

```
        ,Address                    VARCHAR(60)
        ,City                       VARCHAR(15)
        ,Region                     VARCHAR(15)
        ,PostalCode                 VARCHAR(10)
        ,Country                    VARCHAR(15)
        ,Phone                      VARCHAR(24)
        ,Fax                        VARCHAR(24)
      ) END-EXEC.
*>-------------------------------------------------------------
*> COBOL DECLARATION FOR TABLE Customers
*>-------------------------------------------------------------
  01   DCLCustomers.
       03 Customers-CustomerID             SQL TYPE IS
                                           CHAR(5).
       03 Customers-CompanyName            SQL TYPE IS
                                           CHAR(40).
       03 Customers-ContactName            SQL TYPE IS
                                           CHAR(30).
       03 Customers-ContactTitle           SQL TYPE IS
                                           CHAR(30).
       03 Customers-Address               SQL TYPE IS
                                           CHAR(60).
       03 Customers-City                   SQL TYPE IS
                                           CHAR(15).
       03 Customers-Region                 SQL TYPE IS
                                           CHAR(15).
       03 Customers-PostalCode             SQL TYPE IS
                                           CHAR(10).
       03 Customers-Country                SQL TYPE IS
                                           CHAR(15).
       03 Customers-Phone                  SQL TYPE IS
                                           CHAR(24).
       03 Customers-Fax                    SQL TYPE IS
                                           CHAR(24).
*> -------------------------------------------------------------
*> COBOL INDICATOR VARIABLES FOR TABLE
*> -------------------------------------------------------------
  01   DCLCustomers-NULL.
       03 Customers-CustomerID-NULL        PIC S9(04)   COMP-5.
       03 Customers-CompanyName-NULL       PIC S9(04)   COMP-5.
       03 Customers-ContactName-NULL       PIC S9(04)   COMP-5.
```

Listing 29.02 – 2 of 3

Expanded Files

```
03 Customers-ContactTitle-NULL      PIC S9(04)  COMP-5.
03 Customers-Address-NULL           PIC S9(04)  COMP-5.
03 Customers-City-NULL              PIC S9(04)  COMP-5.
03 Customers-Region-NULL            PIC S9(04)  COMP-5.
03 Customers-PostalCode-NULL        PIC S9(04)  COMP-5.
03 Customers-Country-NULL           PIC S9(04)  COMP-5.
03 Customers-Phone-NULL             PIC S9(04)  COMP-5.
03 Customers-Fax-NULL               PIC S9(04)  COMP-5.
```

Listing 29.02 – 3 of 3

Note that you can delete the fields that you do not use from the definitions included for the Customers table. None of the **SQLCA** definitions may be removed however, because they are required by the system. A reduced set of definitions for Customers follows.

As earlier indicated, following the **into** we provide the host variables. They appear in the following format:

```
:Customers-CustomerID:Customers-CustomerID-NULL
```

The first part, `:Customers-CustomerID` , preceded by a colon is the host variable, the second element, `:Customers-CustomerID-NULL`, also preceded by a colon, is a field created and used by Net Express with which you need not be concerned.

Reducing Number of Field Definitions

```
      EXEC SQL INCLUDE Customers END-EXEC
      EXEC SQL DECLARE
      Customers TABLE
      ( CustomerID          VARCHAR(5)
       ,CompanyName          VARCHAR(40)
       ,ContactName          VARCHAR(30)
      ) END-EXEC.
*>-------------------------------------------------------------
*> COBOL DECLARATION FOR TABLE Customers
*>-------------------------------------------------------------
   01   DCLCustomers.
      03 Customers-CustomerID       SQL TYPE IS CHAR(5).
      03 Customers-CompanyName      SQL TYPE IS CHAR(40).
      03 Customers-ContactName      SQL TYPE IS CHAR(30).
```

Figure 29.02 – 1 of 2

Reducing Number of Field Definitions

```
*>------------------------------------------------------------
*> COBOL INDICATOR VARIABLES FOR TABLE
*>------------------------------------------------------------
   01   DCLCustomers-NULL.
        03  Customers-CustomerID-NULL         PIC  S9(04)   COMP-5.
        03  Customers-CompanyName-NULL        PIC  S9(04)   COMP-5.
        03  Customers-ContactName-NULL        PIC  S9(04)   COMP-5.
```

Figure 29.02 – 2 of 2

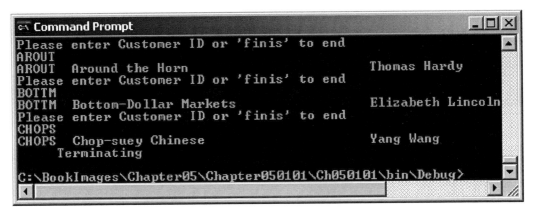

The following table depicts some of the values returned in SQLCODE and the meanings associated with these values.

SQLCODE	Meaning
0	Statement executed successfully
1	The statement executed successfully but returned a warning. The warning is stored in one of the SQLWARN variables.
100	Data not found or end of result set reached
Negative	Execution was unsuccessful. Code is in SQLCODE and message is in SQLERRMC.
Table 13 – Some SQLCODE values	

Summary

- In file systems, where a file system is a collection of unrelated files we find data **redundancy**. Redundancy leads to **inconsistencies**.

- A **database** is a centralized repository of non-redundant data accessible by multiple users. The database organization we will be looking at is the relational model of database. Relational databases are said to consist of associated relations. For our purpose we can see a **relation** as a file. We could therefore picture a relational database as consisting of associated files. Another name for a relation is a **table**. Tables consist of rows called **tuples** and columns called **attributes**. Using the terminology we are used to, we see that a tuple corresponds to a record and that an attribute corresponds to a field.

- For a file to be a relation it must satisfy the following prerequisites:

    - - Each column must pertain to an attribute and contain a single value.
    - Each column must have a name and the name must be unique.
    - The key for a **tuple** must be unique.
    - The sequence of rows is not material.

- **Data Normalization** – When we start normalizing data we will have organized our data in such a way that it will be a collection of fields with some loose association. For our purposes we will see this collection of fields as a file. In normalizing data our objective is to remove insertion, deletion and update anomalies. In removing anomalies, from that one file, a number of files will result. A file may be described as being in first, second or third normal form. Normally we do not go beyond third normal form because that would result in the creation of more files without bringing commensurate advantages.

- **First Normal Form** – A relation is said to be in first normal form if it is free of repeating values. This means that at an intersection of a row and a column there cannot be more than one value. In other words, a tuple may not contain an embedded table. We have anomalies in first normal form if there are attributes that do not depend on the whole key.

- **Second Normal Form** – A relation is said to be in second normal form if it is already in first normal form and does not contain fields that are not functionally dependent. The anomalies in second normal form arise from the fact that there are fields that are not functionally dependent on the key.

- **Third Normal Form** – A relation is said to be in third normal form if it is already in second normal form and does not have transitive dependencies. To remove transitive dependencies we remove the transitive dependent fields and create a new relation. Notice that to allow navigation, one of the transitive dependent fields must be left behind. This field is described as a **foreign key**.

- **Relationships between relations** – When we have our relations in third normal form, we must ensure that we are able to navigate the database. Foreign keys provide the mechanism that enables us to traverse the database. Notice that we must be able to ascertain to which customer an order belongs, but there is no way of linking from Customer to Orders.

- **SQL** – When accessing the database we do not use COBOL commands, instead we use SQL commands. SQL, which stands for **S**tructured **Q**uery **L**anguage, is an international standard that caters for the interaction between program and database. Although the word Query is part of the name, the language does not restrict itself to queries.

- **OpenESQL Assistant** – To facilitate the creation of SQL statements that are required for the program to interact with the database, Net Express comes to the assistance of the programmer through the presence of the OpenESQL Assistant. The assistant is able to generate the required statements through an interactive dialogue.

Complete

1. Relational databases seek to reduce _____ through the elimination of _____.

2. Another name for a database file is _____ or _____.

3. Another name for rows in a relation is _____.

4. Another name for the fields in a row is _____.

5. In first normal form there may not be _____ values for an attribute.

6. We are said to be in the presence of _____ _____ if for a single value of productCode there is a _____ value for description.

7. We have _____ _____ if a field depends on another field that is not part of the key.

True/False

1.   Relational databases attempt to maximize inconsistencies.

2.   Redundancy leads to the presence of inconsistencies.

3.   A relation in first normal form may not have repeating items.

4.   Navigation between relations is possible through foreign keys.

5.   A relation may be in second normal form and not be in first normal form.

Exercise

1.   Using the Northwind database from the Microsoft Access database, prompt the user for Employee ID and then select from the database EmployeeID, FirstName, LastName and Title. The retrieved data should then be displayed on the screen.

Chapter 30

Introduction to SQL

Topics Covered

- Selects
- Different Selects
- Select with > or =
- Select 'LIKE'
- Select Using 'AND', 'OR' and 'IN'
- Avg, Min and Max
- Sum and COUNT(*)
- Select Distinct
- The Join
- Insertions
- Deletions
- The Update
- Summary
- Complete
- True/False
- Exercises

Selects

In the preceding chapter we looked at a **select** that enables us to randomly retrieve a desired record. This facility is very useful and we could not do without it. However, at times we need to be able to do a pass through the database.

We know that the program processes one record at a time. Going back to our experience with files, the I/O system retrieves a number of records into the buffer and then passes these records from the buffer to the program, one at a time.

With a database we have a similar mechanism that enables us to do a pass through the file, accessing each and every record. To do this we need a **cursor**. In our example, as we retrieve a record we place it on the screen. On the screen, the cursor advances to the next line and that determines where the record will be placed. The cursor for the database behaves in a similar fashion. It will advance to the next record and pass it to the program.

To obtain a cursor we must declare it. Because it is a **declarative** statement we can place it either in the **data** or **procedure** division.

Obtaining a Cursor

```
EXEC SQL
    DECLARE CSR10 CURSOR FOR SELECT
        A.CustomerID
        ,A.CompanyName
        ,A.ContactName
    FROM Customers A
END-EXEC
```

Figure 30.01

The name of the cursor is **CSR10** and it is to be used to retrieve the named columns from relation Customers. Before we can use the cursor we must open it. The **declare** created the cursor, but to use it we need to open it. The place to position the **open** is before retrieval of database records is initiated.

Note that as we place the file read in an iteration, we will also need to place database record retrieval in a loop. The statement that retrieves the records from the database is the **fetch**.

A Fetch to Retrieve Records from the Database

```
EXEC SQL
  FETCH CSR10 INTO
       :Customers-CustomerID:Customers-CustomerID-NULL
      ,:Customers-CompanyName:Customers-CompanyName-NULL
      ,:Customers-ContactName:Customers-ContactName-NULL
END-EXEC
```

Figure 30.02

The full program follows. We have used a variable to count the number of records displayed. We pause every 10 records.

Accessing the Database

```
$set sql(dbman=ODBC)
 identification division.
 program-id. DB2.

 working-storage section.
 01  ctr                  pic 99 value 0.
     EXEC SQL INCLUDE Customers END-EXEC
     EXEC SQL INCLUDE SQLCA END-EXEC
 01  sql-code             pic S9(9) comp-5
     88  valid sql-code            value 0.
     88  no-more-records           value 100
     EXEC SQL
         DECLARE CSR10 CURSOR FOR SELECT
             A.CustomerID
            ,A.CompanyName
            ,A.ContactName
         FROM Customers A
     END-EXEC
 procedure division.
 A100-start.
     EXEC SQL
         CONNECT TO 'Customers in Northwind' USER 'admin'
     END-EXEC
     if  SQLCODE not = 0
         display SQLCODE " " SQLERRMC
     end-if
```

Listing 30.01 – 1 of 2

Accessing the Database

```
      EXEC SQL   OPEN CSR10 END-EXEC
      if  SQLCODE not = 0 display SQLCODE " " SQLERRMC
      end-if
      move SQLCODE to sql-code
      PERFORM UNTIL not valid-sql-code

          EXEC SQL
            FETCH CSR10 INTO
                :Customers-CustomerID:Customers-CustomerID-NULL
               ,:Customers-CompanyName:Customers-CompanyName-NULL
               ,:Customers-ContactName:Customers-ContactName-NULL
          END-EXEC
          move SQLCODE to sql-code
          IF  valid-sql-code
              perform A100-ShowData
          else
              if not no-more-records
                  display SQLCODE " " SQLERRMC
              end-if
          END-IF
      END-PERFORM
      EXEC SQL   CLOSE CSR10 END-EXEC
      EXEC SQL
          DISCONNECT CURRENT
      END-EXEC
      if  SQLCODE not = 0
          display SQLCODE " " SQLERRMC
      end-if
      stop run.
   A100-ShowData.
      add 1 to ctr
      if  ctr > 10
          accept ctr
      end-if
      display Customers-CustomerID '   '
              Customers-CompanyName
              Customers-ContactName.
```

Listing 30.01 – 2 of 2

    If **SQLCODE** is less than zero there is an error that precludes processing of the relation. Display **SQLCODE** to find out the cause of the error. Furthermore, the error message explaining the cause of the error will be in **SQLERRMC** and you are advised to display this field as well.

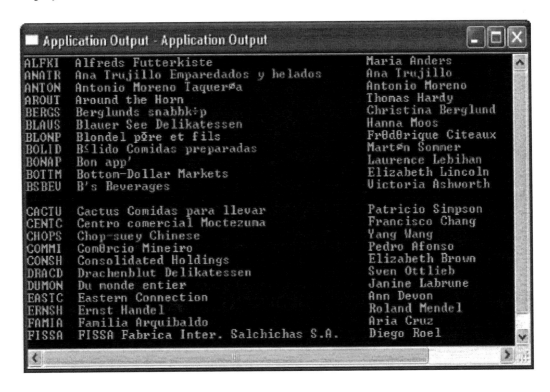

In using the OpenESQL Assistant to obtain a cursor we would select as shown following:

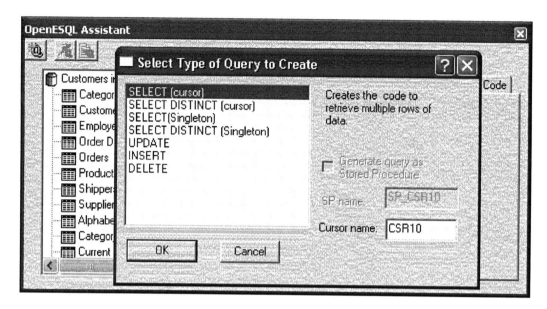

The query secured is shown below. When we store it, we will copy the cursor declaration and place it in the data division.

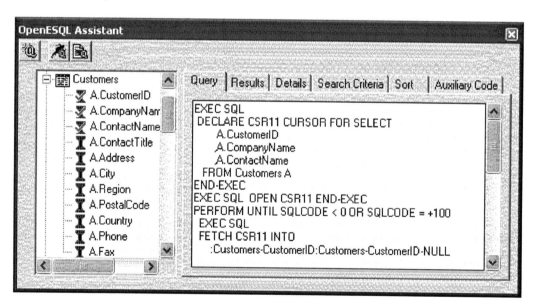

As you can see, the Assistant is very useful. But it is not able to do everything for you. When we need to specify a condition, we will code the **where** ourselves.

Different Selects

We have to be able to format the select so as to satisfy our requirements. The following are only a few of the options open to us:

Select with > or =

In the following example we will be using the products relation. See how we declare the cursor. The **fetch** remains unchanged:

Select with a Relational Operator

```
EXEC SQL
    DECLARE CSR13 CURSOR FOR SELECT
            A.ProductID
           ,A.ProductName
           ,A.UnitPrice
    FROM Products A
            where UnitPrice >= 50
END-EXEC
```

Figure 30.03

We have seen how the **fetch** resides inside a loop but we have not yet commented on the conditions in the **perform**.

PERFORM UNTIL SQLCODE < 0 OR SQLCODE = +100

The condition 'SQLCODE < 0' means an error. Successful execution will return 0 into SQLCODE. The other condition 'SQLCODE=+100' means end of result set. Let us see the execution:

```
Application Output - Application Output
+0000000009  Mishi Kobe Niku                      97.00
+0000000018  Carnarvon Tigers                     62.50
+0000000020  Sir Rodney's Marmalade               81.00
+0000000029  Th"ringer Rostbratwurst             123.79
+0000000038  C[te de Blaye                       263.50
+0000000051  Manjimup Dried Apples                53.00
+0000000059  Raclette Courdavault                 55.00
```

Only products with a unit price in excess of 50 were reflected.

Select 'Like'

The **like** enables us to select records for which we do not know the whole key. In the example we know only one character. We are saying that the key contains at least one 'O'. The '%' on either side, signifies any characters.

Using Like with %

```
EXEC SQL
    DECLARE CSR10 CURSOR FOR SELECT
          A.CustomerID
          ,A.CompanyName
          ,A.ContactName
    FROM Customers A
          where CustomerID LIKE '%O%'
END-EXEC
```

Figure 30.04

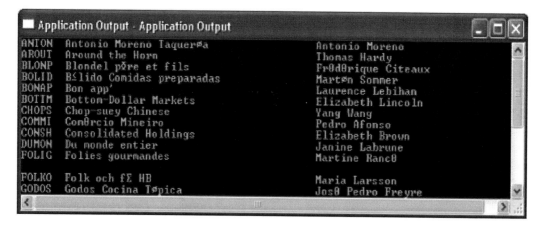

In the following example we are saying that the 'O' is preceded by three characters and followed by any number of characters '___O%'. If we wanted to indicate that the 'O' was preceded by two characters and followed by two characters we would specify '__O__'.

Using Like with __

```
EXEC SQL
    DECLARE CSR10 CURSOR FOR SELECT
            A.CustomerID
            ,A.CompanyName
            ,A.ContactName
    FROM Customers A
            where CustomerID LIKE '___O%'
END-EXEC
```

Figure 30.05

```
ANTON   Antonio Moreno Taquerøa          Antonio Moreno
DUMON   Du monde entier                  Janine Labrune
GODOS   Godos Cocina Tøpica              Josß Pedro Freyre
LACOR   La corne d'abondance             Daniel Tonini
LINOD   LINO-Delicateses                 Felipe Izquierdo
SIMOB   Simons bistro                    Jytte Petersen
```

Select Using 'AND', 'OR' and 'IN'

We may tailor the select through the use of **and** and **or**. In the example that follows we employ the **and** to restrict the search to a narrow range. We use the Assistant in specifying the **and**.

In the example we used a cursor. Because the **and** implies a condition, we clicked on the Search Criteria and proceeded to specify the condition. We used a literal and, as the following window depicts, we were provided with an appropriate window in which we were able to specify the literal.

The primary condition is 'greater than' and the secondary condition following the **and** is 'less than'.

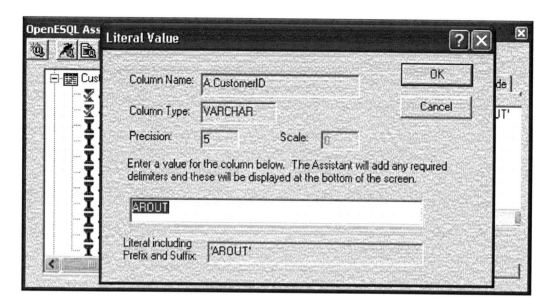

Once the search criteria have been established we click on the right arrow, with the result shown in the following window. The condition is depicted in the box on the right.

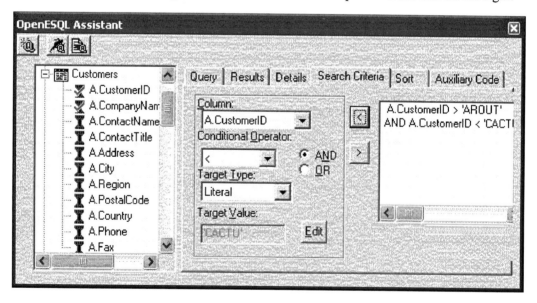

We now click on the left arrow to incorporate the condition into the query. The resulting query is as follows:

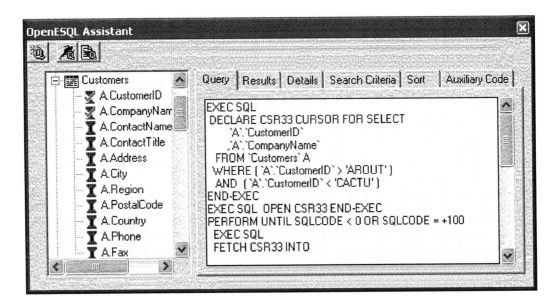

The program listing follows:

Using Conditional Operators (and)

```
$set SQL(dbman=ODBC)
$set sourceformat 'free'
 program-id. Andor1.
 working-storage section.
 01   sql-code              pic S9(9) comp-5
      88   valid-sql-code              value 0.
      88   no-more-records             value 100.
      EXEC SQL INCLUDE Customers END-EXEC
      EXEC SQL INCLUDE SQLCA END-EXEC


      EXEC SQL
          DECLARE CSR33 CURSOR FOR SELECT
                 `A`.`CustomerID`
                ,`A`.`CompanyName`
          FROM `Customers` A
              WHERE ( `A`.`CustomerID` > 'AROUT' )
              AND   ( `A`.`CustomerID` < 'CACTU' )
      END-EXEC
```

Listing 30.02 – 1 of 2

Using Conditional Operators (and)

```
procedure division.
    EXEC SQL
        CONNECT TO 'Customers in Northwind' USER 'admin'
    END-EXEC
    if  SQLCODE not = 0
        display SQLCODE " " SQLERRMC
    end-if
    EXEC SQL  OPEN CSR33 END-EXEC
    if  SQLCODE not = 0
        display SQLCODE " " SQLERRMC
    end-if
    Move SQLCODE to sql-code
    perform until not valid-sql-code
        EXEC SQL
        FETCH CSR33 INTO
            :Customers-CustomerID:Customers-CustomerID-NULL
            ,:Customers-CompanyName:Customers-CompanyName-NULL
        END-EXEC
        Move SQLCODE to sql-code

        IF  valid-sql-code
            perform A100-Display
        else
            if  not no-more-records
                display SQLCODE " " SQLERRMC
            END-IF
        END-IF
    END-PERFORM
    EXEC SQL  CLOSE CSR33 END-EXEC
    EXEC SQL
        DISCONNECT CURRENT
    END-EXEC
    if  SQLCODE not = 0
        display SQLCODE " " SQLERRMC
    end-if
    stop run.
A100-Display.
    display  Customers-CustomerID  ' '
            Customers-CompanyName.
```

Listing 30.02 – 2 of 2

```
Application Output - Application Output
BERGS  Berglunds snabbk÷p
BLAUS  Blauer See Delikatessen
BLONP  Blondel pŏre et fils
BOLID  B£lido Conidas preparadas
BONAP  Bon app'
BOTTM  Bottom-Dollar Markets
BSBEV  B's Beverages
_
```

We will not use a cursor for the **or**, instead we will get one record at a time.

Using Conditional Operators (or)

```
$set sql(dbman=ODBC)
 program-id. SQL14Or.
 working-storage section.
     EXEC SQL INCLUDE Customers END-EXEC
     EXEC SQL INCLUDE SQLCA END-EXEC
 procedure division.
     EXEC SQL
         CONNECT TO 'Customers in Northwind' USER 'admin'
     END-EXEC
     if  SQLCODE not = 0
         display SQLCODE " " SQLERRMC
     end-if
     EXEC SQL
       SELECT
            `A`.`CustomerID` ,`A`.`CompanyName`
       INTO
         :Customers-CustomerID:Customers-CustomerID-NULL
        ,:Customers-CompanyName:Customers-CompanyName-NULL
       FROM `Customers` A
           WHERE ( `A`.`CustomerID` = 'AROUT' )
           OR    ( `A`.`CustomerID` = 'CACTU' )
           OR    ( `A`.`CustomerID` = 'VINET' )
     END-EXEC
     display  Customers-CustomerID '  ' Customers-CompanyName
     EXEC SQL
         DISCONNECT CURRENT
     END-EXEC
```

Listing 30.03 – 1 of 2

```
if  SQLCODE not = 0
    display SQLCODE " " SQLERRMC
end-if
stop run.
```

Listing 30.03 – 2 of 2

The **in** replaces the **or** and introduces a simpler format though not as clear. The output produced would be the same in both cases. Below we show only how the select has changed:

Using the In

```
EXEC SQL
  SELECT
      `A`.`CustomerID`
    , `A`.`CompanyName`
  INTO
      :Customers-CustomerID:Customers-CustomerID-NULL
    , :Customers-CompanyName:Customers-CompanyName-NULL
  FROM `Customers` A
    WHERE  `A`.`CustomerID` in('AROUT', 'CACTU', 'VINET' )
END-EXEC
```

Figure 30.06

Avg, Min and Max

A database management system needs to provide services and facilities that go beyond insertion and retrieval of data. Thus, **SQL** provides a number of functions that enable the user to extract values from the database and, if necessary, perform arithmetic on them. The program that follows determines the lowest, highest and average values for unit price.

You will notice that we do not need to do a pass through the database to obtain the required values. We know this because, had this not been so, we would have needed to declare a cursor. Instead, we just used the Select:

Min, Max and Avg

```
$set sql(dbman=ODBC)
$set sourceformat "free"
 identification division.
 program-id. DB6.
 working-storage section.
 01  EditMax                  pic ZZZ,ZZZ.99.
 01  EditMin                  pic ZZZ,ZZZ.99.
 01  EditAvg                  pic ZZZ,ZZZ.99.
 01  maxPrice                 pic 9(5)V99.
 01  minPrice                 pic 9(5)V99.
 01  avgPrice                 pic 9(5)V99.
     EXEC SQL INCLUDE Products END-EXEC
     EXEC SQL INCLUDE SQLCA END-EXEC

 procedure division.
     EXEC SQL
         CONNECT TO 'Customers in Northwind' USER 'admin'
     END-EXEC
     if  SQLCODE not = 0
         display SQLCODE " " SQLERRMC
     end-if

     EXEC SQL
        SELECT
             max(`A`.`UnitPrice`),
             min(`A`.`UnitPrice`),
             avg(`A`.`UnitPrice`)
        INTO
             :maxPrice,
             :minPrice,
             :avgPrice
        FROM `Products` A
     END-EXEC

     perform A100-ShowData
     EXEC SQL
         DISCONNECT CURRENT
     END-EXEC
```

Listing 30.04 – 1 of 2

Min, Max and Avg

```
        if  SQLCODE not = 0
            display SQLCODE " " SQLERRMC
        end-if
        stop run.
    A100-ShowData.
        move maxPrice to EditMax
        move minPrice to EditMin
        move avgPrice to EditAvg
        display 'Highest price is: ' EditMax
        display 'Lowest  price is: ' EditMin
        display 'Average price is: ' EditAvg.
```

Listing 30.04 – 2 of 2

```
c:\ Command Prompt                                    _ □ ×
Highest price is:     263.50
Lowest  price is:       2.50
Average price is:      28.86
```

Sum and COUNT(*)

Sum and **COUNT(*)** are two functions also provided by **SQL**. The first returns the sum of the values and the second the number of values added; in other words, how many records participated in the operation. The following program depicts the implementation of the two functions:

Sum and Count(*)

```
$set sql(dbman=ODBC)
$set sourceformat "free"
  identification division.
  program-id. DB6.
  working-storage section.
  01  EditSum                  pic ZZZ,ZZZ.99.
  01  EditNum                  pic ZZZ,ZZZ.
  01  sumPrice                 pic 9(5)V99.
  01  numOfRecords             pic 9(5).
```

Listing 30.05 – 1 of 2

Sum and Count(*)

```
    EXEC SQL INCLUDE Products END-EXEC
    EXEC SQL INCLUDE SQLCA END-EXEC

procedure division.
    EXEC SQL
        CONNECT TO 'Customers in Northwind' USER 'admin'
    END-EXEC
    if  SQLCODE not = 0
        display SQLCODE " " SQLERRMC
    end-if
    EXEC SQL
        SELECT
            sum(`A`.`UnitPrice`),
            count(*)
        INTO
            :sumPrice,
            :numOfRecords
        FROM `Products` A
    END-EXEC
    perform A100-ShowData
    EXEC SQL
        DISCONNECT CURRENT
    END-EXEC
    if  SQLCODE not = 0
        display SQLCODE " " SQLERRMC
    end-if
    stop run.

A100-ShowData.
    move sumPrice to EditSum
    display 'The sum of prices is:     ' EditSum
    move numOfRecords to EditNum
    display 'The number of records is: ' EditNum.
```

Listing 30.05 – 2 of 2

```
Command Prompt                                          _ □ ×

The sum of prices is:    2,222.71
The number of records is:     77
```

Select Distinct

The **Distinct** is used when we want only one row returned, however many there may be for the columns being processed. Consider the following table:

The **Distinct** will return one row for Sup1 because both rows are for PartA. For Sup3 however, there will be two rows printed because one will be for PartC and the other for PartD.

Distinct

```
$set sql(dbman=ODBC)
 program-id. DB7.
 working-storage section.
     EXEC SQL INCLUDE Supplier END-EXEC
     EXEC SQL INCLUDE SQLCA END-EXEC
 01  sql-code              pic S9(9) comp-5.
     88  valid-sql-code           value 0.
     88  no-more-records          value 100.
     EXEC SQL
       DECLARE CSR22 CURSOR FOR SELECT DISTINCT
               `A`.`SupID`
              ,`A`.`PartNO`
          FROM `Supplier` A
     END-EXEC
```

Listing 30.06 – 1 of 2

Distinct

```
procedure division.
    EXEC SQL
        CONNECT TO 'Supplier Distinct' USER 'admin'
    END-EXEC
    if  SQLCODE not = 0
        display SQLCODE " " SQLERRMC
    end-if
    EXEC SQL  OPEN CSR22 END-EXEC
    if  SQLCODE not = 0
        display SQLCODE " " SQLERRMC
    end-if
    Move SQLCODE to sql-code
    PERFORM UNTIL not valid-sql-code
        EXEC SQL
            FETCH CSR22 INTO
              :Supplier-SupID:Supplier-SupID-NULL
              ,:Supplier-PartNO:Supplier-PartNO-NULL
        END-EXEC
        Move SQLCODE to sql-code
        IF  valid-sql-code
            perform A100-ShowData
        else
            if not no-more-records
                display SQLCODE " " SQLERRMC
            END-IF
        END-PERFORM
    EXEC SQL  CLOSE CSR22 END-EXEC
    if  SQLCODE not = 0
        display SQLCODE " " SQLERRMC
    end-if
    EXEC SQL
        DISCONNECT CURRENT
    END-EXEC
    if  SQLCODE not = 0
        display SQLCODE " " SQLERRMC
    end-if
    stop run.

A100-ShowData.
    display  Supplier-SupID
             Supplier-PartNO.
```

Listing 30.06 – 2 of 2

In obtaining **select distinct** the cursor was obtained via the following window:

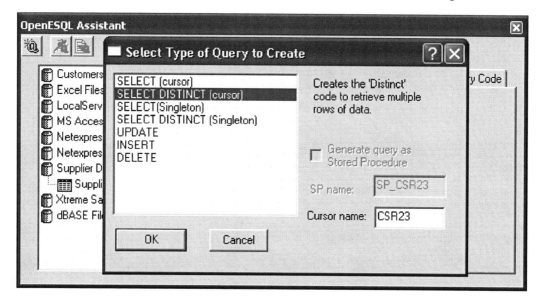

The Join

The **Join** is one of the operations provided by SQL and it combines selected fields from two files. The **Assistant** assists us in joining files and we will see what we will have to do to join the Customers relation to the Orders relation.

- Open the Assistant and select customers.

- In the Type of Query window choose '**SELECT(cursor)**'. The following query will be produced:

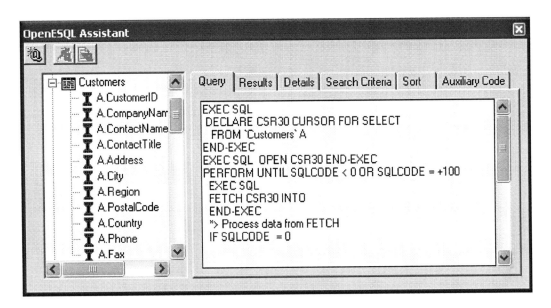

- Further select CustomerID and CompanyName

- Select Auxilliary Code and do as before namely, select Connect, Disconnect, SQLCA Declaration and Host Variable Declaration.

- Once the preceding steps have been taken, select the Orders icon, as shown below:

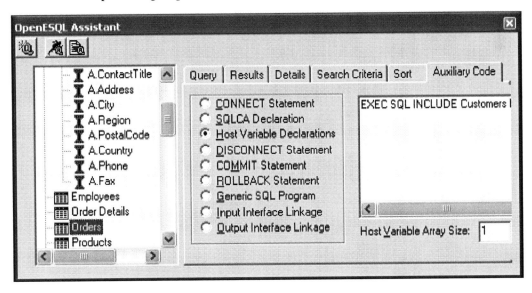

- The following window will be returned. You see that it understands that since you are selecting another relation, it is because you want to join the two.

- The Assistant then goes through the fields in each of the tables and determines the fields from each of the tables that are most likely to be of use in a join and prepares a condition involving the selected fields.

- You will notice that the field from the Customers table is prefixed by an 'A' and the corresponding field from the Orders table is prefixed by a 'B'. You will notice also that all the fields from the primary table are preceded by an 'A' and the fields from the secondary table are preceded by a 'B'.

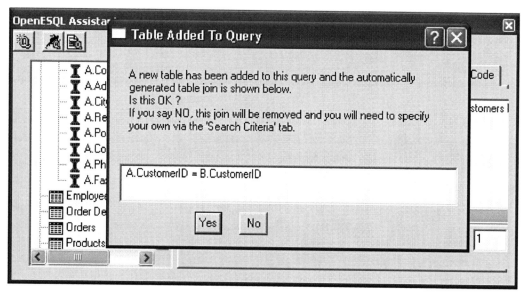

- You may accept the join provided and it will be incorporated into the query or you may reject it. If you reject, it is up to you to provide the appropriate condition.

- We have accepted the join and have selected the fields we want from the Orders file. The query now looks as follows:

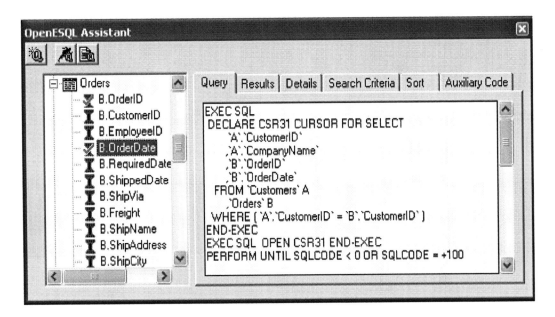

- Now select Auxiliary Code and in there select Host Variable Declarations. Notice the include:

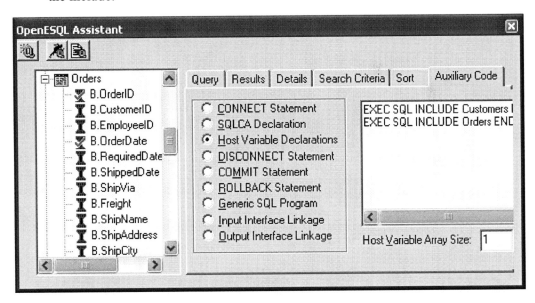

The program up to this point would look as follows:

Listing Database Records

```
$set SQL(dbman=odbc)
$set sourceformat 'free'
 program-id. DB9.

working-storage section.
01   ctr                   pic 99     value 0.
01   w-date                pic X(10).
01   sql-code              pic S9(9) comp-5.
     88   valid-sql-code              value 0.
     88   no-more-records             value 100.
     EXEC SQL INCLUDE SQLCA END-EXEC
     EXEC SQL INCLUDE Customers END-EXEC
     EXEC SQL INCLUDE Orders END-EXEC

     EXEC SQL
       DECLARE CSR29 CURSOR FOR SELECT
               `A`.`CustomerID`
             , `A`.`CompanyName`
             , `B`.`OrderID`
             , `B`.`CustomerID`
             , `B`.`OrderDate`
          FROM `Customers` A
             , `Orders` B
         WHERE ( `A`.`CustomerID` = `B`.`CustomerID` )
     END-EXEC

 procedure division.
     EXEC SQL
         CONNECT TO 'Customers in Northwind' USER 'admin'
     END-EXEC
     if  SQLCODE not = 0
         display SQLCODE " " SQLERRMC
     end-if
     EXEC SQL  OPEN CSR29 END-EXEC
     if  SQLCODE not = 0
         display SQLCODE " " SQLERRMC
     end-if
     move SQLCODE to sql-code
```

Listing 30.07 – 1 of 2

Listing Database Records

```
      PERFORM UNTIL not valid-sql-code
         EXEC SQL
            FETCH CSR29 INTO
               Customers-CustomerID:Customers-CustomerID-NULL
               ,:Customers-CompanyName:Customers-CompanyName-NULL
               ,:Orders-OrderID
               ,:Orders-CustomerID:Orders-CustomerID-NULL
               ,:Orders-OrderDate:Orders-OrderDate-NULL
         END-EXEC
         move SQLCODE to sql-code
         IF  valid-sql-code
            perform A100-ShowData
         else
            if  not no-more-records
               display SQLCODE " " SQLERRMC
            END-IF
         END-IF
      END-PERFORM
      EXEC SQLCLOSE CSR29 END-EXEC
      if  SQLCODE not = 0
         display SQLCODE " " SQLERRMC
      end-if
   EXEC SQL
         DISCONNECT CURRENT
      END-EXEC
      if  SQLCODE not = 0
         display SQLCODE " " SQLERRMC
      end-if
      stop run.

 A100-ShowData.
      add 1 to ctr
      if  ctr > 20
         accept ctr
      end-if
      move  Orders-OrderDate to w-date
      display Customers-CustomerID ' ' Customers-CompanyName
            Orders-OrderID '  ' w-date.
```

Listing 30.07 – 2 of 2

```
ALFKI   Alfreds Futterkiste                        +0000010643  1997-08-25
ALFKI   Alfreds Futterkiste                        +0000010952  1998-03-16
ALFKI   Alfreds Futterkiste                        +0000010692  1997-10-03
ALFKI   Alfreds Futterkiste                        +0000010835  1998-01-15
ALFKI   Alfreds Futterkiste                        +0000011011  1998-04-09
ALFKI   Alfreds Futterkiste                        +0000010702  1997-10-13
ANATR   Ana Trujillo Emparedados y helados         +0000010759  1997-11-28
ANATR   Ana Trujillo Emparedados y helados         +0000010926  1998-03-04
ANATR   Ana Trujillo Emparedados y helados         +0000010308  1996-09-18
ANATR   Ana Trujillo Emparedados y helados         +0000010625  1997-08-08
ANTON   Antonio Moreno Taquería                    +0000010682  1997-09-25
ANTON   Antonio Moreno Taquería                    +0000010535  1997-05-13
ANTON   Antonio Moreno Taquería                    +0000010365  1996-11-27
ANTON   Antonio Moreno Taquería                    +0000010573  1997-06-19
ANTON   Antonio Moreno Taquería                    +0000010856  1998-01-28
ANTON   Antonio Moreno Taquería                    +0000010507  1997-04-15
ANTON   Antonio Moreno Taquería                    +0000010677  1997-09-22
AROUT   Around the Horn                            +0000010741  1997-11-14
AROUT   Around the Horn                            +0000010383  1996-12-16
AROUT   Around the Horn                            +0000010355  1996-11-15
```

Insertions

So far we have looked at the **Select** in order to retrieve records. For the select the records must already be there. What we are now going to look at is how we go about inserting records. We use the **insert** for the purpose. The format of the **insert** is as follows:

```
Insert into TableName
        ('field1', 'field2', 'field3')
values
        ('field11', 'field22', 'field33')
```

The fields field1, field2 and field3 are the database fields that will be receiving the data. The fields that will provide the data follow the **values** keyword and are field11, field22 and field33.

The Assistant comes to our help and from the Type of Query window we select Insert.

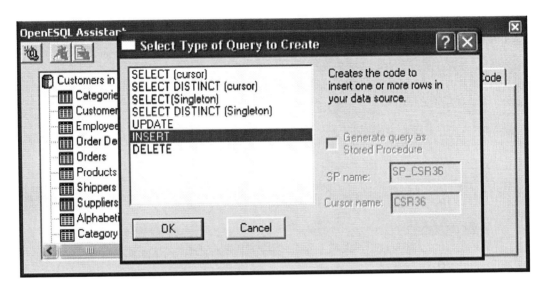

The format of the resulting query follows. Notice that we have selected only two fields. We have done this to keep the examples within a reasonable size. Two fields or 20 fields introduces nothing new but makes the code appear more complicated than it actually is.

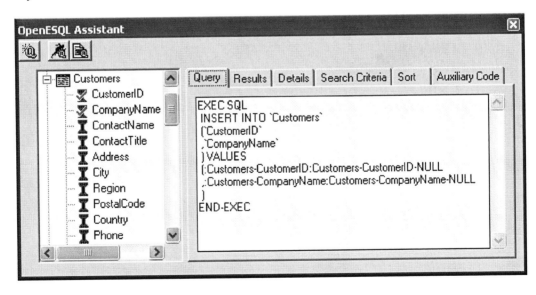

We click on the icon to transfer the code to the program. The program is as follows:

Insertion

```
$set SQL(dbman=odbc)
$set sourceformat 'free'
 program-id. DB9.
 working-storage section.
 01  ctr                     pic 99 value 0.
     EXEC SQL INCLUDE Customers END-EXEC
     EXEC SQL INCLUDE SQLCA END-EXEC

procedure division.
     EXEC SQL
         CONNECT TO 'Customers in Northwind' USER 'admin'
     END-EXEC
     if  SQLCODE not = 0
         display SQLCODE " " SQLERRMC
     end-if
     perform A200-Prompt
     move SQLCODE to sql-code
     perform A100-Insert
     if  not valid-sql-code
         display 'SQLCODE is:  ' SQLCODE
         display 'SQLERRMC is: ' SQLERRMC
     end-if
     EXEC SQL
         DISCONNECT CURRENT
     END-EXEC
     if  SQLCODE not = 0
         display SQLCODE " " SQLERRMC
     end-if
     stop run.

 A100-Insert.
     EXEC SQL
       INSERT INTO `Customers`
       (`CustomerID`
       ,`CompanyName`
       ) VALUES
          (:Customers-CustomerID:Customers-CustomerID-NULL
          ,:Customers-CompanyName:Customers-CompanyName-NULL
          )
     END-EXEC
```

Listing 30.08 – 1 of 2

Insertion

```
    if  SQLCODE not = 0
        display SQLCODE " " SQLERRMC
    end-if
    EXEC SQL
        commit
    END-EXEC.

     if  SQLCODE not = 0
        display SQLCODE " " SQLERRMC
     end-if
  A200-Prompt.
     display 'Enter Customer ID: ' no advancing
     accept  Customers-CustomerID
     display 'Company name: ' no advancing
     accept Customers-CompanyName.
```

Listing 30.08 – 2 of 2

We have inserted a record and then, immediately thereafter, used the **commit**, causing the insertion to be passed to the database. Every time we write to the database there is an I/O operation. Having I/O operations for single records is ineffective. It would be better to **commit** after a number of records are ready to be written. This is what we have done in the following example:

Writing Groups of Records

```
$set SQL(dbman=odbc)
 identification division.
 program-id. DB9.
 Data division.
 working-storage section.
 01  sub          pic 99 value 0.
 01  tab-data.
     05           pic X(23)  value 'AVANTWines of the World'.
     05           pic X(23)  value 'AVENTBrazilian Delights'.
     05           pic X(23)  value 'AVINTFoods of the World'.
     05           pic X(23)  value 'AVONTAEats and Drinks  '.
     05           pic X(23)  value 'AVUNTTai Cooking       '.
     01  tab redefines tab-data occurs 5.
        05  tab-key          pic X(05).
        05  tab-info         pic X(18).
```

Listing 30.09 – 1 of 2

655

Writing Groups of Records

```
        EXEC SQL INCLUDE Customers END-EXEC
        EXEC SQL INCLUDE SQLCA END-EXEC

    procedure division.
        EXEC SQL
            CONNECT TO 'Customers in Northwind' USER 'admin'
        END-EXEC
        if  SQLCODE not = 0
            display SQLCODE " " SQLERRMC
        end-if
        perform A100-Insert 5 times
        EXEC SQL
            commit
        if  SQLCODE not = 0
            display SQLCODE " " SQLERRMC
        end-if
        END-EXEC.

        EXEC SQL
            DISCONNECT CURRENT
        END-EXEC
        if  SQLCODE not = 0
            display SQLCODE " " SQLERRMC
        end-if
        stop run.
    A100-Insert.
        add 1 to sub
        move tab-key(sub)   to Customers-CustomerID
        move tab-info (sub) to Customers-CompanyName
        EXEC SQL
            INSERT INTO `Customers`
            (`CustomerID`
            ,`CompanyName`
            ) VALUES
            (:Customers-CustomerID:Customers-CustomerID-NULL
            ,:Customers-CompanyName:Customers-CompanyName-NULL)
        END-EXEC
        if  SQLCODE not = 0
            display 'SQLCODE is:  ' SQLCODE
            display 'SQLERRMC is: ' SQLERRMC
        end-if.
```

Listing 30.09 – 2 of 2

We progress through the table and only **commit** once all the records in the table have been exhausted. The following window shows that the records have been written to the database:

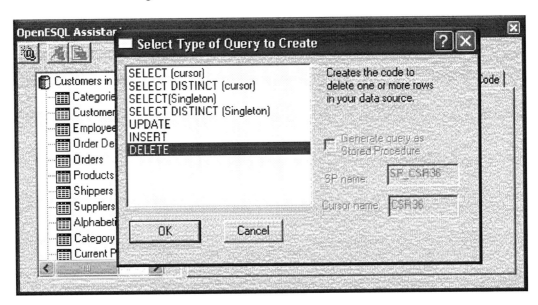

Deletions

The **delete** enables us to remove records from a table. We request the help of the Assistant and in the following window we would select delete:

The selection gives rise to the following query:

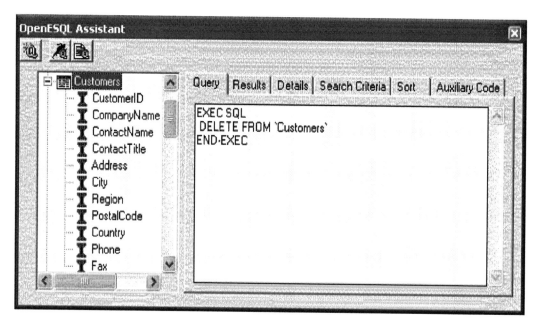

The next step is to establish the search criteria. We must name the key of the record we wish to delete and when that field is equal to the key field that will be the record to be deleted. The following window depicts the selection criteria:

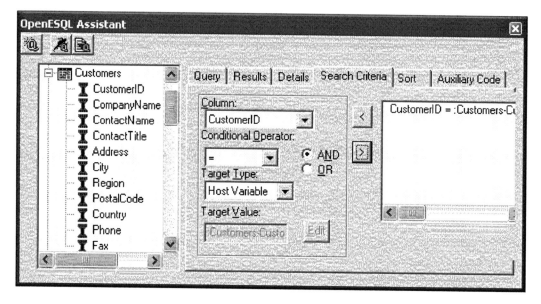

We click on the left arrow to incorporate the search criteria into the query. The full query would then look as follows:

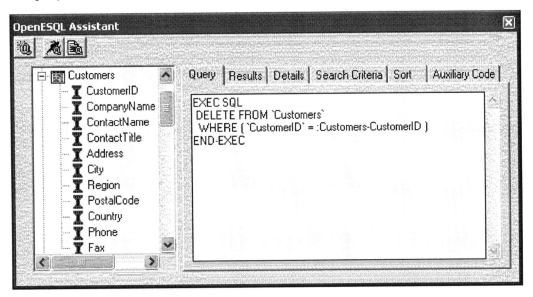

The program reflecting the required code follows. Again, because it is only for you to see the code, we delete one record and then commit. As indicated earlier, it is advisable to commit when an associated set of operations is complete.

Commiting

```
$set SQL(dbman=odbc)
$set sourceformat 'free'
 program-id. DB12.
 working-storage section.
     EXEC SQL INCLUDE Customers END-EXEC
     EXEC SQL INCLUDE SQLCA END-EXEC
 procedure division.
     EXEC SQL
         CONNECT TO 'Customers in Northwind' USER 'admin'
     END-EXEC
     If  SQLCODE not = 0
         display  SQLCODE  ' ' SQLERRMC
     end-if
     perform A100-Prompt
     EXEC SQL
        DELETE FROM `Customers`
           WHERE ( `CustomerID` = :Customers-CustomerID )
     END-EXEC
     If  SQLCODE not = 0
         display  SQLCODE  ' ' SQLERRMC
     end-if
     EXEC SQL
          COMMIT
     END-EXEC
     If  SQLCODE not = 0
         display  SQLCODE  ' ' SQLERRMC
     end-if
 A100-Prompt.
     display 'Please enter CustomerID: ' no advancing
     accept Customers-CustomerID.
     If  SQLCODE not = 0
         display 'SQLCODE: ' SQLCODE
         display 'Error message: ' SQLERRMC
     else
         display 'Record Deleted'
     end-if
```

Listing 30.10 – 1 of 2

Commiting

```
EXEC SQL
    DISCONNECT CURRENT
END-EXEC
If  SQLCODE not = 0
    display  SQLCODE  ' '  SQLERRMC
end-if
stop run.
```

Listing 30.10 – 2 of 2

The Update

In updating a database record, we read the record, change it and then rewrite it. However, if you already know the change you wish to implement you may, as we have done in the example, just put the changes into effect. This means that as in the delete, a prior read of the record is not required.

Again, we go through the assistant and select update.

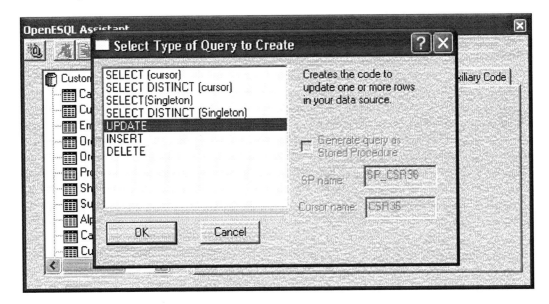

The query will be generated and from there we will go to select the search criteria. After selection the query will have the following format:

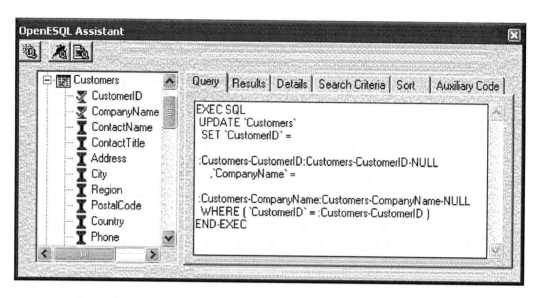

In the update, we name the table that will be updated. Following that, the set is used to assign the host variables to the database fields. After the update the table will reflect the change.

Update

```
$set SQL(dbman=odbc)
$set sourceformat 'free'
 program-id. DB13.
 working-storage section.
     EXEC SQL INCLUDE Customers END-EXEC
     EXEC SQL INCLUDE SQLCA END-EXEC

 procedure division.
     EXEC SQL
         CONNECT TO 'Customers in Northwind' USER 'admin'
     END-EXEC
     If  SQLCODE not = 0
         display  SQLCODE  ' ' SQLERRMC
     end-if
     perform A100-prompt
     EXEC SQL
         UPDATE `Customers`
             SET `CustomerID` =
             :Customers-CustomerID:Customers-CustomerID-NULL
              ,`CompanyName` =
             :Customers-CompanyName:Customers-CompanyName-NULL
             WHERE ( `CustomerID` = :Customers-CustomerID )
     END-EXEC
     if  SQLCODE not = 0
         display 'SQLCODE is: ' SQLCODE
         display 'Message is: ' SQLERRMC
     end-if
     EXEC SQL
         COMMIT
     END-EXEC
     If  SQLCODE not = 0
         display  SQLCODE  ' ' SQLERRMC
     end-if
     EXEC SQL
         DISCONNECT CURRENT
     END-EXEC
     If  SQLCODE not = 0
         display  SQLCODE  ' ' SQLERRMC
     end-if
     stop run.
```

Listing 30.11 – 1 of 2

Update

```
A100-Prompt.
    display 'Enter Customer ID : ' no advancing
    accept Customers-CustomerID
    display 'Enter company name: ' no advancing
    accept Customers-CompanyName.
```

Listing 30.11 – 2 of 2

The execution would produce the following result:

```
c:\ Command Prompt                                    _ □ ×

Enter Customer ID : AVANT
Enter company name: Avionics
```

The following program incorporates the **select**, **insert**, **delete** and **update**. You will see that one paragraph will be allocated to each of the functions. The output will show that the functions work.

Select, Insert, Delete and Update

```
$set SQL(dbman=odbc)
$set sourceformat 'free'
 program-id. DB14IUD.
 working-storage section.
 01   SelectionCode            pic 9 value 0.
 01   msg                      pic x(65) value
      'Enter: 1-Select, 2-Insert, 3-Delete, ' &
      '4-Update, 9-End: '.
      EXEC SQL INCLUDE Customers END-EXEC
      EXEC SQL INCLUDE SQLCA END-EXEC
 procedure division.
 main section.
      EXEC SQL
          CONNECT TO 'Customers in Northwind' USER 'admin'
      END-EXEC.
```

Listing 30.12 – 1 of 3

Select, Insert, Delete and Update

```
    If  SQLCODE not = 0
        display  SQLCODE  ' ' SQLERRMC
    end-if
    perform A100-Selection until SelectionCode = 9
    EXEC SQL
        DISCONNECT CURRENT
    END-EXEC
    If  SQLCODE not = 0
        display  SQLCODE  ' ' SQLERRMC
    end-if
    stop run.
A100-Selection.
    display msg no advancing
    accept SelectionCode
    evaluate SelectionCode
        when 1 perform  B100-Select
        when 2 perform  B200-Insert
        when 3 perform  B300-Delete
        when 4 perform  B400-Update
        when other move 9 to SelectionCode
    end-evaluate.
B100-Select.
    display 'Please enter Customer ID: ' no advancing
    accept Customers-CustomerID.
    EXEC SQL
      SELECT
            `A`.`CustomerID`
          , `A`.`CompanyName`
        FROM `Customers` A
          WHERE ( `A`.`CustomerID` = :Customers-CustomerID )
    END-EXEC
    If  SQLCODE not = 0
        display  SQLCODE  ' ' SQLERRMC
    end-if
    perform C100-CheckCode.
B200-Insert.
    display 'Please enter Customer ID: ' no advancing
    accept Customers-CustomerID.
    display 'Please enter Company name: ' no advancing
    accept Customers-CompanyName
```

Listing 30.12 – 2 of 3

Select, Insert, Delete and Update

```
      EXEC SQL
          INSERT INTO `Customers`
          (`CustomerID`
          ,`CompanyName`
          ) VALUES
          (:Customers-CustomerID:Customers-CustomerID-NULL
          ,:Customers-CompanyName:Customers-CompanyName-NULL
          )
      END-EXEC

      If  SQLCODE not = 0
          display  SQLCODE  ' ' SQLERRMC
      end-if
      EXEC SQL COMMIT END-EXEC
      If  SQLCODE not = 0
          display  SQLCODE  ' ' SQLERRMC
      end-if
      perform C100-CheckCode.

  B300-Delete.
      display 'Please enter Customer ID: ' no advancing
      accept Customers-CustomerID.
      EXEC SQL
          DELETE FROM `Customers`
              WHERE ( `CustomerID` = :Customers-CustomerID )
      END-EXEC
      If  SQLCODE not = 0
          display  SQLCODE  ' ' SQLERRMC
      end-if
      EXEC SQL COMMIT END-EXEC
      If  SQLCODE not = 0
          display  SQLCODE  ' ' SQLERRMC
      end-if
      perform C100-CheckCode.

  B400-Update.
      display 'Please enter Customer ID: ' no advancing
      accept Customers-CustomerID.
      display 'Please enter Company name: ' no advancing
      accept Customers-CompanyName
```

Listing 30.12 – 3 of 4

Select, Insert, Delete and Update

```
      EXEC SQL
         UPDATE `Customers`
            SET `CustomerID` =
            :Customers-CustomerID:Customers-CustomerID-NULL
               , `CompanyName` =
            :Customers-CompanyName:Customers-CompanyName-NULL
            WHERE ( `CustomerID` = :Customers-CustomerID )
      END-EXEC
      If  SQLCODE not = 0
          display  SQLCODE   ' ' SQLERRMC
      end-if
      EXEC SQL COMMIT END-EXEC
      If  SQLCODE not = 0
          display  SQLCODE   ' ' SQLERRMC
      end-if
      perform C100-CheckCode.
  C100-CheckCode.
      if  SQLCODE = 0
          perform Z100-Display
      else
          display SQLCODE ' ' SQLERRMC
      end-if.
  Z100-Display.
      display  Customers-CustomerID '  '
               Customers-CompanyName.
```

Listing 30.12 – 4 of 4

The execution follows:

- We start with an insertion by entering the code 2. The key is AVANT and the company name is Aviation Unlimited.

- We enter a code of one, which is for **Select**. The code is AVANT and Aviation Unlimited is returned.

- We enter a code of four, which is for **Update**. The company name is changed to Avionics.

- Next we enter a code of one to **Select**. The key is Avant and the company name Avionics is returned.

- We enter a code of three to **Delete**. Next we enter a code of one to ascertain whether the record was deleted. The record was not found, showing that it was deleted.

```
Enter: 1-Select, 2-Insert, 3-Delete 4-Update 9-End: 2
Please enter Customer ID: AVANT
Please enter Company name: Aviation Unlimited
AVANT   Aviation Unlimited
Enter: 1-Select, 2-Insert, 3-Delete 4-Update 9-End: 1
Please enter Customer ID: AVANT
AVANT   Aviation Unlimited
Enter: 1-Select, 2-Insert, 3-Delete 4-Update 9-End: 4
Please enter Customer ID: AVANT
Please enter Company name: Avionics
AVANT   Avionics
Enter: 1-Select, 2-Insert, 3-Delete 4-Update 9-End: 1
Please enter Customer ID: AVANT
AVANT   Avionics
Enter: 1-Select, 2-Insert, 3-Delete 4-Update 9-End: 3
Please enter Customer ID: AVANT
AVANT   Avionics
Enter: 1-Select, 2-Insert, 3-Delete 4-Update 9-End: 1
Please enter Customer ID: AVANT
SQLCODE is: 00000000000100
Message is:
Enter: 1-Select, 2-Insert, 3-Delete 4-Update 9-End: 9
```

Summary

- If we need to iterate through the records in a database, in order to process a record, before advancing to the next record, we will need a **cursor**. To obtain a cursor we must declare it. The declarative statement may reside in the data division or the procedure division. The records returned are termed a **result set**.

```
EXEC SQL
        DECLARE CSR10 CURSOR FOR SELECT
        A.CustomerID
        ,A.CompanyName
        ,A.ContactName
        FROM Customers A
END-EXEC
```

- **Fetch** – The fetch returns one record at a time. In the fetch we name the cursor we are using. The fetch is placed inside a loop. The fetch returns a code. If the code is less than zero there is an error. SQLCODE contains the error code. You are advised to display the preceding field as well as the field SQLERRMC, that contains a description of the error. A value of +100 signifies end of result set.

- **Where** – We do not always want to process all the records. Instead of looking at all the customers, we would prefer to receive only the ones for whom amount owing exceeds the limit. For the preceding example, we introduce a condition into the **cursor** declaration using a **where**.

- **Like** – Sometimes we don't know the whole key but only part of the key. The **like** comes to our assistance. Two characters are used with the like. The % signifies any number of characters on that side. Thus, if we have the names Lincoln, Dodge and Ford and we ask for all names containing an 'o' we would code %o% and we would get all three names. We can be more restrictive by using the '_'. Specifying '____o__' would mean four characters preceding the 'o' and two characters following the o. Specifying '_o%' would get us those names having one character preceding the 'o' followed by any number of characters.

- **And, Or and In** – The And, Or and In connectors enable the programmer to specify compound conditions. The In does the same thing as the Or but is more streamlined.

- **Avg, Min and Max** – SQL provides the database user with a facility for determining the average, minimum and maximum values in a database file.

669

- **Sum and Count(*)** – The facility is provided by SQL. Sum obtains the total of the values in the specified field and Count(*) will establish how many values were involved in obtaining the total.

- **Distinct** – The facility will return one record, however many records there may be for the fields involved.

- **Join** – The Join enables us to combine fields from two files based on a field common to both files. SQL offers us this facility.

- **Insert** – The insert provides us with the possibility of adding records to the database. The format is as follows:

```
Insert into TableName
      ('field1', 'field2', 'field3')
values
      ('field11', 'field22', 'field3')
```

- The first arguments are the database fields. Following the keyword **values** come the fields containing the data. The positions in the two sets of arguments correspond.

- **Delete** – The delete accomplishes the removal of the specified record from the database. The format follows:

```
EXEC SQL
     DELETE FROM 'Customers'
     WHERE ('CustomerID' = :Customers-CustomerID )
END-EXEC
```

- **Update** – The update enables us to read a database record, change it and then write it back to its original position in the database.

Complete

1.   The cursor declaration may appear in the _____ or in the _____ division.

2.   Once we have a cursor, we use the _____ to retrieve records from the data-base.

3.   End of result set is indicated by a value of _____ in SQLCODE. +100

4.   To specify a condition we use the _____ .

5.   If we wanted all employees with a salary greater than 16 000 we would code ... where _____ .

6.   If we wanted all employees where firstName contains a 'c' as the third character and is followed by any number of characters we would code ...where _____ .

7.   For a loop to retrieve a result set with any number of records the loop condition would be perform until _____ or _____ .

8.   The min function does _____ require a _____ through the database.

9.   To count the number of records in a database file we would use _____ .

10.   When we only want one record of a set we code select _____ distinct

11.   For an insertion we do not need to _____ a _____ declare.

12.   In an insertion following the keyword _____ we have the fields containing the data to be inserted.

13.   An error in database access is reflected in a _____ error code.

14.   To make a change to the database persistent we need to use the _____ com-mand.

15.   In an update, to assign the new values we use the _____ command.

True/False

1.   A cursor must be declared in the data division.

2.   To use the cursor we must first open it.

3.   We use the fetch to retrieve a record from the database without the need for a cursor.

4.   A negative value in SQLCODE signifies an error.

5.   When using min to determine the lowest value in the database we need a pass through the database.

6.   The connector AND should only be used with the Insert.

7.   The values keyword is used with insert as well as with update.

8.   Database persistence requires the commit command.

9.   When we have declared a cursor, we use the select…into.

10.   The like can only be used when we know at least one character and its position in the name.

11.   The in is easier to use than the or.

12.   The join combines selected records from two files based on the key.

13.   When we use select distinct there will be only one record selected per key.

14.   The set command is used in the insert to assign values to the database fields.

15.   The avg command can only operate if a cursor has been declared.

16.   When using the sum command, the select uses into.

17.   The end of result set returns +100.

Exercise

1.   Using the Northwind database from the Microsoft Access database, process the following transactions:

   ▪   Insert the records depicted in the table below:

CustomerID	CompanyName	ContactName
ALBAA	Cycling Wizards	L. Armstrong
ALBAB	Cantiflas	Mario Moreno
ALBAC	Uphill Experts	Jose Azevedo

   ▪   Delete row with CustomerID ALBAC

   ▪   Update row with CustomerID ALBAB and change Cantiflas to Cantinflas Ltd.

Appendix A
Solutions

Complete – Chapter 1

1.   The number of possible combinations in a byte is 2 to the power of **8**.
2.   The maximum value that may be stored in four bits is **15**.
3.   **4** is the value corresponding to bit 3 where bit 0 is the rightmost bit.
4.   **CPU** is the part of the computer that processes the data.
5.   The bit representation 1100 0101 corresponds to the hexadecimal value **C5** .
6.   The bit configuration 0100 0000 corresponds to the decimal value **64**.
7.   Peripheral storage will reside on **tape or disk**.

True/False – Chapter 1

1.   Operations in the CPU are carried out in hexadecimal. **False**
2.   Hexadecimal 31 is equivalent to decimal 49. **True**
3.   Decimal 38 is equivalent to hexadecimal 24. **False**
4.   Generating test data should precede program design. **True**
5.   Hexadecimal E is equivalent to decimal 13. **False**

Complete – Chapter 2

1.   The paragraph in the identification division is the **program-id** paragraph.
2.   The **space** precedes the word division.
3.   A **period** immediately follows the word section.
4.   The **first** character in a program name must be alphabetic.
5.   The **space** is a word separator.
6.   The **data** division is the third division in a program.
7.   The **file-name** immediately follows the word select.
8.   If the program uses three files, it will have **three** select statements.
9.   Area A comprises columns **1** to **8**.
10.   The first section in the environment division is the _configuration_ section.
11.   Another name for the external file is **physical file**.

12.   Another name for the internal file is **logical file**.
13.   If format is fixed, area B comprises columns **12** to **72**.
14.   The hyphen may not be the **first** or the **last** character in a data name.
15.   Select statement is coded in the **input-output** section.
16.   Another name for the external file is **physical** file.
17.   The source-computer paragraph names the computer where the program will be **compiled**.
18.   The object-computer paragraph names where the program will be **executed**.

True/False – Chapter 2

1.   The internal file name follows the keyword Select. **True**
2.   The Select is part of the Configuration section. **True**
3.   The Procedure Division is the fourth division in a program. **True**
4.   A routine may not bear the name 67118. **False**
5.   A field may have the name 3333-44. **True**
6.   The program name 100Pay is valid. **False**
7.   The Environment Division is compulsory. **False**
8.   The program name may not contain numeric characters. **False**
9.   Programid is a reserved word and may not be used as a field name. **False**
10.   The field name 12345A is invalid. **False**
11.   The field name A12345 is valid. **True**
12.   The field name 12345 is invalid. **True**
13.   The field name 1234-5 is valid. **True**

Complete – Chapter 3

1.   When processing sequentially, we **buffer** input/output operations.
2.   According to the COBOL 85 standard the maximum size of a numeric field is **18** digits.
3.   According to the COBOL 2002 standard the maximum size of a numeric field is **31** digits.
4.   The picture of a numeric signed field with five integers and three decimal positions is **9(5)V9(3)**.
5.   In a numeric field, we have an **implied** decimal point.
6.   For every sequential file we will have **double** buffers.
7.   The highest numeric level number possible for a group field is **48**.
8.   A byte in an alphanumeric field may have any of the **256** possible combinations.
9.   Select statements are coded in the **input-output** section.
10.   In a numeric field the ASCII code for a negative value is **7**.
11.   The highest level, numerically, for a numeric field is **49**.
12.   The data in an alphanumeric field may have **any** of the **256** possible bit configurations.
13.   The possible characters in an alphabetic field are **A** to **Z** and the **space**.
14.   Under the FD we would define fields that are part of **input and output**.
15.   Fields that are not part of input or output are coded in the **working-storage** section.

True/False – Chapter 3

1.   The maximum size for an alphanumeric field is 160 bytes. **False**
2.   The maximum size of a numeric field is 32 bytes. **False**
3.   If a program reads a file and writes to a file, two Select statements will be required. **True**
4.   The number of records in a buffer is given by the blocking factor. **True**
5.   A group field may or may not have a picture clause. **False**
6.   Elementary fields have a picture clause. **True**
7.   A level 01 is always a group field. **False**
8.   A level 49 may be a group field. **False**
9.   Fields that are part of input or output are defined in the Working-Storage section. **False**
10. In the FD we specify the physical file name. **False**
11. An Input/Output file needs two Selects. **False**
12. A group field with only numeric subordinates is implicitly numeric. **False**
13. It is possible to have a group field without subordinates. **False**
14. In a signed field, the sign takes up one additional byte. **False**
15. The data type of a group field is implicitly alphanumeric. **True**
16. The FD contains a period at the end of each line. **False**
17. A group level field should be defined starting in column eight. **False**
18. An identifier bearing the following name '12345' may be described as having a stupid name but it will at times be a valid identifier. **True**

Complete – Chapter 4

1.   In the case of volatile storage, data is lost when the **power** goes **down**
2.   The open secures the **availability** of the file.
3.   The open positions the **pointer** at the beginning of the file.
4.   The **at end** enables us to specify actions to take when there are still more records to be read.
5.   The **not at end** enables us to specify actions to take when there are still more records to be read.
6.   The **not at end** enables us to specify while there are still records available.
7.   The open acquires **buffer** space to hold the records read.
8.   The close releases **buffer** space.
9.   The read enables us to process records in working-storage or in the **buffer**.
10. Literals may be **numeric** or **alphanumeric**.
11. Alphanumeric literals are enclosed in **inverted commas** .
12. In a numeric literal the '.' may not be the **rightmost** character.
13. The '+' or the '-' sign, when present, must be the **leftmost** character.
14. Low-values is a **figurative** constant.
15. The copy verb is used to incorporate a **copy book** into the program.
16. When using the replacing option with the copy, the replacing text **precedes** the text to be replaced.

True/False – Chapter 4

1. The open, for different types of I/O, requires that we specify input files, followed by output files, followed by I/O files. **False**
2. The open establishes a link between the program and the file. **True**
3. The maximum length for a numeric field in COBOL 2002 is 31. **True**
4. The open positions the file pointer to point to any record in the file. **False**
5. The maximum length for a numeric field in COBOL 85 is 16. **False**
6. The open acquires buffer storage and fills both buffers with records. **False**
7. In the close we specify the name of the internal file. **False**
8. A numeric literal may only contain the characters zero to nine and the sign. **False**
9. An alphanumeric literal may contain any value in the collating sequence. **True**
10. The first read will fill both buffers. **True**
11. COBOL 85 does not require a close statement if the stop run is being used. **True**
12. The logical and the intrnal files are different types of files. **False**
13. The close will cause any unwritten records to be written to the file. **True**
14. In the read we specify the name of the external file. **False**
15. The FD, select and open set, must all name the same file. **True**
16. If you no longer need a file you should immediately close it. **True**
17. The stop run will close all open files to ensure that all files are closed before the program terminates. **True**
18. Alphanumeric literals must be enclosed in doulble quotes. **False**
19. The copy verb incorporates a copy book into the program. **True**
20. In 'all literal' the literal may be numeric. **False**

Complete – Chapter 5

1. The procedural approach uses **functional decomposition** to resolve complexity.
2. Cohesion means one routine for **one** function.
3. The type of cohesion we find when a set of diverse operations needs to be executed at the same time is called **temporal** cohesion.
4. An in-line perform must end on **end-perform**.
5. If the condition in the perform says 'until ctr > limit' then every time the routine executes, control returns to the instruction **following** the condition.
6. The display is for low volume output.
7. The clause that will enable two displays to display on the same line is the **no advancing** clause.
8. To accept the date with a four-digit year we code a picture of **YYYY**.
9. To get a seven-digit Julian date we code a picture of **YYYYDDD**.
10. The display incorporates a **carriage return**.
11. If an accept follows a display and we want the data to be entered on the same line as the data displayed, we would code the clause **no advancing**.
12. If the day of week is returned, **1** is for Monday and **7** is for Sunday.
13. If two displays follow one another, the data will be displayed on **two** line/s.

14.   A read that incorporates a condition must end on **end-read**.
15.   The field that receives high-values must be of type **alphanumeric**.

True/False – Chapter 5

1.   A perform until... executes while true. **False**
2.   In a hierarchy chart 'Close File' would appear on the left of the iteration. **False**
3.   In a hierarchy chart the read follows the open. **True**
4.   A perform ... varying does not require prior setting of the condition field. **True**
5.   The inline perform may end on an end-perform or a period. **False**
6.   The display verb has an explicit carriage return. **False**
7.   The accept... from date returns a four-digit year. **False**
8.   We may use the accept to place data into one or more fields. **False**
9.   A perform varying ctr from 1 by 1 until ctr > 5 will execute four times. **False**
10.   A perform varying ctr from 1 by 1 until ctr > 5 will execute five times. **True**
11.   A read must always end on end-read. **False**
12.   The advantage of the in-line perform is that we can follow the logic without looking at another part of the program. **True**
13.   The accept catering for time returns hours, minutes and seconds. **False**
14.   With the perform varying you must always vary from one. **False**
15.   With the perform varying you may vary by whatever value you find appropriate. **True**
16.   With the following code: perform until ctr > 5 you must increment ctr inside the loop. **True**
17.   In the preceding question you do not need to set the ctr before the perform. **False**

Complete – Chapter 6

1.   The with test after clause forces execution even if the **condition** is satisfied.
2.   The with test before causes execution to be **by-passed** if the condition is satisfied.
3.   The code: `perform with test before varying`
               `ctr from 0 by 1 until ctr = 20`
      will cause execution to be repeated **20** times.
4.   The code: `perform with test after varying`
               `ctr from 0 by 1 until ctr = 20`
      will cause execution to be repeated 21 times.
5.   In arithmetic, the corresponding clause may be used only with the **add** and the **subtract**.
6.   The corresponding clause references **group** fields.
7.   The corresponding clause operates only on fields with the **same** name.
8.   The second operand in an arithmetic statement may name **more** than **one** field.
9.   The field or fields following the giving clause may be of type **numeric** or **numeric-edited** .
10.   After execution res would contain_006.90_ and rem would contain_000.10_.

True/False – Chapter 6

1.   The clause with test after bypasses the loop if the condition is already satisfied. **False**

2.   Given the statement: `add flda to fldb`, after execution fldb would contain 300+.
      True

3.   Given the statement: `add fldb to flda`, after execution flda would contain 300+.
      True

4.   Given the statement: `add flda fldb to flde`, after execution flde would contain
      300+. **True**

5.   Given the statement: `add flda fldb to fldd flde`, after execution fldd would
      contain 100+ and flde would contain 300+. **True**

6.   Given the statement: `add 500 to flda fldc fldd`, after execution flda = 600+
      fldc = 00+ fldd = 500+. **False**

7.   Given the statement: `add 100.5 to flda`, after execution flda would contain 200+.
      True

8.   Given the statement: `add flda to fldd`, after execution fldd would contain 100-.
      False

9.   Given the statement: `add flda to fldd giving flde`, after execution flde would
      contain 100+. **False**

10.   Given the statement: `add flda to fldc`, after execution fldc would contain 400+.
      False

Complete – Chapter 7

1.   A numeric field may be moved to a **numeric** and to an **alphanumeric** destination.
2.   An alphanumeric field may be moved to a **numeric**,
      alphanumeric, **alphabetic** destination.
3.   An alphabetic field may be moved to an **alphabetic** or **alphanumeric** destination.
4.   The condition 'not greater than or equal to' may be expressed as **less than**.
5.   The condition 'not less than or equal to' may be expressed as **greater than**.
6.   The alternate way of showing 'not less than' is **greater than or equal**.
7.   Assume that if month is 12 we don't do anything otherwise we add 1 to ctr. if month = 12
      continue else...
8.   You have: 'move '999' to alfanum', defined as pic X(3). The test 'if alfanum numeric'
      display 'OK' would display **OK**.
9.   If x = y and z could be replaced by **if x = y and x = z**.
10.   If x not = y and < z is equivalent to **if x not = y and x < z**.
11.   Not negative means **positive** or **zero**.
12.   Not positive means **negative or zero**.
13.   A numeric field may not be moved to an alphanumeric field if it contains **decimals**.
14.   A **literal** may not serve as a destination in a move statement.
15.   The return from a perform is always to the **first** instruction **following** the perform.

True/False – Chapter 7

1. An alphanumeric field may be moved to a numeric field. **True**
2. A numeric field may not be moved to an alphanumeric field. **False**
3. An alphabetic field may be moved to a numeric field. **False**
4. Where we use a literal we may use a field name. **True**
5. Where we use a field name we may use a literal. **False**
6. 'Greater than or equal to' may be replaced by 'not less than'. **True**
7. An in-line perform may have no more than one period between perform and end-perform. **False**
8. When we code: perform rout-x 5 times, the word times may be dispensed with. **True**
9. You have defined Source PIC X(5) and Dest PIC X(4). Source contains 'SMITH'. Furthermore, you code move Source to Dest. After execution, Dest will contain the value 'SMITH'. **False**
10. A period is always required at the end of a paragraph. **True**
11. We may initialize fields defined in working-storage at compile time. **True**
12. We may initialize fields defined in the file section at compile time. **False**
13. The value clause is only used in the working-storage section. **False**
14. The word FILLER provides addressability to the area. **False**
15. The CONTINUE statement operates like the NEXT SENTENCE. **False**
16. An IF must always have a matching ELSE. **False**
17. An Else must always have a matching IF. **True**

Complete – Chapter 8

1. A numeric packed field may be moved to an alphanumeric field if it does not contain **decimals**.
2. Moving a packed numeric field to an alphanumeric field will **unpack** the data.
3. In moving a numeric field to an alphanumeric field, if the destination is longer than the source **padding** will occur on the right.
4. If you define a numeric field with the picture 9(5)V99 and you move the value 7523.9 to it, the value in the receiving field will be **752390**. (Show all bytes)
5. You have defined a field with the picture X(6) JUSTIFIED. You move the value September to it. After the move the field will contain the value **tember**.
6. You have defined a field with the picture X(7). You move ALL 'Yes' to the field. After the move the field will contain the value **YesYesY**.
7. You have defined a field with the picture X(7) JUSTIFIED. You move ALL 'Yes' to the field. After the move the field will contain the value **YesYesY**.
8. You have a group field and its subordinates contain the value 98765. You move the group field to a numeric field with picture 9(4). After the move, the numeric field will contain **9876**.
9. You have an alphanumeric field defined with the picture X(06). After moving the value 'Five' to it, it will contain **Five^**. (The ^ indicates a space)
10. The sign in a packed field is in the **digit** component of the **low order** byte.

11.   The sign in an unpacked field is in the **zone** component of the **low order** byte.

True/False – Chapter 8

1.   We may not move a packed field to an alphanumeric field. **True**
2.   Data moved to an alphanumeric field aligns on the left. **True**
3.   Numeric data moved to a numeric field always aligns on the right. **True**
4.   Moving packed data to a numeric unpacked field will unpack the data. **True**
5.   If you moved 5000 to an alphanumeric field defined as X(6) after the move, the field will contain 500000. **False**
6.   When packed data is moved to an alphanumeric field, the data is unpacked. **True**
7.   We may move an alphanumeric field containing packed data to a numeric unpacked field and the data will be unpacked. **True**
8.   If for a group field we code 'value zero', the group field will be set to all zeros. **True**
9.   If for a group field we code 'value 0', the group field will be set to a zero on the left. The remaining bytes will be set to spaces. **True**
10.   To determine the size of a packed field given its picture, we divide the number of digits by 2, subtract 1 and round upwards. **False**
11.   You have a numeric field defined as 9(3) containing the value 123. You move this field to a field defined as X(6). You move the alphanumeric field back to the numeric field. The numeric field will now contain the value 000. **True**
12.   We may not use the JUSTIFIED clause on a field defined as numeric. **True**
13.   Specifying the JUSTIFIED clause on an alphanumeric field will cause the data to align on the left. **False**
14.   ALL 'Literal' does not respect the JUSTIFIED clause. **True**

Complete – Chapter 9

1.   You want to use a binary field to store temperatures in the range – 20 to +50. The field would be defined as **PIC S99** comp.
2.   For a binary field definition we may employ the usage COMP or **binary** or **comp-4**.
3.   On a PC binary fields align on a **byte**.
4.   On a mainframe, the address of a binary halfword must be divisible by **2**,
5.   On a mainframe, the address of a binary fullword must be divisible by **4**,
6.   You need to place a value of 95000.74 into a binary field. The picture for the field would be PIC **S9(7)V99** binary.
7.   The **synchronized** clause causes binary fields to be aligned on a proper boundary.
8.   Using the new binary types introduced by the standard, to store a value of 25325 you would define the field as usage **binary-short**.
9.   Using the new binary types introduced by the standard, to store a value of + or -25325 you would define the field as usage **binary-short signed**.
10.   Float-short corresponds to **comp-1** and float-long corresponds to **comp-2**.
11.   You wish to place the value 1,234,567 in a binary field. The picture should be **PIC S9(9)** comp-5.

12.   Anding 1111 0000 with 0110 1001 produces **0110 0000**.
13.   Oring 1111 0000 with 0110 1001 produces **1111 1001**.
14.   Not 1111 0000 is **0000 1111**.
15.   Exclusive oring 1100 1001 with 0011 0110 produces **1111 1111**.

True/False – Chapter 9

1.   Binary fields may not contain decimals. **False**
2.   The PIC clause enables us to specify maximum and minimum values as well as intermediate values. **False**
3.   A signed fullword binary field may hold a value of 4294967295. **False**
4.   Fullword fields align on a boundary that is divisible by 4. **True**
5.   Usage is comp and usage is binary yields the same results. **True**
6.   To a signed binary-char field, we may assign any character that has a bit configuration not greater than 127. **True**
7.   Binary-char occupies two bytes. **False**
8.   The value 1001 0110 anded with 0110 1001 yields 1111 1111. **False**
9.   The value 1001 1111 ored with 1111 0000 will yield 1111 1111. **True**
10.   The value 1001 1111 exclusive ored with 1111 0000 will yield 0110 1111. **True**
11.   Float-extended and binary-double have the same size. **True**
12.   You have a field defined as float-short. You move the following value to it: 123456789987. If you display the field, the following would be displayed 123456790000000000. **False**
13.   The precision for float-extended is 16 digits. **False**
14.   The Net Express program that carries out anding is 'cbl-and'. **True**
15.   To interpret a negative binary number we find the value of the bit position to the immediate left of the leftmost zero. To that value we add all bits on to the right of that bit. **True**
16.   The not implements the two's complement. **False**

Complete – Chapter 10

		Picture	Data	Edit Picture	Result
1.	Given:	9(4)V99	0025V75	$$$9.99	^^$25.75
2.	Given:	9(4)V99	0045V62	$***9.99	$**45.62
3.	Given:	9(4)V99	0125V75	ZZ.99	25.75
4.	Given:	9(4)V99	0136V752	$Z,ZZZ.99	$^^136.75
5.	Given:	9(6)	000005	ZZZ.999	^^5.000
6.	Given:	9(4)V99	0000V85	$$,$$9.99	^^^^$0.85
7.	Given:	9(4)V99	0005V25	$$,$$9.99	^^^^$5.25
8.	Given:	S9(6)	−000364	ZZZZ9BCR	bb364^CR
9.	Given:	S9(6)	+001234	++,+++,++9	^^^^+1,234
10.	Given:	9(3)V99	255V15	$ZZZ.99	$255.15
11.	Given:	S9(2)V99	00V13	$ZZ.99+	$^^.13+

12.	Given:	S9(2)V99	+00V29	$ZZ.99-	$^^.29^
13.	Given:	S9(4)V99	-0517V87	Z,ZZ9.99-	^^517.87-
14.	Given:	9(6)	132547	ZZZBZZ9	132^547
15.	Given:	S9(6)	-123456	----,--9	-123,456
16.	Given:	S9(3)	-321	$ZZZ.99BDB	$321.00^DB
17.	Given:	S9(2)V99	-00V45	$ZZ.99BCR	$^^.45^CR
18.	Given:	9(3)	100 99 blank when zero		^^
19.	Given:	9(4)V999	0043V123	$ZBZZZ.99	$^^^43.12
20.	Given:	S9(4)V99	0035V67	$$$$.99	^$35.67

True/False – Chapter 10

	Picture	Data	Edit Picture	Result	
1.	S9(3)V9(3)	000V000	ZZ9.99	^^0.00	T
2.	S9(4)V9(2)	0000V00	ZZZZ.ZZ	^^^^.^^	F
3.	S9(4)V9(2)	0000V55	Z,ZZZ.99	^^^^.55	F
4.	S9(4)V9(2)	2500V15	ZBZZ9.99	2^500.15	T
5.	S9(5)V9(2)	-12345V30	ZBZZ9.99+	12^345.30-	F
6.	S9(5)V9(2)	10000V00	ZBZZZ.ZZ	^^^^^^^^	T
7.	S9(5)V9(2)	15000V00	+Z,ZZZ.99	+5,000.00	T
8.	S9(6)V9(2)	123456V00	+,+++,+++.++	^+123,456.00	T
9.	S9(6)V9(2)	123456V15	+++,+++.++	+123,456.15	F
10.	S9(5)V9(2)	10000V00	-,---.--	^^^^^^^^	T
11.	S9(4)V9(2)	5125V34	Z,ZZZ.99BDB	5,125.34^^^	T
12.	S9(4)V9(2)	-6323V45	Z,ZZZ.99BCR	6,323.45CR	F
13.	S9(5)V9(2)	15545V56	$Z,ZZ9.99	15,545.56	F
14.	S9(5)V9(2)	5656V67	$,$$$.99	^$656.67	T
15.	S9(5)V9(2)	10000V00	Z,ZZZ.ZZ Blank when zero	^^^^^^^^	T
16.	S9(4)V9(2)	5375V00	$$,$$$.$$	$5,375.00	T
17.	S9(4)V9(2)	0000V00	*B***.**	*****.**	T

18. Should we wish to use a comma as the decimal point, we would code "decimal point is ','" in the special names paragraph. **F**

Complete – Chapter 11

1. In reading ahead, the first read follows **file** open and precedes the **find-low**.
2. If we are applying the read ahead the **last** thing we do inside the loop is **read**.
3. In applying the read ahead we **read** the next record when we have finished processing the **preceding** record.

4.   We are reading randomly and we prompt the reader for the record key and will loop until the user enters 'xxx'. We should **prompt** before entering the loop.

5.   The detail line receives data **before** testing for end of page.

6.   You have paper that is 50 lines. You leave five lines at the top and five lines at the bottom. There are five heading lines. The body of the report is **35** lines.

7.   In writing to the printer we use the **write from**.

8.   Write print-rec from detail-line **after advancing** 2.

9.   In the heading routine we move **zero** to the line-ctr.

10.   When we are processing sequentially and have requested dynamic access to retrieve a record we use **read next**.

11.   Assume you have a field Start-key that has the point from which you want to start processing and that mast-file is sequenced on mast-key. Before using the start statement you would code 'move **Start-key** to **mast-key**'.

12.   Assuming the information from the preceding question, your start statement would be: '**start mast-file key is > mast-key**.

13.   Records in a relative file must be **fixed** length.

14.   In a relative file, records are all written **next** to each other.

15.   The delete requires a **file** name.

True/False – Chapter 11

1.   The read requires the file name. **True**

2.   The write requires the record name. **True**

3.   The rewrite requires the file name. **False**

4.   The after advancing clause has a default of two lines. **False**

5.   When printing we can print either before or after advancing. **True**

6.   We move 0 to the line-ctr after printing the last line on the page. **False**

7.   If the page is able to hold 50 detail lines, moving 51 or 52 to line-ctr has the same effect. **True**

8.   To delete a record we must first read it. **False**

9.   The delete carries out logical deletion only. **False**

10.   The record key in an indexed sequential file must be defined in the record defined under the FD. **True**

11.   The file status field should be defined in working storage as a pic xx field. **True**

12.   The values returned into the file status field are all numeric. **True**

13.   If we specify access is dynamic, we can specify read next or read prior. **False**

14.   The start statement calls for a key field that has the same length as the file key. **False**

15.   Relative access provides random access based on the relative position of the record, either from the beginning or the end of the file. **False**

16.   When processing a relative file to delete a record we should first read it. **True**

17.   The rewrite applies to the record retrieved by the immediately preceding read. **True**

Complete – Chapter 12

1.   Matching records have the same **key**.
2.   If m-key is five and t-key is five, the value in low-key will be **5**.
3.   If we are using the grandfather, father, son method of backup, the file that receives the output becomes the **son**.
4.   If we are using the grandfather, father, son method of backup, the file that is providing the input is the **son** and becomes the **father**.
5.   The file that is overwritten is always the **grandfather**.
6.   In a sequence it is not **generally** important what we do first.
7.   The three logical constructs required to solve any logic problems are **sequence, selection** and **iteration**.
8.   We read the next record once we have processed the **preceding** record.
9.   When creating a compound key, each level as we go up **contains** one more field.
10. In the match, the test is **mast-key = low-key**.
11. In the match, if there is a master we store the master and read the next master. We do this because if there is no master we already have the **next** master.
12. To find whether we have transactions to process we code until **tran-key** not = **low-key**.
13. If we are processing an addition, store-master should have **spaces**.
14. The match is **subordinated** to the control break.
15. Any loop for transactions must be **subordinated** to the match.

True/False – Chapter 12

1.   Master files are temporary and transaction files are permanent. **False**
2.   With sequential processing, we use the delete verb to delete a record. **False**
3.   The read ahead principle ensures that at the top of the loop we always have a new record to process. **True**
4.   In a sequence the order in which the parts are executed is always important. **False**
5.   Low-key must be determined prior to entering the loop. **True**
6.   When mast-key is not = low-key, we have the next master. **True**
7.   When mast-key is not = low-key we do not have a transaction. **False**
8.   To add a new record to the file mast-key must be = low-key. **False**
9.   If tran-key not = low-key we have a master without transactions. **True**
10. If store-master = spaces we do not write out a master. **True**
11. The match involves groups of records. **False**
12. Compound keys enable the programmer to reduce the number of comparisons required in a condition. **True**
13. If we have a match and control breaks, the match will be subordinated to the control breaks. **True**
14. In merging, if a record from one of the files is equal to low-key we do not have to read the next record for this file. **False**

Complete – Chapter 13

1. The redefined and the redefining items **cannot both** be in storage at the **same** time.
2. The redefined and the redefining items will have the same **address**.
3. The redefined and the redefining items must be the same **length**.
4. If redefined and the redefining items share a format such as a key field, we may address either **redefined** or the **redefining** item.
5. Redefinition at 01 level in the file section is **implied**.
6. Redefinition at level 05 in the file section must be **explicit**.
7. If we apply the value clause at group level we will have **implied** redefinition.
8. The renames uses level **66** and applies to the **immediately preceding** level 01.
9. The renames enables the programmer to ascribe a new name to a field. The old name **remains** in effect.
10. A condition name enables the programmer to allocate a **name** to a **value** in a field.
11. To place a value in the conditional variable we may use the **set** verb.
12. To place the value one in the conditional variable associated with condition name EOF, we would code **set EOF to true**.
13. When a list follows the value clause, the items in the list may be separated by ',' or **space** or a ';'.
14. When a list follows the value clause, the set verb will use the **first** item in the list.
15. The concatenation operator **&** concatenates two **strings**.

True/False – Chapter13

1. The redefined and redefining items occupy the same storage. **True**
2. The redefined and redefining fields may be in storage at the same time. **False**
3. The redefined and redefining fields have the same address. **True**
4. Redefinition in the file section is implied at 05 level. **True**
5. The redefined and redefining fields should be of the same length. **True**
6. We may have implied redefinition at level 05 using the value clause. **True**
7. The renames clause applies to the immediately preceding 01 level. **True**
8. The renamed item may no longer be used. **False**
9. A condition name names a value associated with a conditional variable. **True**
10. The set verb may be used to set a condition name to false. **False**
11. When the set verb must select from a list it will always select the first item in the list. **True**
12. When setting the conditional variable to multiple values with the value clause we may use the 'thru' if the values are in succession. **True**
13. The value clause may be used in the file section as long as it is used to set a value. **False**
14. When continuing an alphanumeric literal we must open and close inverted commas on every continued line. **False**
15. The concatenation operator may be used to concatenate up to three literals. **False**
16. The concatenation operator is able to concatenate a literal and a string. **False**
17. For qualification to operate, the group fields must be unique. **True**

Complete – Chapter 14

1.   The entries in a table must all have **the same** format.
2.   The entries in a table must all be the same **length** .
3.   A subscript value must lie between **1** and the **table length**.
4.   A table is defined using the **occurs** clause.
5.   To define a table with 25 entries you would code: 05 Tab **occurs 25**.
6.   To reference a table entry we can use either a **subscript** or an **index**.
7.   To subscript we may use either a **literal** or a **field-name**.
8.   To define a variable length table we use the **depending on** clause.
9.   The **depending on** clause for a variable length table names a **numeric** field.
10.   When defining a variable length table we can specify **minimum** and **maximum** sizes.
11.   In looping through a table in the body of the loop, we add one to the subscript at the **bottom** of the loop.
12.   An item containing the **occurs** clause may not be **redefined**.
13.   To initialize a table we can use _**implicit redefinition**_ using the value clause.
14.   In preparing for an iteration we would move **1** to the subscript.
15.   Relative subscripting means that we are adding a **literal** to the value in the **subscript**.
16.   To increment an index by five you would code **set** ind **up by** 5.

True/False – Chapter14

1.   The entries in a table need not have the same format as long as they are all of the same size. **False**
2.   The word 'times' which follows the length in the occurs clause is compulsory. **False**
3.   In subscripting, if we use a literal, to change it we have to recompile the program. **True**
4.   In looping through a table, we increment the subscript in the body of the loop. **True**
5.   The space for a variable length table is reserved at execution time. **False**
6.   If you code occurs 50 depending on tab-size and tab-size never has a value in excess of 25, then the space used up does not exceed the space required for 25 entries. **False**
7.   A table is defined using the occurs clause. **True**
8.   If we loop through a table at the end of the loop, the value in the subscript will be greater than the table size. **True**
9.   If there is a possibility of a not found condition, the condition name(sub) = st-name must appear before the condition sub > tab-size. **False**
10.   We may only subscript items for which the **occurs** clause has been coded. **False**
11.   A condition name may be subscripted. **True**
12.   We do not need to define an index; the compiler generates a fullword when we use the indexed by clause. **True**
13.   To increment an index ind, we would code add 1 to ind. **False**
14.   We may compare an index to a number as in if ind > 50. **True**

Complete – Chapter 15

1.   Two dimensional tables have **rows** and **columns**.
2.   The table has 100 byte entries and there are 10 rows and 10 columns, the table would occupy **10 000** bytes in storage.
3.   A two dimensional table has one **occurs clause** per dimension.
4.   In a two dimensional table we have a field that exists only in the rows, the field will occupy a position to the _left_ of the columns table.
5.   In a two dimensional table we have a field that exists only in the rows, to reference that field we would need only one _subscript_.
6.   The **search** verb is applied to the item at the level where the _occurs_ is coded.
7.   In the **when**, the **or** is implied for _multiple_ conditions.
8.   In the **when**, the **and** is not a **valid** connector.
9.   When using the **search** verb the at end exit is taken for a **not found** condition.
10.   The **search** requires that the **at end** clause be used.
11.   We may vary a **numeric** field or an **index** field.
12.   We may vary an index from **another** table.
13.   The **search all** carries out a **binary** search.
14.   In the **search all**, in the when, the **and** is the only connector allowed.
15.   When using the **search all**, the table must be in **sequence** by a **key** field.

True/False – Chapter 15

1.   In referring to a two dimensional table, we would code entry(row, column). **True**
2.   A two dimensional table requires one occurs clause and two indexes. **False**
3.   In a two dimensional table we have a field that occurs only in the rows. The field must be coded so that it will be on the left of the columns. **True**
4.   In a two dimensional table, if the row is coded at level 15 then the columns would be coded at level 20. **True**
5.   The varying clause causes a change in the index to be reflected in the field being varied. **True**
6.   If you vary an index you will vary an index other than the first index specified for the dimension. **True**
7.   In a two dimensional table, the second dimension lies inside the first dimension. **True**
8.   When sequential searches are involved we place the most frequently referenced items at the end of the table. **False**
9.   When using the search all we should place the most frequently referenced items at the beginning of the table. **False**
10.   When using the search, multiple whens are explicitly connected by or. **False**
11.   When using the search, in a when, multiple conditions may be connected by and. **False**
12.   When using the search all, multiple whens must be connected by and. **False**
13.   The sort verb enables us to sort the entries in a table in ascending sequence on one field and in descending field on another field. **True**
14.   The table to be sorted must be indexed. **False**

Complete – Chapter 16

1. Reference modification enables the programmer to **select** a group of bytes in a field, rather than the **whole** field.
2. In reference modification, we must always specify the **starting position**.
3. In reference modification, we need not always specify the **end position** of bytes to be transferred.
4. A reference modified field is implicitly **alphanumeric**.
5. Reference modified fields may not be used in **arithmetic** operations.
6. If reference modified data is moved to an alphanumeric destination, alignment will be on the **left**.
7. If we have a reference modified numeric destination field, alignment will be on the **left** .
8. When applying reference modification to a table entry, the reference modification comes **after** the subscript.
9. The data type to which we may apply reference modification is **display**.
10. You have defined a field pic 9(6) with the value 54321. The first byte contains the value **0**.
11. If the value 48.55 were being returned by an intrinsic function, the function would be of type **numeric**.
12. When using **alphanumeric** intrinsic functions we generally use the move verb.
13. The integer-of-day intrinsic function is of type **date conversion.**
14. When invoking a programmer created function, we do not use the keyword **function**.

True/False – Chapter 16

1. We may not move a reference modified source to a packed destination. **True**
2. When data is moved to a reference modified numeric field it will align on the right. **False**
3. We may not reference modify a packed field. **True**
4. A packed field may not serve as a destination for a reference modified source. **True**
5. We may omit the starting position in reference modification as long as we do not omit the number of bytes. **False**
6. We may omit the number of bytes in reference modification. **True**
7. If the starting position is omitted in reference modification, it is as if a starting position of 1 had been specified. **False**
8. If the field is eight bytes long, starting position is four and number of bytes has not been specified, four bytes would be transferred. **False**
9. In a programmer created function we do not code the word function. **True**
10. The function must have the returning clause in the procedure division statement. **True**
11. The item returned may be defined in the working-storage section. **False**
12. The last line of code in the function is Exit Function. **False**
13. When compiling the function we need a compiler directive to update the repository. **True**
14. If the seed for the random function is always the same, the same random number will be returned each time. **True**
15. Numeric intrinsic functions return an integer variable. **False**

Complete – Chapter 17

1. Large programs are difficult to **maintain**.
2. The **using** clause is required to pass as well as to receive data.
3. Data at the source are changed when the called program changes a field passed by **reference**.
4. Data are not changed at the source when the called program changes a field passed by **value** or by **content**.
5. In passing a numeric literal we need to use the **value** keyword.
6. In the static call, called and calling programs are **link edited** together.
7. In the case of a dynamically called program, the program is loaded when the program is **called**.
8. We specify: call field-name using… in the case of a **dynamic call**.
9. Received items are defined in the **linkage section**.
10. If the call to a program is not successful we should take the **on overflow** exit.
11. A program will be an initial program when the word initial follows the **program name**.
12. An initial program will have all initialized variables re-initialized every time the **program** is **called**.
13. The cancel will terminate a **dynamically called** program.
14. A cancelled program will be loaded once more when the program is **called**.
15. The returning clause in a called program is coded following **goback**.

True/False – Chapter 17

1. A program is only able to see the data it defines. **True**
2. The data that passes between called and calling programs must have the same name in called and calling programs. **False**
3. Fields passed must be in the same sequence in called and calling programs. **True**
4. Unless data are returned they cannot be used by the calling program. **False**
5. If a level 05 field is passed it must be defined in the linkage section as a level 05. **False**
6. For control to revert to the calling program we code goback or exit-program. **True**
7. We use the dynamic call when we know the name of the program to be called at compile time. **False**
8. The default is passing by reference. **True**
9. **On exception** and **on overflow** do very much the same thing. **True**
10. The **initial** keyword causes data to be reinitialized on the first call. **False**
11. The **cancel** keyword causes data to be reinitialized on the first call. **True**
12. The files in a cancelled program will be closed before termination. **True**
13. A return code of zero generally indicates an error. **False**
14. The entry statement enables us to specify multiple entry points. **True**
15. For the entry to take effect the program must already be loaded. **True**
16. When there is only one entry point all the arguments are passed whether needed or not. **True**

17.   We may not code the returning clause in the procedure division statement of a
        called program. **True**

Complete – Chapter 18

1.   For the external clause to function, all programs must have **identical** definitions of the ex-
        ternal data.
2.   The external clause may only be specified at level **01**.
3.   The **value** clause may not be specified for a field bearing the external clause.
4.   An item defined in the linkage section is seen as **internal**.
5.   A 05 item subordinated to a 01 defined as external is also **external**.
6.   An external item may be defined in the **working-storage** section and the **file** section
7.   If the external clause is applied to a field that has been redefined, the redefining field is **also**
        external.
8.   A program that has a nested program is a **containing** program.
9.   An indirectly contained program is not seen by the **indirectly containing** program.
10.   A common program is accessible by its **siblings** and by any programs these may **contain**.
11.   Nested programs are precluded from using the **returning** clause.
12.   If we want other programs lower in the containing hierarchy to see a variable we define it
        using the keyword **global**.
13.   The global keyword may be used in the **working-storage** section and in the **file** section
14.   If the global clause is specified in the FD contained programs may **do** I/O.

True/False – Chapter 18

1.   In the **linkage** section, the external clause may be specified at level 77. **False**
2.   To pass external fields to a contained program the using clause is required. **True**
3.   The goback or exit program must always end on a period. **False**
4.   We may use the global keyword at level 01 in the linkage section. **False**
5.   If a redefined field is external, the redefining field will also be external. **False**
6.   In the working-storage section the external clause may be specified at level 05 as well as
        level 01. **False**
7.   The value clause may not be specified for an external field. **True**
8.   If the external clause is specified in the FD, other programs may access the I/O area but we
        must first open the file. **False**
9.   A common program may only be accessed by its siblings and not by the programs they con-
        tain. **False**
10.   When using the returning clause in a nested program, the clause must be specified in the
        procedure division header. **False**
11.   The fields to which the global clause is applied will be visible to all containing and con-
        tained programs. **True**
12.   The global clause must be defined at level 01 in the file section or in the FD. **True**
13.   The global clause may be specified in the working-storage section but not in the linkage
        section. **False**

14. When using the global clause, in the case of redefinition, it applies independently to the item for which it is specified. **True**
15. If the global clause is specified in the FD, directly and indirectly contained programs may perform I/O on the file. **True**

Complete – Chapter 19

1. In the **string** statement transfer starts on the **left** and proceeds **byte** by **byte**.
2. If we string numeric data it must not contain **decimals**.
3. Delimited by size is the **default**.
4. If the field is too small to receive the data, the data will be **truncated**.
5. If the data to be transferred is 99 bytes, the pointer field must be able to hold the figure **100**.
6. It is up to the programmer to **initialize** the pointer field before using it.
7. If there is **overflow** on the pointer field, transfer of data will stop.
8. A value of **zero** in the pointer field will cause overflow.
9. If the pointer field has been defined as pic 99, a value of **100** will cause overflow.
10. All fields participating in the string or the unstring must have been defined implicitly or explicitly, as usage is **display**.
11. In the unstring, a receiving field may be numeric and contain **decimals**.
12. If in the unstring a receiving field is numeric and contains decimals, the decimals will be **zeros**.
13. Count in counts the **number** of **bytes** transferred.
14. In the unstring, the pointer option specifies the starting position in the **source** field.
15. The tallying option counts the **number** of **fields** that received data.
16. A value of **0** in the pointer field will cause overflow.

True/False – Chapter 19

1. The pointer option in the string enables us to stipulate from which point in the source field to start transferring. **True**
2. A value of zero in the pointer field will cause overflow. **True**
3. In the unstring, a receiving field may be numeric but may not contain decimals. **False**
4. The string will accept a numeric field as long as it does not contain decimals. **True**
5. In the unstring you may have one delimited by clause. **True**
6. The string will concatenate a number of fields into a group or an elementary field. **True**
7. In the **string** the delimited by applies only to the field for which it is specified. **False**
8. The overflow exit will be taken for the string when the pointer field becomes one. **False**
9. Literals specified as delimiters may be numeric or alphanumeric. **False**
10. Delimited by '   ' will cause the unstring to treat two spaces as a delimiter. **True**
11. Delimited by spaces will cause any number of spaces to be treated as a single space. **True**
12. The count in clause is used to count the number of fields that received data. **False**
13. The tallying option counts the number of characters transferred to a given field. **False**
14. The pointer option in the unstring enables us to start transferring data from a point other than the first byte. **True**

15.   The overflow option will be taken in the unstring if the pointer field contains zero. **True**

Complete – Chapter 20

1.   You wish to count all the occurrences of the characters 'th' in a field. The code would be: inspect field-1 **tallying** ctr for **all** 'th'.
2.   You wish to count the number of asterisks on the left of the field. You would code: inspect field-1 **tallying** ctr for **leading** '*'.
3.   You wish to know how many bytes occur in the field before a '/' is encountered. Inspect field-1 **tallying** ctr for **characters before** '/'.
4.   You wish to replace all characters preceding '/' by '0'. You would code: Inspect field-1 **replacing characters before** '/' by '0'.
5.   You wish to replace the first occurrence of 'XK' by 'SLR' following '...'. You would code: inspect field-1 **replacing first** 'XK' by 'SLR' **after** '...'.
6.   You wish to replace zeros on the left of the field by '#'. You would code   inspect field-1 **replacing leading** zeros by '#'.
7.   You wish to change 'abc' to '123'. Assume that field-1 contains 'abc'.   Inspect **converting field-1 to '123'**.

True/False – Chapter 20

1.   Before and after calls for either a literal or a field name but the character must not be more than one character in length. **False**
2.   When using the tallying option we must use all or leading but not characters. **False**
3.   When using before or after the initial keyword is optional. **True**
4.   The keyword first may be used with tallying. **False**
5.   When using replacing with leading we have to specify the leading character. **True**
6.   Characters means any character in the alphabet. **True**
7.   Characters and leading do not go together. **True**
8.   Characters may be used with before or after. **True**

Complete – Chapter 21

1.   The intention of the initialize is to permit a **group** or multiple **fields** to be initialized.
2.   Using the initialize, a numeric field will be set to **zero**.
3.   Using the initialize, an alphanumeric field will be set to **spaces**.
4.   Using the initialize, a numeric-edited field will be set in accordance with its **picture**.
5.   Using the initialize, an alphanumeric-edited field will be set in accordance with its **picture**.
6.   A field defined as pic S9(3) comp-3 is initialized. Show the contents of the field: **000C** .
7.   Using the initialize, an alphabetic field will be set to **spaces**.
8.   Following the replacing, we specify the **type** of the target field.
9.   When using the replacing, the type of the source field must be **compatible** with the target field.

10.   The target W10-data is alphanumeric and you are going to replace it with 1234. You would code: initialize **W10-data replacing alphanumeric** by 1234.

11.   The target W10-edit is numeric-edited. You are going to replace it with 567.5. You would code: initialize **W10-edit replacing numeric-edited** by 567.5.

12.   The target W10-data is a group field containing an alphanumeric field and a numeric edited field. You are going to initialize W10-data with 'Good!' and W10-edited with 6543.75. You would code: initialize **W10-data replacing alphanumeric** by 'Good!' **numeric-edited** by 6543.75.

True/False – Chapter 21

1.   In the initialize you can only initialize group fields. **False**
2.   Alphanumeric fields will be initialized to spaces. **True**
3.   Numeric-edited fields will be initialized in accordance with the picture. **True**
4.   Alphanumeric-edited fields will be initialized to spaces. **False**
5.   Alphabetic fields will be initialized in the same way as alphanumeric fields. **True**
6.   Following replacing, we code the name of the target field. **True**
7.   Fillers are initialized to spaces. **False**
8.   In the initialize, the source and the target need not be compatible. **False**
9.   The type of data specified in the replacing must be the same type as the target. **True**
10.   When using the replacing option, source and target fields must be of the same type. **False**
11.   The replacing option enables us to initialize an alphanumeric field using a fractional number. **False**
12.   When an alphanumeric field is initialized using a fractional number say 123.45, the alphanumeric field will contain the value '123.45'. **False**
13.   When we use a numeric value to initialize an alphanumeric field, using the replacing, we would be coding: initialize W10-data replacing alphanumeric by '123.45'. **True**
14.   Using …replacing all numeric by 100 has the advantage of being explicit. **True**

Complete – Chapter 22

1.   In order for a sort to be possible, the records to be sorted must have a **key**.
2.   The actual sort operation is carried out in the **work file**.
3.   The select for the sort work file is a select for a **sort definition** file.
4.   The sort key must be defined in the **SD**.
5.   The **using** clause is used if no processing is done prior to passing the records to the sort.
6.   The **giving** clause is used when no **processing** is done on the sorted records.
7.   The **with duplicates in order** clause is coded to maintain the sequence of records with the same key.
8.   The sort is associated with **sequential** applications.
9.   The using and the giving use **any** file organization.
10.   When there are no more records to be passed to the sort, the **sort** receives control.
11.   When the sort has finished sorting, **control** reverts back to the **program**.
12.   Records are obtained from the sort by means of the **return** statement.

13.   The input and the output procedure both have an **exit** mechanism at the end of each procedure.
14.   The invocation of the sort and the return of control to the program are **automatic**.
15.   Records are passed to the sort by means of the **release** statement.

True/False – Chapter 22

1.   The sort keys are specified minor to major key. **False**
2.   The input procedure invokes the **sort** by means of a perform, but the sort returns control to the program automatically. **False**
3.   When the using is employed, we do not use the **release** statement. **True**
4.   When the giving is employed, we can only create a sequential file. **False**
5.   The using only allows input of sequential files. **False**
6.   When the using is employed, it is up to the programmer to open the file. **False**
7.   When the using is employed, the program cannot read the file. **True**
8.   When the using is employed, the program cannot release records to the sort. **True**
9.   The file used by the sort must be given the name sort-work-file. **False**
10.   The sort key must be defined in the file section. **True**
11.   We may sort in ascending key on some fields and descending key on others. **True**
12.   With duplicates in order means that records with the same key will remain in the sequence in which they were read. **True**
13.   In an EBCDIC file that is sorted, 123 will precede ABC. **False**
14.   In an ASCII file that is sorted, 123 will always precede ABC. **True**
15.   The input procedure may not contain a sort verb. **True**
16.   Control must reach the return statement from within a sort statement because return only has meaning in association with the sort. **True**
17   An input procedure need not contain a release statement. **True**

Complete – Chapter 23

1.   Procedural programming uses **functional** decomposition as the mechanism for resolving complexity.
2.   Encapsulation hides the **implementation**.
3.   Communication with a class is through the **interface**.
4.   A class does not see another class until you create a **reference** to the class and **load** it.
5.   A class **reference** must be loaded with the **address** of the class before it can be used.
6.   In OO COBOL, **methods** are inherited but **attributes** are not.
7.   The relationship found in inheritance is the **a kind of** relationship.
8.   The paradigm of polymorphism is reflected in the phrase, one **interface** many **implementations**.
9.   To call a method of another class we use the **invoke** verb.
10.   To receive data from another class, the call to the method utilizes the **returning** clause.
11.   The factory object uses the returning verb to return the reference. The returning clause is coded in the **procedure division** statement.

12.   The keyword **super** is used to refer to the class from which the present class inherits.
13.   The reference that can only point to the class in which it is coded is the **active-class** reference.
14.   Objects that are no longer used but are still using up memory give rise to **memory leaks**.

True/False – Chapter 23

1.   All class instances will have the same attributes and the same functions. **True**
2.   A method can have only one paragraph. **False**
3.   The most basic of classes is the Object class or the base class. **True**
4.   A reference enables us to refer to a class object. **True**
5.   To use a class we need to know what its implementation looks like. **False**
6.   Function overriding makes one form of polymorphism possible. **True**
7.   We use **self** when we wish to refer to a method in the base class. **False**
8.   Super is used to refer to a method in the same class. **False**
9.   A method may not have working-storage, only local storage. **False**
10.   The factory object relies on the base class to create the object requested. **True**
11.   Initialization code present in the factory object may only be executed once the object is created. **True**
12.   Objects of a class may access the working-storage of the factory object of the containing class. **False**
13.   Factory data applies to the whole class rather than to particular objects of the class. **True**
14.   Memory leaks refer to memory usage that is no longer required but is not released. **True**
15.   The verb that releases storage that is no longer required is 'liquidate'. **False**
16.   The returning clause that in the factory object returns the reference may be coded in the procedure division or in the exit method statement. **False**
17.   The method 'new' in the factory object could be called by another name. **True**

Complete – Chapter 24

1.   When doing analysis, the analyst obtains information from the **domain expert**.
2.   Each iteration in the production of the system involves going through **analysis**, **design**, **implementation** and **testing**.
3.   Risk assessment is of three types namely, **requirements**, **technological** and **skills**.
4.   Program testing should be an integrated process where **execution** of the program to be tested involves **execution** of the testing program.
5.   The layered approach involves the layers **user interface**, **business** and **data access**.
6.   When using the layered approach a change to the user interface will **not affect** the other two layers.
7.   A use case reflects the **interaction** between an actor and the system.
8.   An actor is shown as a **stick figure**.
9.   An actor may be a **person** or another **system**.
10.   An include points to a possibility of reducing **duplication** of code.
11.   The extend points to **addition** of functionality in the **derived** class.

True/False – Chapter 24

1.   Before proceeding to the next module in the delivery of a system we obtain approval of the preceding module by the user. **True**
2.   The steps in an iteration in the system production process are as follows: Analysis, design and implementation. **False**
3.   The preliminary evaluation seeks to produce a cost/benefit analysis. **True**
4.   Requirements risk refers to the possibility of providing the wrong solution to the user. **True**
5.   The business layer is concerned with the burden of securing the required results. **True**
6.   A way of finding the actors is through the presence of verbs in the description. **False**
7.   A way of finding scenarios is to locate the nouns in the requirements description. **False**
8.   The include relationship reflects the presence of a function that is required by only one scenario. **False**
9.   The extends relationship points to the need for additional functionality in the derived class. **True**
10.   In a base class/derived class relationship, the base class is the more generalized class. **True**

Complete – Chapter 25

1.   The class diagram will depict the **relationship** between two classes.
2.   The specification perspective enables us to specify the **structure** of the class.
3.   The relationship between classes is established via the **interfaces**.
4.   A relationship established between classes which is not established via the interface is the **inheritance** relationship.
5.   The specification perspective is mainly concerned with the **interface**.
6.   A **foreign key** enables an Orders file to link back to Customer.
7.   A method that returns data may be classified as a **query** or as a **getter**.
8.   A method that changes the value of an attribute may be described as a **modifier** or as a **setter**.
9.   If we have a base class Person and a derived class Student, the name would be in the **base** class.
10.   A base class shares its **methods** with the derived class.

True/False – Chapter 25

1.   Class diagrams must always be used when analysing a system. **False**
2.   The conceptual perspective provides the most detail. **False**
3.   All relationships between classes are established via the interface. **False**.
4.   The relationship between orders and line items is a one to many relationship. **True**
5.   An orders file must have at least one line item pending. **False**
6.   A getter operation is equivalent to a query operation. **True**
7.   If you were accumulating total amounts outstanding from customers, the variable used for the accumulation would be classified as an attribute. **False**
8.   A setter operation is equivalent to a modifier operation. **True**

9.   The interface of the base class may never be bigger than the interface of one of its derived classes. **False**
10.   An order may originate from only one customer. **True**

Complete – Chapter 26

1.   Diagrams depicting interaction between classes are called **interaction** diagrams.
2.   Sequence diagrams use an **arrow** to show the connection to another class.
3.   In the sequence diagrams shown in the chapter an **X** was used to show a return point.
4.   Some of the UML diagrams may be **dispensed** with because they are difficult to update when changes are introduced.
5.   Collaboration diagrams are not good at showing **behavior**.
6.   Activity diagrams are poor at showing **dynamic** behavior.
7.   Activity diagrams enable us to show **simultaneity** whereas flowcharts do not.
8.   The **join** terminates the simultaneous process.
9.   In a CRC card the class is the **class** under examination.
10.   In a CRC card collaboration depicts the classes with which this class **interacts**.

True/False – Chapter 26

1.   Interaction diagrams depict interaction between methods. **False**
2.   Return arrows from the class instance that received control are always shown. **False**
3.   In a sequence diagram, the lifeline may be a dashed line or an elongate rectangle. **True**
4.   A collaboration diagram serves the same purpose as a sequence diagram. **True**
5.   If we use sequence diagrams we must use collaboration diagrams. **False**
6.   In a collaboration diagram, it is not easy to depict behavior. **True**
7.   The fork initiates a simultaneous process. **True**
8.   Responsibilities consist of what the class needs to do. **True**
9.   Collaboration refers to what this class will do for others. **False**
10.   CRC cards facilitate group interaction and discussion. **True**

Complete – Chapter 27

1.   Inheritance is one of the mechanisms contributing towards **reusability**.
2.   The class that inherits is the **derived** class and the class from which inheritance takes place is the **base** class.
3.   The implementation contains **private** items and the interface contains **public** items.
4.   In COBOL the **implementation** is not inherited.
5.   A data item defined with the property clause causes the compiler to generate an **accessor** with the **same** name as the data item.
6.   A reference to the property must be included in the **repository** paragraph.
7.   The reference to the property must be made in the **external** repository.
8.   The keyword property must be provided at the level of the **method-id**.
9.   The keyword property must be preceded by the word **get** or **set**.

10. A property called finalValue would end on **end method**.
11. A secondary interface contains the **prototypes** for methods.
12. When a class inherits an interface it must **implement** all the methods contained in the interface.
13. An interface B specifies three method prototypes. Interface B inherits interface A which specifies two method prototypes. If a class implements interface B, it must implement **five** methods.
14. A class may inherit **multiple** interfaces.
15. An interface definition starts with **interface-id** and ends with **end interface**.

True/False – Chapter 27

1. The class from which all classes inherit is class Object. **False**
2. In COBOL, the data form part of the implementation. **True**
3. In COBOL, both data and methods are inherited. **False**
4. To gain access to a field associated with a property, we need a reference to the class containing the property. **True**
5. In the class containing the property a reference to the property must be included in the repository paragraph. **False**
6. When a class inherits another class a reference to the base class must be included in the repository paragraph. **False**
7. When a reference to the base class is included in the repository paragraph, the 'inherits from' in the class-id is no longer required. **False**
8. When a class is inherited, the class must be registered in the external repository. **False**
9. When coding your own property, the 'end method' does not take the property name. **True**
10. When you code your own property, the definition of the field associated with the property must carry the keyword property. **False**
11. When defining an interface, the interface ends on 'end interface'. The name of the interface is not required. **False**
12. When a method inherits an interface, the interface must be reflected in the repository paragraph. In addition, at object level we must use the implements keyword followed by the name of the interface. **True**
13. If interface B inherits from interface A, interface B must have 'inherits from A'. **True**

Complete – Chapter 28

1. Collections are also known as **containers** in other languages.
2. Array class instances grow **manually**.
3. The index for Array class objects must be of type **pic X(4) comp-5**
4. The method **withByteLengthValue** creates an instance of class CharacterArray.
5. The getValue method of class CharacterArray receives a **reference** to a string.
6. The **display** method displays the string pointed to by the invoking reference.
7. The **atPut** method is used to add elements to an Array class instance.
8. In a bag items are placed in the **sequence** in which they were **entered**.

9.   To store **strings** in a bag we use the ofReferences method.
10.   To store intrinsic data in a bag we use the **ofValues** method.
11.   The remove method from the bag class removes the item to which the **reference** passed is **pointing**.
12.   Bags grow **automatically**.
13.   ValueSets **do not** allow duplicates.
14.   ValueSets **will** grow automatically.
15.   To insert an item into a ValueSet we use the **add** method.
16.   When testing for the presence of an item in a ValueSet we use the **occurrencesOf** method or the **includes** method.
17.   An OrderedCollection will grow **automatically**.
18.   To add at the beginning of an OrderedCollection we would use the **addFirst** method.
19.   To implement a stack using an OrderedCollection we would use the **addLast** method.
20.   To implement a queue using an OrderedCollection we would use the **addFirst** method.
21.   To remove from a stack we use the method **last**.
22.   When retrieving from an OrderedCollection, the item returned has two components, a **reference** component and a **data** component.
23.   The value returned by the occurrencesOf method must be placed into a field defined as **pic X(4) comp-5**.
24.   SortedCollections grow **automatically**.
25.   SortedCollections use the **add** method to insert an item in the collection.
26.   If a SortedCollection is to contain strings it is created using the **ofReferences** method.
27.   If a SortedCollection is to contain intrinsic data we will us the **ofValues** method to create it.
28.   Dictionaries have two components, a **key** component and a **data** component.
29.   An **association** relates the two components of a Dictionary instance.

True/False – Chapter 28

1.   Array class objects are indexable. **True**
2.   The Array class instances grow by using the **increase to** method. **False**
3.   The getValue method of class CharacterArray returns a string. **True**
4.   Bags are not indexable. **True**
5.   In a bag, duplicates are not allowed. **False**.
6.   The remove method receives a reference. **True**
7.   We may not retrieve an element from a bag. **True**
8.   Bags require manual intervention to grow. **False**
9.   To insert an item into a ValueSet we use the atPut method. **False**
10.   If we want to know if there is more than one particular item in a ValueSet we would use the includes method. **False**
11.   In an OrderedCollection, duplicates are not allowed. **False**.
12.   To implement a stack using an OrderedCollection, we would use the addLast method. **True**
13.   To implement a queue when using an OrderedCollection, we would use the addLast method. **False**

14.   A SortedCollection provides indexed access. **True**
15.   A Dictionary has both pointer and data components. **False**
16.   To relate the two components of a Dictionary instance we use a Relation. **False**

Complete – Chapter 29

1.   Relational databases seek to reduce **inconsistencies** through the elimination of **redundancy**.
2.   Another name for a database file is **relation** or **table**.
3.   Another name for rows in a relation is **tuple**.
4.   Another name for the fields in a row is **attributes**.
5.   In first normal form there may not be **repeating** values for an attribute.
6.   We are said to be in the presence of **functional dependency** if for a single value of productCode there is a **unique** value for description.
7.   We have **transitive dependency** if a field depends on another field that is not part of the key.

True/False – Chapter 29

1.   Relational databases attempt to maximize inconsistencies. **False**
2.   Redundancy leads to the presence of inconsistencies. **True**
3.   A relation in first normal form may not have repeating items. **True**
4.   Navigation between relations is possible through foreign keys. **True**.
5.   A relation may be in second normal form and not be in first normal form. **False**

Complete – Chapter 30

1.   The cursor declaration may appear in the **data** or in the **procedure** divisions.
2.   Once we have a cursor, we use the **fetch** to retrieve records from the database.
3.   End of result set is indicated by a value of **+100** in SQLCODE.
4.   To specify a condition we employ the **where**.
5.   If we wanted all employees with a salary greater than 16000 we would code … where **Salary > 16000**
6.   If we wanted all employees where firstName contains a 'c' as the third character and is followed by any number of characters we would code …where **firstName like '__c%'** .
7.   For a loop to retrieve a result set with any number of records the loop condition would be perform until **SQLCODE < 0** or **SQLCODE = +100**.
8.   The min function does **not require a pass** through the database.
9.   To count the number of records in a database file we would use **count(*)**.
10.   When we only want one record of a set we code select **distinct** .
11.   For an insertion we do not need to **declare** a **cursor**.
12.   In an insertion following the keyword **Values** we have the fields containing the data to be inserted.
13.   An error in database access is reflected in a **Negative** error code.

14.   To make a change to the database persistent we need to use the **commit** command.
15.   In an update, to assign the new values we use the **Set** command.

True/False – Chapter 30

1.   A cursor must be declared in the data division. **False**
2.   To use the cursor we must first open it. **True**
3.   We use the fetch to retrieve a record from the database without the need for a cursor. **False**
4.   A negative value in SQLCODE signifies an error. **True**
5.   When using min to determine the lowest value in the database we need a pass through the database. **False**
6.   The connector AND should only be used with the Insert. **False**
7.   The values keyword is used with insert as well as with update. **False**
8.   Database persistence requires the commit command. **True**
9.   When we have declared a cursor, we use the select…into. **False**
10.   The like can only be used when we know at least one character and its position in the name. **False**
11.   The in is easier to use than the or. **True**
12.   The join combines selected records from two files based on the key. **True**
13.   When we use select distinct there will be only one record selected per key. **False**
14.   The set command is used in the insert to assign values to the database fields. **False**
15.   The avg command can only operate if a cursor has been declared. **False**
16.   When using the sum command, the select uses into. **True**
17.   The end of result set returns +100. **True**

INDEX

A

Accept verb   65
     Accept date   65
     Accept date with pattern   65
     Accept time   65, 66
     Day-of-week   66
     Gregorian date   66
     Julian date   66

Actors   506
Add   72
     Corresponding   75
After advancing   179
All "Literal"   47
Alphabetic data type   29
Alphabetic editing   152
Alphanumeric data type   29
Alphanumeric editing   153
Alphanumeric field max size   29
And   94
Arithmetic statements   72
Array class   558
     Grow   558
     Grow to   558,
     ofReferences   564,
ASCII character set   5, 25
ASCII signed field   26
Association   516
at   559, 561
At end   44
atPut   559, 561
Attributes   472, 516, 598
Automatic   485
Avg (SQL)   640

B

Bag   566
     Add   568, 569
     Includes   568, 569
     ofReferences   567
     ofValues 567
     Remove   568, 569
Base Class   473
Before advancing   179
Behavior   472
Binary   126 – 130
     Binary fields   127
     Field capacity   126
     Alignment   130
Binary system   4
Binary-char   131
Binary-double   131
Binary-long   131
Binary-short   131
Bitwise And   136
Bitwise Or   138
Blank when zero   165
Block contains   34
Blocking factor   32
Bottom of page   177
Buffer   32
Buffer addressability   33
Business layer   504

C

Call   356
     By content   362
     By reference   362
     By value   362
     Dynamic   361

D